Avid Media Con 6.x Cookbook

Over 160 highly effective and practical recipes to help beginning and intermediate users get the most from Avid Media Composer 6 editing

Benjamin Hershleder

PUBLISHING

BIRMINGHAM - MUMBAI

Avid Media Composer 6.x Cookbook

First published: December 2012

Production Reference: 1131212

Published by Packt Publishing Ltd.
Livery Place
35 Livery Street
Birmingham B3 2PB, UK.

ISBN 978-1-84969-300-4

www.packtpub.com

Cover Image by Benjamin Hershleder (ben@contactben.com)

Credits

Author
Benjamin Hershleder

Reviewers
Oliver Peters

Michael Phillips

Roger Shufflebottom

Acquisition Editor
Kartikey Pandey

Lead Technical Editor
Sweny M. Sukumaran

Technical Editors
Kaustubh S. Mayekar

Devdutt Kulkarni

Copy Editor
Insiya Morbiwala

Project Coordinator
Michelle Quadros

Proofreaders
Jonathan Todd

Lauren Tobon

Indexers
Hemangini Bari

Rekha Nair

Tejal Soni

Production Coordinator
Nitesh Thakur

Cover Work
Nitesh Thakur

About the Author

Benjamin Hershleder (`Hershleder.com`) currently freelances as an Avid Editor and Director. He has been teaching Avid Media Composer since 1995, and became an Avid Certified Instructor in 1997. He teaches as an adjunct professor at the American Film Institute in Los Angeles, at Avid Authorized Training Partner institutions, and also provides private, customized training to individuals and facilities.

Hershleder is an award-winning Producer-Director and accomplished Editor. He has produced and/or directed a variety of projects for such companies as Shapiro/West, The Spark Factory, and Old Fashioned Pictures. This work includes co-writing and directing the award-winning (including an Emmy and the Gold Ebenseer Bear) short film "Paul McCall" and directing and editing the Telly award-winning documentary "The Bronx Boys – Hosted by Carl Reiner", which aired on PBS and as part of the Cinemax anthology series "Reel Life". Benjamin is currently completing the follow-up to this film. It is again hosted by Carl Reiner and is titled "The Bronx Boys – Still Playing At 80".

His other credits include developing, producing, and directing the pilot of "Spoilers" (not to be confused with Kevin Smith's new production of the same name), serving as a Consulting Producer on comedian Andy Kindler's concert film "I Wish I Was Bitter", and editing Paramount Studios' "The Original Latin Kings Comedy" (George Lopez, Paul Rodriguez, Cheech Marin). His background in post-production also includes editing the indie-feature film "Hollywood Capri", two years as an editor for E! Entertainment Television, and editing an hour-long pilot episode of "In Search Of..." for Fox.

Acknowledgement

I would like to thank Michael Phillips, Oliver Peters, and Roger Shufflebottom, who were Technical Reviewers on this book. I would also like to thank Andrew Balis, Steve Bayes, George Bellias, Christie Carr, Bryan Castle, Cecil Daniels III, Ron Diamond, Ron Friedman, Nini Hadjis, Doug Hansel, Alex Hepburn, Jim Hershleder, Stan Hershleder, Robert Jones, Tamera Martin, Mike McNulty, Patty Montesion, Eric Naughton, Paul Petschek, Tom Quick, Katie Riccio, Leah Riccio, Samantha Riccio, Tom Riccio, R. Bandit Rivera, George Rizkallah, Larry Rubin, Ben Rock, Carolyn Rae Schultz, Jeff Sengpiehl, Wes Sewell, Greg Staten, Alan Stewart, Todd Smelser, Tracy Smith, Paul Stephan, Rik Swartzwelder, Jim Turner, and Paul Valdez.

Thanks to all those with the willingness and patience to teach me throughout my life. Thanks to all my students over the many years; I learned a lot from you, too.

About the Reviewers

Oliver Peters has worked in the television, film, and entertainment industries since 1970. He has accrued a diverse range of experience in all facets of production, post-production, instructional development/design, and project management. His credits include national and international TV and film projects, which have won awards such as the NATPE Iris, Telly, ITS Monitor, a national Addy, and others.

During his career, he worked for numerous years at Century III, the resident post-production facility at Universal Studios, Florida, which he helped design and manage. He currently owns his own post-production services company, working as an Independent Project Manager, Editor, and Colorist.

He is also a contributing Editor to Digital Video magazine and the Creative Planet websites, writing and lecturing about editing and post-production technologies and products. Other books that he has reviewed, include *The Art and Technique of Digital Color Correction, Steve Hullfish, Focal Press; Mastering MultiCamera Techniques, M. Jacobson, Focal Press;* and *The Avid Handbook, Steven Bayes and Greg Staten, Focal Press.*

Michael Phillips is an award-winning Filmmaker, Producer, Editor, and Industry Technologist. Michael's contributions to the industry have been for the co-invention and design of Avid's Media Composer, Film Composer, and Symphony product lines, which offer professional digital online and offline editing, and finishing, earning him a 1994 Academy Award® for Scientific and Engineering Achievement from the Academy of Motion Picture Arts and Sciences. In 1999, Michael and Avid were rewarded with an Oscar® for their continued efforts in enhancing and developing the Avid Film Composer. That same year, Michael was recognized with a Massachusetts Innovator of the Year award.

His producing and editing credits include, "Johnny Slade's Greatest Hits", "Patriots", "Jack in the Box" for editing, and "Leon" (The Professional), "Milk", and the award-winning documentary "Cinematographer Style" for digital post consultation and supervision; and recently completing the DI conform on "The Iceman".

Michael has lectured around the world on the ever-changing nature of digital processes, spoken at industry forums, and conducted workshops on digital post-production. He co-wrote the book "Digital Filmmaking, The Changing Art Form of Making Movies". He has been awarded over 10 patents from the United States Patent Office for digital synchronization of picture and sound, and other editing technologies pertaining to 24 frame editing, as well as compositing, interactive media (transmedia), and surround sound technologies. Michael is currently developing tools for story discovery.

Michael was chosen as the Post Supervisor for the Sundance Institute Director's Summer Labs 2012.

Michael is currently CTO of Cineworks, a full service film and digital cinema facility with locations in New Orleans, Los Angeles, Miami, Baton Rouge, and Shreveport. Michael is directing research and development of new technology solutions for the digital production process extending workflow consulting to Cineworks clients as well as industry manufacturers on workflow.

Roger Shufflebottom is an Editor living and working in the United Kingdom. He started editing documentaries and TV series on 16-mm film and got his hands on an Avid system for the first time in 1992. He proudly says that he never did any tape-to-tape editing professionally!

He became one of the first cohort of UK Avid Certified Instructors in the 1990s and has since run training courses in Europe, the Middle East, Africa, and the USA. He has written Media Composer, NewsCutter, Unity and Interplay training courseware for Avid in the U.K, and Focal Press published his book *Video Editing with Avid* in 2001.

He now teaches editing in the Media School at Bournemouth University, Dorset, U.K.

www.PacktPub.com

Support files, eBooks, discount offers and more

You might want to visit www.PacktPub.com for support files and downloads related to your book.

Did you know that Packt offers eBook versions of every book published, with PDF and ePub files available? You can upgrade to the eBook version at www.PacktPub.com and as a print book customer, you are entitled to a discount on the eBook copy. Get in touch with us at service@packtpub.com for more details.

At www.PacktPub.com, you can also read a collection of free technical articles, sign up for a range of free newsletters and receive exclusive discounts and offers on Packt books and eBooks.

http://PacktLib.PacktPub.com

Do you need instant solutions to your IT questions? PacktLib is Packt's online digital book library. Here, you can access, read and search across Packt's entire library of books.

Why Subscribe?

- ▶ Fully searchable across every book published by Packt
- ▶ Copy and paste, print and bookmark content
- ▶ On demand and accessible via web browser

Free Access for Packt account holders

If you have an account with Packt at www.PacktPub.com, you can use this to access PacktLib today and view nine entirely free books. Simply use your login credentials for immediate access.

Table of Contents

Preface

Whether you're just beginning your use of Avid Media Composer or you've been using it for some time, I believe this book contains a great deal of useful, time-saving, and frustration-reducing information for users at all experience levels. Further, I believe this book fills a particular gap in the Avid Media Composer publications that are currently available.

Because the features and abilities of Avid Media Composer are so broad, encompassing editing, sound design, color correction, and visual effects, I decided to focus this book primarily on the core story-telling needs we have every day; essentially, getting footage into the system, editing, and audio mixing.

I first began learning Avid Media Composer in 1994 through trial and error. Nonlinear editing and the Internet were still in their infancy, and there weren't any books on Avid Media Composer. So, I did my best to learn by reading the manual. My frustrations came when I'd read about a procedure or tool in the manual, but it didn't include a definition of it or context for when it would be useful. So, in addition to providing the step-by-step instructions, as cookbooks published by Packt Publishing promise, I've included many definitions of industry and Media Composer-specific terms, explanations of why tools and functions behave as they do, and situations when they would be helpful. In many ways, this is one of the books I wish I had had all those years ago.

I'd also like to mention that some incredibly knowledgeable people have helped me by reviewing this book's content while I was writing it: Michael Phillips, Oliver Peters, and Roger Shufflebottom. These very generous gentlemen are talented professionals whom you may find yourself meeting, consulting, or working with in the future. I encourage you to read their biographies, which are included in this book, and you'll see how fortunate I was to have them on the team.

Lastly, I truly hope you find this book to be helpful.

What this book covers

Chapter 1, Getting Assets into Your Media Composer Project, gets you thinking about organization, provides you with some common workflows, and gives you some tips to hopefully make your work easier and/or more productive.

Chapter 2, Customizing Your Work Environment, has a goal to show you some great features to help you work more comfortably, swiftly, and efficiently.

Chapter 3, Polishing Gems, explains that there are many useful features, gems if you will, that go underutilized. This chapter shines and polishes a few of them up by revealing some functions' hidden abilities, explaining their behavior, and/or giving you a few new ideas about how you might use them.

Chapter 4, Creating Split Edits, examines several methods to create a Split Edit, which is also known as an L Cut, Prelap, **Postlap**, or more simply, a Split.

Chapter 5, Maintaining and Regaining Sync, focuses on giving you a solid understanding of why Avid Media Composer works the way it does regarding sync, how you can be in complete control of staying in sync when using any of the editing modes (without Sync Locks enabled), what Sync Locks do and how they work, and what to do if you find yourself out of sync.

Chapter 6, Managing Your Media Files, has a goal to take some of the mystery out of dealing with media files, using the Media Tool, and helping you through some common media management situations.

Chapter 7, Mono and Stereo Audio Mixing, centers on many of the common audio mixing and effects tasks and challenges when working on a mono or stereo project.

Chapter 8, Editing with Group Clips and MultiCamera Mode, covers several methods to sync all the footage from different cameras used in a multiple-camera production, and how to edit with this footage in an efficient way using the features that Media Composer provides.

Chapter 9, Output Tips and Tricks, includes topics for creating bars and tone; adjusting your sequence to accommodate bars, tone, and slate; an overview of exporting still images and QuickTime movies; and familiarizing yourself with the Timecode Burn-In effect.

Chapter 10, Time Savers in the Title Tool is not present in the book but is available as a free download from the following link: `http://www.packtpub.com/sites/default/files/ downloads/Time_Savers_in_the_Title_Tool.pdf`.

This chapter examines some of the commonly overlooked behaviors and features of the Title Tool.

Appendix A, Additional Tips, Tricks, and Explanations, has additional helpful information about various functions and features that did not fit into the step-by-step format of a cookbook published by Packt Publishing.

Appendix B, Details on Trimming, Slipping, Sliding, and Segment Mode, provides helpful background and supplemental information for users at all levels to help demystify, and get more use from, Trim Mode and Segment Mode.

Appendix C, Helpful Details about MultiCamera Editing, provides supporting information for *Chapter 8, Editing with Group Clips and MultiCamera Mode*, which is beneficial to users at all levels.

What you need for this book

In addition to this book, you will need Avid Media Composer software, running on either a Mac or a PC. You can download a 30-day free trial of Avid Media Composer at `Avid.com`. While this book focuses on Avid Media Composer Version 6, because Avid has done a great job of preserving the majority of functionalities as the software has evolved, a great deal of the information will still be useful to those using other releases of the software.

Who this book is for

This book is intended as an additional resource for Avid Media Composer users ranging from those just beginning through intermediate users looking for a deeper understanding of the functionality of the software, tips, and tricks.

Conventions

In this book, you will find a number of styles of text that distinguish between different kinds of information. Here are some examples of these styles, and an explanation of their meaning.

Code words in text are shown as follows: "Project settings are located inside the `Project` folder along with the bins and folders that you created."

New terms and **important words** are shown in bold. Words that you see on the screen, in menus or dialog boxes for example, appear in the text like this: "On the **Record Track Selector Panel**, enable only the **V1** Track Selector."

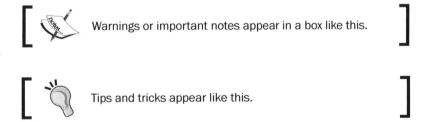

Warnings or important notes appear in a box like this.

Tips and tricks appear like this.

Reader feedback

Feedback from our readers is always welcome. Let us know what you think about this book – what you liked, or may have disliked. Reader feedback is important for us to develop titles that you really get the most out of.

To send us general feedback, simply send an e-mail to feedback@packtpub.com, and mention the book title via the subject of your message.

If there is a topic that you have expertise in and you are interested in either writing or contributing to a book, see our author guide on www.packtpub.com/authors.

Customer support

Now that you are the proud owner of a Packt book, we have a number of things to help you to get the most from your purchase.

Errata

Although we have taken every care to ensure the accuracy of our content, mistakes do happen. If you find a mistake in one of our books – maybe a mistake in the text or the code – we would be grateful if you would report this to us. By doing so, you can save other readers from frustration and help us improve subsequent versions of this book. If you find any errata, please report them by visiting http://www.packtpub.com/support, selecting your book, clicking on the **errata submission form** link, and entering the details of your errata. Once your errata are verified, your submission will be accepted and the errata will be uploaded on our website, or added to any list of existing errata, under the Errata section of that title. Any existing errata can be viewed by selecting your title from http://www.packtpub.com/support.

Piracy

Piracy of copyright material on the Internet is an ongoing problem across all media. At Packt, we take the protection of our copyright and licenses very seriously. If you come across any illegal copies of our works, in any form, on the Internet, please provide us with the location address or website name immediately so that we can pursue a remedy.

Please contact us at copyright@packtpub.com with a link to the suspected pirated material.

We appreciate your help in protecting our authors, and our ability to bring you valuable content.

Questions

You can contact us at questions@packtpub.com if you are having a problem with any aspect of the book, and we will do our best to address it.

1

Getting Assets into Your Media Composer Project

In this chapter we will cover:

- ▶ A strategy for project organization at the desktop level
- ▶ Understanding Media Creation settings
- ▶ Mixing frame rates
- ▶ Tape capture tip: Adding Markers while Capturing
- ▶ Tape capture tip: Making Subclips while Capturing
- ▶ Logging clips tip: Logging from the keyboard
- ▶ Logging clips tip: Keeping the Capture Tool active after logging a clip
- ▶ Quickly calculating total duration of clips (or any items in a bin)
- ▶ Combining available drive space and/or controlling where media is stored
- ▶ Making sure your Batch Capture continues without you
- ▶ Modifying clips before capture
- ▶ Modifying clips after capture: Adding tracks
- ▶ Modifying clips after capture: Deleting tracks
- ▶ Capturing and editing at the same time
- ▶ Preparing to use AMA (Avid Media Access): Getting the plug-ins
- ▶ AMA (Avid Media Access) linking
- ▶ Getting the AMA file's image to display as desired
- ▶ Consolidating (copying) AMA Master Clips

- ▸ Transcoding AMA linked clips before beginning to edit
- ▸ Transcoding AMA Master Clips after editing has begun
- ▸ Consolidating an AMA sequence or subclips
- ▸ Transcoding an AMA sequence
- ▸ Importing stills and video files such as QuickTime
- ▸ Importing audio
- ▸ Adjusting audio levels before editing
- ▸ Adjusting audio pan settings before editing
- ▸ Setting stereo-audio tracks

Introduction

You've created your project, and now comes the sometimes time-consuming task of acquiring your assets. In this chapter, I'll get you thinking about organization, provide you with some common workflows, and give you some tips to hopefully make your work easier and/or more productive.

A strategy for project organization at the desktop level

Some words to the wise to help you avoid some common pitfalls.

How to do it...

Following are the steps for organizing the project at the desktop level:

1. Determine a location for a folder that will hold items relating to your project that will not require being moved.
2. Create a folder and name it something that is clear and concise, for example, either `[Project Name] Materials` or `[Project Name] Assets`.
3. Inside that main folder, create additional folders for `Avid Project Backups`, files you will link to using the **Avid Media Access** (**AMA**) feature, `Music`, `Sound Effects`, `Imports_Stills`, `Imports_Motion Graphics`, `Photoshop Masters`, `Fonts`, `After Effects Projects`, and any others you think you'll need.

How it works...

By keeping everything organized and in a consistent location, you will have a much easier time keeping track of assets and changes to assets. Further, backing up, moving, archiving, or re-importing the assets will be easier.

The trick is to remember to copy assets into this folder before putting them to use in any way within your project. For example, copy music and sound effects from a CD to this folder, then import the audio file that's in the folder (rather than directly off the CD) into a Media Composer, or copy into this folder any fonts that you download before adding them to your operating system.

Understanding Media Creation settings

It's important to spend some time setting up your **Media Creation** settings. Essentially **Media Creation** settings allow you to set defaults, which will help ensure that the media files you create (for example, render files, imports, and so on) are stored where you want them and are of the resolution you need. Plus, it will save you time making selections in various dialog boxes and tools throughout the workday.

Getting ready

In your **Project** Window select the **Format** tab. Select the format of the media that you will be capturing, importing, and/or rendering. Media Composer will remember your **Media Creation** settings for each format that you configure. So, for example, if you're mixing SD and HD footage, you'll configure your **Media Creation** settings for each. Once your preferences are set in the **Media Creation** tool for each format, Media Composer will automatically switch to your customized settings whenever the format itself is switched.

How to do it...

The following steps will guide you through using the Media Creation Tool:

1. Go to the **Tools** menu at the top of your screen.
2. Select **Media Creation**.
3. Proceed section by section to set defaults for the resolution of the media that you create, as well as for the destination for that media. See the following *How it works...* section for details.

How it works...

The settings are separated by tabs, described as follows:

Drive filtering and indexing

▶ **Filter Network Drives Based on Resolution**: Selecting this will not allow media files to be placed on any network drives that Media Composer feels will not be able to reliably capture or playback files of a particular resolution. For example, you open your **Capture Tool** and set the resolution to **1:1**. Then when you go to select a drive to store your media files on, you may see that one is grayed out and not selectable. If you then change your resolution to **3:1**, you may find that it is now selectable as a storage drive.

▶ **Filter Out System Drive**: Selecting this will not allow the media files to be stored on the same drive that your operating system is installed on.

▶ **Filter Out Launch Drive**: Selecting this will not allow the media files to be stored on the same drive that your Media Composer software is installed on.

Video resolution

Under each tab you can select a default resolution. You are not locked into this resolution. Tools and dialog windows will still allow you to override this default whenever you want.

Apply to All: If you'd like to set a specific resolution and have it applied to all the different media type tabs, rather than having to do it one by one, simply click on the **Apply to All** button.

The benefit of breaking the media types into categories, such as **Capture**, **Render**, and **Import**, is that you can then set different defaults for each. For example, on a project with many hours of taped footage, you might elect to capture all of your footage at a low resolution in order to increase how much media will fit onto your drive(s). This will mean that when the project is creatively finished, you will go through a second process to recapture just the video portions that are being used at a much higher resolution, a process frequently called the Up-Res, so that the image quality will be higher. You may prefer to not have to go through a similar process for all of the titles, still images, and motion graphics, so you could elect to set the default for these media types at the level where you need them to be for the final master (for example, **1:1**).

Video drive/Audio drive

Under each tab, you can select a default location for the media types to be stored. You are not locked into this. Various tools and dialog windows will still allow you to override this default when desired.

This selection is helpful for ensuring files go where required, and it allows you to send render files (known in Avid terminology as `Precompute` files) to a specific drive if required by your facility.

Apply to All: If you want the storage drive to be the same for all the different media type tabs, rather than having to do it one by one, simply click on the **Apply to All** button.

Media type

Changing this is only possible for SD video, as HD will always be in the MXF format. **Media Creation** settings will default to the file format called **Material Exchange Format (MXF)**. You should not change this unless you are in the unique situation where you are generating media on one workstation that will have to be used on a much older workstation that can only play the **Open Media Framework (OMF)** file format.

Mixing frame rates

Yes, it's possible to mix footage with different frame rates. However, at the time of writing, the Media Composer only allows each Project to be at one frame rate. So, here's one method to make the mixing of frames rates possible.

Getting ready

You will create two separate projects, each at the required frame rate. Be sure to label them accordingly to avoid confusion. For example, one project would be named [Project Title] 29-97 (project names cannot contain a period) and the other would be named [Project Title] 24p.

How to do it...

The following are the steps to mix footage with different frame rates:

1. **Capture** and/or **import** your video into the corresponding projects based on the frame rates.

2. Decide which project will be the main/primary project that you will actually work within to edit and craft your movie. Most likely, this will be the project that contains the majority of your footage or matches the final delivery format that is required.

3. In your main project, ensure that no bins are currently selected in the **Project** Window.

4. Go to the **File** menu and select **Open Bin...**. (Alternatively, you will find the **Open Bin...** selection under the **Project** Window's **Fast Menu** as well as in the menu that will appear when you right-click in the **Project** Window.)

5. In the dialog window, navigate to the project that's at the other frame rate and contains the bin file that you want to open.

6. Select the bin and either double-click on it or click on the **Open** button in the dialog window.

7. The bin will open in your Project and you can access the contents.

8. Once the bin is open, it will be inside a folder created by Media Composer labeled `Other Bins`. This is short for other projects' bins. It means that the bin file does not reside inside the same folder as your Project's bin files.

At this point you can elect to begin editing right from those bins, or you may elect to copy the clips into a bin that does reside in your Project folder. See the next *There's more...* section for two methods of copying clips, called Duplicating and Cloning.

There's more...

There are two methods you can use to copy the clips (making a Duplicate or a Clone), each with a unique behavior. Whether you Duplicate or Clone a clip, you will never create any new media files, but will simply create an additional clip that refers (or you could say points) to the media file(s). Media Composer calls this reference a link and would say that the clip is linked to the media file(s).

▶ **Duplicating a clip**: Each clip acts independently of the other. For example, one clip could be named `Horse` and contain several Markers while the Duplicated clip could be named `White Horse Runs` and have no Markers. Making changes to the name, adding/removing I/O marks, and adding/removing Markers to one Duplicated clip does not have any affect on the other. Further, the creation date of a Duplicated clip will reflect the new date and time it was created.

▶ **Cloning a clip**: Cloned clips are able to communicate to their cloned brethren. For example, if you change the name of one Cloned clip, the other's name will also change. The same is true for adding and removing Markers as well as **In** and **Out** points. The creation date for all Cloned clips will be the same (the original date).

Duplicating clips

The following are the steps for duplicating clips:

1. Select the clips you want to Duplicate.

2. Go to the **Edit** menu.

3. Select **Duplicate**. Alternatively, you could right-click on one of the selected clips and choose **Duplicate** from the **Contextual** menu, or use the keyboard shortcut *cmd + D* (Mac) or *Ctrl + D* (PC).

4. New clips will be created and will have `.copy` added to the end of their names.

5. Create a new bin by clicking on the **New Bin** button in your **Project** Window, or go to the **File** menu and select **New Bin**.

6. Move the clips that you just created to the new bin.

7. If you no longer want to have the borrowed bin appear in the Other Bins folder, select the borrowed bin and either press the *Delete* key or right-click and select **Delete Selected Bins** from the **Contextual** menu. It's helpful to note that you are not actually permanently deleting the bin file, but rather just telling Media Composer that you no longer want to use it. The bin is still intact inside the other project's folder. For emphasis, this only applies to bins that are inside the Other Bins folder. Deleting a bin created within the currently open Project will place it into the Trash.

Cloning clips

The steps for Cloning the clips are as follows:

1. Create a new bin by clicking on the **New Bin** button in your **Project** Window, or go to the **File** menu and select **New Bin**.

2. Select the clips you want to **Clone**.

3. Press and hold the *Alt/option* key while you drag the selected clips to the new bin.

4. New clips will be created in the desired bin when you release the mouse button. These clips will *not* have .copy added to them.

5. If you no longer want to have the borrowed bin appear in the Other Bins folder, select it and either press the *Delete* key or right-click and select **Delete Selected Bins** from the **Contextual** menu. It's helpful to note that you are not actually deleting the bin file, but rather just telling Media Composer that you no longer want to use it. The bin is still intact inside the other Project's folder.

Sequences will never be Cloned

On a related topic, you can use either of the methods mentioned previously on a sequence. Both of the methods will produce a Duplicate of the sequence. In other words, both of the methods will make a sequence with the word .Copy added to it, and no matter which method you used to create that sequence, it will never, ever, communicate with another sequence in any way. They will always be totally independent. The changes made to one sequence will never be replicated in another.

Motion Adapters

Note that when you edit mixed frame rate clips into your **Sequence**, they are automatically adjusted. You'll see a small green dot on the clip that indicates that it contains what Avid calls a Motion Adaptor. The method used to adjust the image (for example, **Blended Interpolated** or **Both Fields**) can be changed by promoting the clip to a **Timewarp** effect. The Motion Adaptor is applied only to the video and preserves the original duration of the clip; further, the audio is not altered in any way.

Tape capture tip: Adding Markers while Capturing

This simple feature allows you to accomplish multiple tasks at the same time. As you capture material off tape, you can simultaneously add Markers to help you locate the takes you like and the takes that the members of the creative team like. For example, while Capturing and watching the footage with your director, you might use red Markers for what you deem to be useful takes and yellow Markers for the ones that the director likes.

Getting ready

This tip works when you're actively Capturing from the tape (the red light is blinking). Note that this tip does not work when Batch Capturing.

How to do it...

The steps that follow indicate how to add a Marker while Capturing:

1. Open the **Capture Tool** by going to **Tools** menu | **Capture Tool**.
2. Begin the Capture from tape (the red light is blinking).
3. While the capture is in progress, press any of the keys *F3* or *F5* through *F12* on your keyboard. *F3* or *F5* = Red Marker, *F6* = Green, *F7* = Blue, *F8* = Cyan, *F9* = Magenta, *F10* = Yellow, *F11* = Black, and *F12* = White.
4. See the *There's more...* section of this recipe for details.

How it works...

When the **Capture Tool** is active, it takes control of your *F* keys. Whatever you've mapped there for editing is replaced with several different functions, including the ability to add Markers.

There's more...

You can even add notes inside a Marker while capturing.

Adding notes in a marker during capture

1. While the capture is in progress, add a Marker using one of the *F* keys mentioned in the previous *How to do it...* section.
2. Press the *Tab* key to tell Media Composer you want to add a comment to that Marker (rather than naming the clip).
3. Type your comment.

4. Press the *F4* key to tell the **Capture Tool** that the Marker entry is completed. This will return the **Capture Tool** to its previous behavior of allowing you to name and comment on Master Clips and Subclips.

5. The markers will be visible once the capture is finished and the bin is saved.

Tape capture tip: Making Subclips while Capturing

While Capturing a long Master Clip, you have the ability to divide it into Subclips at the same time, which will save you time since you won't have to perform the Subclipping and labelling in a separate step. For example, you have a tape of an interview with the President of the United States and you need to get it into your Media Composer immediately. You can begin capturing from the start of the tape and by using the tip that follows in the next recipe, you'll also be able to create Subclips of each question and answer.

Note that this tip produces different types of subclip behavior depending on whether you are in a film Project or a video Project. If you set up your Project as a film project (for example, 16 mm or 35 mm) when you first created it, then the Subclips will be locked in their duration and cannot be trimmed longer in the **Sequence**. This is intentional in order to protect vital Key Code/Key Number information that is specific to film projects.

Getting ready

This tip works while you're actively capturing from the tape (the red light is blinking). Note that this tip does not work when Batch Capturing.

How to do it...

The steps that follow help us make Subclips while capturing:

1. Begin capturing (red light is blinking).

2. Press the *F1* key when you want to begin a new Subclip. If you want to update the location for the beginning of that Subclip to a later point, press the *F1* key again. You can update the **In** point at any time. It is not locked in until the *F2* key is pressed.

3. Begin typing to name the Subclip, if you want to.

4. You, optionally, can also press the *Tab* key to move the cursor into the Comment Entry Box and begin typing to add a comment.

5. Press the *F2* key to end the Subclip. If you want to update the location for the end of that Subclip to a later point, then press the *F2* key again. You can update the **Out** point at any time. It is not locked in until the *F1* key is pressed again.

6. Press the *F1* key to begin a new Subclip and repeat the preceding steps.

How it works...

During this process, you are creating one Master Clip that will refer to, point to, or, as Avid says, link to the media file(s) of video and/or audio. The Subclips do not create new media files; they are just shorter references to, or subsections of, the longer Master Clip.

Logging clips tip: Logging from the keyboard

This is a quick tip to aid in the faster logging of Master Clips from a tape during the Batch Capture process.

You may be aware that when the **Capture Tool** is selected and is in Capture Mode, that pressing the *F4* button will begin the Capture from the tape. Many are not aware that when the **Capture Tool** is in Log Mode, the *F4* key will send the logged clip into your designated bin. Further, this button can be mapped to wherever you prefer on your keyboard.

How to do it...

The following steps indicate how to log from the keyboard:

1. Open or create a bin.
2. Open the **Tools menu | Capture Tool**.
3. In the **Capture Tool** there is a pull-down menu labeled as **Bin**. From that menu, select the bin where you'd like your logged clips to be placed.
4. At the top of the **Capture Tool**, change the tool's mode from **Capture** to **Log**. To do this, click on the button near the **Trash Can** icon that says **CAP** so that it reads **LOG** and displays a pencil icon.
5. Log clips using the keyboard. You can control the following features using the keyboard keys:
    -   Control the deck with the *J*, *K*, and *L* keys
    -   Mark the start and end of your Master Clips with the *I* and *O*, or *E* and *R* keys
    -   Use the **Tab** key to navigate to the name and comment entry boxes
    -   Select/deselect the **V1**, **V2**, **A1**, **A2**, **A3**, and **A4** keys using the *7, 8, 9, 0, -,* and *=* keys respectively
6. Use the *F4* key to log a clip into your selected bin.

There's more...

You can map this logging feature to another location on your keyboard.

1. Go to the **Project** Window.
2. Click on the **Settings** tab.
3. Open your **Keyboard** settings by double-clicking on it.
4. Go to the **Tools** menu.
5. Select the **Command Palette**.
6. Click on the tab labeled **Play**.
7. In the bottom-left of the **Command Palette**, select **Button to Button Reassignment**.
8. Drag the **Record** button to your desired location.

 If you use the _J_, _K_, and _L_ keys to control the tape deck, consider mapping the **Record** button to either the _H_ or colon/semicolon key.

See also

- ▶ The _Logging clips tip: Keeping the Capture Tool active after logging a clip_ recipe in this chapter
- ▶ _Chapter 2, Customizing Your Work Environment_ includes an additional discussion of keyboard mapping as well as interface and work environment customization

Logging clips tip: Keeping the Capture Tool active after logging a clip

This is a quick tip to help with logging Master Clips from tape during the Batch Capture process.

When you are logging, once the clip is sent to the bin, the bin becomes active. This allows you to immediately begin naming the clip in the bin. However, what if you already named the clip in the **Capture Tool**, or are in a hurry to log, and plan on naming the clips more precisely later? In such cases, you may prefer that the **Capture Tool** always stays selected, so that you can log the clip to the bin and quickly return to shuttling the tape and logging more clips without having to select the **Capture Tool** again. The following setting will allow that.

How to do it...

These are the steps to keep the **Capture Tool** active after logging a clip:

1. Open the **Capture Settings** by either of the following methods:
   - In the **Project** Window, select **Settings tab | Capture Settings**
   - Right-click on **Capture Tool** and select **Capture Settings...**
2. In the **Capture Settings** window, click on the tab labeled as **General**.
3. Deselect the setting labeled as **Activate bin window after capture**.

Even though the name of the setting refers to capturing, this works for logging as well (that's why it's a bit of a hidden tip).

See also

▶ The *Logging clips tip: Logging from the keyboard* recipe earlier in this chapter

Quickly calculating total duration of clips (or any items in a bin)

After logging many clips you'll Batch Capture them. However, it's helpful to know the total duration of all the clips added together so you can make sure that your drive can accommodate that amount of media.

How to do it...

Below are the steps to calculate the total duration of selected clips:

1. Select all the clips that you want to calculate the duration for. Methods include *Shift +* clicking to select a range of clips, or going to the **Edit** menu and choosing the **Select-All** command.
2. Right-click on one of the selected Master Clips.
3. From the menu select **Get Bin Info**.
4. The **Console** window will open.

5. There will be an entry in the **Console** that reads **Total duration of selected items:**. The duration is displayed as Hours:Minutes:Seconds:Frames (refer to the screenshot below).

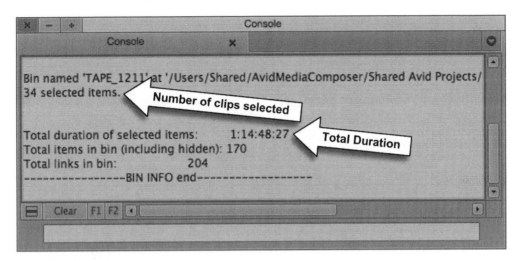

There's more...

This is also useful for calculating the total duration of multiple sequences (for example, if your movie or TV program is still divided into separate sequences for each act).

Combining available drive space and/or controlling where media is stored

The **Capture Tool** has a feature that lets you create a Drive Group that designates more than one drive for Media Composer to be used for media storage. This is helpful in the following situations:

▶ You want to make sure that the media files go to the drive(s) that you want when one becomes full, rather than Media Composer simply selecting the drive that happens to have the most free space

▶ You have a large amount of media to capture but there is not one single drive that has enough space

▶ Making a Drive Group is especially helpful when you want to leave the Capture process unattended

How to do it...

1. Open the **Tools menu | Capture Tool**.

2. Click on the **Drive Selection** menu. It's located directly below the **Bin Selection** menu and the **Resolution Selection** menu (refer to the next screenshot).

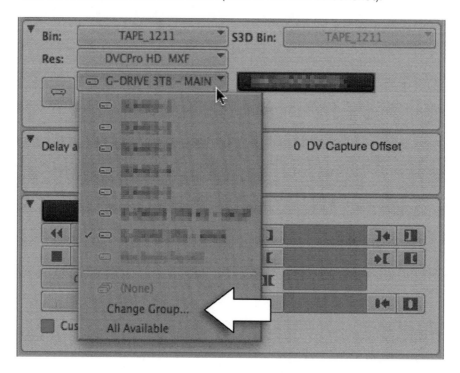

3. From the **Drive Selection** menu select **Change Group....**

4. A dialog window will open, listing all the available drives.

5. Press *cmd/Ctrl* and click to select your desired drives.

6. Press the **OK** button.

See also

▶ If you're Batch Capturing, also see the *Making sure your Batch Capture continues without you* recipe

▶ The *Quickly calculating total duration of all logged clips (or any items in a bin)* recipe may be helpful as you'll generally want to determine how much space is required for your media

Making sure your Batch Capture continues without you

You've logged many clips and are ready to begin Batch Capturing. You'd like to start the capture process and then run out for lunch. You just need to make sure that if the drive you've selected becomes full before capturing all the clips' media, that Media Composer won't stop and wait for you to tell it which drive to switch to. Further, you want to make sure that, if it has trouble capturing a clip, it will try a couple of times and then move on, rather than stopping on that one clip and waiting for you to tell it what to do.

How to do it...

Following are the steps to make sure your Batch Capture continues without you:

1. Open the **Capture Settings** by either of the following methods:
   - From the **Project** Window select **Settings** tab | **Capture Settings**
   - Right-click on the **Capture Tool** and select **Capture Settings...**

2. In the **Capture Settings** window, click on the tab labeled as **Batch**.

3. Enable the selection labeled **Switch to emptiest drive if current drive is full**.

4. Enable the selection labeled **Log errors to the console and continue capturing**.

There's more...

As an added measure and for more control, you may also want to create what Avid calls a Drive Group as discussed in the *Combining available drive space and/or controlling where media is stored* recipe.

Modifying clips before capture

There will come a time when something needs to be changed before a clip is captured (modifying clips after they have been captured is covered in the next section). The following are the typical issues:

- The clips were logged by hand using the incorrect type of **Timecode**
- The clips were associated with the wrong tape
- The clips were created with the wrong tracks

How to do it...

Below are the steps to modify clips before capture:

1. Select the clips. Some methods include *Shift* + clicking to select a range of clips or going to the **Edit** menu and choosing the **Select-All** command.

2. Open the **Modify** window by using either of the following methods:

    ❑   From the **Clip** menu, select **Modify**

    ❑   Right-click on any of the selected Master Clips and choose **Modify**

3. In the **Modify** window, click on the pull-down menu.

4. In order to change the:

    ❑   Type of **Timecode**, choose **Set Timecode Drop/Non-Drop**

    ❑   Tape association, choose **Set Source**

    ❑   Add or remove tracks, choose **Set Tracks**

Modifying clips after capture: Adding tracks

It's possible that you don't discover that you need additional tracks off the tape until after the capture is completed. You'll find that once a clip is captured, some modifications, such as setting tracks, are not possible without a little extra work called **Unlinking**.

Before we go through the process, an overview will be helpful. Unlinking is temporarily breaking the connection (in Avid terminology, the **Link**) between the clips and their media files. After Unlinking, you'll modify the clips to add the tracks you want. Then, you'll Relink the clips to the existing media. After the Relink, you'll capture the media that's missing.

How to do it...

Here are the steps to modify clips (adding tracks) after capture:

1. Select the clips. Some methods include *Shift* + *clicking* to select a range of clips, or going to the **Edit** menu and choosing the **Select-All** command.

2. Press the *Shift* key and the *cmd/Ctrl* key at the same time. As you're pressing these modifier keys, it changes the menu selection from **Relink** to **Unlink**.

3. Select the **Unlink** command by either:

    ❑   Selecting **Clip** menu | **Unlink**

    ❑   Right-clicking on any of the selected Master Clips and choosing **Unlink**

4. If the clips have become unselected, be sure to select them.

5. Open the **Modify** window by either:

    ❏ Selecting **Clip** menu | **Modify...**

    ❏ Right-clicking on any of the selected clips and choosing **Modify...**

6. In the **Modify** window, click on the pull-down menu.

7. Choose **Set Tracks**.

8. Select the tracks you want to add.

9. Click on **OK**.

10. If the clips have become unselected, be sure to select them.

11. Open the **Relink** window by either:

    ❏ Selecting **Clip** menu | **Relink...**

    ❏ Right-clicking on any of the selected Master Clips and choosing **Relink...**

12. Relink the clips.

13. If the clips have become unselected, be sure to select them.

14. Begin the Batch Capture process by either:

    ❏ Selecting **Clip** menu | **Batch Capture**

    ❏ Right-clicking on any of the selected Master Clips and choosing **Batch Capture**

15. Optionally, if you only want Media Composer to capture the media that's missing, then in the **Batch Capture** dialog window, enable the selection that says **Offline media only**.

16. Optionally, if you also need to capture new media files and at the same time get rid of the previous ones, then in the **Batch Capture** dialog window, deselect the option that says **Offline media only**. For example, you realize that you need to recapture the video at a different resolution.

> Deselecting this option deletes the existing media before it recaptures the new media.

See also

▶ If you need to delete tracks rather than add tracks, there are a few more important steps involved. See the *Modifying clips after capture: Deleting tracks* recipe.

Modifying clips after capture: Deleting tracks

It's possible you don't discover that you have tracks that you don't need until after the capture is completed. In this case you'll want to:

▶ Delete the unnecessary media to free up the drive space and ensure that you don't have orphan media files that are not linked to any clips.

▶ Modify the clips so they no longer refer to media files that don't exist (since you deleted them). This will help avoid confusion during the editing process.

Before we get into the specifics, here is an overview of the process. First you're going to use the **Media Tool** to delete the specific media files that you don't need. Then you'll find that once a clip has been captured, some modifications, such as setting tracks, are not possible without a little extra work called **Unlinking**. This temporarily breaks the connection (in Avid terminology, the Link) between the clips and their media files. After Unlinking, you'll modify the clips to remove the unnecessary tracks, and, finally, you'll relink the clips to the media that remains.

How to do it...

The following are the steps to modify clips (deleting tracks) after capture:

1. First, you're going to determine where the media files have been stored. Select the bin that contains all of your clips in order to make it active.

2. Change the bin display to **Text View** from the **Bin Display** menu at the bottom-left of the **Bin** window.

3. Open the **Bin Column Selection** window using any of the following methods:

   ❑ In the **Clip** menu, choose **Columns**

   ❑ Right-click in the bin and select **Choose Columns**

   ❑ Right-click in the **Column Headings** section at the top of the bin and select **Choose Columns** from that menu

4. The **Bin Column Selection** window opens. From the list of possible columns of information types, select **Drive** and click on **OK**.

5. Take note of the media drive(s) your clips are referring to.

6. Open the **Media Tool** by going to the **Tools** menu and selecting **Media Tool**.

7. In the **Media Drives** column of the **Media Tool**, select only the media drive(s) that your clips are referencing (those listed in the Drive column in your bin).

8. Click on the button labeled as **Current Project**, since you'd generally want to display media that belongs only to the currently open project and no other. If you did want to display media from other projects, you can *Shift* + click to select the additional project names.

9. Select the Master Clips checkbox. Note that in the end, you'll still be looking at media files. It's just that they will be displayed in a more familiar way, as Master Clips.

10. Deselect both the check boxes for **Precompute Clips** and **Media Files** and click on **OK**.

11. A window will open titled **Media Tool**. This window has all the features of a bin.

12. Arrange your **Bin** window and the **Media Tool** window so you can see both of them at the same time.

13. The next few steps are going to ensure that only the correct clips become selected in the **Media Tool**. Start by selecting the clips *in your bin*.

14. Go to the **Bin Fast Menu** at the bottom-left corner of the bin and choose **Select Media Relatives**. Note that the clips in your **Media Tool** have become selected.

15. Click on the top title portion of the **Media Tool** so that it is selected/active. Make sure that when you select the **Media Tool**, you don't mistakenly deselect the clips.

16. Press the *Delete* key on your keyboard.

17. The **Delete Media** dialog window will open.

18. Enable the check box for each track of media you want to permanently delete and click on **OK**.

19. Another dialog window will open. If you are positive that you want to permanently delete the media files you've selected, click on **OK**.

20. Close the **Media Tool**.

21. The unnecessary media is now deleted, but you are left with clips in your bin that are still looking for that media even though it isn't there or, in other words, is **Offline**. This can be very confusing during editing, so the next set of steps will fix that. If the clips have become unselected in your bin, be sure to select them before continuing.

22. In order to modify the clips, we have to temporarily break the connection (the Link) between the clip(s) and the media file(s), which is called Unlinking. To do this, press and hold the *Shift* key and the *cmd/Ctrl* key at the same time (this changes the **Relink** menu selection to **Unlink**).

23. Select the **Unlink** command by either:

   ❑ Selecting **Clip** menu | **Unlink**

   ❑ Right-clicking on any of the selected Master Clips and choosing **Unlink**

24. If the clips have become unselected, be sure to select them.

25. Open the **Modify** window by either:

    ❑   Selecting **Clip** menu | **Modify**

    ❑   Right-clicking on any of the selected Master Clips and choosing **Modify**

26. In the **Modify** window, click on the pull-down menu and choose **Set Tracks**.

27. Deselect the tracks that no longer have media to link to, since you just deleted it. In other words, make sure only the tracks that still have media available on the drive(s) are selected. Click on **OK**.

28. If the clips have become unselected, be sure to select them.

29. Open the **Relink** window by either:

    ❑   Selecting **Clip** menu | **Relink...**

    ❑   Right-clicking on any of the selected Master Clips and choosing **Relink...**

30. Relink the clips. Additional information on Relinking is available in the **Avid Media Composer Help**.

Capturing and editing at the same time

If you're in a hurry, it's possible to edit the clip(s) being captured into the **Sequence** at the same time that you capture from the tape.

How to do it...

Here are the steps to capture and edit at the same time:

Create a new sequence or load an existing sequence into the **Timeline** Window.

1.   In the case of an existing sequence, clear any existing **In** and/or **Out** Marks.

2.   Place the blue Position Indicator where you'd like to begin adding the clips.

3.   Open the **Capture Tool** using any of these methods:

    ❑   **Tools** menu | **Capture Tool**

    ❑   **Workspaces** menu | **Capture**

    ❑   *cmd/Ctrl + 7*

4. Open the **Capture Settings** by either:

   ❑ Right-clicking on the **Capture Tool** and choosing **Capture Settings**

   ❑ Going to the **Project** window, selecting the **Settings** tab, and double-clicking on the **Capture Settings**

5. In the **Capture Settings** window, click on the tab labeled **Edit**.

6. Select/enable the feature labeled as **Enable edit to timeline (splice, overwrite)**. Click on **OK**.

7. Look at your **Capture Tool**. At the top, two new buttons have appeared, one for Splicing and the other for Overwriting.

8. Select/enable either the **Splice** or **Overwrite** function in the **Capture Tool**.

9. Begin capturing a portion of the tape.

10. End the capture of that clip.

11. That clip will automatically be edited into the **Sequence**.

12. Continue to capture to add more clips to the **Sequence**.

13. When you are finished, to avoid unintentional editing into the **Sequence** during a future capture session, be sure to either:

    ❑ Deselect the **Splice** or **Overwrite** button in the **Capture Tool**

    ❑ Disable this feature in the **Capture Settings**

Preparing to use AMA (Avid Media Access): Getting the plug-ins

AMA allows you to almost immediately begin editing with file-based video, without first having to go through another process, such as Transcoding or Importing. Essentially, you point Media Composer directly to the native files, and because of AMA programming/architecture, it recognizes them and links to them. However, Media Composer needs to be given the ability to recognize the files first. This is done by installing free plug-ins for each camera and/or video format (note that the QuickTime AMA plug-in is an exception and is installed by default). Using plug-ins means that they can be updated at any time independently from the Media Composer program, and, as new video formats are created, their AMA plug-ins can be made available by the manufacturer at the same time.

How to do it...

Here are the steps to get the AMA plug-ins:

1. You will need to access the Internet.

2. To get to the AMA plug-ins page at `Avid.com`, either:

   ❑ To open the **AMA Settings**, go to the **Project** Window, select the **Settings** tab, and double-click on **AMA Settings**. In the **AMA Settings** window, click on the tab labeled **Volume Mounting**. At the bottom of the **Volume Mounting** window is a link labeled **Check for additional or updated AMA plug-ins at Avid.com**.

   ❑ At the time of writing, you may visit one of the following links:

      i. `http://www.avid.com/ama`

      ii. `http://www.avid.com/products/Avid-Media-Access`

3. On the `Avid.com` web page, you'll see a link labeled **Download** and/or there will be three tabs near the top labeled **Overview**, **Features**, and **Plug-ins**.

4. Click on either the **Download** link or the **Plug-ins** tab.

5. Before downloading a plug-in, make sure the file formats will work with AMA and your version of Media Composer. At the time of writing, there is a link below the **Downloads** column that states **Please refer to the 'AMA Plug-ins and Media Composer Version Compatibility' table for software requirements**.

6. Download the AMA plug-ins for the formats that you'll be using and that correspond to the version of Media Composer that you're using.

7. Each plug-in has its own installer and will guide you through the installation process.

Avid also provides helpful, in-depth AMA user guides for different video formats on the same page as the download links. I highly suggest downloading them for the formats you will be using. They provide a good deal of helpful information that is outside the scope of this book.

There's more...

You can verify what plug-ins have been installed or check which version of a plug-in is installed.

1. Open the **Console** window by either:

   ❑ Selecting **Console** from the **Tools** menu

   ❑ Pressing *cmd/Ctrl* + 6

2. In the text entry box at the bottom of the **Console** window, enter the following:
   `AMA_ListPlugins`

3. Press **Return** (Mac) or **Enter** (PC).

4. A table will be generated in the **Console** window that lists the plug-in name(s) and its version number.

AMA (Avid Media Access) linking

AMA allows you to almost immediately begin editing with file-based video formats, such as P2, XDCAM, QuickTime, RED, and others, without first having to endure the very time-consuming Import or Transcode process before editing.

 Before undertaking a project using the AMA feature, it is highly recommended that you perform a small-scale test of the process to familiarize yourself with the options and results. Ideally, you would be able to perform your small-scale test prior to receiving the mission-critical files and prior to the intensity of working under a deadline.

Avid provides helpful AMA user guides for the different video formats. You'll find them on the same page as the AMA plug-in downloads (URLs provided below). They provide a good deal of helpful information that is outside the scope of this book. At the time of writing, you may visit one of the following links:

▶ `http://www.avid.com/ama`

▶ `http://www.avid.com/products/Avid-Media-Access`

On the `Avid.com` web page, you'll see a link labeled **Download** and/or there will be three tabs near the top labeled **Overview**, **Features**, and **Plug-ins**. Click on either the **Download** link or the **Plug-ins** tab. You will find the AMA user guides there.

Getting ready

First, perform the steps as detailed earlier in the *Preparing to use AMA (Avid Media Access): Getting the plug-ins* recipe.

How to do it...

Following are the steps to link to files with AMA:

1. Configure your **AMA Settings** by going to the **Project** Window, selecting the **Settings** tab, and then double-clicking on **AMA settings**.

2. In the **Bins** tab, you may select how Media Composer will react when it automatically detects that you've mounted a volume (for example, a P2 card or a removable drive). This also becomes the action that Media Composer will perform when you manually AMA link to a volume, and in the **Bin Selection** dialog window that will open during the AMA linking process, you select **Bin(s) Based On Current AMA Settings**.

   ❑ To use active bin, in this case, you would first select an open bin inside your Project before mounting or manually linking to the volume through AMA

   ❑ Create a new bin:

      i. Default bin naming convention: The bin that's automatically created will have the name of the Project (with an incrementing number added for each new bin).

      ii. Volume name: The bin that's automatically created will have the name of the card or drive.

      iii. Specify bin name: The bin that's automatically created will have the text that you type into the entry box

3. Some video formats provide multiple files with varying compression. In the **Quality** tab, you may select which files the AMA process will initially link to. Note that the files that are linked to can be changed later, and this is discussed in the later recipe titled *Changing the link between different resolutions of media*.

4. Link Options sets a default for how to treat the audio tracks (for example, mono or stereo). Note that this can be changed later by selecting the clips and using the **Modify** command from the **Clip** menu.

5. Click on the **OK** button to close the **AMA Settings** window.

6. You're now ready to begin the AMA linking process. The following steps cover linking to files that have been copied off a camera card. You will see this referred to as linking to a **Virtual Volume**. If you want to link to the files directly off of the camera card, see the *There's more...* section that follows this section for details. The following steps presume that:

   ❑ You have copied the files off the original camera card and organized them in a fashion as discussed at the beginning of this chapter, in the recipe titled *A strategy for project organization at the desktop level*.

   ❑ The original file and folder structure on the card has been kept perfectly intact during the copy process to a drive. In other words, there are no differences between the contents of the card and the copy on the drive. Note that this is very important and is something you should discuss with the production team prior to shooting.

> ❑ You have chosen to allow Media Composer to make a new bin when it creates the AMA link, rather than selecting a current bin.

7. From the **File** menu, select **Link to AMA Volume**.

8. The browser window will open.

9. Browse to the location of your files keeping the following in mind:

   > ❑ XDCAM files: Select one folder above the **Clip** folder
   >
   > ❑ XDCAM EX files: Select one folder above the **BPAV** folder
   >
   > ❑ P2 files: Select one folder above the **Contents** folder
   >
   > ❑ RED files: Navigate to the root directory
   >
   > ❑ GFCAM files: Navigate to the root directory
   >
   > ❑ QuickTime files: Navigate to the folder that contains the files

10. Click on **OK**.

11. A dialog window may open (usually when Media Composer detects multiple folders within a directory that contains media) and ask you how you would like to have the bin created.

    > ❑ **Bin(s) based on current AMA setting**: This is the default selection. Use this if you want the bin to follow your AMA settings.
    >
    > ❑ **Single bin named**: This method allows you to override your AMA settings for this moment and set a specific name.
    >
    > ❑ **Single bin based on selected folder**: If you made a main folder named AMA Media, and then placed the contents of three different P2 cards inside it (each card having its own folder) and named each P2 card's folder as card_1, card_2, and card_3, Media Composer would make just one bin named AMA Media, and the clips from card_1, card_2, and card_3 would all be placed within it.
    >
    > ❑ **Bin(s) based on subfolders**: If you made a main folder named AMA Media, then placed the contents of three different P2 cards inside (each card having its own folder) and named each P2 card's folder as card_1, card_2, and card_3, Media Composer would make three separate bins. The bins would be named card_1, card_2, and card_3.

There's more...

Some more aspects of linking are mentioned in this section.

Linking to files on a camera card

If you choose to work directly off the camera card rather than copy and organize your files, as discussed earlier in this chapter in the *A strategy for project organization at the desktop level* recipe, then follow the next set of steps:

1. Launch Avid Media Composer.

2. Insert the card into the card reader attached to your system.

3. When the card is recognized by the computer and is mounted, Media Composer will scan the volume (the card).

4. A bin will be created and named based on your AMA settings.

5. Media Composer will grab the clip data from the card and create Master Clips. Then, it will link the Master Clips to their media files.

6. After successfully linking, each Master Clip will display a chain link icon attached to it.

Changing the link between different resolutions of media

If your media type provides you with versions of the files at different resolutions, you may want to switch linking from one resolution to another. For example, you've initially linked to the low-resolution version of the media for editing, and now you'd like to change the link to the high-resolution version for finishing.

1. Select the clips in your bin.

2. Right-click on the selected clips.

3. Choose **Modify AMA Resolutions...** from the menu.

4. The **AMA Resolutions Quality** window opens.

5. Select the video quality that you want for your video.

6. Click on **OK**.

Having trouble with AMA?

You can get more information from the AMA plug-in Log File.

A note from Avid technology:

> *The Avid system creates an AMA plug-in log file when you link clips. The log file records errors and information about the clips. If you experience any problems while you link clips or if you receive an error message, check the AMA log file to get more information about the error (for example, a corrupt file or a bad filename).*

You can view the log file from the following location on your system:

▶ (Windows) drive:\Program Files\Avid\Media Composer\Avid FatalError Reports. The name of the log file is AMALoggerMM_DD_YY.log.

▶ (Macintosh) Volume/Users/Shared/AvidMediaComposer/Avid FatalError Reports. The name of the log file is AMALoggerMM_DD_YY.log.

See also

▶ The *Getting the AMA file's image to display as desired* recipe in this chapter

Getting the AMA file's image to display as desired

If you link to media using the AMA process and the clip does not match the aspect ratio and frame size set in your **Format** tab, then Media Composer will allow you to change the way it is displayed at any time.

An important note from Avid technology:

If you are working in an Interplay environment, do not change the Reformat attribute from the Stretch setting. If you use a different setting, and you then use 'Interplay Transcode' or 'Send to Playback,' the results might not be what you expect.

How to do it...

Below are the steps to display the AMA file's image as desired:

1. Set your bin to be displayed in **Text View** from the **Bin Display** menu in the lower left of your bin.

2. You're going to display the **Reformat** column. Start by going to the **Bin** menu and selecting **Choose Columns**.

3. In the **Bin Column Selection** window choose **Reformat**.

4. Click on **OK** to close the window.

5. Select the clip(s) in your bin for which you want to **Reformat** the display.

6. In the **Reformat** column of the selected clip(s), click to reveal, and also choose, the alternate display options. If multiple clips are selected, you can change the **Reformat** setting for one of the selected clips and have that setting applied to all of the selected clips.

7. Note that if you loaded the clip into the **Source** Window, you will see the **Reformat** display change occur. Whatever you set here will be applied to the clip when it is edited into your sequence. However, if you have already edited the clip into a sequence, the version in the sequence will continue to display in the manner that it was set in when it was first edited into the sequence. This is to prevent changes being applied to the sequences that are considered complete and ready to export or master to tape. If you want to update all the instances of the clip in your sequence to use the new **Reformat** setting, this can be done without having to re-edit the clip(s). Follow the next set of steps:

8. Select the sequence(s) in the bin.

9. Right-click on the selected sequence(s).

10. Choose **Refresh Sequence**.

11. From the submenu select **Reformatting Options**. See the next section for details.

How it works...

Below are the **Reformat** options that are available along with the explanation of each.

▸ **Stretch**: If the Project is set to display 4:3, then a 16:9 image will be stretched vertically. If the Project is set to display 16:9, then a 4:3 image will be stretched horizontally.

▸ **Pillarbox/Letterbox**: This feature scales the image as large as possible within the currently set aspect ratio that you've set for your Project's display. If the Project is set to display 4:3, then a 16:9 image will be letterboxed (black bars on the top and bottom). If the Project is set to display 16:9, then a 4:3 image will be Pillarboxed (black columns on the left and right-hand side of the screen).

▶ **Center Crop**: No scaling occurs in this option. If the project is set to display 4:3, then a 16:9 image will have the left and right hand side portions of the image cropped. If the project is set to display 16:9, then a 4:3 image will have the top and bottom portions cropped.

▶ **Center Keep Size**: If the image is larger, when it is centered in the window, portions of the image on all the sides may be cropped. If the image is smaller, then its native size will be displayed and black color will appear around it.

Changing the project's aspect ratio display

Note that not all formats support multiple aspect ratio displays. Here are two methods that are available:

Method 1: **Project** Window | **Format** tab | **Aspect Ratio** menu.

Method 2: Right-click in either the **Source** Window or the **Record** Window and select **Project Aspect Ratio**, and then select the desired display from the submenu.

Consolidating (copying) AMA Master Clips

Consolidating is Avid Media Composer's method of making copies of media files.

[Consolidating (copying) is a process done by using the Media Composer software. It is not done by simply copying the files at the desktop level.]

The Consolidation process specified in this recipe can be used either before you have begun to edit or at any stage during editing. What you'll be doing is making copies of your AMA files in their entirety. When completed, your Master Clips will link to the copied media (in the Avid MediaFiles folder) and Media Composer will create new clips that will link to the AMA media files. (For the clips that link to the AMA media, Media Composer will put an extension on them that says .old.) If you've already begun to edit, the sequence will link to the copied media rather than the AMA media.

[
Before consolidating all of your files, it is highly recommended that you perform a small-scale test of the process to familiarize yourself with additional options and results. The steps below focus on only one specific result. Ideally, you would be able to perform your small-scale test prior to receiving the mission-critical files and prior to the intensity of working under a deadline.

The AMA linking feature can be very processor intensive, and Avid recommends that users Consolidate the media into what they refer to as the Managed Media environment (which means the Avid MediaFiles folder) as soon as is practical, in order to take advantage of faster processing and a linking architecture that is more mature and robust than AMA.

Some formats cannot be Consolidated (copied) using their original Codec, and Media Composer will alert you that they will also need to have their Codec changed during the copy process. This is referred to as Transcoding. Ideally, you would transcode your Master Clips prior to doing any editing, though there is a process available in case you have already started to edit. Information on this is available in the *Transcoding AMA Master Clips before beginning to edit* and *Transcoding AMA Master Clips after editing has begun* recipes.

If you want to Consolidate only the shorter portions of media that are being used by a sequence or subclips, rather than the entire Master Clip media, see the recipe titled *Consolidating an AMA sequence or subclips.*
]

Getting ready

If your media type provides you with versions of the files at different resolutions, you may want to switch linking from one resolution to another. For example, you've initially linked to the low-resolution version of the media for editing and now you'd like to change the link to the high-resolution version for Consolidating. If this applies to you, then follow the next set of steps; otherwise, proceed to the *How to do it...* section:

1. Select the clips in your bin.
2. Right-click on the selected clips.
3. Choose **Modify AMA Resolutions...** from the menu.
4. The **AMA Resolutions Quality** window opens.
5. Select the video quality that you want for your video.
6. Click on **OK**.

How to do it...

The following are the steps for consolidating the media clips:

1. Select the clips in the bin.
2. From the **Clip** menu select **Consolidate/Transcode**.
3. In the top-left of the **Consolidate/Transcode** window, select **Consolidate**.
4. In the **Video/Data** region of the window, select the drive (also known as the target drive) that you want the copied files to be stored on.
5. Do *not* enable the selection that says **Delete media files when done**. In the case of AMA linked media files, they will not be deleted even if this is selected. Further, Media Composer will not create a Master Clip that links to the AMA media as it should.
6. Click on the **Consolidate** button.
7. The **Copying Media Files** dialog window opens.
8. Select the second option that reads **Relink Master Clips to media on target drive**. This option also includes some helpful text that reads **Selected Master Clips will be relinked to the new media on the target drive. Master Clips with a .old extension will be created and linked to the original media**. In this case, the original media refers to the AMA linked files.
9. Click on **OK** and the Consolidate (copy) process begins.

See also

▸ The *Consolidating an AMA Sequence or Subclips* recipe in this chapter

Transcoding AMA Master Clips before beginning to edit

Some formats cannot be Consolidated (copied) using their original codec. Media Composer will alert you that they will also need to have their codec changed during the copy process, or you may wish to change the codec when you copy the media. This is referred to as Transcoding.

Before you Transcode all of your files, it is highly recommended that you perform a small test of the process to familiarize yourself with any additional options and results. Additional options include, but are not limited to, **Debayer Settings** (found in the **Media Creation** settings) for RED footage, which also need to be configured. Ideally, it is best if you are able to perform your small-scale test prior to receiving the mission-critical files and prior to the intensity of working under a deadline.

 As the title of this recipe suggests, the next set of steps would be used *before* editing and will focus on only one specific result. If you have already begun to edit, see the *Transcoding AMA Master Clips after editing has begun* recipe.

Getting ready

If your media type provides you with versions of the files at different resolutions, you may want to switch linking from one resolution to another. For example, you've initially linked to the low-resolution version of the media for editing and now you'd like to change the link to the high-resolution version for Transcoding. If this applies to you, then perform the following steps, or, if this does not apply to you, then proceed to the paragraph that follows these steps:

1. Select the clips in your bin.
2. Right-click on the selected clips.
3. Choose **Modify AMA Resolutions...** from the menu.
4. The **AMA Resolutions Quality** window opens.
5. Select the video quality that you want for your video.
6. Click on **OK**.

If you are Transcoding Standard Definition video to High Definition or vice versa, then you'll want to ensure the highest quality result using the next set of steps. If this does not apply to you, then proceed to the *How to do it...* section.

1. From the **Project** window, select the **Settings** tab and double-click on **Render Settings**.
2. Select the **Image Interpolation** pull-down menu.
3. Select **Advanced (Polyphase)**.
4. Click on **OK**.

How to do it...

Below are the steps to Transcode AMA linked media before editing:

1. In the **Project** window select the **Format** tab.
2. Select the Project Type and **Aspect Ratio**.

> *Avid states: New clips created through the Transcode operation are in the Project Format. When you Transcode a clip across formats, for example if you Transcode a 16:9 clip in a 4:3 project, the* **Reformat** *bin setting determines how the clip is conformed to the new format.*
>
> For details on the **Reformat** option, see the recipe *Getting the AMA file's image to display as desired.*

3. Select the clips in the bin.
4. **Clip** menu | **Consolidate/Transcode**.
5. In the top-left of the **Consolidate/Transcode** window, select **Transcode**.
6. In the **Video/Data** region of the window, select the drive where you want the copied media files to be stored.
7. Select the video resolution that you want the copied media files to become.
8. Click on the **Transcode** button to begin the process.

> **Transcoding is not magic**
>
> Transcoding cannot increase the quality of the image. For example, if your footage came from a MiniDV tape (the resolution is DV25) and you transcoded it to a resolution of 1:1 (uncompressed), the new file will take up more space on your hard drive but will not look any better. On the other hand, if you transcoded to 20:1, then the file will be compressed and the image quality will be reduced.

See also

▸ The Transcoding AMA Master Clips after editing has begun recipe

▸ The Transcoding an AMA sequence recipe

Transcoding AMA Master Clips after editing has begun

Before Transcoding all of your files after editing has begun, it is a very good idea to perform a small-scale test of the process to familiarize yourself with any additional options and results. Additional options include, but are not limited to, **Debayer** settings (found in the **Media Creation** settings) for RED footage, which also need to be configured. Ideally, you would be able to perform your small-scale test before receiving the mission-critical files and prior to the intensity and pressure of working under a deadline.

When you Transcode Master Clips, Media Composer automatically makes new Master Clips (with the `.new` extension), and those new clips will *not* link to a sequence that was created from them automatically. So, you'll have to make the sequence link to the new Master Clips with a process called Relinking.

Getting ready

The steps given in the *How to do it...* section presume that:

▸ You have begun to edit

▸ You have already followed the steps in the recipe *Transcoding AMA Master Clips before beginning to edit*

▸ You now have a bin(s) with new, Transcoded Master Clips

How to do it...

The following are the steps for Transcoding after editing has begun:

1. Open all the bins that contain the `.new` Transcoded clips.
2. Open the bin containing your sequence.
3. Select all the `.new` Transcoded files in all of the open bins.
4. Select your sequence.
5. Go to **Clip** menu | **Relink**. (You may also right-click on the selected sequence.)

6. In the **Relink** window, enable the selection that says **Selected items in ALL open bins**.

7. At the bottom of the window, make sure to enable the check box that says **Create new sequence** and click on **OK**.

8. At the completion of this process, a new sequence will be created with the text `Relinked` at the end. This sequence is now linked to the Transcoded clips. If you load the sequence into the **Timeline**, you'll see that the clip names will also have the `.new` extension on them.

Consolidating an AMA sequence or subclips

Before consolidating a sequence, it is very highly recommended that you perform a small test of the process on an unimportant sequence to familiarize yourself with additional options and results. Additional options include, but are not limited to, **Debayer** settings (found in the **Media Creation** settings) for RED footage, which also need to be configured. The steps of this recipe focus on only one specific result.

Consolidating a sequence or subclips simply means you'll be making copies of only the portions of media files that are being referred to by your sequence or by the subclips. Essentially, Media Composer will take each shot used in the sequence, or each subclip, and make a brand new Master Clip for it.

You'll have the option to add handles. Handles are additional media added to the head and tail (beginning and end) of the new Master Clips that are not currently being used/seen/heard in the sequence or subclips. Handles are helpful in case, after Consolidating, you need to do some trimming within a sequence or need to add a transition effect like a dissolve.

You'll also have the option to delete the original media after the Consolidate (copy) process is completed. Deleting the original source media would be helpful with a sequence if you had completed all of your editing and wanted to save drive space, or with subclips, if *before you began* editing you only wanted to keep portions of Master Clips. On the other hand, one use of not deleting the original media would be if you wanted to give a coworker a copy of your sequence or a portion of a clip to work with.

Getting ready

Before consolidating a sequence, it is always a very smart idea to make a backup copy of the sequence and place it into its own well-labeled bin (for example, `My Movie Before Consolidate`). This extra version will not only protect you in case you make an error, but will help keep your project organized for future reference (not to mention bring you additional peace of mind).

How to do it...

Here are the steps to consolidate an AMA sequence or subclips:

1. Select the sequence or the subclips.

2. **Clip** menu | **Consolidate/Transcode** (you may also right-click on the selected Sequence or Subclips).

3. The **Consolidate/Transcode** window will open.

4. In the upper left-hand corner of the window, select **Consolidate**.

5. In the **Video/Data** region of the window, select the drive where you want the copied files to be stored.

6. In the **Handle Length** entry box, enter the number of frames you want added to the head and tail of each new Master Clip.

7. If you are Consolidating a sequence, be sure to select the **Create new sequence** check box. Even though I suggested earlier that you make a backup copy manually prior to the consolidate process, this provides an additional layer of protection.

8. For the **Delete original media files when done** choice, my instruction here will be to *not* select this check box. In other words, I am instructing you to *not* delete the original media files after Media Composer has completed making copies of just the portions of media that are being used by your sequence or subclips. If you do indeed want to delete the original media, then you would select this option.

9. Click on the **Consolidate** button at the bottom of the window.

10. The consolidate process will begin.

11. On Completion of the process you will have the following:

   ❏ Master Clips that have the extension `.new` added to them. The duration of each Master Clip will be only whatever it is in the sequence or subclip, plus the added duration of the handles.

   ❏ A new sequence with the addition of `.Consolidated` at the end. This sequence is linked to the `.new` clips.

   ❏ Your original sequence will remain linked to the original Master Clips that you edited from.

   ❏ In the case of subclips, Media Composer creates new Master Clips that are the total duration (including handles) as well the as new subclips that are the duration of the original subclips.

Transcoding an AMA sequence

Before Transcoding a sequence, it is recommended that you carry out a small test of the process to familiarize yourself with additional options and results. These additional options include, but are not limited to, **Debayer** settings (found in the **Media Creation** settings) for RED footage, which also need to be configured. The steps that follow focus on only one specific result. Ideally, you would be able to perform your small-scale test prior to receiving the mission-critical files and prior to the intensity of working under a deadline.

Some formats cannot be Consolidated (copied) using their original codec, and Media Composer will alert you that they will also need to have their codec (also known as resolution) changed during the copy process. This is referred to as Transcoding.

Transcoding a sequence simply means that you'll be making copies of only the portions of the media files that are being referred to by your sequence. (Essentially, Media Composer will take each shot used in the sequence and make a brand new Master Clip for it.) Further, as it generates new media files, it will also be changing the media files' codec.

Unlike Consolidating, Transcoding does not offer the option to delete the original media files after it has completed the Transcoding process.

Getting ready

Before Transcoding a sequence, it is a very wise idea to first make a backup copy and place it in its own well-labeled bin (for example, `My Movie Before Transcode`). This extra version protects you in case you make an error, and will help to keep your project organized for future reference.

How to do it...

The steps to Transcode an AMA linked sequence are as follows:

1. First, review the information presented earlier in this chapter, in the *Transcoding AMA Master Clips before beginning to edit* recipe.
2. In the **Project** Window select the **Format** tab.
3. Select the Project Type and **Aspect Ratio**.

    Important note from Avid Technology:

    New clips created through the Transcode operation are in the project format. When you transcode a clip across formats, for example if you transcode a 16:9 clip in a 4:3 project, the Reformat bin setting determines how the clip is conformed to the new format.

[For details on the **Reformat** option, see the *Getting the AMA file's image to display as desired* recipe.]

4. Select the sequence in the bin.

5. **Clip** menu | **Consolidate/Transcode** (you may also right-click on the sequence).

6. In the top left of the **Consolidate/Transcode** window, select **Transcode**.

7. In the **Video/Data** region of the window, select the drive you want the copied files to be stored.

8. In the **Handle Length** entry box, enter the number of frames you want added to the head and tail of each new Master Clip.

9. Be sure to select the **Create new sequence** check box. Even though I suggested earlier that you make a backup copy manually prior to the Transcode process, this provides an additional layer of protection.

10. Click on the **Transcode** button at the bottom of the window.

11. The **Transcode** process begins.

12. On completion of the process you will have the following:

   ❑ Master Clips that have the extension .new added to them. The duration of each clip will be whatever it is in the sequence plus the added duration of the handles.

   ❑ A new sequence with the addition of .Transcoded at the end. This sequence is linked to the .new clips.

   ❑ Your original sequence will remain linked to the original Master Clips that you edited from.

Importing stills and video files such as QuickTime

We're often given still images in formats such as .jpg, .gif, .png, or even as a layered Photoshop file, all of which can be imported into Avid Media Composer. Further, there will be instances when you'll need to import a QuickTime file rather than AMA link to it. For example, you've been given a motion graphic that contains an Alpha Channel (transparency information) that is meant to be composited on top of video. AMA linking will not recognize the Alpha Channel, so you must import it. Another example is regarding Broadcast Wave Format (BWF) files. AMA should never be used with BWF files as the **Timecode** will be incorrect and offers no control over Pull-up and Pull-down Sample Rates. See **Avid Media Composer Help** for additional information. The search term is BWF.

What does Avid Media Composer mean when it uses the term *Import*? In Media Composer, Import means that new media is created during the import process. The format of the media created is dictated by the settings in your **Project** Window's **Format** tab. The resolution is dictated in your **Media Creation** settings. For comparison, Adobe After Effects also uses the term import, except that in its case it is only pointing (linking) to the file rather than making new media as Media Composer does.

If you want to animate within a still image (often referred to as The Ken Burns Effect), you will most likely not want to import the image since that restricts the image size to that of your current format, which would mean having to scale the image up in order to pan and tilt across it. Scaling up reduces the quality of the image. If you are looking to create the Ken Burns Effect, then you'll want to check **Avid Media Composer Help** regarding the Avid Pan & Zoom effect. If you have the **Boris Continuum Complete** (**BCC**) effects package installed on your system, I also suggest checking out the BCC Pan & Zoom effect. You may also want to investigate other plug-ins available for this effect from the **Marketplace** menu.

Getting ready

Organize your files. Some suggestions are in the *A strategy for Project organization at the desktop level* recipe, earlier in this chapter.

How to do it...

Here are the steps to import video and still image files.

1. **Project** Window | **Format** tab.

2. In the **Format** tab set the Project Type, **Aspect Ratio**, **Color Space**, and **Raster Dimensions** for the media you'll create during the import.

3. Open the **Media Creation** settings using any of these methods:

   - **Tools** menu | **Media Creation**
   - *cmd/Ctrl + 5*
   - **Project** Window | **Settings** tab, and then double-click on **Media Creation**

4. In the **Media Creation** window select the **Import** tab.

5. Set the Video Resolution for the media you'll create during the import.

6. Set the drive where you want the media that you create to be stored.

7. Click on **OK** to close the **Media Creation** window.

8. Open your **Import Settings** by selecting the **Project** Window | **Settings** tab, and then double-clicking on **Import Settings**.

9. In the **Import Settings** window, click on the **Image** tab.

10. In the **Image** tab, you'll select the appropriate options for your situation. A brief explanation of these options is in the *There's more...* section that follows this recipe of steps.

11. Click on the **OK** button to close the **Import Settings** window.

12. You can now import with one of the two following methods:

    ❏ Method 1: Drag the file(s) from their location on a drive directly into a bin. All the settings you previously set will dictate how the media will be created and on which drive the media will be stored. Once you drop the files into the bin, both the Master Clips and media will be created. Layered Photoshop files will open an additional dialog window. Those options are discussed after the *There's more...* section that follows this recipe.

    ❏ Method 2: Select an open bin. Then, either right-click within the bin and select **Import** from the **Contextual** menu or go to the **File** menu and select **Import**.

13. The following steps relate to using Method 2 for import.

14. Be aware that when using Method 2, note that in the **Select Files To Import** window you will have the ability to do the following:

    ❏ Click on the **Options** button to access the **Import Settings**

    ❏ Set the resolution for the media you'll create during the import

    ❏ Set the drive where you want the media you create to be stored

15. In the **Select Files To Import** window, navigate to the file(s) you want to import.

16. Select the file(s).

17. Click on the **Open** button.

There's more...

The **Import Settings** window can be a bit confusing, so let's go over the options in the **Image** tab.

Image size adjustment

This selection relates to how the image will be scaled during the import:

- **Image sized for current format**: This means that the file is the same frame size as the video format you are using. In other words:
    - 648 x 486 square pixels for an NTSC SD 4 x 3 project
    - 864 x 486 square pixels for an NTSC SD 16 x 9 project
    - 1920 x 1080 for a 1080 HD project
    - 1280 x 720 for a 720 HD project

- **Crop/Pad for DV scan line difference**: If your SD project is the full raster of 720 x 486 and you import an image sized for DV (720 x 480), then Media Composer will add in (pad) the six missing lines. On the other hand, if your project is DV and your graphic is 720 x 486, then Media Composer will remove (crop) the extra six lines. By either padding or cropping, it means that your image will not be subtly distorted.

- **Do not resize smaller images**: Images smaller than your video format will not be resized and will appear in the center of the frame. Images with an Alpha channel will have a transparent area surrounding them while those without will have black surrounding them.

- **Resize image to fit format raster**: Whether larger or smaller, the image will be scaled to fit within your video format's size. If your image is longer horizontally, then it will be scaled until it reaches the left and right edges of the frame. If your image is longer vertically, then it will be scaled until it reaches the top and bottom edges of the frame. Any remaining areas will be filled with black. Note that if your release of Media Composer is not allowing this to work within a 16 x 9 SD project, the workaround is to switch to an HD format, import, and then switch back.

File Pixel to Video Mapping

This section relates to how the luminance (brightness) and the chrominance will be interpreted during the import:

- **Computer RGB (0 - 255)**: Choose this if your file came from a computer graphics application such as Photoshop, After Effects, or Apple Motion. Selecting this option tells Media Composer to adjust the image during the import so it fits properly into the broadcast levels. Specifically, the darkest value in the graphic is mapped to the level of video black for your video format and the brightest value is mapped to the level of video white. All other values are adjusted proportionately.

- **Computer RGB, dither image colors**: This is used in the same situation as Computer RGB, except it performs one extra operation on the graphics file. If the file has fine gradients and you notice there is banding in the final imported image, try this. The extra operation it performs adds some noise (dithering) that may help to reduce or hide the banding.

- **601 SD or 709 HD (16 - 235)**: Choose this only if your file is already at the proper broadcast levels for your video format. For files created in other applications, such as Photoshop or After Effects, this will be infrequent. However, good examples of files that are already at broadcast levels include the SMPTE Color Bars file that Avid provides inside the Test_Patterns folder, and video files such as P2 that can be imported.

Additional selections

The following are the additional selections within the **Import** dialog window:

- **Frame Import Duration**: When you import a still image, you can tell Media Composer how long you'd like the duration of the Master Clip to be. Media Composer will only create a frame or two (which Avid calls a Slide) of actual media, so you can set any duration you like without worrying that the media will take up a lot of drive space. This simply instructs Media Composer to refer to the "slide" over and over again for the duration that you specify.

- **Autodetect Sequentially-Numbered Files**: Choose this option if you are given a folder containing many files where each represents one frame (for example, of an animation). They'll be numbered in order (sequentially). During import you would select only the first file in the folder (not all the files). Media Composer will then automatically look for file number two, then file number three, and so on (autodetection). When the import is completed, Media Composer will have assembled all the files (frames) into one single Master Clip.

 Be sure to leave this option deselected if you are not importing sequentially-numbered files for the purpose of assembling them into a single Master Clip upon import.

- **Field Ordering in File**: This is not to be confused with **Field Dominance**; these options only apply to interlaced video formats. If your video format is progressive, these options will not be displayed. Before you can know what to select here, it's pretty helpful to know what the native field order is for different video formats:

  - NTSC is Even (Lower Field First)
  - HD is Odd (Upper Field First)
  - PAL is Odd (Upper Field First)
  - PAL DV is Even (Lower Field First)

With that knowledge, the details on the Field Order import selections, which follow, will be more useful:

- ❑ **Ordered for current format**: Use this for still images without fields, and for importing still images and video files with fields that match the field order of your video format. For example, the video file is NTSC and your project format is NTSC, or your video file is HD and the project is HD.

- ❑ **Odd (Upper Field First)**: Choose this option if there is a mismatch between the graphic file's field order and the video format of your project. Specifically, the file is a format with Odd field order and the project's video format has Even field order.

- ❑ **Even (Lower Field First)**: Choose this option if there is a mismatch between the graphic file's field order and the video format of your project. Specifically, the file is a format with Even field order and the project's video format has Odd field order.

▶ **Alpha Channel**: The Alpha Channel is grayscale and is used to define the opaque and transparent areas.

- ❑ **Invert on Import (white = opaque)**: This is the most common setting choice you'll make and is used when you get a graphic from a designer who has used After Effects, Photoshop, or similar applications to create it. This takes the grayscale Alpha Channel information in the file and inverts it to conform to how Avid Media Composer likes it (black is opaque).

- ❑ **Do not invert (black = opaque)**: You'll rarely use this. However, if a designer's application happens to create the graphic file with the Alpha Channel the way that Media Composer likes it (black = opaque), then this is the choice you'd make.

- ❑ **Ignore**: The Alpha Channel information is discarded during import, and the file that is created will be opaque rather than a Real Time Matte Key.

Layered Photoshop files

When you import a Photoshop file with two or more layers, Media Composer will give you an additional dialog window with the following options:

▶ **Sequence of Layers**: Media Composer brings in each individual layer as a separate Master Clip. It also assembles each Master Clip (layer) into a completed sequence just as in the Photoshop file.

 Media Composer will not recognize Layer Styles (for example, Drop Shadow, Bevel, and so on). If you have applied Layer Styles, you'll want to first duplicate your Photoshop file (as a backup version). Then, within that duplicate, you will need to merge all the layer effects into the layers themselves before importing into Media Composer.

> ▶ **Flattened Image**: All the layers in the graphic file are married together into one single Master Clip.

> ▶ **Select Layers**: This feature allows you to choose just the layers you want from the file. Each layer will become a separate Master Clip. Naming the layers in your graphic file will be very helpful if you plan to use this option.

See also

> ▶ If your file also contains audio, then the *Adjusting audio levels before editing*, *Adjusting audio pan settings before editing* and *Setting stereo-audio tracks* recipes may be helpful

Importing audio

There are a couple different methods to import audio files (or files containing audio), which I'll cover here. Check out the sections that follow for some additional audio tips and settings.

If you are importing BWF (Broadcast Wave Format) audio files, see **Avid Media Composer Help** for additional information. The search term is BWF.

Getting ready

Organize your files before importing. Some suggestions are in the *A strategy for project organization at the desktop level* recipe.

How to do it...

These are the steps to import an audio file:

1. Go to the **Media Creation** settings using any of these methods:
   - ❏ Go to the **Project** Window, select the **Settings** tab, and then double-click on **Media Creation**
   - ❏ **Tools** menu | **Media Creation**
   - ❏ *cmd/Ctrl + 5*

2. Select the **Import** tab.

3. From the **Drive** menu set a destination for the imported media.

4. Click on **OK** to close the **Media Creation** window.

5. This is an optional step: adjust **Import Settings** as discussed in the *Adjusting audio levels before editing, Adjusting audio pan settings before editing,* and *Setting stereo-audio tracks* recipes.

6. You can now import with one of the following two methods:

    ❏   Method 1: Drag the file(s) from their location on a drive directly into a bin. All the settings you previously configured will dictate how the Master Clip will be set (for example, level adjustment and/or stereo tracks) and on which drive the media will be stored. Once you drop the files into the bin, both the Master Clips and media will be created.

    ❏   Method 2: Select an open bin. Then, either right-click and select **Import** from the **Contextual** menu or go to the **File** menu and select **Import**.

7. The following steps relate to using Method 2 to import.

    When using Method 2 note that in the **Select Files To Import** window, you have the ability to do the following:

    ❏   Click on the **Options** button to access the **Import Settings**

    ❏   Set the drive where you want to store the media you will be creating

    ❏   Set the Resolution for the video media that you may create during the import

8. In the **Select Files To Import** window, navigate to the file(s) you want to import.

9. Select the file(s).

10. Click on the **Open** button.

See also

▶   The *Adjusting audio levels before editing, Adjusting audio pan settings before editing,* and *Setting stereo-audio tracks* recipes

Adjusting audio levels before editing

There will be times when a Master Clip's audio levels are too loud (as is very often the case with imported audio) or too low, and you want to adjust the level setting before playing it in the **Source** Window or editing it into your sequence. There are three methods available. The steps that follow present one method, and the other two can be found in the *There's more...* section. None of the methods make any changes to the actual media file(s). Each method just applies a setting for the Master Clip that can be adjusted at any time, including in the sequence.

How to do it...

This method is a fast and simple way to adjust one or more clips in a bin:

1. Import or capture clips into a bin.
2. Select the clip(s) you want to adjust.
3. **Clip** menu | **Apply Gain**.
4. The **Apply Clip Gain** window opens.
5. Enter the value that you want to be applied.
6. Click on **OK**.

There's more...

The following are two additional methods to adjust audio levels before editing clips into the sequence:

Using Import settings

This is particularly helpful when importing music and sound effects, as they generally come in very loud. I find that adjusting to a level of **-14** is a good starting point, as it can always be adjusted later:

1. Open the **Import** settings: **Project** Window | **Settings** tab | double-click on **Import**.
2. Select the **Audio** tab.
3. Enable/check the setting that says **Apply attenuation/gain effect on Import**.
4. In the entry box, type in the level value that you want to be applied.
5. If you want this setting to be applied only to audio coming from a CD rather than from all the audio files, check the box that says **CD Only**. Since I organize my files as discussed in the recipe titled *A strategy for project organization at the desktop level*, I leave this selection disabled/unchecked.
6. Now, when you import an audio file (or a video file containing audio), this level setting will automatically be applied.

Using the Audio Mix tool

This method only affects one clip at a time:

1. Open the **Audio Mixer** tool from the **Tools** menu.
2. Set the **Audio Mixer** to **Clip Volume and Pan mode**, which is abbreviated simply as **Clip**. This is done by clicking on the **Audio Mixer Mode** button in the upper right-hand corner of the **Audio Mixer** tool.

3. Load a Master Clip into the **Source** Window.

4. With the **Source** Window active, the level adjustment you make to the Master Clip using the **Audio Mixer** will be applied before you edit it into your sequence.

Adjusting audio pan settings before editing

This is particularly helpful when you have a mono clip (for example, a voice over) or separate mics on each channel of a multitrack clip (for example, an interviewer on channel one and the interview subject on channel two). In these instances, there's no need to edit the audio onto two tracks to make it play out of both the left and right speakers (channels). Instead you can set the clip to split the one signal out to both the left and right channel, so you only have to edit it onto one track. This panning operation goes by several names (center pan, mid, or mono), but it all means the same thing.

One thing to be aware of is that when you center pan a clip, the audio level will be reduced by about 3 dB due to the nature of how Media Composer deals with how we perceive audio levels when panned (called the Pan Law). So, depending on your situation, you may find that after setting a clip to mid you will need to increase the level by 3 dB in order to return it to its level prior to being center panned.

There are three methods available to center pan a clip depending on your needs. This recipe presents one method, and the other two can be found in the *There's more...* section. None of the methods make any alterations to the actual media file(s). This is just a setting that is applied to the Master Clip that can be adjusted at any time, including in the sequence.

How to do it...

This method is a fast and simple way to adjust one or more clips in a bin to center pan. It's also important to note that this method will affect all the tracks in a Master Clip.

1. Import or capture your audio file(s) into a bin.

2. Select the clip(s) you want to adjust.

3. Go to the **Clip** menu and select **Center Pan**.

4. A confirmation window opens.

5. Click on **OK**.

There's more...

The following are two additional methods to adjust audio pan before editing clips into the sequence:

Using the Audio Mix tool

This method affects only one clip at a time:

1. Open the **Audio Mixer** tool from the **Tools** menu.

2. Set the **Audio Mixer** to **Clip Volume and Pan mode**, which is abbreviated simply as **Clip**. This is done by clicking on the **Audio Mixer Mode** button in the upper right-hand corner of the **Audio Mixer** tool.

3. Load a Master Clip into the **Source** Window.

4. Select the pan entry/display box (see the following screenshot).

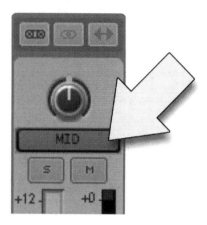

5. Enter one of the following values:

   ❑   0 (zero) to set the pan to **MID**

   ❑   -100 to set the pan to 100% left channel

   ❑   +100 to set the pan to 100% right channel

6. Press **Enter**.

Using Import settings

This method only works if the source audio file is mono to begin with.

1. Open the **Import** settings: **Project** Window | **Settings** tab | **Import**.

2. Select the **Audio** tab of the Import settings.

3. Enable/check the setting that says **Automatically center pan monophonic clips**.

4. Now, when you import an audio file (or a video file containing mono audio), this pan setting will automatically be applied.

Setting stereo-audio tracks

In Avid Media Composer, you can have Master Clips that are interpreted by the software as mono, stereo, 5.1 surround, and 7.1 surround. Each type can only be edited onto matching tracks in your sequence. For example, a stereo Master Clip can only be edited onto a stereo track.

There are three methods available, depending on your situation and needs. The recipe will present one method and you'll find two alternative methods in the *There's more...* section.

How to do it...

This method is used on one or more clips in a bin:

1. Import or capture your clip(s) that contains audio tracks into a bin.

2. Select the clip(s) you want to effect.

3. Go to the **Clip** menu | **Modify....** (You may also right-click on the selected clips and choose **Modify....**)

4. The **Modify** dialog window opens.

5. From the pull-down menu select **Set Multichannel Audio**.

6. From the menu below the tracks, configure how you want the audio tracks to be interpreted by Media Composer (for example, as stereo).

7. Click on **OK**.

There's more...

Here are the two additional methods for setting tracks to stereo:

Using Import Settings

The steps that follow indicate how to set tracks to stereo using **Import Settings**:

1. Open the **Import Settings** by going to the **Project** Window, selecting the **Settings** tab, and then double-clicking on **Import Settings**.

2. Select the **Audio** tab.

3. In the section labeled **Multichannel Audio**, click on the button labeled **Edit**.

4. The **Set Multichannel Audio** dialog window opens.

5. From the menu below the tracks, configure how you want the audio tracks to be interpreted by Media Composer.

6. Click on **OK**.

7. Now, when you import the clips containing audio, they will automatically be configured as you set.

During capture from tape

Following are the steps to set tracks to stereo during the capture from tape:

1. Open the **Capture Tool**.

2. From the menu below **Audio Track Selectors**, configure how you want the audio tracks to be interpreted by Media Composer.

2
Customizing Your Work Environment

In this chapter, we will cover:

- ▶ Settings overview
- ▶ Creating Site Settings
- ▶ User Profile Settings – transferring to another workstation
- ▶ Interface settings
- ▶ Font size adjustment
- ▶ Creating Bin Views
- ▶ Creating Timeline Views
- ▶ Customizing Workspaces
- ▶ Creating Bin Layouts
- ▶ Linking Bin Layouts with Workspaces
- ▶ Linking other settings with Workspaces
- ▶ Mapping Workspaces and Bin Layouts
- ▶ Mapping buttons and menu selections

Introduction

It's a demanding work day in the editor's chair, and the more comfortably, swiftly, and efficiently you can get through it, the better. In this section the goal is not only to show you some great features built into the software and how to make them work, but also to get you thinking about how you work and how you might use these features, so that you can have more time to be creative.

Settings overview

There is a great deal of customizability in Avid Media Composer; much of it can be achieved through various settings. The following discussions provide a helpful overview.

Types of settings

Media Composer has three types of settings as follows:

- **User Settings**: These apply to modifications you make and are stored as part of your unique User Profile settings in the `Avid Users` folder. User settings include things such as customized keyboards, render settings, Timeline Views, Bin Views, and more. User Settings are entirely separate from Projects, which allows you to use them along with any Project and at any workstation. We will see more information on User Profile Settings later in this chapter.

- **Project Settings**: Project Settings are located inside the `Project` folder along with the bins and folders that you created. Changes made to Project Settings affect it and any other editor(s) who work with that Project. Project Settings include information about the video format, audio configuration (for example, sample rate), video display, and more.

- **Site Settings**: The word "site" in this case means your computer workstation and/or associated hardware such as tape decks connected to that system. Site Settings are useful for making specific settings available to all new projects and new users. For emphasis, Site Settings will only be put into effect when a new Project or a new User Profile is created. When Media Composer creates a new Project or new User, it first looks at the `Site Settings` file before loading any Project and User Settings that are not in that file. This can be a real time saver for things that are used over and over again, for example custom Export Settings, Deck Configuration Settings, Safe Color settings, Interplay settings, and more. Information on customizing Site Settings will be covered later in this chapter.

Duplicating settings to create alternate versions

Settings can be duplicated and then customized, so you can have alternate versions available when you need them.

One thing to be aware of is that when you display your settings (**Project Window | Settings tab**), the selections within the **Project** window's **Fast Menu** (the hamburger-looking icon in the top-left corner of the **Project** Window) will be different from when the **Project** Window is set to display bins. If the menu is set to display only the active settings, rather than all settings, it can often cause confusion when you duplicate settings as they will not be visible immediately. For emphasis, make sure that when you're duplicating settings that the **Project** Window's **Fast Menu** is set to display all settings.

To duplicate a setting, perform the following steps:

1. Go to **Project window | Settings tab**.

2. Click on a setting to select it.

3. Use any of these methods to duplicate the setting:

   ❑ Select **Edit menu | Duplicate**

   ❑ Press *cmd/Ctrl + D*

   ❑ Right-click on a setting and select **Duplicate**

Naming settings

Start by hovering your cursor over the setting name. As you slowly move your cursor to the right, you'll see it change from the hand icon to the arrow icon, which will allow you to click into that entry cell and type in.

Activating alternate settings

When there are multiple settings available, only one can be active at a time. It's the one with the check mark that Media Composer pays attention to. You can change which alternate setting is enabled by clicking just to the left of it. This will move the check mark and make that setting active. There are two notable exceptions to this, however. Custom Bin Views and custom Timeline Views can only be activated using the **Bin View Menu** located at the bottom of every bin or the **Timeline View Menu** located at the bottom of the Timeline Window.

Alternate settings ideas

The following are some useful alternate settings to get you started:

► **Keyboard**: You could create several keyboard layouts, each customized for a specific task (for example, editing, capturing, multicamera editing, audio mixing, and so on). My suggestion is to start with your personalized editing keyboard that already has your customized mappings for various functions, Workspaces, Timeline Views, and so on. Then duplicate that keyboard, rename it, and make the specific (most likely minor) changes you want for the new task.

► **Grid**: You may find that it's faster to preset a couple of different grid display settings and then switch between them by moving the check mark than having to reconfigure it each time. For example, I have several different grid displays for different aspect ratios along with varying combinations of Safe Title, Safe Action, and assorted grid lines displayed. More information on grid settings can be found in *Chapter 3, Polishing Gems*.

> ▸ **Import**: You may find that it's faster to preset a couple of different common Import settings and then switch between them by moving the check mark than having to reconfigure it. This is especially helpful if you use the drag-and-drop import method.

> ▸ **Composer**: Composer settings allow you to customize such settings as **Always Display Two Rows of Data** above the **Source** and **Record** windows, **Undo Only Record Side Events**, enable **Single Mark Editing**, and make some choices for when you're editing in MultiCam Mode or in Stereo 3D, and to control the behavior of the Fast Forward and Rewind functions.

Deleting settings and two warnings

Deleting a setting is as easy as selecting it, and performing either of the methods below:

> ▸ Press the *Delete* key.

> ▸ Right-click on it and select **Delete**.

The following are some warnings and some good news about deleting settings:

> ▸ **Warning number one**: The setting will instantly be deleted. Media Composer will not give you an additional dialog box when deleting a setting, which would allow you to cancel the operation.

> ▸ **Warning number two**: Once a setting is deleted, it can not be brought back by using the Undo command. Instead, you would have to rebuild it all over again.

> ▸ **Good news**: You cannot delete an active setting, so you'll never be left without a keyboard setting, for example. Further, this would be a good time to point out that you should save some backup copies of your User Settings in case you mistakenly delete something or if they become corrupted.

Restoring a setting back to default

The following is useful if/when you've made modifications to a setting and if you want to revert back to the default selections later, as they were when Media Composer was first installed. Perform the following steps to restore a setting back to default:

1. Go to **Project window | Settings tab**.

2. Select a setting.

3. You may then do either of the following:

   ▫ Go to **Special menu | Restore To Default**

   ▫ Right-click on the setting and select **Restore To Default**

4. A dialog box will open, which will allow you to simply restore the setting, or to save your customized version of the setting as well as provide you with a restored version.

Creating Site Settings

More information about the Site Settings is included in the discussion titled *Settings overview*. Next we'll cover how to make them:

1. Open a Project that contains one or more settings you want to use as Site Setting(s).

2. Access User and Project settings via **Project Window | Settings tab**.

3. Open Site Settings. From the **Special** menu, select **Site Settings**.

4. The **Site Settings** window will open.

5. In your **Settings** list, select one or more settings.

6. Drag-and-drop the selected setting(s) into the **Site Settings** window to copy them.

7. Close the **Site Settings** window.

User Profile Settings – transferring to another workstation

User Profile Settings ("User Settings" for short) are several files that are collected together in a folder (location detailed ahead). When I talk about backing up your User Settings in a moment, it's important to understand that I'm talking about backing up the entire folder, not simply the contents of that folder. Further, it's important to note that you should not rename the User Profile Settings folder. Media Composer requires that the folder name and some of the files inside be named identically.

Your User Settings should be backed up in a few locations so that you can easily access them during the workday. User Settings are notorious for becoming corrupt and then causing any number of strange, unpredictable, and decidedly unpleasant behaviors. Having a backup of your personal User Settings means you can easily replace the bad ones if/when you have to, and quickly get back to editing.

Transferring your User Settings between workstations and between platforms is possible, which saves you a lot of time not having to rebuild your custom keyboard, Timeline Views, Bin Views, and so on. If you are transferring User Settings created with the same version of Media Composer which is installed on the destination system you will be using, then all you have to do is copy them into the appropriate location (see below). However, if your User Settings were created on a different version of Media Composer than what is installed on the new system you will be using, then it's not recommended to simply copy your User Settings folder over. Because of differences in the platforms and across the different versions of software, simply copying User Settings between platforms and/or versions can cause very odd and quite objectionable behaviors while editing. So, Avid provides a very simple procedure, detailed below.

It should also be noted that Avid recommends that if/when possible, it is best to create brand new, fresh User Settings rather than using the import process explained next.

Getting ready

First, it's crucial to know where User Settings are located. They can be found at the locations, as explained below:

Macintosh: `Users | Shared | Avid Media Composer` (or `Avid Symphony`) `| Avid Users`. Your User Settings will be based on the following:

- ▶ If you're the only user on that system and have not created any additional User Settings, then your settings will be the folder immediately inside the `Avid Users` folder

- ▶ If you're one of several editors who use that workstation, then your settings will be inside the folder with the logged-in user's name

Windows XP: `Documents and Settings | All Users | Shared Documents | Avid Media Composer` (or `Avid Symphony`) `| Avid Users`. Your user settings will be based on the following:

- ▶ If you're the only user on that system and have not created any additional User Settings, then your settings will be the folder immediately inside the `Avid Users` folder

- ▶ If you're one of several editors who use that workstation, then your settings will be inside the folder with the logged-in user's name

Windows 7 / Windows Vista: `Users | Public | Public Documents | Avid Media Composer` (or `Avid Symphony`) `| Avid Users`. Your user settings will be based on the following:

- ▶ If you're the only user on that system and have not created any additional User Settings, then your settings will be the folder immediately inside the `Avid Users` folder

- ▶ If you're one of several editors who use that workstation, then your settings will be inside the folder with the logged-in user's name

How to do it...

Now that you have some background information about User Settings and know where they reside, let's go through the import process. Perform the following steps:

1. Make your previously saved, original User Settings (the ones you want to import) accessible. So, download them from your cloud storage (for example, iCloud, DropBox, etc.), mount your flash drive, or insert your CD.

2. Go to the **Project** Window and select the **Settings** tab.

3. Directly below the **Settings** tab is the User Profile selection drop-down menu, as shown in the following screenshot:

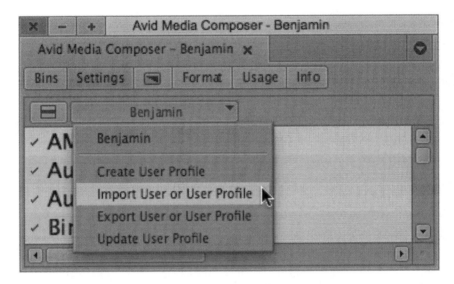

4. From the User Profile Selection Menu, choose **Import User or User Profile**.

5. The **Select User Directory** window opens.

6. Navigate to your original User Settings folder (on your flash drive, or maybe you've copied them to the desktop).

7. Select your original User Settings folder.

8. Click on the **Choose** button at the bottom of the **Select User Directory** window.

9. Media Composer will then create a brand new User Settings Profile and place it within the workstation's currently logged-in user's User Settings folder.

Interface settings

Interface settings are not a difficult area to experiment with on your own, but I wanted to make sure to mention them so you'll check them out, as they've changed a bit over the last several releases.

Further, if you happen to be using a version of Media Composer released before version 6, there is a programming bug to be aware of—if you set your interface brightness to its lightest/brightest level, then you may find that the columns in your Effect Palette display as black. The fix for this is simply to set your interface brightness to one level darker.

How to do it...

To customize Interface settings, perform the following steps:

1. Go to the **Project** window, select the **Settings** tab, and double-click on **Interface**.

2. Modify the settings as desired. You can test them out before committing to them by clicking on the **Apply** button.

3. See earlier in this chapter for more information about duplicating, deleting, restoring, and naming settings. If you have multiple Interface settings by default, or if you have created more, then only one of them will have a small check mark just to the left of it. The one with the check mark is the one that is active and is telling Media Composer how to look. You can change which alternate setting is active by clicking to the left of it. This will move the check mark and put that setting into action.

Font size adjustment

As computer screens have increased in resolution, icons and fonts have decreased in size. Personally, I find that the default font sizes are too small in most of Media Composer's windows and tools (even for some with younger eyes than mine).

As of this writing, it's possible to change the font display only at the following locations:

▸ The **Project** Window

▸ The **Composer** Window (also known as the **Source/Record** Window)

▸ Timeline Views

▸ Bins (also see the section titled *Additional Bin Font Programming* later in this chapter)

▸ The **Effect Editor** window (for this, see the section titled *Effect Editor font size later* in this chapter)

How to do it...

To adjust font size, perform the following steps:

1. Select the **Project** Window, **Composer** Window (also known as the **Source/Record** Window), **Timeline** Window, or a bin to make it active.

2. Go to the **Edit** menu and select **Set Font**.

3. The **Set Font** box opens.

4. Select a font style and/or type in a font size.

5. Click on the **OK** button.

There's more...

The following are two additional tips regarding font size:

Additional bin font programming

At the time of writing, the feature I will mention here is currently not working in Version 6, but does work in earlier releases. I'm including it for those who may be using earlier releases of Media Composer, and in the hope that it will be returned in future versions.

Whenever you change the font style and/or size in a bin you are also telling Media Composer to repeat that choice for all the bins you create from that point on. This is helpful because when you create a new Project you can set the first bin as you prefer and know that the many new bins you'll create from that point on will have the attributes you like.

Effect Editor font size

There's not much flexibility with font size in the **Effect Editor** window, but it is possible to enlarge it a bit. Perform the following steps to do so:

1. Go to the **Project** window, click on the **Settings** tab, and double-click on **Effect Editor**.

2. Enable/check the selection that says **Large Text**.

3. Click on **OK**.

Creating Bin Views

Bin Views are customized displays of information you can access when a bin is placed into Text View. These customized Bin Views are available to any bin (and the **Media Tool**) by using the Bin View menu at the bottom of each bin window (see the following screenshot).

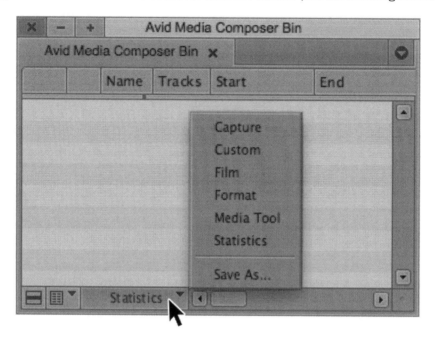

In addition to the columns of information that Media Composer comes with, you can create as many custom columns of information as you like (for example, best performance, shot type, quality, and so on).

After the basic recipe for creating a Bin View, there is information on creating custom columns and changing an existing Bin View in the *There's more...* section.

How to do it...

Perform the following steps to create Bin Views:

1. Open a bin.

2. Place the bin into Text View from the display menu in the lower-left corner of the bin window (it's the menu right next to the **Fast Menu**).

3. Open the **Bin Column Selection** Window by one of these methods:

   ❏ Right-click in an open area of the bin and select **Choose Columns** from the contextual menu

   ❏ Go to the **Bin** menu and select **Choose Columns**

4. The **Bin Column Selection** Window opens.

5. Select and/or Deselect to set the information you would like to have displayed.

6. Click on the **OK** button.

7. Arrange the columns by clicking onto the column heading (for example, **Name**, **Creation Date**, **Tracks**) and dragging the column to the left or right. When you reach the desired position, release the mouse button.

8. Click on the **Bin View** Menu at the bottom of the bin.

 The text in the **Bin View** Menu will be displayed in italics to let you know that changes to the current Bin View have not been saved.

9. Select **Save As**.

10. The **View Name** dialog box opens.

11. Enter a name.

12. Click on **OK**.

13. Notice that the name of your Bin View appears in the **Bin View** Menu and is not in italics.

There's more...

Closely related to creating Bin Views is creating custom columns where you can insert information that is helpful to you (for example, shot type, director's notes, and so on). Next, along with creating custom columns, we'll also cover changing an existing Bin View.

Creating a custom column

To create a custom column, perform the following steps:

1. Set the bin to Text View using the display menu in the lower-left corner of the bin window (it's the menu right next to the **Fast Menu**).

2. Create an open area in the columns by clicking onto any column heading (for example, **Name**, **Creation Date**, **Tracks**) and dragging that column by a short distance to the right (making the column that you're moving just slightly overlap the one to its right). When you release the mouse button, you'll see the selected column push the other columns over to the right. Repeat this process until you have an open area.

3. Place your cursor in the open column heading name area that you just created (the row at the top of the bin that includes other headings such as **Name** and so on).

4. Click the mouse button to create the text entry box, and type the column heading's name.

5. When you've completed typing, you can do either of the following:

    ❑   Hit *Enter* or *Return*

    ❑   Click the mouse's cursor in an open area of the bin

6. If you need to make a correction to a custom column heading, then press the *option/Alt* key when you click your cursor in the column heading name region.

7. Now that you have created a custom column, you can add text in the cells by clicking within that column when your cursor is across from a Clip or Sequence.

Changing an existing Bin View

You can add columns of information and rearrange the columns at any time. You remove a column from being displayed by selecting its column heading name and pressing the *Delete* key. Deleting columns of information that come standard with Media Composer will simply hide them and no data will actually be erased. Deleting custom columns of information that you created will open a second dialog box where you can choose to either permanently delete the column and all the information that has been entered into it, or to simply hide it from view. Hidden custom columns can be selected in the **Bin Column Selection** Window at any time. You'll find them in the bottom portion of the list.

Also be aware that whenever you make a change to an existing Bin View, its name in the **Bin View** Menu will appear in italics to indicate that any changes you've made have not yet been saved. You then have the option of either saving the Bin View as a new one, or updating the existing one. To save it as a new Bin View, perform the following steps:

1. Click on the **Bin View** Menu at the bottom of the bin.

2. Select **Save As** and the **View Name** dialog box opens.

3. Enter a name.

4. Click on **OK**. Notice that the name of your Bin View appears in the **Bin View** Menu and is not in italics.

To update an existing Bin View, perform the following steps:

1. Press and hold the *option/Alt* key.

2. Click on the **Bin View** Menu at the bottom of the bin. A list of existing Bin Views will appear that includes the word **Replace** before each of them.

3. Select the one that you want to update/replace.

4. A confirmation dialog box will open. Click on the **Replace** button. When you're done, notice that the name of your Bin View appears in the **Bin View** Menu and is not in italics.

See also

▶ The *Settings overview* discussion for more information about activating, naming, duplicating, deleting, and restoring settings

▶ The *Font size adjustment* recipe

Creating Timeline Views

Creating Timeline Views is one of the easiest things you can do to make your workday more efficient. Timeline Views allow you to create a library of different ways you like to have your Timeline displayed for various tasks. Timeline Views can be customized with the following:

▶ Font style and size (see the *Font size adjustment* recipe in this chapter).

▶ Settings found in the **Timeline Window Fast Menu** (hamburger-looking icon) in the lower-left corner of the **Timeline** Window. The settings there include things such as track color and the ability to enable/disable features such as **Dupe Detection**, **Waveform Display**, **Clip Color** display, and more.

Creating custom Timeline Views is very easy. After the recipe, there will be some ideas and tips for Timeline Views in the *There's more...* section.

How to do it...

To create Timeline Views, perform the following steps:

1. Load a Sequence into the **Timeline** Window.

2. Adjust the attributes and enable/disable features such as (but not limited to) the following:

   ❑ **Track Height**

   ❑ **Track Control Panel Display**

   ❑ **Waveform Display**

   ❑ **Volume Display**

   ❑ **Dupe Detection**

   ❑ **Clip Color Display**

   ❑ **Font Style** and/or **Size** (see the *Font size adjustment* recipe in this chapter)

3. Click on the **View** Menu at the bottom of the **Timeline** Window.

4. Select the **Save As** option.

5. The **View Name** dialog box opens.

6. Type in a name.

7. Click on **OK**.

There's more...

Next we'll take a look at some additional topics that will help you get more out of using Timeline Views.

Default Timeline View

Media Composer provides an easy way to get back to its preset default (you'll find it as the very first selection in the **Timeline** Window's **Fast Menu**, labeled as **Default Setup**). Further, you may want to consider creating your own Timeline View that you prefer to be your own personal default, so that you can access it quickly.

Updating Timeline Views

After making a change to a Timeline View, Media Composer adds a **.1** at the end of the name and makes the name display in italics. There are two ways to save the updated view without creating an entirely new one, as follows:

▶   From the **View Menu** select **Save As**. In the **View Menu** dialog box erase the **.1** that was added. When you press the **OK** button, another dialog box will ask you to either cancel or confirm the update.

▶   Hold down the *option/Alt* key. When you click on the **View Menu**, you'll see that each selection now includes the word **Replace** before it. Select the appropriate Timeline View to update. Another dialog box will ask you to either cancel or confirm the update.

Offline warning

I suggest that within all the different Timeline Views that you create, you should include the Offline warning color display. Perform the following steps:

1. Go to the **Timeline View Fast Menu** and select **Clip Color**.

2. The **Clip Color** dialog box opens.

3. Enable/check the selection at the top labeled as **Offline**.

4. Click on the **OK** button.

5. As long as the active Timeline View includes the **Offline** color being enabled, any time you have offline clips in your sequence they will be displayed as bright red and easy to detect.

Timeline background color

At the time of writing, this feature is currently not working in version 6. However, I'm including it for anyone using an earlier release, as well as in the hope that it will be returned in the future.

The default **Timeline** Window has a gray background color. You can actually set it to be whatever you prefer. My personal choice is to make the **Timeline** Window's background black. I like the higher contrast and find it easier on my eyes over a long workday. To change the **Timeline** Window's background color, perform the following steps:

1. Start with doing one of the following:

    □ Deselect/turn off all the Track Selectors in the **Timeline** Window.

    □ Clear the **Timeline** Window from displaying any sequence. Above the **Record Monitor**, where you see the name of your sequence, there is actually a menu (Avid calls it the **Record Monitor Clip Name Menu**). Click there and choose **Clear Monitor**.

2. Go to the **Timeline Window's Fast Menu** and select **Background Color** (note that if any tracks are enabled, this selection will read as **Track Color**).

3. Select a color from the palette (also see the *More color selections* section ahead).

Switch Timeline Views from the keyboard

When you map Timeline Views to the keyboard or interface (note that mapping buttons and menu selections are discussed in more detail later in this chapter), Media Composer assigns whatever happens to be the first Timeline View in your settings list as **Timeline View #1**, the second in the list as **Timeline View #2**, and so on. Perform the following steps:

1. Go to the **Project** Window and click on the **Settings** tab.

2. Locate your Timeline Views.

3. Update each Timeline View name by placing a number before it (for example, **1. Audio Mixing**, **2. Effect Editing**, and so on). While this is not technically necessary, it will make your life a bit easier when mapping them and will keep them from shifting position if you change the name in the future.

4. Open your **Keyboard** settings by double-clicking on them in the settings list.

5. Open the **Command Palette** by selecting the **Tools** menu and then choosing **Command Palette**.

6. In the lower-left corner of the Command Palette, enable the selection that says **Button To Button Reassignment**.

7. Select the tab labeled as **More**.

8. Now you can drag-and-drop the "T1" through "T8" buttons onto the keyboard.

See the discussion earlier in this chapter titled *Settings overview* for more information about activating, naming, duplicating, deleting, and restoring settings.

More color selections

When selecting colors for your Timeline tracks or background, you can expand your choices beyond what the Media Composer palette gives you. Perform the following steps:

1. Hold down *option/Alt*.

2. Go to the **Timeline Window's Fast Menu** and select **Track Color** or **Background Color**.

3. The Media Composer color palette appears.

4. Select any color from the palette.

5. The custom color picker associated with your computer's operating system will open.

6. Create a custom color.

7. Click on **OK**.

See also

- ▸ The *Settings overview* discussion for more information about activating, naming, duplicating, deleting, and restoring settings.

- ▸ The *Font size adjustment* recipe

- ▸ The *Mapping buttons and menu selections* recipe

- ▸ The *Keyboard mapping ideas* section

- ▸ The *Activating alternate settings* section

Customizing Workspaces

Prior to Media Composer Version 6, the software included both Workspaces and Toolsets. They accomplished the same thing, but were set up by the user in different ways. In version 6, the old Workspaces feature and the Toolsets feature were essentially combined and simply named as **Workspaces**. With that out of the way, let's discuss what they are.

Workspaces are a task-focused feature which you create so that, with just a visit to a menu or a quick push of a button you can instantly reveal the tools and windows you need for a particular type of work. For example, you go to **Windows | Workspaces | Audio Editing**. After selecting **Audio Editing**, your **Source/Record** window instantly reduces in size, the timeline expands taller, the **Audio Tool** opens, the **Audio Mixer** opens, and the **Audio Suite** opens. Not only do these windows change size and the tools open, but they are then placed on your screen(s) exactly where you like them. Again, this all happens because you set it up that way.

By default, Media Composer provides you with some Workspaces that have been pre-named and waiting for you to set them up. You can also create your own Workspaces.

More time-saving features related to Workspaces are discussed after this. See the *Creating Bin Layouts*, *Linking Bin Layouts with Workspaces*, and *Mapping Workspaces and Bin Layouts* recipes.

How to do it...

To customize Workspaces, perform the following steps:

1. Go to **Windows** menu | **Workspaces**.

2. From the submenu, do either of the following:

   ❑ Select an existing Workspace

   ❑ Select the **New Work Space** command

3. Once a Workspace is selected or created, it is activated and is said to be the "current" Workspace. The currently active Workspace will have a check mark next to it in the menu.

4. Customize the work environment to your needs and taste. Open the tools you want to help you perform a specific task. Arrange and resize the tools, the **Timeline Window** and the **Source/Record** window exactly as you'd like them, including placing tools into tabbed sets.

5. Once your tools and interface windows (Bin Layouts are discussed in the next section) are arranged as you like, you'll make Media Composer remember that Workspace layout. Go to **Windows** menu | **Workspaces** | **Save Current**. You must do this step or the Workspace layout will not be saved. Remember to select **Save Current**.

6. Once the Workspace is saved, you may move and close interface windows and tools as needed without actually updating the layout. Because you don't save those changes, the next time you select that Workspace it will return to its previously saved configuration. If you make changes and you do indeed want to update the currently active Workspace, then select **Windows** menu | **Workspaces** | **Save Current**. If you find yourself updating your Workspaces frequently, you may find it convenient to map the **Save Current** menu selection to a button in the interface or on the keyboard. See the *Mapping buttons and menu selections* recipe later in this chapter for more information.

There's more...

To get you thinking more about how you might customize Workspaces, the following is an additional example:

Workspace example

If your currently active Workspace is named "Effects Editing" and you want to customize it, then you'd open the **Effect Palette** and the **Effect Editor** from the **Tools** menu. You might resize the **Source/Record** window so that it only displays the Record Monitor*. This is accomplished by grabbing the right edge of the **Source/Record** window (a small, black, horizontal arrow will appear) and dragging it to the left-hand side until the **Source** window disappears. Once you have only the Record Monitor* showing, you might grab the lower-right corner of it (a small, black, diagonal arrow will appear) and drag diagonally to make it larger or smaller. Resize and reposition your **Timeline** window, **Project** window, and the **Effect Editor** and **Effect Palette** windows. With everything as you like it you'd then select **Windows | Workspaces | Save Current**.

*When in Effect Mode, the Record Monitor technically becomes the "Effect Monitor," just in case you see it referred to like that in any Media Composer documentation.

See also

- ▸ The *Creating Bin layouts* recipe
- ▸ The *Linking Bin layouts with workspaces* and *Mapping workspaces and Bin layouts* recipes

Creating Bin Layouts

Bin Layouts made their debut in Media Composer version 6. Like Workspaces, they are a task-focused feature that, with just a visit to a menu or a push of a button, allow you to instantly reveal the bins you want and to have them arranged just as you've saved them, including in tabbed sets.

Bin Layouts can be activated independently of Workspaces, or they can be activated automatically at the same time you activate a Workspace. Avid refers to this as **linking**. That feature is covered in the *Linking Bin Layouts with Workspaces* and *Mapping Workspaces and Bin Layouts* recipes.

An important note is that Bin Layouts are not saved as part of your User Settings. They are actually specific to a particular Project. See the *There's more...* section in this recipe for additional information on this.

How to do it...

To create Bin Layouts, perform the following steps:

1. Go to **Windows** menu | **Bin Layout**.

2. From the submenu, do one of the following:

   ❑ Select an existing Bin Layout

   ❑ Select the **New Bin Layout** command

3. Once a Bin Layout is selected or created, it is activated and is said to be the "current" Bin Layout. The currently active Bin Layout will have a check mark next to it in the menu.

4. Open the bins you want to help you perform a specific task. Arrange and resize them, including placing bins into tabbed sets and arrange them on your screen(s) as needed.

5. Once your bins are arranged as you like, you'll make Media Composer remember that layout. Go to **Windows** menu | **Bin Layout** | **Save Current**.

6. Once the Bin Layout is saved, you may move and close them as needed without actually updating the Layout. Because if you don't save those changes, the next time you select that Bin layout it will return to its previously saved configuration. If you make changes and you do indeed want to update the currently active Bin Layout, then go to **Windows** menu | **Bin Layout** | **Save Current**. If you find yourself updating your Bin Layouts frequently, you may find it convenient to map the **Save Current** menu selection to a button in the interface or on the keyboard. See the *Mapping buttons and menu selections* recipe later in this chapter for more information.

 At the time of writing, if a new bin is opened and the current Bin View is not saved to include this bin, then the bin will close if/when that Bin View is reselected (either manually or because that Bin View is linked to a Workspace). Further, if a bin that is included in a Bin View is deleted and the layout has not been resaved, then you may get an error message when that Bin View is reactivated.

There's more...

For easier access, you can map your Bin Layouts to buttons in the interface and/or on the keyboard. Further, you can link them to one or more Workspaces so that they become active when that Workspace is activated. This is covered in the *Linking Bin Layouts with Workspaces* and *Mapping Workspaces and Bin Layouts* recipes later in this chapter.

However, since Bin Layouts are Project-specific settings, rather than part of your User Profile Settings, the question arises—what happens if you map a Bin Layout to a button and/or link it to a Workspace and use those settings with another Project?

Here's an example. While in a Project called "Wisconsin" you created a Bin Layout for three bins@ one for music, one for sound effects, and one for voiceover. You named this Bin Layout "Music+SFX+VO". You wanted to use this Bin Layout frequently, so you mapped it to a button on your Timeline Toolbar and you linked it to your Audio Editing Workspace. While in the "Wisconsin" project, the button appears on the Timeline Toolbar with a line below the abbreviation.

A month later, the "Wisconsin" project gets completed and you begin working on another project called "California". When working on the "California" project, you use your previously saved User Settings that include the button mapping and linking you did in the "Wisconsin" project for the Bin Layout called "Music+SFX+VO". Since that Bin Layout doesn't exist in the "California" Project, when you activate the Audio Editing Workspace, no bins open and, in the Timeline Toolbar, the mapped button's abbreviation is now italicized and no longer has a line beneath it.

If you want that Bin Layout to be activated while in the "California" project, then do the following:

1. Create a new Bin Layout and name it exactly as it was named when it was originally mapped and/or linked. In this example, it would be named "Music+SFX+VO". You must pay particular attention to spaces, symbols, and uppercase/lowercase letters. If the name is not identical in all respects, then it will not work. If it is named identically, then the text appearing on the button it is mapped to will not be italicized and will have a line underneath the abbreviation.

2. While that Bin Layout is active, create and/or open the bins you want associated with it. There do not have to be the same number of bins as before, nor do the names have to be the same as before.

3. Arrange the bins as needed for that Bin Layout.

4. Save the Bin layout by selecting **Windows | Bin Layout | Save Current**.

Linking Bin Layouts with Workspaces

There are three things you can do to make using Workspaces and Bin Layouts even faster and more useful. The first is linking a Bin Layout with a Workspace so that when you select/activate a Workspace, the linked Bin Layout simultaneously becomes active too, saving you time having to activate it separately. We'll cover that in this recipe. Immediately following this recipe are discussions about linking other settings with Workspaces, and mapping Workspaces and Bin Layouts to your keyboard and/or interface.

How to do it...

To link Bin Layouts with Workspaces, perform the following steps:

1. Start with one of the following:

    ❑ Go to **Windows | Workspaces** and select the Workspace you want to link with a Bin Layout. Once it is activated (a check mark will appear next to it in the menu), then go to the **Workspaces** and select **Properties**.

    ❑ Go to the **Project** Window, click on the **Settings** tab, and then go to **Workspaces**. Double-click to open the Workspace you want to link with a Bin Layout.

2. The **Workspace View Setting** dialog box will open.

3. From the **Bin Layout** Menu, select the name of the Bin Layout you want to link with that Workspace.

4. Click on **OK** to close the **Workspace View Setting** dialog box.

Linking other settings with Workspaces

When you select/activate a Workspace, it is possible to have other settings in addition to Bin Layouts simultaneously becoming active (discussed in the previous recipe), saving you time and frustration having to activate them one at a time. The following are two examples:

▶ **Example one – audio mixing**: You go to the **Windows | Workspaces** and select **Audio Editing**. Instantly, several tools open and the interface windows adjust themselves to your preset (the method to accomplish this is discussed in the earlier section about Workspaces). But the really cool thing is that the Timeline View also simultaneously switches to your preferred display setup because you linked it.

▶ **Example two – color correction**: You go to **Windows | Workspaces** and select **Color Correction**. Instantly, tools open, the interface windows adjust themselves to your preset, the interface color changes from light gray to black, and the Timeline View simultaneously switches to your desired display. Once again, this is all possible because you linked these settings to be activated together.

For the following steps, I'll be referring to example two (color correction). More information on duplicating, naming, and activating settings can be found at the beginning of this chapter.

How to do it...

We'll begin the process by customizing the interface. Perform the following steps:

1. For the Interface settings, go to the **Project** window, click on the **Settings** tab, and select **Interface**.

2. Duplicate the current Interface setting.

3. Name the new Interface setting as "CC1". Note that you can name settings with any name you'd like, this is simply an example.

4. Activate the new "CC1" Interface setting by placing the check mark next to it.

5. Open the new "CC1" Interface setting and set the interface brightness to its darkest setting (black). You may also make any other changes to that setting that you'd like (for example, highlight color).

6. Click on **OK** to close the Interface setting. Note that you may want to re-activate the previous light gray Interface setting so you can see the changes occur when you activate the **Color Correction** Workspace. Further, you'll need to repeat the full process outlined here to link your light gray interface to your **Source/Record** Workspace. If you do not do this, then the black interface will remain activated when you switch back to the **Source/Record** Workspace.

7. Now we'll customize a Timeline View. Go to the **Project** window, click on the **Settings** tab, and select a **Timeline View**. Duplicate the existing Timeline View that you want to link with a Workspace. One method to duplicate is to go to the Edit menu and select Duplicate.

8. In this example, name the duplicated Timeline View as "CC1". Note that when typing identical names for multiple settings, pay attention to spaces and uppercase/lowercase letters. The naming has to be identical for the linking to work. To ensure that the names are identical, you could copy the name from one setting and paste it for the other setting(s). Further, you may want to repeat the full process outlined here to link a different Timeline View to your **Source/Record** Workspace. If you do not do this, then the CC1 Timeline View will remain activated when you switch back to the **Source/Record** Workspace.

9. To link the Interface and Timeline View settings to a Workspace, start with one of the following:

   ❑ Go to the **Windows | Workspaces** and select the Workspace you want to link with other settings. In this example you would select the **Color Correction** Workspace. Once it is activated (a check mark will appear next to it in the menu), then go to **Windows | Workspaces | Properties**.

   ❑ Go to the **Project** window, click on the **Settings** tab, and scroll to **Workspaces**. Double-click to open the Workspace you want to link with other settings. In this example you would open the **Color Correction** Workspace.

10. The **Workspace View Setting** dialog box will open.

11. Enable the setting labeled as **Link to named settings**.

12. In the text entry box, type in the name of the setting(s) you want to link with that Workspace. In this example you'd type in CC1. Note when typing the name for the setting(s) to link to, pay attention to spaces and uppercase/lowercase letters. The naming has to be identical for the linking to work. To ensure that the name is identical, you could copy the name from one setting and paste it into this text entry box.

13. Click on **OK** to close the dialog box.

14. You'll need to repeat this process for the other Workspaces in order to link your other desired Interface settings and Timeline Views to them. If you do not do this, then the "CC1" Interface setting and Timeline View will remain activated when you switch back to another Workspace. Note that you can link any User Settings that you like (for example, keyboard); Interface and Timeline Views were used here simply as an example.

15. Optionally, you can map Workspaces to buttons in the interface or on the keyboard for added speed and convenience. See the *Mapping Workspaces and Bin Layouts* and *Mapping buttons and menu selections* recipes later in this chapter.

Mapping Workspaces and Bin Layouts

You'll find that mapping your Workspaces and Bin Layouts to buttons in the interface or buttons on the keyboard will speed up your work and save you some frustration.

The engineers for Avid Media Composer Version 6 have implemented a new method for mapping Workspaces and Bin Layouts. In the Command Palette, there is now a new tab labeled as **Workspaces**, which provides you with 12 buttons to which either Workspaces or Bin Layouts can be assigned. It's important to note that the only way to map custom Workspaces and Bin Layouts is to use these buttons. You can not use the traditional Command Palette + "Menu to Button Reassignment" mapping method (discussed in the *Mapping buttons and menu selections* recipe in this chapter) with custom Workspaces or Bin Layouts. However, the original six Workspaces still do work with the traditional Command Palette + "Menu to Button Reassignment" mapping method. This is good news if you have more than 12 of these that you'd like to map. The original six Workspaces that can be mapped with the traditional method are—**Audio Editing**, **Color Correction**, **Source/Record Editing**, **Full Screen Playback**, **Effects Editing**, and **Capture**.

How to do it...

To map Workspaces and Bin Layouts, perform the following steps:

1. This first step is an option: Open your keyboard settings by going to the **Project** window, clicking on the **Settings** tab, and double-clicking on **Keyboard**.

2. Open the Command Palette by clicking on **Tools menu | Command Palette**.

3. Select the **Workspace** tab.

4. Using the menu that appears next to a button, assign a Workspace or Bin Layout to that button. In the menu, Workspaces are above the dividing line and Bin Layouts are below it.

5. In the lower-left corner of the **Command Palette**, enable **Button to Button Reassignment**.

6. Drag-and-drop the desired button(s) from the **Command Palette** to one or more buttons in your interface or on the keyboard.

7. Close the **Command Palette**.

See also

▸ The *Mapping buttons and menu selections* recipe

Mapping buttons and menu selections

You can increase your speed and efficiency simply by placing access to tools, functions, and menu selections in convenient locations.

When you open the **Command Palette** (**Tools menu | Command Palette**), you'll see the button functions conveniently organized in tabbed sections. You'll also see the following three enable buttons at the bottom of the window:

▸ **Button to Button Reassignment**: Enable this selection to map button functions from the palette to your interface and keyboard, to move around existing button functions on the keyboard and interface, and to copy an existing button function to another location.

▸ **Active Palette**: Enable this selection so that you can leave the palette open and regain the ability to edit as well as to actually use/click on any function that's on the palette. For emphasis, when the Command Palette's button or menu reassignment functions are enabled, you will not be able to edit. To return to editing, either enable **Active Palette** or close the **Command Palette**.

▸ **Menu to Button Reassignment**: Enable this selection to put items from various menus onto keyboard or interface buttons.

You can custom map buttons and menu items to the following places:

- ► Multibutton mouse
- ► Keyboard Top Level (keys displayed when not pressing the *Shift* key)
- ► Keyboard Shift Level (keys displayed while pressing the *Shift* key)
- ► Buttons below the **Source** and **Record** windows
- ► Timeline Toolbar
- ► The **Fast Menu Tool Palette**

You can map selections from the following menus:

- ► All the main menus at the top of the screen (for example, **File**, **Clip**, **Tools**, **Windows**, and so on).
- ► The **Timeline** Window's **Fast Menu** (the hamburger-looking icon in the lower-left corner of the **Timeline** window).
- ► The **Clip Name** Menu (the menu above the **Source** window or **Record** window that includes selections such as **Clear Monitor** and **Load Filler**).

How to do it...

This recipe will focus on mapping buttons; see the *There's more...* section for details on mapping menu selections. To map buttons perform the following steps:

1. Start with one or more of the following:
   - ❑ Open the keyboard settings by going to the **Project** window, clicking on the **Settings** tab, and double-clicking on **Keyboard**
   - ❑ Open the mouse settings by going to the **Project** window, clicking on the **Settings** tab, and double-clicking on **Mouse**
   - ❑ Open the **Fast Menu Tool Palette** by clicking on it, and then drag the palette up or down to "tear it off" and keep it open for mapping and resizing

2. Open the **Command Palette** by clicking on **Tools menu | Command Palette**.

3. Enable **Button to Button Reassignment** in the lower-left corner of the palette window.

4. Locate a button function from any of the tabbed sections.

5. Drag-and-drop a button function to the button location of your choice in the interface, on the keyboard, or on the mouse. If there is already a function there, then what you map will replace it. Remember that you can map to both the top level and the shift level of the keyboard.

See the There's more... section for additional information and see the *Settings overview* discussion for more information about activating, naming, duplicating, deleting, and restoring settings.

There's more...

The method for mapping a menu selection to a button is slightly different than simply mapping a button function. The details for mapping menu selections are presented below. After that you'll also find some useful tips along with some ideas on keyboard mapping.

Mapping menu items using the command palette

Perform the following steps:

1. Start with one or more of the following:

    ❑   Open the keyboard settings by going to the **Project** window, clicking on the **Settings** tab, and double-clicking on **Keyboard**

    ❑   Open the mouse settings by going to the **Project** window, clicking on the **Settings** tab, and double-clicking on **Mouse**

    ❑   Open the **Fast Menu Tool Palette** by clicking on it, and then dragging the palette up or down to "tear it off" and keep it open for mapping and resizing

2. Open the **Command Palette** by clicking on **Tools menu | Command Palette**.

3. Enable **Menu to Button Reassignment** in the lower-right of the palette window.

4. Click on the button you want to place a menu item onto in order to select it. Notice when you click the cursor on a button that the cursor's icon has changed to look like a tiny menu. If there is already a function there, then what you map will replace it. For emphasis, you must first select a button so Media Composer knows where you want to place the menu item. Remember that you can map to both the top level and the shift level of the keyboard.

5. Once a button is selected, it will be highlighted.

6. Go to the necessary menu.

7. Select the menu item you want to map.

8. When the menu item is chosen, it will be mapped to the button. You'll then see on the button either an abbreviation of the menu item or, in the case of some tools, you may see an icon.

See the section in this chapter titled *Keyboard mapping ideas*. Also see the discussion in this chapter titled *Settings overview* for more information about activating, naming, duplicating, deleting, and restoring settings.

Erasing a button

If you want to remove a Media Composer function from a button, then you can use the **Blank** button function found in the **Other** tab of the **Command Palette**. Note that you can not use the Undo command to reverse this action. Instead you'll have to remap the function that was there originally.

Moving a button

When the **Command Palette** is open and the **Button to Button Reassignment** selection is enabled, you can move a button from one location to another within a button region (for example, below the **Source** and **Record** Window, on the keyboard, on the Timeline Toolbar, or on the **Fast Menu Tool Palette**) and it will swap positions with the button function that is already there.

Copying a button

When the **Command Palette** is open and the **Button to Button Reassignment** selection is enabled, and when you move a button from one button region of the interface to another, it will be copied. For example, moving an existing button function from below your **Source** window to your Timeline Toolbar will copy it.

Keyboard mapping ideas

Are you worried that you'll mess up your keyboard? See the discussions of duplicating settings, activating alternate settings, and restoring settings to default at the beginning of this chapter in the section called *Settings overview* to put your mind at ease.

Are you wondering where to start mapping? Start with the "F" keys. Be aware that if you're operating a PC, then the *F1* key is not available for mapping. It's reserved for the Help system of the Windows OS.

My suggestion is to start slowly, only mapping one or two things every day or so, rather than to make a lot of changes all at once. Give yourself time to get used to having a function or tool at your fingertips in a particular location. Let your mapping grow and change as you need it and evaluate it. Be attentive for the first few days with new mappings and assess whether the position of a function is working as well as it could for you. Don't be afraid to experiment in finding just the right location(s). Also, don't worry about replacing default button functions, because once you have a function in a comfortable spot, it won't take long before it's embedded in your memory.

The following are some ideas to get you thinking:

▶ **Mnemonic devices**: This is just a fancy way of saying to place a tool or a function onto a button that helps remind you what is mapped there. For example, the following are some of mine:

   ❏ *Shift + T*: **Enable Transition Manipulation**

   ❏ *Shift + R*: **Render At Position / Render In to Out**

   ❏ *Shift + I*: **Start the Import process**

   ❏ *Shift + E*: **Enter Effect Mode**

   ❏ *Shift + A*: **Open the Audio Mix Tool**

▶ **Move the default JKL Functions**: If you use your right hand for the mouse and use your left hand for the keyboard, then you may find it helpful to move the **Play Reverse**, **Pause**, and **Play Forward** functions from their default locations (*J*, *K*, and *L*) to wherever you feel is the best fit for you. I, along with many other Media Composer editors, have moved those functions onto the *S*, *D*, and *F* keys. The advantages of doing this are as follows:

   ❏ **Mark In** and **Mark Out** are already available above on the *E* and *R* keys.

   ❏ The pinkie on your left hand is close to the *Shift*, *Ctrl*, *option/Alt*, and *Command* keys.

   ❏ The Space bar is really easy to hit with your thumb to perform a loop playback when in Trim Mode.

   ❏ Faster/easier to type since your left hand is already in place on the keyboard, so you don't have to shift position.

   ❏ If you're wondering what I did with the default functions that are on the *S*, *D*, and *F* keys, I placed them on the Shift level. For example, if I want to clear an **In Mark**, I press *Shift + D*.

- **More Detail and Less Detail**: Zooming in and out in the Timeline is something we do dozens of times a day. The keyboard shortcuts for these are found in the **Timeline** Window's **Fast Menu** (the hamburger-looking icon) in the lower-left corner of the **Timeline** Window. However, it is even better using the menu to button mapping to make these functions a one button push operation. Some popular locations on the keyboard for **More Detail** and **Less Detail** are as follows:
  - ❏ Up and down arrow keys
  - ❏ Left and right arrow keys
  - ❏ Left bracket and right bracket keys
  - ❏ *Q* and *W* keys

- **Workspaces and/or Bin Layouts**: Mapping these to the keyboard will speed you up (as well as amaze your clients).

- **Waveforms**: First a hat tip to Steve Cohen, who brought this mapping idea to my attention. Make toggling the waveform display on/off for all tracks quick and easy by mapping it to the keyboard. You'll find it in the **Timeline** Window's **Fast Menu** (the hamburger-looking icon) in the lower-left corner of the **Timeline** Window and then by selecting **Audio Data | Waveform**. I've chosen to map this selection to *Shift + W*.

- **Track Control Panel**: Toggle the **Track Control Panel** open and closed by mapping it to the keyboard. You'll find it in the **Timeline** Window's **Fast Menu**, and then selecting **Track Control Panel**.

- **Timeline Views**: In the *Creating Timeline Views* recipe earlier in this chapter, see the *Switch Timeline Views from the keyboard* subsection.

3
Polishing Gems

In this chapter, we will cover:

- ► Understanding Track Sensitivity
- ► Snapping actions for the Position Indicator and in Segment Mode
- ► Enabling and disabling all Track Selectors from the keyboard
- ► Enabling and disabling Track Selectors using the Shift key plus drag method
- ► Enabling and disabling Track Selectors using the Lasso
- ► Replace Edit: How and why
- ► Sync Point Editing: How and why
- ► Seeing source material in the Timeline Window
- ► Clipboard tips
- ► Using the Match Frame function
- ► Using the Reverse Match Frame function
- ► Setting clip colors in a bin
- ► Setting clip colors in the Timeline Window

Introduction

There are a lot of useful tools and features, gems if you will, in Media Composer. Unfortunately, not all of them are completely understood or get the attention they deserve. My hope with this chapter is to do one or more of the following:

- ► Introduce you to a variety of functions you may not have known about
- ► To reveal some functions' hidden abilities
- ► To explain why some of them behave the way they do
- ► And/or to give you a few ideas about how you might put some of them to use

Be sure to take a look at *Appendix A, Additional Tips, Tricks, and Explanations.*

Understanding Track Sensitivity

The results you get when using several functions depends on which tracks are enabled/ selected in the **Timeline** window and how the transitions are constructed (i.e. straight cuts or split edits/"L-Cuts"). I call this **Track Sensitivity**. The functions that have this programming behavior are as follows:

▸ **Fast Forward & Rewind**

▸ **Mark Clip**

▸ **Go to Previous Edit and Go to Next Edit**

How to do it...

Let's use the **Fast Forward** function to present the basic steps, and to point out the differences in the results, depending on what **Track Selectors** are enabled. In this example recipe, it's important to understand that we have several different segments (shots) in the sequence that have been placed on tracks **V1**, **A1**, and **A2**, and that the transition between each shot is a split edit (in other words, the cuts between shots are not straight, but are instead staggered. This is frequently referred to as an **L** cut). Follow these steps:

1. On the **Record Track Selector Panel**, enable *only* the **V1** Track Selector.

2. Place the blue **Position Indicator** line at the beginning of the sequence.

3. Click on the **Fast Forward** function and notice that the **Position Indicator** jumps to the next transition (cut) on the **V1** track.

4. Click on the **Fast Forward** button a second time. Again, it jumps to the next transition on the **V1** track.

5. Now, along with the **V1** Track Selector, also, enable the **A1** and **A2** Track Selectors. In other words, enable all the Track Selectors.

6. Place the **Position Indicator** at the beginning of the sequence.

7. Click on the **Fast Forward** function. Notice that the **Position Indicator** does not jump to the next transition on the video track. Instead, it has jumped farther down the sequence. Potentially, it has even jumped to the very end of the sequence.

How it works...

Whenever you use **Mark Clip**, **Fast Forward/Rewind**, or **Go to Previous/Next Edit**, Media Composer is always looking for edit points (transitions) to pay attention to. When you have two or more tracks enabled, Media Composer is looking for the transitions that exist at the same time on all the tracks that are enabled.

Below is a comparison of two situations, using the **Mark Clip** function as an example.

In the first example, you have only the **Video** track enabled and you park your **Position Indicator** (blue line) within the segment you want to mark, as shown in the following screenshot:

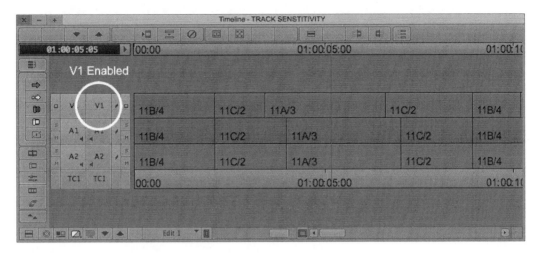

When you click on the **Mark Clip** button, you can imagine that Media Composer sends out radar (metaphorically, of course) in both directions from the **Position Indicator**, as shown in the following screenshot:

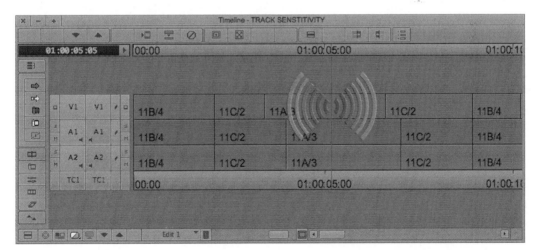

On the selected track, when it detects a transition to the left-hand side, it places the **Mark In**, and when it detects a transition to the right-hand side, it places the **Mark Out**. Refer to the following screenshot:

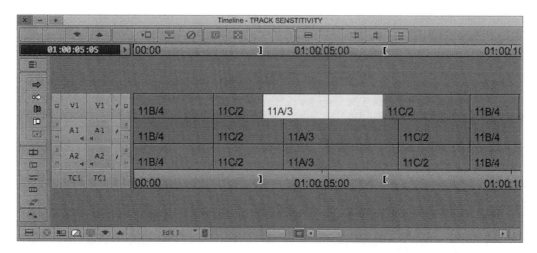

That's easy enough. But what happens when there are multiple tracks enabled? In these cases, the metaphorical radar is looking for transitions that occur at the same time on all the tracks that are enabled.

In this second example, let's look at the same **Sequence** as earlier, but let's enable **V1**, **A1**, and **A2**, as shown in the following screenshot:

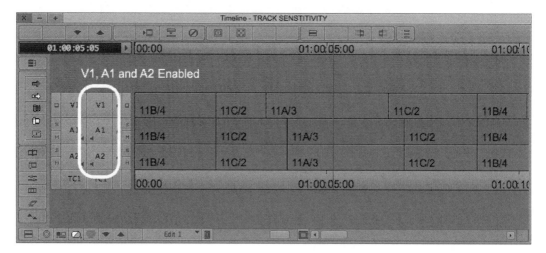

When you click on the **Mark Clip** button, Media Composer sends out its radar in both directions from the **Position Indicator**, as shown in the following screenshot:

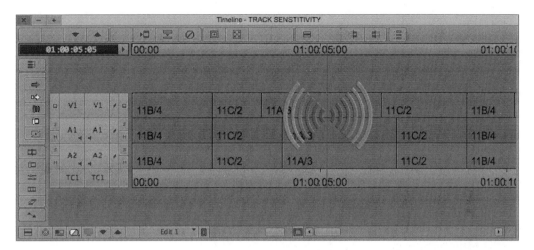

When it detects a simultaneous transition on all the selected tracks to the left-hand side, it places the **Mark In** and when it detects a simultaneous transition on all the selected tracks to the right-hand side, it places the **Mark Out** as shown in the following screenshot:

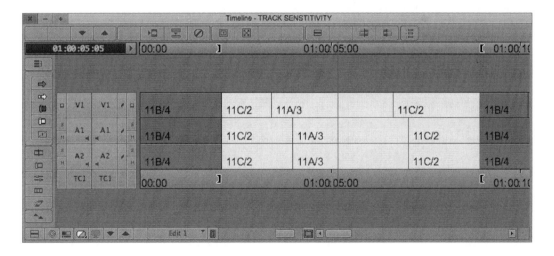

Fast Forward/Rewind and **Go to Next/Previous Edit** pay attention to the Track Selectors and transitions in the same way as **Mark Clip**, except the radar is sent out in just one direction (either to the left or to the right).

There's more...

You can tell these functions not to pay attention when multiple tracks are enabled. In other words, you can make Media Composer ignore the Track Selectors. If you do this, then the radar pays attention to *every* transition on *every* track. This can be accomplished in different ways, depending on the function, and is discussed below.

Fast Forward/Rewind

These are the two methods that allow you to alter the default behavior:

▶ Method 1: Press the *option/Alt* key while using either **Fast Forward** or **Rewind**. Now the **Position Indicator** stops at every edit point (transition) on every track no matter what tracks are enabled.

▶ Method 2: Make **Fast Forward** and **Rewind** always ignore the Track Selectors (and save yourself the need of pressing the *option* or the *Alt* key). Go to the **Project Window** | **Settings** tab | **Composer** settings | **FF/REW** tab, and then enable the selection that says **Ignore Track Selectors**.

Mark Clip and Go to Previous/Next Edit

Below are the two methods that allow you to alter the default behavior:

▶ Method 1: Press the *option/Alt* key when using the **Go To Previous/Next Edit** or **Mark Clip** functions. Using *option/Alt* key along with **Go to Previous/Next Edit** makes the **Position Indicator** stop at every edit point (transition) on every track. Using *option/Alt* key along with **Mark Clip** will mark the duration based on the two closest transitions from the **Position Indicator** on any track. This is useful enough that I have both **Mark Clip** as well as *option/Alt* + **Mark Clip** (see Method 2) mapped to my keyboard.

▶ Method 2: Unlike **Fast Forward/Rewind**, there isn't a setting to change the way **Mark Clip** and **Go to Previous/Next Edit** behave, but all is not lost. If you'd rather not hold down the *option/Alt* key with these functions, you can add the *option/Alt* modifier right to the button, so it becomes a one button-push operation. I'll use the **Go to Previous/Next Edit** function in their default locations on the *A* and *S* keys for the example of how to do this below.

Follow these steps:

1. Open your **Keyboard** settings by clicking on the **Project** Window | **Settings** tab | **Keyboard**.

2. Open the **Command Palette** by clicking on **Tools menu** | **Command Palette**.

3. Enable the **Button to Button Reassignment** selection in the lower left side of the **Command Palette**.

4. On the **Command Palette**, select the tab labeled as **Other**.

5. In the first column of buttons on the **Command Palette** you'll see a button labeled **Add Option Key** (on Mac) or **Add Alt Key** (on PC).

6. Drag-and-drop the **Add Option Key** function or the **Add Alt Key** function right onto the **Go to Previous Edit** button on your keyboard (if it's still in its default location, it's on the letter *A key*).

7. After adding this, get out your magnifying glass. If you look closely, you'll see a very small black dot has appeared just below the arrow symbol to indicate that the *option/Alt* modifier has been added.

8. Repeat step 6 for the **Go to Next Edit** button.

Snapping actions for the Position Indicator and in Segment Mode

With just a couple of keyboard shortcuts, you can make your **Position Indicator** snap right to the transition you want, and in the exact position you need, exactly on the head frame (first frame) or on the tail frame (last frame).. Plus, the convenient thing is that Media Composer uses the same keyboard shortcuts for segments when you're moving them around.

How to do it...

Let's begin by making the **Position Indicator** or a segment **Snap to Head**. Follow these steps:

1. Press and hold the *cmd* (on Mac) or *Ctrl* (on PC) keys.

2. To make the Position Indicator snap, drag it forward or backward in the sequence, or click the cursor near a transition, to make the **Position Indicator** snap to the **Head Frame** (first frame) of a segment.

3. To make a segment snap, do the following: Select a segment with either **Segment Mode** arrow (red or yellow). Now, when dragging segments, holding the cmd or Ctrl key makes the beginning (left-hand side, or head) of the segment snap to transitions that exist on *any* track.

4. Next we'll make the **Position Indicator** or a segment **Snap to Tail**.

5. Press and hold the keys *cmd + option/Ctrl + Alt*.

6. Drag the **Position Indicator** forward or backward in the sequence, or click the cursor near a transition, to make the **Position Indicator** snap to the **Tail Frame** (last frame) of a segment.

7. Select a segment with either **Segment Mode** arrow. Now, when dragging segments, holding *cmd + option/Ctrl + Alt* makes the end (right-hand side, or tail) of the segment snap to transitions that exist on any track.

There's more...

Below are two additional keyboard shortcuts that apply only when you're using **Segment Mode**, along with some helpful details about snapping with the **Position Indicator** and placing Marks.

Additional Segment Mode shortcuts

Press the *cmd* + *Shift* keys (on Mac) simultaneously or *Ctrl* + *Shift* keys (on Windows) simultaneously – this is useful when you want to move segment(s) from one track to another without getting out of sync. This keyboard shortcut will lock (constrain) segments into their current place in time on the Timeline when you move them up or down to another track. It should be noted that, at the time of writing, when you use this keyboard shortcut and move a segment, you will hear an alert sound. This is actually telling you that you have either enabled or disabled what Avid refers to as **Four Frame Display**. Using this keyboard shortcut was how **Four Frame Display** was enabled and disabled in the past. Now that it has been programmed to constrain segments to moving only up or down, it has become a bit of an annoyance. I'm sure that the enable/disable programming will be removed in a future release.

Press *option* (on Mac) or *Alt* (on Windows) – this keyboard shortcut actually doesn't control snapping, but since it has to do with moving segments, it made sense to include it here. Press the *option* key or *Alt* key while moving segments (and moving slowly) to ensure that you are moving just one frame at a time, regardless of the level of detail (how zoomed in or out you are) in the **Timeline** window.

Details about snapping

When you have snapped the **Position Indicator** line to the head of a segment, Media Composer will display a rather small, white, for lack of a better term I'll call it a bracket symbol, in the lower left-hand side corner of the **Record Monitor**. When you've snapped to the tail, the bracket symbol will be displayed in the lower right-hand side corner of the **Record Monitor**. Refer to the following screenshot:

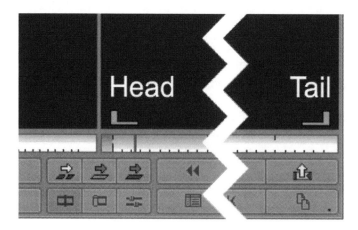

Paying attention to where you place the **Position Indictor** is important as you edit. Notice that when you zoom in (using **More Detail** or the **Scale Bar**) to take a very close look at the **Position Indicator**, you'll see that the blue line isn't one single line at all. This is because the **Position Indicator** parks on, and designates, one frame. It's actually made of two lines. The solid line of the **Position Indicator** is on the left-hand side (the head) of the frame and the dotted line is on the right-hand side (the tail) of the frame. When you set a **Mark In**, it's placed on the head side, and when you set a **Mark Out**, it's placed on the tail side. The following screenshot shows that just one frame has been marked:

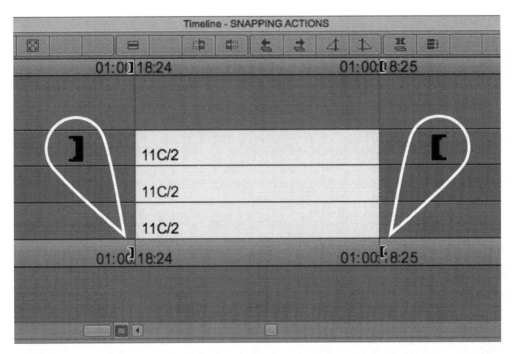

Enabling and disabling all Track Selectors from the keyboard

There will be a variety of instances when enabling or disabling all the Track Selectors will be necessary or helpful. One example is when you have many tracks and before you make an edit, you have to scroll up or down to check the status (enabled or disabled) of the hidden tracks. However, with the help of the next simple recipe, you can enable/disable all the tracks (even the ones you can't see).

How to do it...

Follow these steps:

1. Select the **Source** Window, **Record** Window, or the Timeline Window.

2. Use one of these keyboard shortcuts found in the **Edit** Menu:

   ❑ *Press cmd and A keys (on Mac) or Ctrl + A keys (on Windows) simultaneously to select all tracks*

   ❑ *Press* the A key along with **Shift** and Cmd (on Mac), or **Shift** and **Ctrl** (on Windows) to deselect all tracks

There's more...

Media Composer also allows you to map all 24 video Track Selectors and all 24 audio Track Selectors to the keyboard. You'll find them in **Tools** menu | **Command Palette** | **Tracks** tab (see the *Mapping buttons and menu selections* recipe in *Chapter 2, Customizing your Work Environment* for more information if you are unfamiliar with mapping). However, by default, Media Composer lets you enable or disable Track Selectors from the keyboard for a small number of tracks. Here is the default Track Selector keyboard mapping: **V2** on the *7* key, **V1** on the *8* key, **A1** on the *9* key, **A2** on the *0* key, **A3** on the – key, and **A4** on the = key.

Enabling and disabling Track Selectors using the Shift key plus drag method

There will be times when you want to enable or disable a series of adjacent Track Selectors. Some examples would be enabling or disabling all the video tracks or all the audio tracks, or perhaps you have 10 audio tracks that are disabled and you want to enable only **A5**, **A6**, **A7**, and **A8**. This recipe of steps is a fast way to enable or disable a number of adjacent tracks in one quick swiping movement with your cursor.

How to do it...

Follow these steps:

1. Press and hold the *Shift* key.

2. Click and hold the mouse button down on any Track Selector on either the **Source** side or the **Record** side of the Track Selector Panel.

3. Quickly drag the cursor either up or down over the Track Selectors.

   ❑ If the initial click on a Track Selector disables it (turns it off), then as you drag, it will only disable the ones that is enabled

   ❑ If the initial click on a Track Selector enables it (turns it on), then as you drag, it will only enable the ones that are disabled

How it works...

To demonstrate how this works, let's say I have eight video tracks in my **Sequence**. Currently enabled are **V1**, **V3**, **V5**, and **V7**. To quickly disable all of my video tracks with this method, I would hold down the **Shift** key, then I'd click and hold down the mouse button on the **V1** Track Selector. Finally, I would quickly drag the cursor upward across the other video Track Selectors. The result: all the video tracks would be disabled.

Enabling and disabling Track Selectors using the Lasso

There will be instances when you would like to reverse the status (enabled or disabled) of one or more Track Selectors. One example would be if all the video and audio Track Selectors were enabled and you needed to quickly disable all of the video Track Selectors. See the *How it works...* section for another example.

How to do it...

Follow these steps:

1. Click and hold the mouse button down in an area of the **Timeline** window (not within the tracks of the sequence) that is either above or below the Track Selectors for either the **Source** side or the **Record** side.

2. Drag the cursor across the Track Selectors. Note that you will see a ghosted box (the **Lasso**), and that you do not have to surround the Track Selectors with the **Lasso**. You only have to make the **Lasso** come into contact with a Track Selector.

3. Release the mouse button.

How it works...

Here is another example to illustrate how lassoing within the **Track Selector Panel** could be useful: I have four video tracks and six audio tracks in my **Sequence**. All the video tracks are enabled (turned on) and all the audio tracks are disabled. To quickly flip this around, I would click the cursor in the **Timeline** window above the video Track Selectors and hold down the mouse button. Then I would drag down across all the video and audio Track Selectors to create the **Lasso**. When I release the mouse button, all the video tracks would be turned off and all the audio tracks would be turned on.

Note that for anyone familiar with, or currently using, earlier releases of Avid Media Composer, in the past you could press the *Ctrl* key, which allowed you to lasso inside the **Track Selector Panel** (for example, lassoing over just **V1**, **A1**, and **A2**). At the time of writing, that is not currently available due to changes in programming that affected the *Ctrl* key.

Replace Edit: How and why

By default, you can find **Replace Edit** in the **Fast Menu Tool Palette** (the **Fast Menu** that, by default, is between the **Splice In** and **Overwrite** buttons as well as in the **Timeline Toolbar**), and in the **Command Palette** (**Tools** menu | **Command Palette** | **Edit** tab).

I often call **Replace Edit** the mysterious blue arrow, because so many don't know what it does and avoid using it. This is too bad because **Replace Edit** is a very useful tool that allows you to quickly replace existing segments (shots) in your **Sequence** as well as to sync a specific frame of video to a specific frame of audio (or vice versa).

Since I call it the mysterious blue arrow, which sounds like the name of a cartoon super hero, let me first explain its two super powers, which are as follows:

- ▸ You don't have to Mark In or Out in either the **Source** Window or the **Record** Window when you use it. **Replace Edit** knows how much to edit into the **Sequence** based on the duration of the segment that's already in the **Sequence**.

- ▸ It is always syncing whatever frame your **Position Indicator** is parked on in the **Source** Window to the spot where your **Position Indicator** is parked in the **Sequence**.

If this seems confusing, don't worry. After I go through the general steps, I'll also give you some specific examples.

How to do it...

When using **Replace Edit**, you can replace video only, audio only, or video and audio at the same time. It's simply a matter of what Track Selectors you've enabled.

As an example, this is a simple set of steps for replacing only a video segment. Additional information is in the *There's more* section that comes after these basic steps:

1. Load the desired shot into the **Source** Window.

2. In the **Source** Window, place the **Position Indicator** on the first frame of video you want to place into the **Sequence**. You do not need to **Mark In** or **Mark Out**.

3. In the **Sequence**, park the **Position Indicator** on the first frame of the segment (shot) you want to replace. You do not need to **Mark In** or **Mark Out**.

4. Patch the **Source Video** Track Selector to the **Sequence** video track that contains the shot you want to replace.

5. On the **Source Track Selector Panel**, enable the video track.

6. On the **Record/Timeline Track Selector Panel**, enable *only* the video track.

7. Click on **Replace Edit**.

There's more...

Let's take a look at another way to use Replace Edit, and two applications of **Replace Edit**:

In and Out Marks work too

In addition to using existing transitions (edit points) in the **Timeline** window to determine the duration of video and/or audio to edit into the sequence, **Replace Edit** will also pay attention to a duration that you set in the **Sequence** using **Mark In** and **Mark Out**.

Syncing example with Replace Edit

You have edited a music track into your **Sequence** and have edited images on top of it. At one point in the music, there is a loud drum beat and you decide to replace the existing shot at that point in the **Sequence** with video of a hammer hitting a nail. Specifically, you want the frame when the hammer hits the nail to sync with the loud drum beat. Below are the steps to accomplish this:

1. In the **Source** Window, park the **Position Indicator** on the frame where the hammer first comes into contact with the nail. **Mark In** and **Mark Out** are not required.

2. In the Sequence, park the **Position Indicator** on the loud drum beat. **Mark In** and **Mark Out** are not required. If it helps you, an option is to display the audio waveform so you can see the exact location of the loud drum beat.

3. Patch the **Source Video** Track Selector to the **Sequence** video track that contains the shot you want to replace.

4. Enable the **Video** Track Selector for the **Source**.

5. Enable *only* the **Video** Track Selector for the **Record** side.

6. Press **Replace Edit**.

7. The result is that the previous shot is replaced and the image of the hammer hitting the nail occurs at the same moment as the drum beat.

Fast montage creation

Here's a classic tip that is great when you want shots placed at precise intervals. One example of this would be having your shots change on the beat of the music.

Since **Replace Edit** uses existing transitions (edit points) to determine how much video and/or audio to place into the **Sequence**, what you're going to do first is to quickly create a series of transitions on an empty video track, and then use **Replace Edit** to swap the **Filler** for video.

Follow these steps:

1. First you need to map the **Add Edit** function to a convenient button on the keyboard. You can find **Add Edit** by going to **Tools** menu | **Command Palette** | **Edit** tab (see the *Mapping buttons and menu selections* recipe in *Chapter 2, Customizing Your Work Environment* if you need information about how to map this).

2. Edit the music into your sequence.

3. If you do not already have an empty video track, then create one by going to **Clip** menu | **New Video Track**.

4. Enable *only* the Track Selector for the empty video track.

5. Play your sequence.

6. Now you're going to tap to the beat of the music. As the music plays, tap the **Add Edit** function you mapped on the keyboard. Note that the edits you create will not appear until playback has stopped.

7. After stopping the playback, you'll have a series of transitions in the video track that correspond to the beats in the music. If you missed a beat by a frame or two, the transition can be double-roller trimmed to adjust its position at any time, even if there's only **Filler** on the track.

8. You can now use **Replace Edit** to replace the segments of **Filler** between each **Add Edit** with video.

See also

▶ The *Sync Point Editing: How and why* recipe in this chapter

▶ The *Replacing Edit versus Sync Point Editing* recipe in this chapter

Sync Point Editing: How and why

Sync Point Editing is an extra ability you temporarily give to the **Overwrite** edit function when you need it. After using it, you turn this ability off. **Sync Point Editing** allows you to perform an **Overwrite** edit and at the same time tell Media Composer to sync a specific frame of audio and/or video in the **Source** Window with a specific frame of audio or video in the **Sequence**. You use the **Position Indicators** in the **Source** window and in the **Timeline** window to establish the sync point.

Getting ready

For this example, imagine that you have edited a documentary about boxing and you now want to add in a sound effect of a punch to enhance the knockout blow. You have imported a clip of punch sound effects off of a CD, and the clip contains 12 different punch sounds. Some are louder and more forceful than others, so you'll have a choice to make. Further, you want the sound effect to sync with the moment the champion boxer hits the challenger.

How to do it...

Follow these steps:

1. Load the sound effect clip into the **Source** Window.
2. Determine the specific punch sound effect that you like.
3. **Mark In** and **Mark Out** around the entire desired sound effect.
4. While still in the **Source** Window, park your **Position Indicator** on the very first frame of the punch sound effect. See the *There's more* section for some options on accomplishing this.
5. In the **Sequence**, park your **Position Indicator** on the video frame you want to sync the audio to. In this example, I would park it on the first frame that the champion's glove makes contact with the challenger's jaw.
6. Patch the **Source** audio tracks to your desired **Sequence** audio tracks.
7. On the **Source** side, enable the necessary **Audio** Track Selector(s).
8. On the **Record** side of the Track Panel, enable only the necessary **Audio** Ttack Selector(s).

9. Now you need to tell Media Composer that when you make the **Overwrite** edit to pay attention to the frame that the **Position Indicator** is parked on in the **Source** Window and to place that frame where the **Position Indicator** is parked in the **Sequence**. To do this, we'll give the **Overwrite** edit function the **Sync Point Editing** ability by following either of these methods:

   ❑ Method one: Right-click in either the **Source** Window or the **Record** Window (it doesn't matter which). From the contextual menu that appears, select **Sync Point Editing**. Once you have done this, take a close look at the **Overwrite** button. You will see that the arrow icon has become a bit smaller and, more noticeably, an orange light has turned on below it.

   ❑ Method two: Start by clicking anywhere in the **Composer** Window (also known as the **Source/Record** Window) to make it active. Then, go to the **Special** menu | **Sync Point Editing**. Once you have done this, take a close look at the **Overwrite** button. You will see that the arrow icon has become a bit smaller and, more noticeably, an orange light has turned on below it.

10. Press the **Overwrite** button (which has the orange light now turned on) to make the edit.

11. Once you have completed the edit, you'll want to turn off the **Sync Point Editing** feature. If you use this a lot, consider mapping it from the **Special** menu to a convenient button on the keyboard. See the *Mapping buttons and menu selections* recipe in *Chapter 2, Customizing your Work Environment* for more information on how to do this.

There's more...

Follow these options to locate an audio point:

▶ Option 1 is to use scrubbing to locate the first frame of the sound effect by following these steps:

   1. Enable **Audio Scrubbing** by either pressing and holding the *Shift* key or enabling *Caps Lock*

   2. Using the *Step Forward One Frame* and *Step Backward One Frame* keys (by default mapped to the *3* and *4* keys) to locate the first frame of audio

▶ Option 2 is to use the scrubbing feature of **Play Reverse**, **Pause**, and **Play Forward** (by default on the *J*, *K*, and *L* keys). For example, hold the Pause key and the Play Forward key at the same time to scrub forward.

▶ Option 3 is to enable the **Audio Waveform Display** and also use **Toggle Source/ Record in Timeline** function to see the clip that's in the **Source** Window displayed in the **Timeline** Window in order to locate the first frame of the sound effect. See the *Seeing Source Material in the Timeline* recipe later in this chapter for details if you are unfamiliar with this.

Seeing source material in the Timeline Window

By default, the **Timeline** Window displays the sequence that's loaded in **Record Window**. However, it's possible to have the **Timeline** Window display what's loaded in the **Source** Window. Being able to do this is useful when you have loaded a sequence into the **Source** Window (when you're editing a portion of one sequence into another) and need to see the transitions, or when you want to see the audio waveform for what's loaded in the **Source** Window.

To do this, you use the **Toggle Source/Record in Timeline** function, which is found by default in the bottom left-hand side of the **Timeline** Window next to the **Video Quality** Menu. It's an icon that resembles the **Source** and **Record** Windows, where one window of the icon is dark and the other is light, as shown in the following screenshot:

When you click on it to enable it, the button will turn green. You'll also see that the **Position Indicator** line in the **Timeline** window turns green to remind you that you're looking at material in your **Source** window.

It's important to know that when the **Toggle Source/Record in Timeline** function is enabled, the **Track Selector Panel** is reversed. This means that the **Source Track Selector** buttons are now on the right-hand side and the **Record/Timeline Track Selector** buttons are now on the left-hand side. Media Composer will let you make edits while the **Toggle Source/Record** button **in Timeline** function is enabled and the **Track Selector Panel** is reversed. Personally, I find that disabling **Toggle Source/Record in Timeline**, and switching back to the standard **Timeline** display, avoids confusion when making the edit.

How to do it...

This example is for how to display the audio waveform for material in the **Source** window. Follow these steps:

1. Before enabling the **Toggle Source/Record in Timeline** function, turn the **Audio Waveform** display on for all tracks or for individual tracks using either of these methods:

   - For all tracks, go to **Timeline Window | Fast Menu | Audio Data | Waveform**.

   - For specific tracks, open the **Track Control Panel** with the small arrow located just to the right-hand side of the **Timecode** display in the upper left of the **Timeline** window. Once it's open, you'll see that each track has a variety of small buttons and menus next to it. The one you want to enable is the one furthest to the left-hand side in the panel that looks like a miniature waveform.

2. Once the waveform is displayed, enable the **Toggle Source/Record in Timeline** function, as described previously.

Clipboard tips

First, what is the Clipboard? The Clipboard is Media Composer's memory bank. When certain operations are performed (discussed in just a moment), it places information temporarily into the Clipboard. When the information in the Clipboard is displayed in either the **Source** Window or the **Record** Window, it is also placed as a selection in that window's **Clip Name** Menu above it. For emphasis, I want to repeat that the information is only stored there temporarily. In order to preserve it for long-term, future use, you must make a Sub-Sequence of it and place it in the a bin.

What does the Copy to Clipboard icon look like? In Version 3 of the software, it was updated to look like a paper document with its corner folded over placed on top of another document, also with its corner folded over, as shown in the following screenshot:

Personally, I think the Clipboard is one of the most useful features and is largely underused by many editors. First, I'll take you through how it is used in its default configuration and then I'll give you an alternative that I think is better (at least for me, in the way that I use the Clipboard).

How to do it...

In this example, we'll use the Clipboard in its default configuration. See the *There's more* section for more tips to make the Clipboard even more useful.

1. Load a sequence into the **Timeline** window.

2. Enable only the tracks of the **Sequence** that you want to copy to the Clipboard.

3. **Mark In** and **Mark Out** around the region of the **Sequence** you want to copy to the **Clipboard**.

4. Next, press the Copy to Clipboard button, which is located by default in one of these locations:

    ❑ Under **Record Monitor**, on the far right-hand side of the **button** bar

    ❑ On the **Fast Menu Tool Palette**

    ❑ On the letter *C* on the keyboard

5. Now you must retrieve the material you've copied to the **Clipboard** using one of these methods:

    ❑ From above the **Source** Window, select the **Clip Name** Menu and then choose **Clipboard Contents**.

    ❑ From above the **Record** Window, select the **Clip Name** Menu and then choose **Clipboard Contents**.

    ❑ Use the Clipboard Contents button as follows: First, make either the **Source** Window or the **Record** Window active (whichever window is active determines where the **Clipboard** contents will be displayed). Then press the **Clipboard Contents** button. This button can be found in **Tools** menu | **Command Palette** | **Edit** tab.

See the *Mapping buttons and menu selections* recipe in *Chapter 2, Creating Your Work Environment* for more information if you are unfamiliar with mapping.

There's more...

Let's now see how to make the **Clipboard** a more efficient tool, how you can use it along with **Lift** and **Extract**, and also, I'll give you some examples of how I use it.

Making Copy To Clipboard faster and more efficient

▶ Method 1 is to press *option* and click on **Copy to Clipboard**, or press *Alt* and and click on **Copy to Clipboard**. When you do this, whatever material you have decided to copy to the **Clipboard** will instantly be loaded into the **Source** Window.

▶ Method 2 is to make **Copy to Clipboard** instantly load whatever has been copied into the **Source** Window by default (without having to press the *option* or *Alt* key). You do this by adding the *option* or *Alt* modifier right to whichever **Copy to Clipboard** buttons for which you'd like it to become a one-button push operation. Here's an example of how to modify the **Copy to Clipboard** button that's on the keyboard:

    i. Open your **Keyboard** settings by going to **Project** Window | **Settings** tab | **Keyboard**.

    ii. Open the **Command Palette** by going to the **Tools** menu and selecting **Command Palette**.

    iii. Enable the **Button to Button Reassignment** selection in the lower of the **Command Palette**.

    iv. On the **Command Palette**, select the tab labeled as **Other**.

    v. In the first column of buttons on the **Command Palette**, you'll see a button labeled **Add Option key** (Mac) or **Add Alt Key** (PC).

    vi. Drag-and-drop the **Add Option/Alt Key** function right onto the **Copy to Clipboard** button on your keyboard (if it's still in its default location, it's on the letter *C*).

    vii. If you look very closely, you'll see a small black dot has appeared on the button to indicate that the *option/Alt* modifier has been added.

Using Copy to Clipboard with Lift and Extract

▶ *option/Alt + Lift*

▶ *option/Alt + Extract*

Every time you Lift or Extract, that material is also saved to the **Clipboard**. If you want to Lift or Extract and also have that material become instantly available in the **Source** Window, then all you have to do is press the *option/Alt* key when you perform either of those edits.

Examples of using Copy To Clipboard

Example one is the ability to patch to another track: Media Composer does allow you to Copy and Paste. However, there is a limitation that you can only Paste onto the same track you copied from. If you're making a video effect that requires you to copy some video from **V1** and place it on **V2**, then **Copy to Clipboard** allows you to easily copy it and then to patch it to the required track.

Example two is the ability to move sections of the Sequence: Sometimes using **Segment Mode** to move sections of the sequence is not convenient because the distance is far, because the section you're moving has split edits at one end (or both), or because the section you want to move includes only portions of segments. Rather than having to make a Sub-Sequence first, you can *option/Alt + Lift* or *option/Alt + Extract* a marked section out of the sequence. This not only performs the Lift or Extract but also immediately places that material into the **Source** Window, ready for you to relocate.

Example three is using it as a method to plug holes of silence: Frequently there will be areas in the dialog track that only contain **Filler**. The problem is that **Filler** is totally silent compared to the natural background sound that's included with the dialog. You want the dialog track to flow without any dropouts of silence. The solution is to fill those silent holes of **Filler** with some ambience. Very often the ambience you need will already be available in the **Sequence** at some point where the speaker has paused. If this is the case, you can copy that ambience to the **Clipboard** and then quickly Overwrite the silent **Filler**.

Using the Match Frame function

The icon for **Match Frame** is the same one used for **Master Clips**. By default, the **Match Frame** function can be found under the **Source** Window as well as in the **Fast Menu Tool Palette** in the **Timeline Toolbar**.

Getting Ready

The most common mistake I see made is when people want to use **Match Frame** to match back from the **Timeline** window (as we will be doing in the example recipe in a moment) they mistakenly click on the **Match Frame** button that's under the **Source** Window. Instead, to Match Frame from the **Timeline** window, either use the **Match Frame** button found in the **Fast Menu Tool Palette** or you can map it to a convenient location under the **Record Monitor**, on the **Timeline Toolbar**, or on your keyboard.

See the *Mapping buttons and menu selections* recipe in *Chapter 2, Customizing Your Work Environment* for more information if you are unfamiliar with mapping.

How to do it...

The following recipe of steps demonstrates the default behavior of **Match Frame** when it is used on a sequence that is loaded into the **Record Monitor/Timeline** window. See the *There's more* section for additional methods of using **Match Frame**.

1. Place the **Position Indicator** over a segment in the sequence.

2. Enable the **Track Selector** for the segment you want to match back to, and make sure that Track Selector is also the uppermost selector that is enabled. For emphasis, **Match Frame** pays attention only to the top-most Track Selector that is enabled.

3. Click on the **Match Frame** function that is on the **Fast Menu Tool Palette**, or which you have mapped underneath the **Record Monitor**, onto the **Timeline Toolbar**, and/ or onto your keyboard.

4. The source clip will then be loaded into your **Source** monitor. For example, if you originally edited that shot into your sequence from a **Subclip**, then the **Subclip** will be loaded.

There's more

Next, we'll examine the programming of **Match Frame** in more depth.

Using it with the **Record Monitor** or the **Timeline** – when the **Record Monitor** or **Timeline** is active, **Match Frame** will load the clip your **Position Indicator** is parked on into the **Source** Window. Be aware of the following:

- ▶ You must enable the track that contains the clip you want to use **Match Frame** with (I'll call that the target track).

- ▶ Make sure that no other video Track Selector that's above your target track is enabled. In other words, your target track must be the top-most enabled track.

- ▶ When **Match Frame** loads the clip into the **Source** Window, by default it erases any previous Marks that may have been placed in the clip and places a **Mark In** on the matching frame. In a moment there will be a tip on this topic.

Using it with the **Source** Window; using **Match Frame** on items loaded into the **Source** Window will do the following:

- ▶ **Subclip**: When used on a **Subclip** that's loaded in the Source Window, **Match Frame** will take you back to the original **Master Clip**. Michael Phillips (who helped technically review this book) further relates that track selection is also observed if the **Subclip** is an **AutoSync** clip, where the video and audio have come from two different sources. This means that since the video is from one clip and the audio is from another, if the video track is enabled, then you'll be matched back to the original video-only clip. If you need to match back to the original audio-only clip, then you'll need to deselect the **Video** Track Selector.

- ▶ **Motion Effect Clip**: When you use this on a **Freeze Frame, Slo-Mo,** or **Fast-Mo** clip, **Match Frame** will take you back to the **Master Clip** or **Subclip** used to create it.

  When **Match Frame** loads the clip into the **Source** Window, by default it erases any previous Marks in the clip and places a **Mark In** on the matching frame. See the following for a tip on this topic.

Next, here are some very useful tips when using **Match Frame**:

- ▶ *option/Alt*: Press *option/Alt* and click on **Match Frame** to retain the Marks that were most recently placed in the clip rather than have them erased and a new **Mark In** placed on the matching frame.

- ▶ **Match Frame Track**: When you use **Match Frame** from the **Timeline** Window, you must enable the track that contains the clip you want to use **Match Frame** with (I'll call that the target track) and you have to be sure that no other Track Selector that's above your target track is enabled. In other words, your target track must be the top-most enabled track. This can be a bit frustrating if you have to keep turning tracks on and off. Instead you can **Match Frame** from any track, whether it's enabled or not, by:

- First, park the **Position Indicator** on the clip to which you want to **Match Frame** back (just as we normally do). Then right-click on the Track Selector button for the track that contains your target clip. From the contextual menu that appears, select **Match Frame track**.

- Press *option/Alt* when you use **Match Frame Track** to retain the marks that were most recently placed in the clip rather than have them erased and have a new **Mark In** placed on the matching frame.

Using the Reverse Match Frame function

Reverse Match Frame allows you to search the **Sequence** for a specific frame of source material on whatever **Timeline** tracks have their Track Selectors enabled. Remember, it is only searching for one frame, not an entire shot, and it pays attention to which tracks are enabled.

This function has recently been improved. In the past, it searched the audio tracks and only track **V1**. It will now search all video tracks, if they are enabled.

Getting Ready

Reverse Match Frame can be found in **Tools** menu | **Command Palette** | **Other tab**. You would map it either under the **Source** Window or onto the keyboard (for use when the **Source** Window is active). See *Mapping buttons and menu selections* recipe in *Chapter 2, Customizing Your Work Environment* for more information if you are unfamiliar with mapping.

How to do it...

1. In the **Timeline**, enable the Track Selectors for the track(s) you want **Reverse Match Frame** to search. Optionally, go to **Edit** menu | **Select All**.

2. Load a clip into the **Source** Window.

3. In the **Source** Window, park the **Position Indicator** onto the frame you want **Reverse Match Frame** to search for.

4. In the **Source** Window, enable the Track Selector(s) for the track(s) you want **Reverse Match Frame** to use for the search. Optionally, go to **Edit** | **Select All**.

5. If you've used that frame multiple times, then each time you press the **Reverse Match Frame** button, the **Position Indicator** will jump to each instance of that frame in the **Sequence**.

Setting clip colors in a bin

Note that you can also set different colors for segments (clips) in the **Sequence**. You'll find the details on that in the recipe that follows this one.

How to do it...

Follow these steps to set Clips Colors in a bin:

1. Put your bin into **Text View**. Notice the column of squares to the left side of the clip's name. These are the color swatches.

2. Select the clips and/or sequences.

3. Once selected, set the color with one of the following methods:

    ❑ Right-click on the color swatch of one of the selected items and make a selection from the palette

    ❑ Go to the **Edit** menu, and select **Clip Color**, and make a selection from the palette

4. In the **Timeline** Window, to display the colors you've assigned to the clips in the bin. Go to **Timeline Window Fast Menu** (the hamburger-looking icon in the bottom left side of the **Timeline** Window) | **Clip Color** | **Source**.

Setting clip colors in the Timeline Window

Note that Avid refers to the shots in your sequence as both clips and segments. So, don't let that cause you any confusion.

How to do it...

1. In order to set clip colors in the **Timeline** Window, you must first enable their display. Go to the **Timeline Window Fast Menu** (the hamburger-looking icon in the bottom left-hand side of the **Timeline Window**) | **Clip Color** | **Timeline Local**.

2. Select a clip in the **Sequence** by using either of the **Segment Mode Arrow** tools (it doesn't matter which one you use). To select multiple segments, hold down the *Shift* key as you make selections. Alternatively, you can also select segments by lassoing left to right around one or more of them, or you can use the **Select Left**, **Select Right**, or **Select In/Out** functions.

3.   Once segments are selected, set the color with one of the following methods:

    ❑   Go to **Edit** menu, **Set Local Clip Color**, and make a selection from the palette

    ❑   Right-click in the **Timeline** Window, choose **Set Local Clip Color**, and then make a selection from the palette

> If both the **Source Clip Color** and **Timeline/Local Clip Color** functions have been set for the same clip, and both displays are enabled, then **Timeline** color takes precedence

There's more...

So, what might you use Clip Color for? Here are a few possibilities:

▶   **Stock Footage**: Typically, a stock footage company will initially provide you with clips that have a watermark of some sort on the image. Frequently, the **Watermark** is a timecode window or some other overlay that prevents you from using the footage without properly licensing and paying for it. At the finishing stage, you've got to order replacement footage (without the watermark) for the portions you've actually used. Once you have that, then the watermarked shots need to be replaced with the non-watermarked versions. Using clip color is a great way to make sure you can easily and quickly locate all the stock footage in your **Sequence**. Personally, in the bin, I label all stock footage clips as orange. Then, when I need to see what non-watermarked clips I need to order, or which ones need to be Overwritten, all I have to do is display **Source Clip Color** in the **Timeline** window.

▶   **Camera Angles**: When editing with Group Clips/MultiCam, you can color each camera angle's **Master Clip** with a different color. For example, camera A is rose, camera B is green, camera C is blue, and camera X is yellow. Then, when you display **Source Clip Color**, as you switch cameras in the **Sequence**, the colors will indicate which angle you've switched to. Further, it helps you to later analyze the **Sequence** to get an idea of where, and in what proportions, you've used the different angles.

▶   **Characters**: When editing a scene, you can code each character's **Master Clip** with a different color. When you display **Source Clip Color**, this can help you to analyze the sequence to get an idea of which characters visually dominate the scene.

▶   **Areas For Attention**: You can quickly lasso left to right around a large group of segments in the **Sequence** and then use **Local Clip Color** to label all of them. This can be helpful in marking a section that you need to return to in the future.

▶   Easily locate segments in a sequence that are a different frame rate or format from your **Project** Settings. For example, if your project is 29.97 fps, enable the **Mixed Rates** checkbox so that clips at frame rates other than 29.97 will be highlighted; or if your Project is set as High Definition (HD), then enable the **SD/HD** checkbox and any Standard Definition (SD) material in your sequence will be highlighted.

4

Creating Split Edits

In this chapter, we will cover:

- ▶ Creating a Split Edit with Double Roller or Overwrite Trim
- ▶ Creating a Split Edit with the Extend function
- ▶ Creating a Split Edit with Asymmetric Trimming

Introduction

Typically, when we first cut together a sequence, all the transitions (cuts) between shots are straight. What this means is that both the image and sound from each segment (shot) cut to the next shot at the same time. However, much of the time we don't want straight cuts. Instead, very often you'll want the picture and audio from a shot to cut at different times. Sometimes, you'll want the picture to change to the next shot before its audio does, and vice versa. You'll frequently hear these types of cuts referred to as an **L** cut, a **Prelap**, a **Postlap**, a **Split Edit** or, more simply, a **Split**.

This book focuses on providing recipes – specific procedures that can be detailed in a step-by-step fashion. However, there is a large amount of important and/or helpful supporting information and additional editing methods/techniques that do not fall into the step-by step-format. Therefore, I've placed a good deal of useful information into the appendices. *Appendix B, Details on Trimming, Slipping, Sliding, and Segment Mode* includes a large amount of information about trimming (and more). It covers the following topics:

- ▶ Trimming terminology
- ▶ Trimming icons and colors
- ▶ How Trimming works
- ▶ Using and configuring the Trimming tools
- ▶ Trimming methods

- ▸ Monitoring during Trimming
- ▸ Slipping with **Trim Mode**
- ▸ Slipping outside of **Trim Mode**
- ▸ Sliding in **Trim Mode**
- ▸ Trimming and effects
- ▸ **Smart Tool** overview
- ▸ Using the **Trim** functions in the **Smart Tool**
- ▸ Using **Segment Mode** with the **Smart Tool**
- ▸ Eight **Segment Mode** tips

In my opinion, Trimming is the most powerful editing function in Media Composer. Unfortunately, many do not take advantage of everything that Trimming can do for them. So, I hope that the topics in *Appendix B, Details on Trimming, Slipping, Sliding, and Segment Mode*, those in this chapter, along with the discussion of using and/or re-mapping the default **JKL** functions (see the *Keyboard mapping ideas* section in the *Mapping buttons and menu selections* recipe in *Chapter 2, Customizing Your Work Environment*), and the discussion of staying in sync (see *Chapter 5, Maintaining and Regaining Sync*), will help you to get the most out of Trimming and get you working faster and more intuitively.

Creating a Split Edit with Double Roller or Overwrite Trim

Generally, when we first assemble a sequence, all the transitions between shots are straight. In other words, both the picture and audio cut at the same time from shot to shot. However, a good deal of the time we do not want straight cuts. Instead, very often we want the video to cut to the next shot before cutting to the audio that belongs with it. An example of this is in the top screenshot (see below) where the video cuts to **RICK** before we hear the audio from **RICK**'s shot. And of course, the opposite is also true; sometimes we want the audio from a shot to be heard before we cut to the video that belongs with it. An example of this is in the bottom screenshot below:

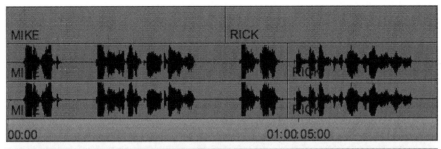

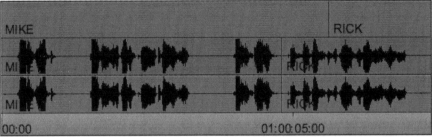

There are several different methods you can use to create **Split Edits** which are discussed in this chapter. I encourage you to familiarize yourself with all three methods as you may prefer one over another, and you may find that one method works better in a particular situation.

Getting ready

In this example, we'll use **Double Roller Trim** or **Overwrite Trim** to create a **Split Edit**. In order to give this some context, the steps below relate to a dialog scene with two characters, **MIKE** and **RICK**. The first shot (the A-side shot) is a closeup of **MIKE**. He says, "Hey Rick! I hear you've started playing tennis. How is it going?". Then, in the second shot (the B-side shot), **RICK** replies, "I think I should have started when I was younger!"

How to do it...

1. The first step is to adjust the pacing between the two shots (see the next screenshot labeled as **A**). Essentially, you'll determine how quickly you want **RICK** to respond to **MIKE**'s question. To do this, you'll have to adjust each shot *separately*, one at a time. Use **Single Roller Trim** on the A-side shot (the shot of **MIKE**) to adjust only the A-side after **MIKE** says the word "going." Then use **Single Roller Trim** on the B-side shot (the shot of **RICK**) to adjust how quickly you want him to respond to **MIKE**'s question. Maybe you have a long pause because you want **RICK** to appear that he's thinking of an answer, or maybe you want him to respond quickly because it will be funnier.

2. Once you've established the pacing between the two shots (see the screenshot below labeled as **B**), you'll change the video from cutting at the same time as the audio. In other words, you'll be creating the **Split Edit**. In this example, I've decided to cut to **RICK**'s reaction just before **MIKE** asks "How is it going?" To do this, use one of the following methods:

   ❏ **Double Roller Trim** (screenshot **C**): Enter **Double Roller Trim** for the video only (one quick method is to lasso just the video transition). Trim the video to either the left or the right to create the **Split Edit**. In the example of the **MIKE** and **RICK** scene, since I want to see **RICK**'s reaction at the same time that **MIKE** says, "How is it going?", I would trim to the left, so that the video cuts to **RICK** just before **MIKE**'s line.

   ❏ **Overwrite Trim** (screenshot **D**): You could accomplish the same result with **Overwrite Trim**, which is the red Trim icon in the **Smart Tool**. If you used this, then you'd want to have the red Trim Roller on the B-side (**RICK**'s shot) as you extended it to the left.

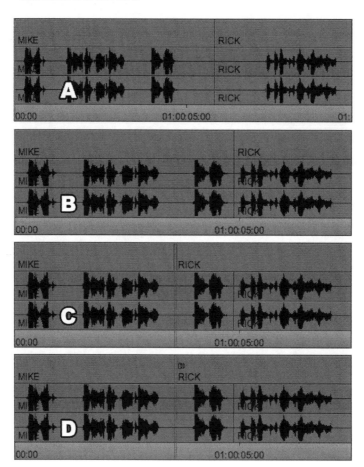

One advantage to using **Double Roller Trim** (the previous screenshot **C**) is that you can use **JKL** Trimming on the keyboard to adjust the position of the cut.

See also

- ▶ *Chapter 5, Maintaining and Regaining Sync*
- ▶ *Appendix B, Details on Trimming, Slipping, Sliding, and Segment Mode*

Creating a Split Edit with the Extend function

By default, you'll find the **Extend** function below the **Record Monitor** and in the **Fast Menu Tool Palette**. It can also be mapped from the **Command Palette** (**Tools** menu | **Command Palette** | **Trim tab**). The icon looks like the following:

In many instances Media Composer offers two or more methods for getting something done. This provides you with choices, depending on your preference or the needs of a particular situation. This is the case with **Extend**. The end result of using the **Extend** function is identical to using **Double Roller Trim** or **Overwrite Trim**. One of the benefits of using **Extend** is that if it's mapped to the keyboard, then all the operations required to use it can be done using the keyboard without even entering **Trim Mode**.

Getting Ready

You'll find it helpful to read the previous *Creating a Split Edit with Double Roller or Overwrite Trim* recipe, if you haven't already, because I'll be using the same scene between **MIKE** and **RICK** for this example too. This will help you to see that you can accomplish the same results with different methods.

How to do it...

1. The first step is to adjust the pacing between the two shots. Essentially, adjust how quickly you want **RICK** to respond to **MIKE**'s question. You will Trim and/or Extract to adjust this.

2. Once you've established the pacing between the two shots, you'll change the video from cutting at the same time as the audio. In other words, you'll be creating the **Split Edit**. In this example, I'll do just as I did in the previous recipe's example and cut to **RICK**'s reaction just before **MIKE** asks, "How is it going?" However, this time I'll use the **Extend** function.

3. Enable only the **V1** Track Selector.

4. Place a **Mark In** just before **MIKE** says the word "How" (see the next screenshot). Placing the **Mark In** is the key to this feature. You might think of the **Mark In** as facing the transition you want to extend to that specific spot. When using a **Mark In**, the shot on the right-hand side of the transition will be extended to the left. On the other hand, if you wanted to extend a shot to the right, then you'd use a **Mark Out**. It's helpful to note that this function is programmed to only pay attention to one Mark placed in the **Timeline** Window. If you happen to have both a **Mark In** and a **Mark Out** placed, the programming tells it to pay attention only to the **Mark In**.

5. Click the **Extend** button. My silly (but hopefully helpful) analogy is that the moment you press the **Extend** button, the **Mark In** (or **Mark Out**, if that's what you've set) is transformed into a powerful magnet that pulls the transition to that spot, with the result being that one shot is made longer and the other is made shorter.

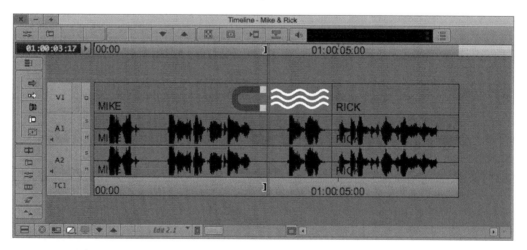

See also

▸ *Appendix B, Details on Trimming, Slipping, Sliding, and Segment Mode*

Creating a Split Edit with Asymmetric Trimming

This recipe will be covering only the essential steps for creating a **Split Edit**. If it's confusing in any way, **Asymmetric** Trimming is explained in much more detail in *Chapter 5, Maintaining and Regaining Sync*. Further, this recipe will be using the *Shift* + click method to configure the **Trim Rollers**, which is discussed in the *Using and configuring the Trimming tools* recipe in *Appendix B, Details on Trimming, Slipping, Sliding, and Segment Mode*.

Getting ready

For this example, you're editing a documentary about auto racing. The first shot (the A-side shot) is of our interview subject, famous race car driver, Teddy Orlando. He says, "I've been racing for 10 years now and I never get tired of it. I absolutely love the feeling of speed." Then, the second shot (the B-side shot) is footage of Teddy's race car loudly speeding around the track.

You make the creative decision to have the video and audio of the race car occur at the same time that Teddy says, "I absolutely love the feeling of speed."

How to do it...

1. Start by using **Overwrite/Lift Segment Mode** (red arrow) to place the audio from the race car footage onto a separate track as pictured in the next screenshot.

2. Enter **Trim Mode** so that you have **Double Roller Trim** at the transition between **TEDDY ORLANDO** and the **RACE CAR** footage, as shown in the following screenshot:

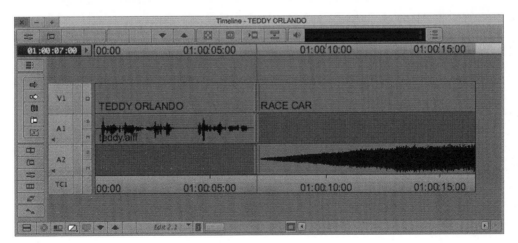

3. Now you'll use the *Shift* + click method to configure the **Trim Rollers** (this method is detailed in the *Using and configuring the Trimming tools* recipe in *Appendix B, Details on Trimming, Slipping, Sliding, and Segment Mode*). Follow the steps below. Remember, the goal is to have the video and audio from the B-side (**RACE CAR** shot) overlap the audio of **TEDDY** saying, "I absolutely love the feeling of speed."

4. Press and hold the *Shift* key, then click to remove the following rollers:

   ❑ On **V1**, remove the B-side roller

   ❑ On **A1**, remove the A-side roller

   ❑ On **A2**, remove the B-side roller

5. You will now have an **Asymmetric** Trim configuration that looks like the following screenshot:

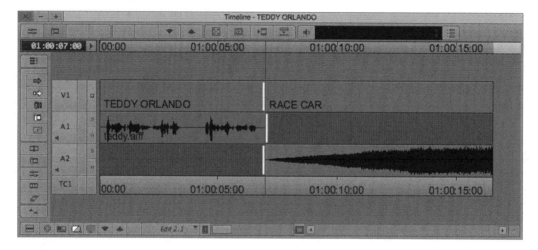

6. Trim in one of the following ways:

   ❑ If you were to grab and drag the rollers in the **Timeline** window (see the next screenshot), in this example, you might choose to grab the A-side roller on the **V1** track and then drag it to the left. This would shorten the video of **TEDDY** as well as the **Filler** on tracks **A1** and **A2**. Note that before you click-and-drag, make sure that the cursor icon's little piece of film extending out from it points to the same side as the **Trim Roller** you're going to grab (in this case, that would be to the left-hand side).

❑ If you wanted to use another Trimming method like **JKL**, the Trim keys, or the numeric key pad, you must first indicate to Media Composer which roller is the leader. You do this simply by clicking on it. However, before you click, make sure that the cursor icon's little piece of film extending out from it points to the same side as the Trim Roller you are clicking on (see the next screenshot). Once you have clicked on it, you can then Trim. In this example, I'd most likely click on one of the A-side rollers on either track **V1** or **A2**, and then trim to the left using the *J* key. This would shorten the video of **TEDDY** as well as the **Filler** on tracks **A1** and **A2**.

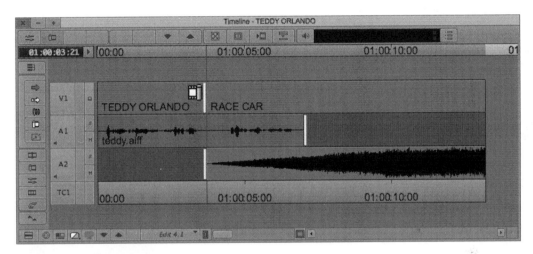

See also

▶ *Chapter 5, Maintaining and Regaining Sync*

▶ *Appendix B, Details on Trimming, Slipping, Sliding, and Segment Mode*

5

Maintaining and Regaining Sync

In this chapter, we will cover:

- ▶ Adding Filler within a sequence with Splice or Overwrite
- ▶ Adding Filler at the end of a sequence
- ▶ Sync Break Indicators: Understanding them and making your own
- ▶ Splicing and Extracting: Methods for staying in sync without Sync Locks
- ▶ Segment Mode: Methods for staying in sync
- ▶ Using the option/Alt + Add Edit method to stay in sync in Trim Mode
- ▶ Asymmetric Trimming type 1: A-Side/B-Side
- ▶ Asymmetric Trimming type 2: Two Heads/Two Tails
- ▶ Opening up the sequence using Splice with Sync Locks enabled
- ▶ Extracting with Sync Locks enabled
- ▶ Extending using Ripple Trim with Sync Locks enabled
- ▶ Shortening using Ripple Trim with Sync Locks enabled
- ▶ Getting back in sync

Introduction

In this chapter, the goal is to give you a solid understanding of *why* the Avid Media Composer system works the way it does with regard to sync, how you can be in complete control of staying in sync when using any of the editing modes without **Sync Locks** enabled, what **Sync Locks** do and how they work, and what to do if you find yourself out of sync.

This introduction itself will cover two topics:

- ▸ Understanding **Filler**
- ▸ The core concepts of **Sync**

First, understanding what **Filler** is will help you to stay in sync. In this chapter, we'll go over all the different methods in which you can add **Filler** to your sequence, including at the end. However, let's begin by discussing what **Filler** is and why Avid Media Composer uses it.

Avid Media Composer is a blend of editing methods, concepts, and terminology, many of which come from film and videotape editing. **Filler** is a concept from film editing. However, in film editing, it isn't called **Filler**, it's called **Slug** or **Leader**. Essentially, **Filler** is a spacer that keeps all the tracks of picture and sound exactly the same length (or duration) and, consequently, keeps them in sync. Just like Slug in film editing, **Filler** occupies space in your sequence just like any other segment (shot) does. A good analogy is that **Filler** is a segment of black video or a segment of silent audio. Understanding that **Filler** is a segment just like all the other segments of picture and sound in your sequence will help a great deal in understanding the behavior of the editing tools in Media Composer.

So you can see what film editing looks like, below is an image of what is called a flatbed, film-editing machine made by a company called Steenbeck. Each of the silver platters holds a roll of film (the picture rolls go on the top two platters and the sound rolls go on the lower two platters). The source rolls would be on the left-hand side and the take-up rolls on the right-hand side.

Photo credit: Benjamin Hershleder

Next is an image of a smaller Steenbeck (only one picture viewer) with the picture and sound rolls loaded. Note that each roll is just like a track in Avid Media Composer.

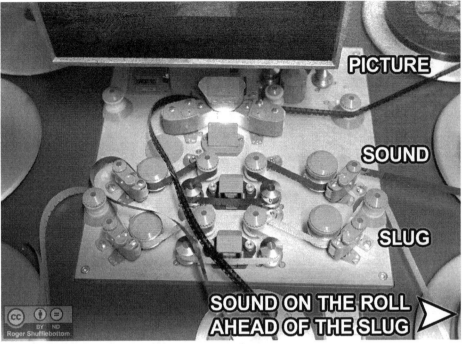

Photo credit: Roger Shufflebottom

Before getting into the specific methods of staying in sync when using the various editing tools in Media Composer, which are discussed in the sections that follow, I feel it's important to provide you with some fundamental information that will help you understand the programming of the software and ultimately to stay in sync. I'll be referring to these concepts a good deal in this chapter. I think of these as the core concepts of sync, which are as follows:

1. Yellow-colored tools (**Splice**, **Extract**, **Ripple Trim**) always change the duration of a track by either adding or removing material. Also, depending on how it's used, the yellow **Extract/Splice-In Segment Mode** tool may also affect the duration of a track. Additionally, even though it's not yellow, there is a function called **Top and Tail** that performs an extraction as part of its programming, so it also affects the duration of a track. The important thing to note is that any function or tool that can change the duration of a track has the capability of placing your tracks out of sync. The behavior of adding and removing material from a track is discussed in more detail in Point #5, below.

2. Red-colored tools (**Overwrite**, **Lift**, **Overwrite Trim**, and the **Lift/Overwrite Segment Mode** tool) do not change a track's overall duration (the only exception to this is if you Overwrite material at the very end of a sequence). Here are some details:

   ❑ **Overwrite** edits and when extending segments with **Overwrite Trim** do not add to a track's duration because they place the new material on top of the previous material. No additional duration is added to the track.

   ❑ **Lift**: The duration of the track is unchanged by removing material and simultaneously replacing it with an equal amount of **Filler**.

   ❑ **Overwrite Trim**: I feel it should be renamed to Overwrite/Lift Trim because when you use it to remove material, it also leaves behind an equal amount of **Filler**, so the overall duration of the track remains unchanged.

   ❑ **Double-Roller Trim** (also known as Dual-Roller Trim): While it is not red, this function will not push material downstream out of sync. **Double-Roller Trim** does not add to a track's duration, because as you extend one segment, it places the new material on top of the other segment. In actuality, no additional duration is added to the track, because as one segment gets longer, the other gets shorter by an equal amount.

   ❑ **Extend**: Although this function is not colored red, it can not push material downstream out of sync. The **Extend** function does not add to a track's duration, because as you extend one segment, it places the new material on top of the other segment. No additional duration is added to the track, because as one segment gets longer, the other gets shorter by an equal amount. Essentially, the **Extend** function is performing a **Double-Roller Trim** without actually being in **Trim Mode**.

3. This is a particularly important concept: As long as you perform the same duration- changing editing operation on all the tracks (which means that you're affecting all the tracks by an equal duration), you will stay in sync. In other words:

   ❑ If you add material to one or more tracks using **Splice** (yellow) or **Ripple Trim** (yellow), then you must add an equal amount/duration of material to all the other tracks to maintain sync

   ❑ If you remove material from one or more tracks using **Extract** (yellow) or **Ripple Trim** (yellow), then you must remove an equal amount/duration of material from all the other tracks to maintain sync

4. **Filler** occupies space in the sequence just like any other segment (shot) does. You can think of **Filler** as a segment of black video or a segment of silent audio. **Filler** was discussed in more detail earlier in the *Introduction* section of this chapter, which covers understanding and adding **Filler**.

5. It is said that editing is the final rewrite of a film. That analogy applies not only to telling the story but also to the way the sequence behaves during editing as well. This is because tracks react to adding and removing material in the same way that a sentence does when you add or remove letters and words:

    ❑   Example 1, **Splicing**: I type the sentence "I went beach this afternoon". I then notice that between the words "went" and "beach" I forgot to type the words "to the". When I insert the words "to the" into the sentence, the words "this afternoon" are pushed down to the right and the sentence becomes longer. This is exactly the same as when I **Splice** (yellow) material into a track or **Ripple Trim** (yellow) a segment making it longer.

    ❑   Example 2, **Extracting**: I type the sentence "I drove down the steep and winding road". I then decide that I no longer want to include the words "steep and". So I highlight those words and press *Delete*. The result is that the words "winding road" move to the left and the sentence becomes shorter. This is exactly the same as when I **Extract** (yellow) material from a track or **Ripple Trim** (yellow) a segment making it shorter.

    ❑   Example 3, **Overwriting**: My intention is to type the name of one of the southern states in the U.S. Due to my poor typing skills, I misspell this state as Mississibbi. I then notice my error; the two b's should instead be p's. I then highlight just the two b's and type "pp". The b's are replaced with an equal amount of letters, so the word does not get any longer. This is exactly what happens when you **Overwrite** (red).

    ❑   Example 4, **Lifting**: Lifting does not really have an exact analogy that corresponds with typing. Since both performing a **Lift** (red) and removing material with **Overwrite Trim** (red) replaces the material it removes with an equal amount of **Filler**, the closest example I can come up with is that I mistype the sentence "I caught thebball". I then notice that I forgot a space between the word "the" and the word "ball", and that I mistakenly typed the letter "b" twice. If I delete the first letter "b" and then also add in the space between "the" and "ball", I have removed something and the sentence remains the same length. Essentially, what takes me two steps in this example, **Lift** does in just one.

Adding Filler within a sequence with Splice or Overwrite

In this recipe, we will see how the programming of Avid Media Composer allows you to edit **Filler** at the beginning of a Sequence, or anywhere between segments of video or audio. However, it does *not* allow you to **Splice** or **Overwrite Filler** at the end of a Sequence (don't worry, Avid gave us a way around that, and it's discussed in the recipe that follows this one).

How to do it...

1. Go to the **Clip Name** Menu above the **Source** Window.
2. From the **Clip Name** Menu select **Load Filler**.
3. By default, Media Composer gives you 2 minutes of **Filler**. **Mark In** and **Mark Out** for the duration you would like to edit into your sequence.
4. Enable the **Source** and **Timeline** Track Selectors as needed.
5. **Splice** or **Overwrite** the selected duration of **Filler** into your sequence.

There's more...

Very frequently the engineers at Avid provide us with multiple methods to accomplish a task, and this is the case with adding **Filler** at the beginning of a sequence.

Additional method for adding Filler at the beginning of a sequence

While you can add **Filler** at the beginning of a sequence with **Splice** or **Overwrite**, Media Composer also has a command called **Add Filler at Start**. By default, the current duration it adds is 30 seconds (in earlier releases it was 1 second). However, this duration can be customized to whatever you'd like. For those of you working in broadcast television in the U.S., you may find it useful to customize the duration to **00;01;29;28** so you can quickly add **Filler** at the beginning of a sequence in order to accommodate the **Color Bars**, **Tone**, **Slate**, and **Countdown** necessary prior to making an output. The path to customize the **Add Filler at Start** duration is **Project** Window | **Settings** tab | **Timeline** settings | **Edit** tab | **Start Filler Duration Entry Box**.

Here are two methods to access the **Add Filler at Start** command:

▸ Method 1: **Clip** menu | **Add Filler at Start**
▸ Method 2: Right-click in the **Timeline** Window | **Add Filler at Start**

See also

▸ The *Adding Filler at the end of a sequence* recipe

Adding Filler at the end of a sequence

Media Composer does not allow you to **Splice** or **Overwrite Filler** at the end of a sequence, but all is not lost. We'll look at two methods you can use. The recipe will look at using **Trimming** to add **Filler** at the end of a sequence, and the *There's more...* section will provide a second method that uses the **Title Tool**.

How to do it...

1. Add a new video or audio track (whichever you prefer) if you do not already have one that is empty at the very end of your sequence.

2. Enable only the Track Selector for the track that is empty at the end of the sequence.

3. If you have **Sync Locks** enabled, then disable all of them (or at least disable it for the track that is empty at the end).

4. Go to the end of the sequence.

5. Make sure that the **Position Indicator** is parked at the end of the sequence and not all the way to the right-hand side and actually parked off the sequence. You may need to move the **Position Indicator** back one or two frames from the very end.

6. Use the **Add Edit** function to put a cut in the **Filler** of the enabled track.

7. Enter **Trim Mode**.

8. Enable **Ripple Trim** (yellow trim) on the **A-Side** (left-hand side) of the cut you placed in the **Filler**.

9. Trim the **Filler**, to make it longer by extending it to the right.

There's more

Here's another approach to adding **Filler** at the end of a sequence that uses the **Title Tool**.

1. Open the **Title Tool** by going to **Tools** menu | **Title Tool**.

2. If presented with a dialog window, select **Title Tool** (not Marquee). If needed, you can regain the dialog window by going to **Project** Window | **Settings** tab | **Marquee Title** | **Create New Title Using** | **Ask Me**.

3. In the lower left-hand side of the **Title Tool**, you'll see a button with a bright green letter **V** on it. This tells Media Composer to make titles with a transparent background so that the video will show through. Click that button to disable this. Now you'll see that the background is a solid color rather than the video, and that the default color is black (if needed, this can be changed by clicking on the black color swatch labeled as **Bg** found next to the **V** button).

4. Go to the **File** menu and select **Save**.

5. A dialog window will open where you will name the title, select the bin that the **Title Clip** will be placed into, select the drive where the media it creates will be stored, and select the resolution of the media that it will create.

6. Click **Save**.

7. Close the **Title Tool** if it's no longer needed.

8. Edit a portion of the title at the end of your sequence.

9. Later, if you need additional **Filler** at the end, you can either:

   ❑ Trim the black title to make it longer

   ❑ Splice in some **Filler** prior to the black title

Sync Break Indicators: Understanding them and making your own

If you are editing without your **Sync Locks** enabled, it is possible to knock one or more tracks out of sync with the others. **Sync Locks** are discussed in more detail later in this chapter.

When the tracks no longer align or sync properly, if the video and audio come from the same clip (or have been AutoSynced), then Media Composer will display what Avid calls **Sync Break Indicators**. These are the small white or black numbers (depending on the color of your tracks) that appear in the segments (shots) when they are out of alignment. Media Composer is able to determine sync breaks because it's programmed to compare a segment's clip source data and timecode across tracks. If the segments on the different tracks come from the same clip and the timecode numbers align, then they are in sync. If they don't align, then that means the timecode numbers do not match and Media Composer can easily calculate the amount of frames for which they are out of sync.

For example, let's imagine that I'm working *without* the **Sync Locks** enabled and I'm editing a dialog scene of a movie in which I have only one video track and one audio track. If I Trim the first shot in my video track 30 frames longer *without also* trimming the audio track 30 frames longer, then this will extend the video segment and push the video segments that follow it down to the right, making them out of sync (out of alignment) with their audio segment mates. The result will be that the actors speaking in my movie will appear as if they are starring in a poorly dubbed version, and the **Sync Break Indicators** will appear.

In this example, the **Sync Break Indicators** in the video track would read as **-30** while those in the audio track would read as **30**. The **Sync Break Indicators** are actually telling you how to fix the sync break. Negative values in Media Composer indicate movement to the left and positive numbers indicate movement to the right. So what Media Composer is telling you in this example is:

▶ In order to get the out of sync segments on the *video track* back in sync with those on the audio track, you need to move them 30 frames to the left

▶ In order to get the out of sync segments on the *audio track* back in sync with those on the video track, you need to move them 30 frames to the right

To regain sync in this example, whichever track you choose to edit is up to you, but it has to be edited *independently* of the other *without* **Sync Locks** enabled. For example, if I were to edit the *video track* to regain sync, I could use any of these methods:

▶ Use **Ripple Trim** (yellow) to trim the video segment that exists just before where the sync break occurs 30 frames shorter; this is my preferred method

▶ **Extract** (yellow) 30 frames from any video segment that exists before the sync break occurs

▶ Place all the video segments *that are out of sync* into **Lift/Overwrite Segment Mode** (red) and move them 30 frames to the left

The topic of regaining sync is discussed in more detail later in this chapter.

Getting ready

In this recipe of steps, we'll discuss making your own **Sync Break Indicators**. This can be helpful because there will be many times when you'll place video and audio from different clips into alignment with each other. For example, you might have some music with a loud cymbal crash and you have placed video of two boxers in sync with it, so that the knockout punch happens at the same time as the cymbal crash. This would be a sync relationship that you created from *different* source clips, and Media Composer will *not* show **Sync Break Indicators** if they get moved out of sync. However, you can create your own visual sync reference using **Markers**.

Before we start the steps of this recipe, here's an overview of what you'll be doing. You'll be adding a **Marker** at the same location on all the video and audio tracks. That way if the segments get knocked out of sync, you'll be alerted, because visually the **Markers** will no longer line up and you'll also have an indication of how much out of sync you are.

Another helpful piece of information before we get into the recipe is that **Markers** are programmed to be placed *only* onto the uppermost track that is enabled, even if the lower tracks are enabled. With that in mind, here's a relatively easy way to add **Markers** as a sync reference.

How to do it...

1. Park the **Position Indicator** in a spot where it crosses all the video and/or audio segments onto which you'd like to place **Markers**.

2. *Enable all* the Track Selectors for the video and/or audio tracks onto which you'd like **Markers** to be placed.

3. The **Add Marker** button can be found by default in the **Fast Menu Tool Palette** between the **Splice** and **Overwrite** buttons underneath the **Source** and **Record** monitors. The icon for Add Marker is a bright, red oval.

4. Add a **Marker** to the uppermost enabled track.

5. Disable the track that just received a **Marker**.

6. Do *not* move the **Position Indicator** line.

7. Repeat steps 4, 5, and 6 until **Markers** have been added at the same location on all the tracks you want them to be on.

Splicing and Extracting: Methods for staying in sync without Sync Locks

When you are editing in **Source/Record mode** you have four main editing functions available. Two functions place material into the sequence (**Splice** and **Overwrite**) and two functions remove material from the sequence (**Extract** and **Lift**). As discussed in the *Introduction* section of this chapter, the functions that affect the duration of a track are colored yellow, specifically **Splice** and **Extract**.

As long as you affect *all* the tracks in your sequence when using **Splice** or **Extract**, you will stay in sync. However, there is a particular situation that can sometimes confuse people so we are going to focus on that.

Below is a screenshot of an example editing situation:

▸ You're editing the scene of a comedy television program

▸ Loaded in the **Source** Window is a clip that contains one video track and two audio tracks

▸ Loaded in the **Timeline** Window is a sequence that contains one video track and four audio tracks

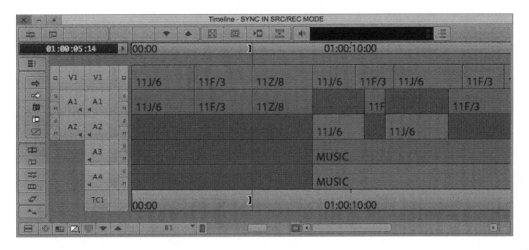

The goals in this example are that:

▸ You want to add only the video to the sequence between the shots **11F/3** and **11Z/8**. It's a close-up shot of one actor's shocked reaction to another actor's line of dialog.

▸ You want to push the other segments (shots) in the sequence down, so that you can later add in the sound of the audience laughing underneath the video of the shocked reaction shot.

▸ You want to accomplish this in as few steps as possible.

Getting ready

If you haven't already read the *Introduction* section of this chapter, which includes an overview of what I call the core concepts of sync, then you may find it helpful.

How to do it...

Follow these steps:

1. In the **Source** Window, **Mark In** and **Mark Out** around the material that you want to add into the sequence.

2. In the sequence, place a **Mark In** between the segments (shots) where you want to insert the reaction shot video.

3. For the **Source** Track Selectors, enable *only* the **Video** Track Selector (see the screenshot below).

4. For the **Sequence** Track Selectors, enable *all* the Track Selectors (see the screenshot below).

5. Splice the material into the sequence. In the screenshot below, we see the result of **Splicing** in the video from shot **11B/2**:

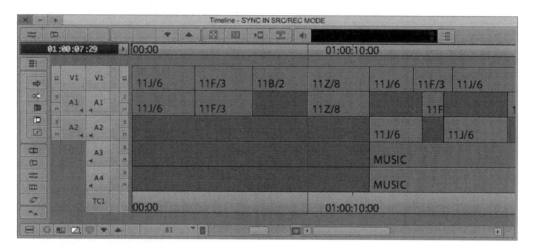

How it works...

This maintains sync because:

▶ By enabling *all* the **Sequence** Track Selectors, you have instructed Media Composer to record on *all* of those tracks.

▶ The video track in the sequence is recording a duration of *video* because the **Video** Track Selector for the **Source** is enabled. In other words, the **Source** video track is *sending* its video and the **Sequence** video track is *recording* that video.

▶ The audio tracks in the sequence are recording a duration of **Filler** because the **Audio** track selectors for the **Source** are not enabled. In other words, the **Source** audio tracks are not sending their audio but the **Sequence** audio tracks are recording something. Specifically, they're recording **Filler**.

▸ As discussed in the *Introduction* section in this chapter, which is about understanding and adding **Filler, Filler** is a segment that occupies space, just like all the other segments of picture or sound in your sequence.

▸ As discussed in the *Introduction* section of this chapter explaining the core concepts of **Sync**, since all the tracks in the sequence are receiving (recording) the same duration of material, everything remains in sync.

Segment Mode: Methods for staying in sync

On the left-hand side of the **Timeline** Window, and included as part of the **Smart Tool**, you'll find the red arrow that points to the right as well as the yellow arrow that points to the right. Together these two features are called **Segment Mode**. This is because they are a separate mode of operation. The red arrow is the **Lift/Overwrite Segment** tool. As its name tells us, it contains both of those editing abilities. The good news is that this tool can never alter the material that is downstream of the edit points causing them to go out of sync. This is because:

▸ At the original location from which the segment(s) is removed, it performs a **Lift** that leaves an equal duration of **Filler** behind

▸ At the new location where the segment(s) is placed, it performs an **Overwrite** that replaces (covers up) the material that was previously there

Then we have the yellow **Extract/Splice-In Segment** tool. As its name suggests, it contains both abilities:

▸ At the original location from which the segment(s) is removed, it performs an **Extraction**

▸ At the new location where the segment(s) is placed, it performs a **Splice**

As discussed in the *Introduction* section of this chapter regarding the core concepts of **Sync**:

▸ Yellow functions have the ability to add or remove material on a track and change its duration

▸ As long as you affect *all* the tracks in your sequence equally when using **Splice** or **Extract**, you will stay in sync

So, you can imagine that *in some situations* this makes it hard to stay in sync using the yellow **Extract/Splice-In Segment** tool when moving one or more segments *without also* moving an equal duration of the segment(s) on the other tracks, as shown in the following screenshot:

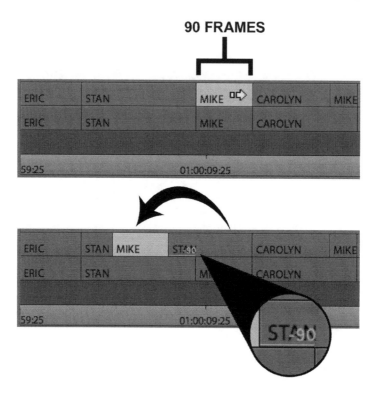

In the example screenshot above, this happened because the segment labeled as **MIKE** (with a duration of 90 frames) was Extracted from its original location and Spliced into its new location within the segment labeled as **STAN**. The Splice operation pushed the material that follows it down to the right, causing it to become out of sync with its audio.

The result would have been even more damaging had the **MIKE** video segment been moved from its original location on track **V1** (upper image of the screenshot below) and placed onto track **V2** (lower image of the screenshot below). In that instance:

▸ The **MIKE** segment would be Extracted from **V1**, causing all of the segments downstream of it on that track to shift to the left

▶ The **MIKE** segment would be spliced onto track **V2**, causing all of the segments downstream of the edit point on that track to shift to the right

Getting ready

If you haven't already read the _Introduction_ section of this chapter, which includes an overview of the core concepts of **Sync**, you may find it helpful.

How to do it...

The sync issues described above can be avoided in the following way when using the yellow **Extract/Splice-In Segment** tool:

1. Enable **Sync Locks** for _all_ the tracks (circled in the following screenshot). **Sync Locks** are discussed in more detail later in this chapter.

2. Enable the setting that will make the yellow **Extract/Splice-In Segment** tool respond to the **Sync Locks**. The path to enable this setting is **Project** Window | **Settings** tab | **Timeline** settings | **Edit** tab, and enable the setting that says **Segment Drag Sync Locks**.

After implementing the steps we just covered, and then repeating the two previous editing examples, we get the following results:

The top screenshot below shows the result of moving the **MIKE** segment to the left on the **V1** track and into the middle of the **STAN** segment. The bottom screenshot below shows the result of moving the **MIKE** segment onto track **V2** as well as into the middle of the **STAN** segment:

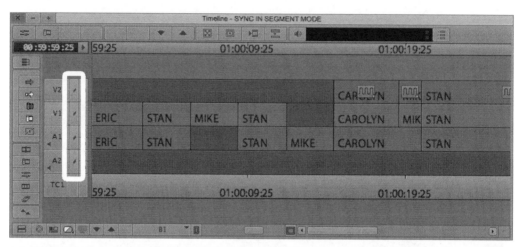

How it works...

Because **Sync Locks** are enabled and because you have enabled the setting that makes the yellow **Extract/Splice-In Segment** tool respond to the **Sync Locks**, sync has been maintained by adding an equal duration of **Filler** to all the tracks.

Using the option/Alt + Add Edit method to stay in sync in Trim Mode

When you use the **Add Edit** function it places a cut in a track wherever the **Position Indicator** is parked and, by default, it's programmed to place the cut onto any track that has its Track Selector enabled. However, if you hold the *option/Alt* key when you use **Add Edit**, it will do the following:

> ▸ In **Source/Record** Mode, it places the cut(s) only in **Filler**. In other words, it will not cut segments of video or audio. Additionally, it will place cuts on a **Filler** track *even if its track selector is not enabled.*

> ▸ In **Trim Mode**, it will do everything it does when used in **Source/Record** Mode but, the great part is that in **Trim Mode**, all the cuts you make will also *automatically become enabled for Trimming*. Because the *option/Alt* + **Add Edit** function only relates to **Filler**, there may be instances where you'll have to then manually configure the **Trim Rollers** on the tracks containing video or audio segments. So be sure to read these related sections:

>> ❑ In this chapter, read the *Using Asymmetric Trimming technically and aesthetically* recipe

>> ❑ The *Enabling and configuring the Trimming tools* section in *Appendix B, Details on Trimming, Slipping, Sliding, and Segment Mode*

The following is an example that provides a general recipe of steps for you. There are multiple video tracks and audio tracks in the sequence. The shot we want to Trim is of **MIKE**, as shown in the following screenshot:

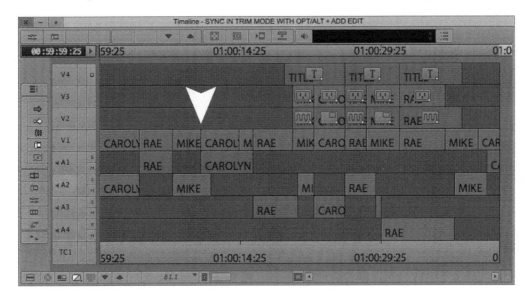

Furthermore for this example, we are working in an area near the beginning of the sequence and are zoomed in, so we can't see very far down to the right to know what's happening on the other tracks (see the screenshot below).

We decide that we want to *only extend the video of the* **MIKE** *shot* on track **V1**. While a straight cut would be much easier to deal with, to further complicate the situation, the transition we want to Trim (between the **MIKE** and **CAROLYN** segments) is a **Split Edit**:

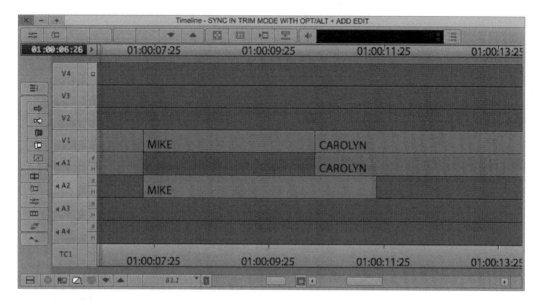

How to do it...

To address the situation described previously, here are the steps:

1. Enter **Trim Mode** at the transition on the **V1** and **A1** tracks only. The method I use most frequently is to lasso. Lassoing is discussed in the *Using and Configuring the Trimming Tools* section in *Appendix B, Details on Trimming, Slipping, Sliding, and Segment Mode*.

2. Select the **A-Side** for Trimming.

3. Perform the *option/Alt* + **Add Edit**. The results of steps 1, 2, and 3 are pictured in the following screenshot:

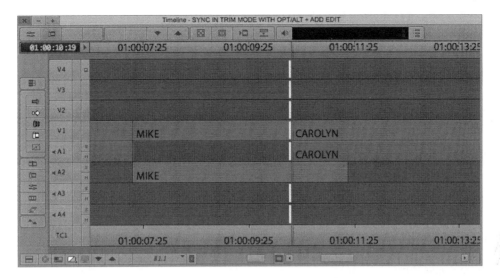

4. Because there is an audio segment on track **A2** and because *option/Alt* + **Add Edit** only places cuts in **Filler**, no cut has been made in the audio segment of **MIKE** and no **Trim Roller** has been enabled on that track. In *this particular instance*, I make the decision that I want to also extend the audio on track **A2**. So I manually add and configure the **Trim Roller** onto the **A-Side** of **Mike's audio segment**, using the **Shift-Click** method discussed in the *Using and configuring the Trimming tools* section in *Appendix B*. The result is pictured in the following screenshot:

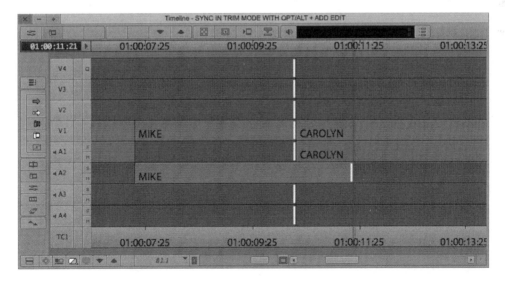

5. Extend the video on track **V1** by trimming it to the right.

How it works...

Sync is maintained because as you trim the video on **V1** to make it longer, all the other tracks are also extended. This is because the **Filler** is being extended too. Because all the tracks are receiving an *equal duration* of material, they all stay in sync. For emphasis, sync is maintained because an equal amount of material is added to *all* the tracks.

Asymmetric Trimming type 1: A-Side/B-Side

The following sections may help you better understand and use **Asymmetric Trimming**, so you may find it helpful to read them first:

- ▸ The *Using and configuring the trimming tools* section in Appendix B, *Details on Trimming, Slipping, Sliding, and Segment Mode*, specifically the portion that details using the **Shift+Click** method to add or remove **Trim Rollers**

- ▸ The *Introduction* section of this chapter

- ▸ The *Using the option/Alt + Add Edit method to stay in sync* recipe of this chapter

Asymmetric Trimming is the "King of Trim". While **Asymmetric Trimming** is an indispensable feature, it can sometimes be a challenging concept. However, it is well worth your time and effort to understand it and to master it.

First, what does **Asymmetric Trimming** mean? Simply, it means trimming in opposite directions at the same time. While this might sound strange, what **Asymmetric Trimming** is doing is shortening or lengthening the tracks by the same duration. However, instead of the **Trim Rollers** all moving in the same direction, they move in opposite directions.

A-Side/B-Side Asymmetric Trimming will be the method you'll find yourself using the majority of the time, and once mastered, will greatly speed up your work because:

- ▸ You'll be able to easily contend with a **Timeline** that has numerous tracks

- ▸ You'll be able to accomplish various, sometimes complicated, edits in less steps

- ▸ You'll be able to always maintain sync while trimming

We'll examine *two* situations as examples for when and how you might use **A-Side/B-Side Asymmetric Trimming**. The first will be presented next and the other will be in the *There's more...* section of this recipe.

Getting ready

In this example, we'll take a look at using **Asymmetric Trimming** to make a change to a sequence with three video tracks and six audio tracks. Here is a screenshot of the example before we do any editing:

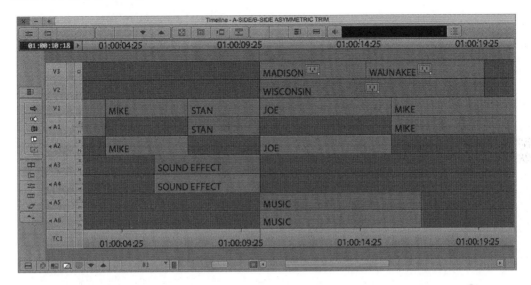

Our goals in this situation are:

- *To extend* (lengthen) the **STAN** video segment on **V1**, because we want a longer pause before the actor (**JOE**) in the next shot speaks

- *To not* extend the dialog on **A1**, because another actor who is off-camera speaks and we don't want to hear them

- *To not alter the segment of* **JOE** *in any way*

- *To not* extend the stereo sound effect on **A3** and **A4**

- *To not alter the music on* **A5** *and* **A6**

- To stay in sync on all the tracks

How to do it...

1. Enable all the Track Selectors.

2. Park the **Position Indicator** near the transition of the **STAN** and **JOE** shots.

3. Enter **Trim Mode** on all the tracks (by default, you'll be placed into the **Double-Roller Trim** configuration).

4. Use the **Shift+Click** method (discussed in the *Using and configuring the trimming tools* recipe in *Appendix B, Details on Trimming, Slipping, Sliding, and Segment Mode*) to select or de-select **Trim Rollers** as needed (detailed in a moment). Just take it slow, track by track. For each track, ask yourself which segment (shot) you want to affect. Then configure the **Trim Roller** on that track so that it's touching the shot that you want to trim. At first, this conversation you have with yourself will take some time, but the more often you do it, you'll find that your internal dialog will move along very quickly. Let's go through it together:

   □ **V3**, **V2**, and **V1**: De-select the **Trim Rollers** on the **B-Side** (the right-hand side) of the transition. In other words, you should have **Trim Rollers** only on the **A-Side**.

   □ **A1**: De-select the **Trim Roller** on the **A-Side** (left-hand side) of the transition.

   □ **A2**: De-select the **Trim Roller** on the **B-Side** of the transition.

   □ **A3** and **A4**: De-select the **Trim Rollers** on the **A-Side** of the transition.

   □ **A5** and **A6**: De-select the **Trim Rollers** on the **B-Side** of the transition. Below is a screenshot of what the sequence looks like after completing the configuration detailed above:

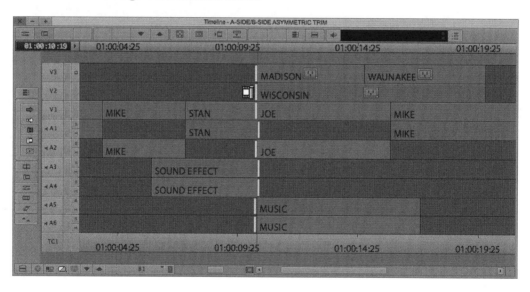

5. Hover the cursor over one of the **A-Side Trim Rollers** on any of the tracks. Make sure that the icon for the cursor also indicates the **A-Side** by having the piece of film that extends out from it pointing to the left (see the previous screenshot).

6. With the cursor being displayed as described in step 5, click-and-drag it to the *right*. The material on tracks **V1**, **V2**, **V3**, **A2**, **A5**, and **A6** will be extended to the *right* while the material on tracks **A1**, **A3**, and **A4** will be extended to the *left*.

Also see the *There's more...* section below for a tip on using **Asymmetric Trimming** along with trim methods other than dragging.

Here's a screenshot of the completed trim:

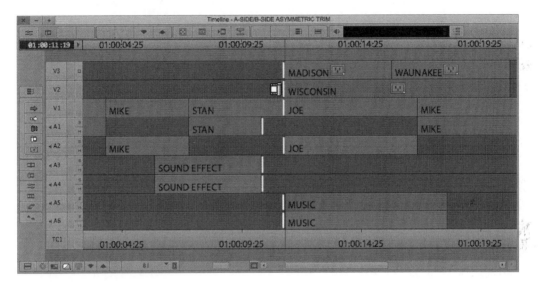

How it works...

The **Trim Rollers** are moving in opposite directions, but they are performing *the same operation* on *all* the tracks, in this case that's *adding the same duration of material*. Specifically, the trimming on track **V1** is extending (adding) to the *video* while the trimming on the other tracks is extending **Filler**. For emphasis, sync is maintained because an *equal* amount of material is added to *all* the tracks.

There's more...

In this second example, we'll take a look at using **Asymmetric Trimming** to create a **Split Edit**. **Asymmetric Trimming** can be used to create a **Split Edit** in a dramatic scene, to get two characters' dialog to overlap (for example, during an argument). However, my example will be a fictitious documentary about film editors Chris Innis and Bob Murawski, who received Academy Awards for Best Editing of The Hurt Locker, directed by Kathryn Bigelow. Here is a screenshot of the editing example before we do any editing:

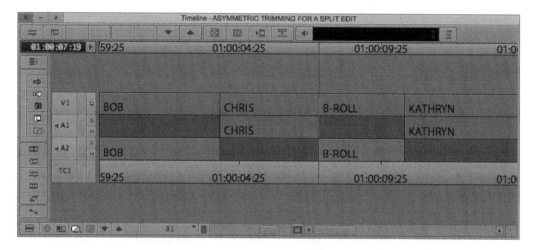

- ▸ My goal in this situation is to bring the **B-ROLL** video and audio in earlier so that it occurs at the same time as the ending portion of Chris' interview sound bite

- ▸ The first shot on the left-hand side of the transition is an interview sound bite from Chris Innis

- ▸ The second shot on the right-hand side is some **B-ROLL** (video that illustrates what is being discussed) from the movie

Here are the steps to use **Asymmetric Trimming** to create the **Split Edit**:

1. Enter **Trim Mode** on all the tracks (by default, you'll be placed into the **Double-Roller Trim** configuration).

2. Use the **Shift+Click** method (discussed in the *Using and configuring the trimming tools* recipe in Appendix B, *Details on Trimming, Slipping, Sliding, and Segment Mode*) to select or de-select **Trim Rollers** as needed (detailed in a moment). Just take it slow, track by track. For each track ask yourself which segment (shot) you want to affect. Then configure the **Trim Roller** on that track so that it's touching the shot that you want to trim. Let's go through it together:

   ❑ **V1**: De-select the **Trim Roller** on the **B-Side** of the transition (the right-hand side). In other words, you should place the **Trim Roller** only on the **A-Side**.

   ❑ **A1**: De-select the **Trim Roller** on the **A-Side** (left-hand side) of the transition.

   ❑ **A2**: De-select the **Trim Roller** on the **B-Side** of the transition. Below is a screenshot of what the sequence looks like after completing the configuration just covered.

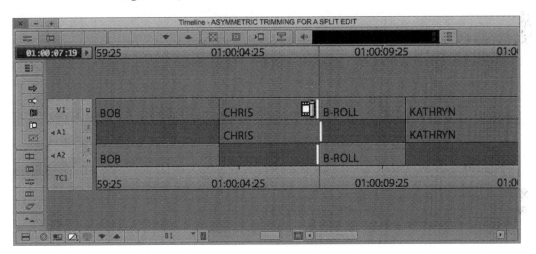

3. Hover the cursor over the **Trim Roller** on the **A-Side** of the video track. Make sure that the icon for the cursor also indicates the **A-Side** by having the piece of film that extends out from it pointing to the *left-hand side* (see the previous screenshot).

4. With the cursor being displayed as described in step 3, click-and-drag it to the *left*. The material on tracks **V1** and **A2** will be shortened to the *left-hand side* while the material on track **A1** will be shortened to the *right-hand side*.

Here's a screenshot of the completed trim:

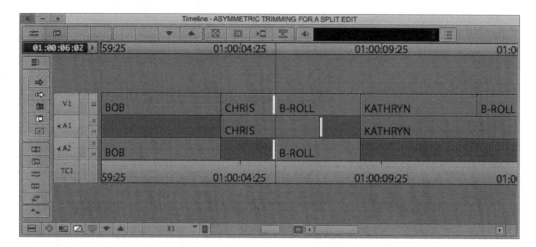

The **Trim Rollers** are moving in opposite directions, but they are performing *the same operation* on *all* the tracks, *removing the same duration of material*. Specifically, the trimming on tracks **V1** and **A2** is removing (shortening) the video and **Filler**, while the trimming on **A1** is removing **Filler**. For emphasis, sync is maintained because an *equal* amount of material is removed from *all* the tracks.

Asymmetric Trimming type 2: Two Heads/ Two Tails

Editor and fellow ACI Paul Petschek assisted me with this example, as well as reminded me that this is an editing capability that was inspired by another editing application called Lightworks. This relatively new addition to the trimming programming in Avid Media Composer is useful in some specific situations. You may not use it every week but when you need it, you'll have it in your bag of tricks. Its most frequent use would come when editing a montage of video that sits on top of a bed of music and/or voiceover, as is often found in music videos, television commercials, and film trailers.

This recipe will take you through the steps to use the **Two Heads/Two Tails Asymmetric Trimming** method, and then for the sake of comparison, an alternate method will be presented in the *There's more...* section of this recipe.

Getting ready

Below is a screenshot of the situation before editing. Note that to help you follow along with what is happening, I've placed white Markers on the first and last frames of the segment labeled as **FLOWER**:

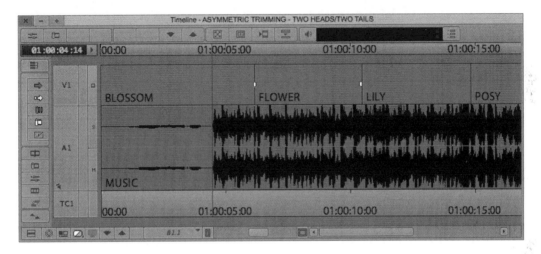

The goals in this situation are:

▶ To move the **FLOWER** shot earlier (to the left) in the sequence so that the transition syncs with the moment that the music first becomes loud and forceful

▶ To *not* change the duration of the shot labeled as **LILY**

▶ To not alter the sync of shots downstream of the **FLOWER** segment

How to do it...

1. Enter **Trim Mode** at the head of the **FLOWER** shot. This will place you into **Double-Roller Trim**, as pictured in the following screenshot:

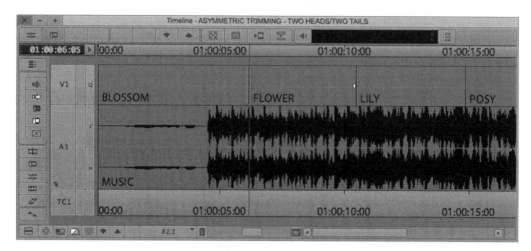

2. Use the **Shift+Click** method (discussed in the *Using and configuring the trimming tools* recipe in *Appendix B, Details on Trimming, Slipping, Sliding, and Segment Mode*) to de-select the **B-Side** (right-hand side) **Trim Roller** and then to also add a **Trim Roller** to the tail of **FLOWER**. You've now configured a **Two Tails Asymmetric Trim**, as pictured in the following screenshot:

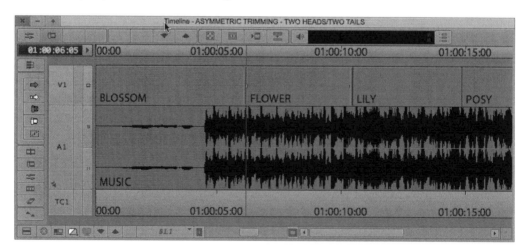

3. Hover your cursor over the **Trim Roller** on the **A-Side** which is on the tail of the shot labeled as **BLOSSOM**. Make sure that the icon for the cursor also indicates the **A-Side**, by having the piece of film that extends out from it pointing to the left-hand side.

4. With the cursor being displayed as described in step 3, click-and-drag it to the left. Go slowly and you'll see that as the **BLOSSOM** shot gets shorter (which moves the **FLOWER** shot earlier/left), the tail of the **FLOWER** shot gets longer by an equal amount, at the same time. See the *There's more* section for a tip on how to perform **Asymmetric Trimming** while using a trim method other than dragging.

5. The result, displayed in the screenshot below, is that the **FLOWER** segment was moved earlier in the sequence so that its transition syncs with the start of the loud music, the **FLOWER** segment was lengthened from its tail, and the **LILY** shot was not altered:

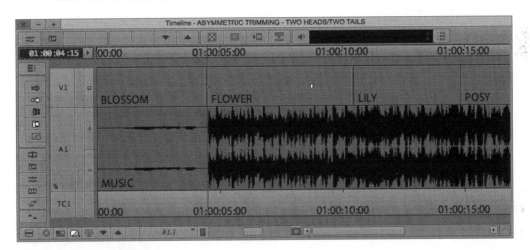

How it works...

The **Trim Rollers** are moving in opposite directions on the same track. Sync is maintained because as material is *removed* from one segment (**BLOSSOM**), an *equal amount is added* to another (**FLOWER**). For emphasis, sync is maintained because the duration of the track remains the same, so it doesn't affect the position of any segments that are downstream (to the right-hand side) of the edit.

There's more...

In this section, you'll find:

▸ An alternate method to that presented above, which achieves the same result

▸ A tip to quickly return to the previously configured **Trimming** setup

▸ A tip for using **Asymmetric Trimming** with trim methods other than dragging

Alternate method

Here is an alternate method that does not use **Two Heads/Two Tails Asymmetric Trimming** to achieve the same result as in the previous recipe:

1. Park the **Position Indicator** on the first frame of the loud music (as pictured previously).

2. Enable the red **Lift/Overwrite Segment Mode** tool.

3. Select the **FLOWER** segment.

4. Hold down the *cmd/Ctrl* key.

5. Drag the **FLOWER** segment to the left. Because you're holding the *cmd/Ctrl* key, the head of the segment will snap to the **Position Indicator**. Release the mouse to place the **FLOWER** segment.

6. Enter **Trim Mode** at the transition that now exists at the tail of the **FLOWER** segment and the head of the **Filler**. This will place you into **Double-Roller Trim**, as pictured in the following screenshot:

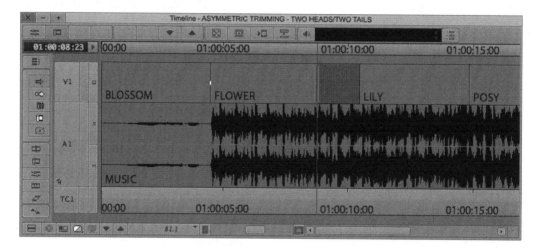

7. Drag the **Trim Rollers** to the right, which will lengthen the **FLOWER** shot and shorten/remove the **Filler**. Note that Media Composer has a nice feature that automatically stops the trim when it encounters a transition.

8. The result is pictured in the following screenshot:

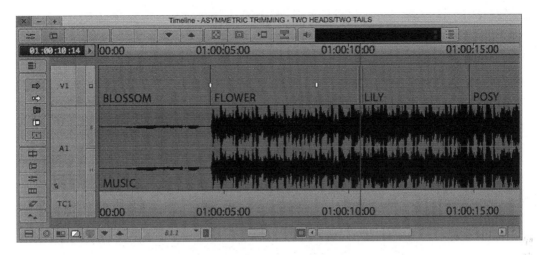

Quickly return to the last used Trim Roller configuration

This is a very useful feature that can be used after exiting from *any* trim configuration. However, this trick is especially helpful when you've just performed a multitrack, **Asymmetric Trim** and want to re-enter **Trim Mode** to make additional adjustments. The steps to do this are as follows:

1. Hold down the *option/Alt* key.
2. Do one of the following:

   ❑ Press the **Trim Mode** button on the keyboard (by default on the letter *U*)

   ❑ Click on the **Trim Mode** button in the interface (for example, on the **Composer** Window below the **Splice** and **Overwrite** buttons)

Asymmetric Trimming with methods other than dragging

When **Asymmetric Trimming**, if you wanted to use another trimming method (that is JKL, the trim keys, or the numeric keypad), you must first indicate to Media Composer which roller is the "leader", so that you can know in which direction to instruct Media Composer to trim. You do this simply by clicking on a **Trim Roller** once. However, before you click, make sure that the cursor icon's little piece of film extending out from it points to the same side as the **Trim Roller** you are clicking on. For example, to designate a **Trim Roller** that is on the **A-Side** (left-hand side) as the leader, the cursor icon's piece of film needs to extend/point to the left-hand side before you click. Once you have clicked on it once, you can then trim it using any trim method.

Opening up the sequence using Splice with Sync Locks enabled

In the previous sections of this chapter, we've learned a lot about staying in sync without using **Sync Locks**, so that you can choose to use them or not. Personally, I like using **Sync Locks** as I find that not only do they protect me from making silly mistakes when I'm in a hurry or tired, but also in many cases allow me to perform various edits in less steps, essentially by reducing the number of tracks that I have to enable to make a **Splice**, an **Extract**, or a **Ripple Trim**.

This recipe, and several that follow it, discuss performing various editing operations while **Sync Locks** are enabled. However, before we get into the recipes themselves, let's get familiar with **Sync Locks** and their behavior:

> ▶ **Sync Locks** are the black, diagonal lines (I call them hash marks) that appear when you click in the narrow **Sync Lock Column** that is immediately to the right-hand side of the **Timeline** Track Selectors, as pictured below. Note that in earlier releases of Media Composer, the **Sync Lock Column** was placed between the **Source** and **Record** Track Selectors.

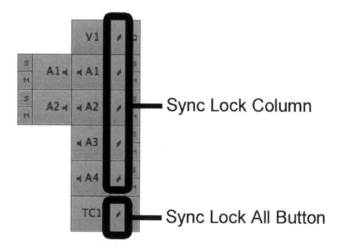

Sync Lock Column

Sync Lock All Button

> ▶ **Sync Locks** work when they are enabled for two or more tracks. In other words, enabling the **Sync Lock** on just one track does nothing.

> ▶ **Sync Locks** can be enabled for any combination of tracks that you need. However, in general, you'll find that you'll have them enabled for all the tracks.

> ▶ You can enable or disable the **Sync Locks** for all the tracks by clicking in the **Sync Lock Column** next to the **Timecode** Track Selector (see the previous screenshot). Avid calls this the **Sync Lock All Button**. You may have to double-click it to get this to work.

- ► **Sync Locks** will respond when you **Splice**, **Extract**, and **Ripple Trim**.

- ► **Sync Locks** will respond to the yellow **Extract/Splice-In Segment Mode** tool only if the **Segment Drag Sync Locks** setting is enabled. The path to enable this setting is **Project** Window | **Settings** tab | **Timeline** settings | **Edit** tab and enable the setting that says **Segment Drag Sync Locks**. This setting and its behavior were discussed in more detail earlier inthis chapter, in the *Segment Mode: Methods for staying in sync* recipe.

- ► **Sync Locks** maintain sync by ensuring that the same duration-changing operation is performed on all the tracks.

- ► When performing a **Trim**, **Sync Locks** are programmed only to be able to adjust **Filler**. In other words, when trimming, **Sync Locks** will not affect segments of video or audio.

Getting ready

Now that you've read the previous introduction and you're a bit more familiar with **Sync Locks**, let's examine what they do and how we can open up the sequence when using **Splice** with **Sync Locks** enabled.

In this situation let's imagine the following:

- ► You're editing a scene of a comedy television program

- ► Loaded in the **Source** Window is a clip that contains one video track and two audio tracks

- ► Loaded in the **Timeline** Window is a sequence that contains one video track and four audio tracks (see the screenshot below)

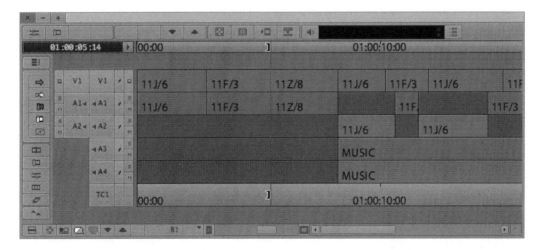

The goals in this example are the following:

▸ You want to add only the video from the source **Clip** into the sequence, between the shots **11F/3** and **11Z/8** (see the previous screenshot). The video you want to add is a close-up shot of one actor's shocked reaction to another actor's line of dialog. You don't want the source **Audio** because you can hear the director talking.

▸ You want to push the other segments (shots) in the sequence down, so that you can later add in the sound of the audience laughing underneath the video of the shocked reaction shot that you will be splicing in.

How to do it...

1. Enable **Sync Locks** for all the tracks by clicking the **Sync Lock All Button** (found in the **Sync Lock Column** next to the **Timecode** Track Selector button) if they are not all already enabled.

2. On the **Source** Track Selectors enable only the video.

3. On the **Record** Track Selectors enable only the video. Note that if the other tracks were enabled, it's okay as the final result would be the same. I'm just doing this to better demonstrate what **Sync Locks** will do.

4. In the **Source** Window, **Mark In** and **Mark Out** around the video that you want to edit into the sequence.

5. In the sequence, place a **Mark In** at the location where you want to Splice in the video.

6. Press the **Splice** button to make the edit. The result is pictured in the following screenshot:

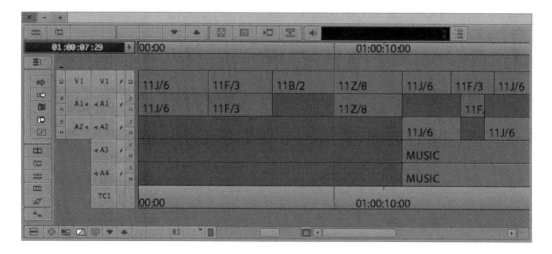

How it works...

Without **Sync Locks** enabled this edit would place you out of sync, because you would be adding a duration of video without adding an equal amount of material to the other tracks. However, *with* **Sync Locks** *enabled*, Media Composer ensures that you are adding an equal duration of material to the other Sync-Locked tracks. It accomplishes this by adding an equal duration of **Filler**. The *Introduction* section of this chapter includes an overview of the core concepts of **Sync**, if you'd like some additional discussion on this topic.

Extracting with Sync Locks enabled

If you haven't already read the introduction to the previous *Opening up the sequence using Splice with Sync Locks enabled* recipe, then you may find it helpful as it includes an overview of Sync Locks as well.

This recipe presents a situation where **Sync Locks** will save us some steps because we won't have to reconfigure the Track Selectors from whatever configuration they happen to be set at a particular moment.

Getting ready

The situation in this example is the following:

- ▶ Loaded in the **Timeline** Window is a sequence that contains one video track and four audio tracks.

- ▶ The last edit was Lifting out some music on track **A4**, so that happens to be the only track that's enabled at the moment. Refer to the following screenshot:

How to do it...

The goal in this example is to Extract a pause in the dialog of shot **11F/3** (see the previous screenshot). Note that this will, of course, create a jump cut in the video and that issue will be corrected by covering it with a reaction shot at a later time.

1. Enable **Sync Locks** for all the tracks by clicking the **Sync Lock All Button** (found in the **Sync Lock Column** next to the **Timecode** Track Selector) if they are not all already enabled.

2. **Mark In** and **Mark Out** in the sequence around the audio that you want to extract. In this example, it would be the pause in the dialog in shot **11F/3** (see the previous screenshot).

3. Press **Extract** to make the edit. The result is pictured in the following screenshot:

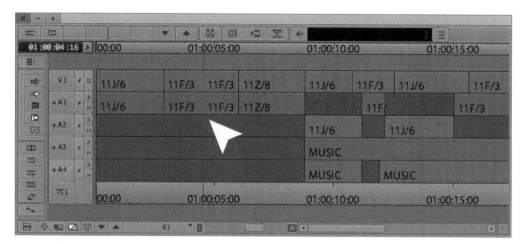

How it works...

Without **Sync Locks** enabled, this edit would place you out of sync because you would be removing a duration of audio *without* removing an equal duration from the other tracks. However, *with* **Sync Locks** *enabled*, Media Composer ensures that you are removing an equal duration of material from the other tracks. It accomplishes this by extracting material from all the sync locked tracks even though the Track Selectors on those other tracks are not enabled. Additional details about sync can be found in the *Introduction* section of this chapter, which includes an overview of the core concepts of **Sync**.

Extending using Ripple Trim with Sync Locks enabled

You may find it helpful to review the introduction to the earlier *Opening up the sequence using Splice with Sync Locks enabled* recipe as it includes an overview of **Sync Locks**.

In this recipe, let's imagine that, as assumed earlier in the chapter, you're editing a scene of a comedy television program.

Getting ready

The goals in this example are that:

▶ You want to extend only the video of segment **64B/18** (pictured in the next screenshot). It's a close-up shot of one actor's shocked reaction to another actor's line of dialog.

▶ You want to push the other segments (shots) in the sequence down, so that you can later add in the sound of the audience laughing underneath the video of the shocked reaction shot.

How to do it...

1. Enable **Sync Locks** for all the tracks (by clicking on the **Sync Lock All Button** found in the **Sync Lock Column** next to the **Timecode** Track Selector) if they all are not already enabled.
2. Enter **Trim Mode** at the transition for the segment (shot) that you want to extend. In this example it's the transition between segments **64B/18** and **64A/11** (see the following screenshot).
3. Select the segment that you want to extend. In this example I've selected the **A-Side** (segment **64B/18**), as pictured in the following screenshot:

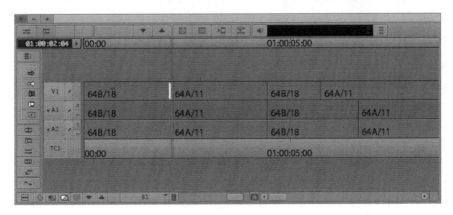

4. Using your preferred method of trimming, extend the segment. In this example, we would trim to the right in order to extend the video. The result is pictured in the following screenshot:

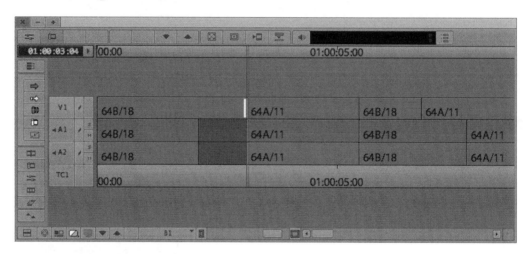

How it works...

Without **Sync Locks** enabled, this edit would place you out of sync because you would be adding a duration of video *without* adding an equal amount of material to the other tracks. However, *with* **Sync Locks** *enabled*, Media Composer ensures that you are adding an equal duration of material to the other tracks. It accomplishes this by adding an equal duration of **Filler**. Details about this can be found in the *Introduction* section of this chapter, which includes a discussion of the core concepts of **Sync**.

Shortening using Ripple Trim with Sync Locks enabled

The introduction to the earlier *Opening up the sequence using Splice with Sync Locks enabled* recipe includes an overview of **Sync Locks**. You may find it helpful to review it before moving on to this recipe.

Getting ready

In this recipe, let's imagine that, as assumed earlier in the chapter, you're editing a scene of a comedy television program.

The goals in this example are as follows (see the next screenshot):

▶ Previously you had extended only the video for segment **64B/18** (a close-up shot of one actor's shocked reaction to another actor's line of dialog, which added **Filler** on tracks **A1** and **A2**). Later you plan to add some audience laughter to cover the silent region of **Filler**.

▶ You've watched the timing of shots **64B/18** and **64A/11** and you feel that **64B/18** is lasting a bit too long before cutting to **64A/11**. So you want to shorten the video.

How to do it...

1. Enable **Sync Locks** for all the tracks by clicking the **Sync Lock All Button** (found in the **Sync Lock Column** next to the **Timecode** Track Selector) if they all are not already enabled.

2. Enter **Trim Mode** at the transition for the segment (shot) that you want to shorten.

3. Select the segment that you want to shorten. In this example I've selected the **A-Side**, which is labeled as shot **64B/18** (see the next screenshot):

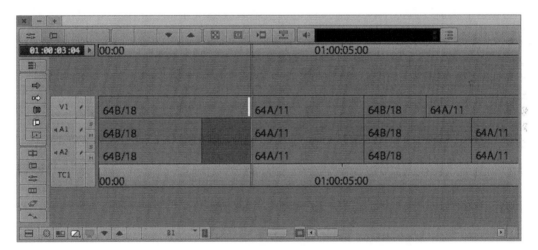

4. Using your preferred method of trimming, shorten the segment. In this example, we would trim to the left in order to shorten the video. The result is pictured in the following screenshot:

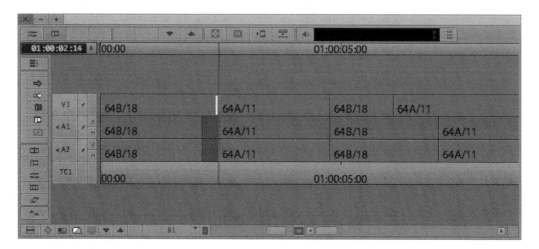

How it works...

Without **Sync Locks** enabled, this edit would place you out of sync because you would be removing a duration of video without also removing an equal duration from the other tracks. However, *with* **Sync Locks** *enabled*, Media Composer makes sure that you're removing an equal duration of material from the other tracks. It accomplishes this by removing an equal duration of **Filler** from all the sync-locked tracks even though the Track Selectors on those tracks are not enabled.

As a reminder, **Sync Locks** are programmed *only* to be able to adjust **Filler**. In other words, when trimming, **Sync Locks** will *not* affect segments of video or audio. If/When you have no **Filler** on a track while shortening, Media Composer will stop you from trimming any further. At such a time you'll have to enable and manually configure the **Trim Rollers** on the necessary tracks.

- The *Enabling and configuring the trimming tools* recipe in *Appendix B, Details on Trimming, Slipping, Sliding, and Segment Mode*, specifically the portion that discusses using **Shift+Click** to add or remove **Trim Rollers**

- The *Asymmetric Trimming type 1: A-Side/B-Side* recipe

- The *Introduction* of this chapter, which includes an overview of the core concepts of **Sync**

Getting back in sync

You may make an edit that causes your tracks to go out of sync with one another, and you may not notice it until much later, after making many other edits.

This recipe addresses the situation when the **Sync Break Indicators** begin at a point in the sequence and then continue on down to the end. For emphasis, unlike a sync break caused by a Slip or Slide, where the **Sync Break Indictors** are isolated to one segment or one area, in this instance, the **Sync Break Indicators** ripple down to the very end of the sequence.

The solution to a sync break problem caused by adding or removing material to one or more tracks without also adding or removing the same duration of material to *all* the other tracks is corrected by doing the opposite to those same tracks. In other words, if you added material to a track and that caused the tracks to become out of sync, then you must remove material from that track to regain sync (and vice versa).

While any of the duration-changing operations (**Ripple Trim**, **Extract**, or **Splice-In**) will work to solve a sync break issue like this, my preferred method is to use **Ripple Trim**. So, that is what I'll be using in the steps of the recipe in a moment. Also see the *There's more...* section for additional discussion on this topic.

Getting ready

You may find it helpful to review the previous *Sync Break Indicators: Understanding them and making your own* recipe.

How to do it...

1. Become the Sherlock Holmes of the editing room. Examine the sequence from left to right (from start to end). Take note of where the **Sync Break Indicators** first appear. Also make note if the sync break value is consistent or changes. If the sync break value changes, then possibly multiple edits were made that broke the sync between the video and the audio. In this example, I see two different sync break values. On the video track, the first is **-14**, and further down the sequence, I see a value of **20**.

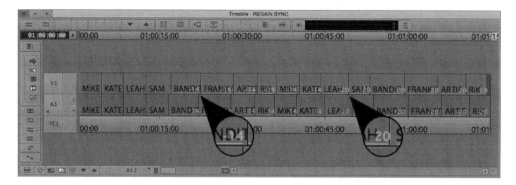

2. If enabled, turn off **Sync Locks** for the tracks that are out of sync.

3. Begin repairing the sync break problem at the first (leftmost/closest to the beginning) edit in the sequence. This is because just as the offending edit ripples down, so will the corrective edit.

4. In the previous example screenshot, the first sync break is **14** frames out of sync. To correct this, you can choose to trim either the video or the audio segment, it doesn't matter which. For this example, I choose to trim the video.

5. Enter **Trim Mode** at the transition prior to where the sync break first appears.

6. Select either the **A-Side** or **B-Side** segment. It doesn't matter which you select, since after repairing the sync problem, you'll refine the transition aesthetically. For this example I've chosen the **A-Side**, as pictured in the following screenshot:

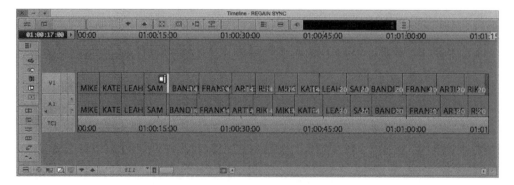

7. The **Sync Break Indicator** on the video track says **-14**. This is actually telling me how to fix the sync break by moving the video track **14** frames to the left. So I trim the segment labeled as **SAM** to be shorter by 14 frames. The result is pictured in the following screenshot:

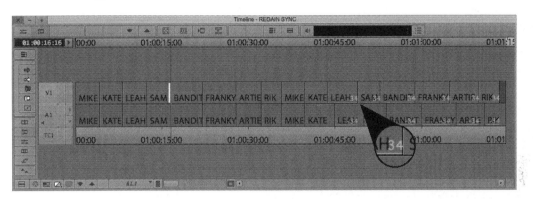

8. Having corrected this, I see that it has repaired sync for several other segments downstream. However, I now see that there is another sync break that ripples down to the end of the sequence. Without realizing it, I must have made two separate edits that broke sync. So now I set about repairing that problem.

9. The **Sync Break Indicators** tell me that I'm 34 frames out of sync. As earlier, I decide to use **Ripple Trim** on the video track to tackle the problem. While I could have selected either the **KATE** or **LEAH** shot to be trimmed, I've selected the **KATE** shot:

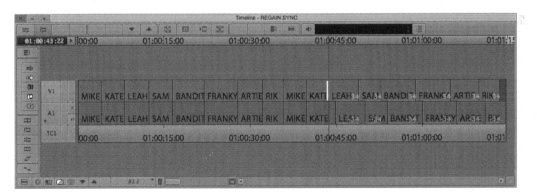

10. To correct this, I trim 34 frames to the right. The result is pictured in the following screenshot:

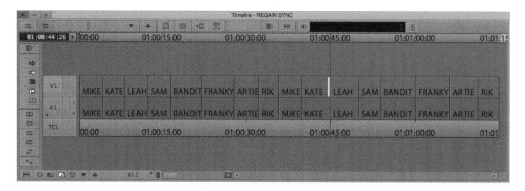

11. If there were more sync break problems, I would work my way down the sequence (moving from left to right), repeating the process detailed above.

12. Once you've regained sync in your sequence, return to the edit points that you adjusted in order to regain sync. Review them to make sure that they work aesthetically. If they don't, then you'll make any necessary corrections.

There's more

The following are some additional methods to consider if/when you find that you're out of sync:

Method one: Undo (cmd/Ctrl + Z)

Especially for new users, I encourage after making an edit that you immediately review it. This way if there is a problem, not only will you catch it (and undo it), but also you'll be able to easily make a connection between the cause and the result, and learn from it.

Method two: Slip/Slide

If you notice that the **Sync Break Indicators** are isolated to one segment or one area and do *not* ripple down to the end of the sequence, then this indicates that either a **Slip** or **Slide** has occurred to place them out of sync. Whatever you did that got you out of sync, you'll use the same operation (**Slip** or **Slide**) to correct the sync problem. Here's an example for correcting a segment that has been slipped out of sync:

- ▶ I'm editing a dialog scene of a movie in which I have only one video track and one audio track.

- ▶ Imagine that **Sync Break Indicators** for just one segment on the video track are displayed as **-30**, while the ones on the audio track are displayed as **30**. The **Sync Break Indicators** are actually telling you how to fix the sync break. Negative values in Media Composer indicate movement to the left and positive numbers indicate movement to the right. So to correct this:

   Enter **Trim Mode** and configure Slipping for either the video segment or the audio segment, but *not* both. In this example, I make the choice to slip just the *video* segment. In this example, the video segment displays **-30**. This indicates that I need to slip 30 frames to the *left* in order to regain sync with the audio segment.

6
Managing Your Media Files

In this chapter, we will cover:

- ► Moving media files
- ► Copying a borrowed clip's media
- ► Sharing clips/backing-up clips
- ► Consolidating Subclips
- ► Consolidating Sequences
- ► Transcoding Sequences for archiving or before up-res
- ► Transcoding Sequences of mixed SD and HD video
- ► Changing the Sample Rate of clips in bin before editing them into your Sequence
- ► Changing the mismatched audio that has been edited into your Sequence
- ► Prevent editing with audio that does not match the Project's Sample Rate
- ► Setting the Media Tool display
- ► Borrowing a clip from another Project
- ► How to determine where media files are stored and how to move them
- ► Isolating video of a specifc resolution
- ► Deleting specific media files from clips (for example, just the A3 and A4 files)
- ► Deleting unused media files: Just Master Clips, just Precomputes, or both
- ► Locking Clips and Sequences
- ► Locking Sequences to make them less easily editable

Introduction

The goal of this chapter is to take some of the mystery out of dealing with media files and take you through some common situations. Before we dive in, here are some important and/or helpful things to be aware of:

1. The topics covered, and recipes of steps provided in this chapter, are geared towards those using local media drives for storage, for example, the internal hard drive, fixed hard drive(s), and/or a relatively small, local RAID.

2. Those working at a facility with Avid Unity, Avid ISIS, Avid Interplay, or another shared storage solution must consult with their facility's technical administrators or lead assistant editors before carrying out any media management functions in a shared storage environment. Failing to do so can cause inadvertent loss of media and/or employment.

3. Before Consolidating or Transcoding clips or sequences, it is highly recommended that you perform a small-scale test of the process to familiarize yourself with additional options and results. Ideally, you would be able to perform your small-scale test prior to receiving the mission-critical files and prior to the pressure and intensity of working under a deadline.

4. I suggest you take a moment to read *Appendix B, Details on Trimming, Slipping, Sliding, and Segment Mode* since it covers helpful information about how clips and media files work together. Understanding this relationship is crucial to understanding what happens during processes, such as Consolidating, Transcoding, Decomposing, and Sample Rate conversion.

5. It's important to distinguish this topic from copying/duplicating clips using the **Duplicate** command method (from the **Edit** menu) or using the *option/Alt* + drag to a different bin method (which Avid calls "Cloning."). In those instances, you are only making a duplicate of the clip information that links to (refers to) the media, but not the media itself. The topic of copying/duplicating versus Cloning clips is discussed in the *Mixing frame rates* recipe in *Chapter 1, Getting Assets into Your Media Composer Project (see the There's more... section).*

6. Every time you create media files by Capturing, Importing, Rendering, Consolidating, or Transcoding, they become associated with the Project that was open when they were created. In other words, they get a stamp on them that says **I belong to 'Project X'**. This knowledge will become helpful when we discuss copying media files, as well as using the **Media Tool**, in this chapter.

7. To perform the tasks of moving, copying, and Consolidating media files, we use a function called **Consolidate/Transcode** (found in the **Clip** menu). First, let's demystify those terms.

   Consolidate, in the context of Avid Media Composer, is essentially just a fancy word for copy. You can instruct Media Composer to do some other things in addition to copying media files, but at its core, that's all the **Consolidate** function does: make copies. Note that you may only Consolidate files supported by Media Composer's Codec library. RED files are an example of files that can not be Consolidated directly without first Transcoding them.

   Transcode is making a copy too, but with an additional process applied. When you Transcode a clip's video media file, during the copy process, you are also changing its compression/codec. I'll discuss this in more detail in the Transcode section.

Moving media files

Please review items 1, 2, and 3 in the *Introduction* section of this chapter.

There are a few common reasons you may find yourself in need of moving media files:

▶ You've captured, imported, Consolidated, or rendered media files onto the wrong hard drive or partition (for example, a drive that belongs to another editor or project)

▶ A drive is failing and you need to get the media onto a healthy drive

▶ You may want to take a copy of all your media, or just a specific portion of it, outside of your editing room to be edited with a laptop system on set, in a client's office, or on an airplane

▶ A drive or partition is getting very full and you want to create space to give the Media Database files room to increase in file size

It is not possible to simply pick up a bundle of ones and zeros and move them from one location to another in the same way that you'd move a chair from one room to another. So, in this recipe are the steps to accomplish moving media files and then following that you'll find an explanation of what's actually happening in the *How it works* section.

Getting ready

You may want to do one or more of the following:

▶ Check available hard drive/partition space. One way to do this is to use the **Hardware Tool** found here: **Tools menu | Hardware Tool**.

▶ Determine where media resides. Select a bin (or the **Media Tool** window, discussed later in this chapter) by going to the **Bin** menu, choose **Columns**, select the **Drive** column, and click **OK**. Then:

- ❏ Within a bin (in other words: not using the **Media Tool**), to display render files (also know as Precompute files) that *are linked* to (being used by) a sequence, select a bin containing a sequence(s), then go to the **Bin** menu, **Set Bin Display**, and enable **Rendered Effects**. For emphasis, only media files that are *linked to, and being used by,* the sequence(s) in the bin will be displayed. Later in this chapter is a discussion of determining (and deleting) *unused* media using the **Media Tool**. It should also be noted that media can be moved using the **Media Tool** as well. Again, the **Media Tool** is discussed later in this chapter.

- ❏ Within a bin (in other words, not using the **Media Tool**), to display media files (captured, consolidated, imported, or AMA linked) that *are linked* to (being used by) a sequence, select an open bin containing a sequence(s), then go to the **Bin** menu, **Set Bin Display**, and enable **Show Reference Clips**. For emphasis, only clips and media files that are *linked to, and being used by,* the sequence(s) in the bin will be displayed. Later in this chapter is a discussion of determining (and deleting) *unused* media using the **Media Tool**. It should also be noted that media can be moved using the **Media Tool** as well. Again, the **Media Tool** is discussed later in this chapter.

How to do it...

Follow these steps to move media files:

1. In a bin, select the clips whose media files you want to move. If you've chosen to display render files, then you could select them if you wanted/needed to. Note that an alternative to selecting clips and/or render files in a bin is to instead use the **Media** Tool. The **Media** Tool is discussed later in this chapter.

2. With the clips and/or render files selected, go to **Clip** menu | **Consolidate/ Transcode**. The **Consolidate/Transcode** dialog window will open.

3. Select the following:

   ❑ In the upper left-hand side corner, select **Consolidate**.

   ❑ Under the heading **Target Drives**, enable the checkbox for **Video, Audio, and Data on same drive** (it will most likely be enabled by default).

   ❑ In the **Video/Data** list box, select the destination drive/partition you want to move the media file(s) onto.

   ❑ Enable the checkbox for **Delete original media files when done**. This is the key to moving the media files, rather than copying them. This will be discussed in the *How it works* section later.

4. In the bottom right corner of the dialog window, click the **Consolidate** button to begin the process. Depending on the number of files, and the size of those files, this process may take some time.

5. If for any reason you need to stop the process (for example, it's taking a long time and you realize you better get back to editing and do the media moving later), you can do this at any time by pressing *cmd/Ctrl* + the period(.) key. This will stop the process for the media file currently being copied. Any previously copied media will remain intact on the destination drive you selected. When you return to this task later, follow the steps above with the addition of enabling one more checkbox: **Skip media files already on target drive**. This will prevent copying files that are already copied and making the process take longer than necessary.

How it works...

Since we can't move digital files in the same way that we move an object from one location to another, we instead copy the files, delete the originals, and then Relink the **Master Clips** to the copied media. Let's follow one **Master Clip** (named **PATTY**) and its media files on their journey being moved from drive **A** to drive **B**. The next picture is a simplified illustration of the following:

▶ The internal hard drive, which holds the Avid Projects folder (not pictured), which holds *your* Avid Project, which holds the bin file, which holds the **Master Clip** named **PATTY**

▶ The **PATTY** Master Clip is linked to three media files on drive **A**

▶ Those three media files are inside a folder named `Avid MediaFiles`

▸ There are three media files, because one of them is the video, one of them is track 1 audio, and the other is track 2 audio:

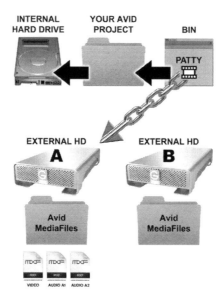

The next image shows the three media files being copied from drive **A** onto drive **B**:

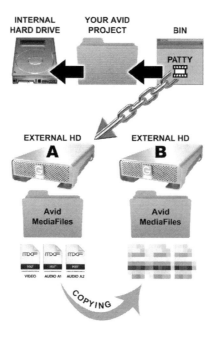

The final image (below) shows that once the media files have been copied onto drive **B**, the original media files are deleted from drive **A**. Additionally, we see that the **PATTY** Master Clip has been relinked to the media on drive **B**. The final result is that the same Master Clip now links to media on drive B. The magic trick is now complete; the media files have been moved.

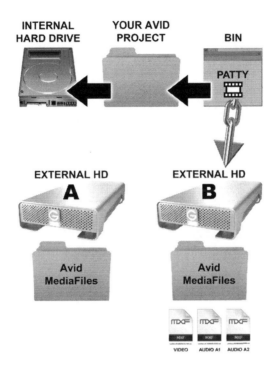

Copying a borrowed clip's media

Please review items 1, 2, 3, 4, and 5 in the *Introduction* section of this chapter.

There are a couple of common reasons you may find yourself in need of copying media files, which will be the focus in this recipe section and the recipe that follows it.

The focus of this first recipe is that you've borrowed a clip from another project and you want to permanently have a copy that is associated with your currently active project.

Getting ready

It's important to emphasize that when you borrow a *Clip*, what you are doing is creating a copy of just the *Clip* that links (refers) to the actual picture and audio media files. You are *not* creating new media. Further, the media you are linking to is still associated with the project in which it was originally created.

While you can definitely edit with a clip borrowed from another project, there are a couple of potential drawbacks if *you* do not have control over the other project's *media*:

> ▶ If you borrowed a clip from your workmate's project and she doesn't know you're using it, she may delete the media. If she deleted the media files, then you'd still have the clip but, unfortunately, it would not be linked to any media. In other words, the media would be Offline.

> ▶ If you had to move your workstation (computer and external hard drives) to another location and if you didn't have your own copy of the media on your own drive, then when you relocated (*without* your workmate's media drive) the clip would be Offline.

So, those are two examples why you may want/need to make a copy of the *media* so that it is associated with *your* project, and *you* have control over it. However, before you can perform the copying, you have to perform the *borrowing*. There are two methods to borrow clips presented, which are as follows:

Let's take a look at the first method of borrowing a clip through opening a bin from another project:

1. Create a new bin or open an existing bin. This will be the bin you'll eventually copy your borrowed clip(s) into.

2. Select the **Project** Window to make it active (but do not select any bins).

3. Go to the **File** menu and choose **Open Bin**.

4. Navigate to the `Project` folder that contains the bin (which holds the clip) you want to open/borrow.

5. Select the bin you want to open/borrow.

6. Click the **Open** button.

7. The bin will open. Furthermore, the bin will reside inside a folder that Media Composer creates in your **Project** Window called **Other Bins**. The italics remind you that these bin files are not part of your project (meaning inside your project's folder). To discontinue borrowing a bin(s), select them and press the *Delete* key. In this instance, you are not actually deleting the bin file. You're simply telling Media Composer that you no longer want to borrow it. For emphasis, the original file is okay and continues to reside in the other project's folder.

8. Select the clip(s) you want to borrow. Then go to the **Edit** menu | **Duplicate**. This creates a duplicate of the clip(s). Note that the difference between a Duplicated clip and a Cloned clip is discussed in the *Mixing frame rates* recipe in *Chapter 1, Getting Assets into Your Media Composer Project (see the There's more... section)*.

9. Move the duplicates into the bin discussed in step 1.

10. Close the bin which you borrowed. Optional: in the **Project** Window, check the **Other Bins** folder, select the bin, and press the *Delete* key to discontinue borrowing it.

Now let's look at the second method of borrowing a clip from another project by using the **Media Tool**:

1. Create a new bin or open an existing bin. This will be the bin you'll eventually copy your borrowed clip(s) into.

2. Open the **Media Tool** by going to the Tools menu | **Media Tool**.

3. In the **Media Tool** dialog window, select the following:

   ❑ In the **Media Drives** display region, select the drive where the media resides. If you're not sure, then you can select them all by clicking the **All Drives** button.

   ❑ In the **Projects** display region, select the name of the project from which you want to borrow a clip(s).

   ❑ Of the three checkboxes, *select only* the one labeled **Master Clips** and click on **OK**. The **Media** Tool window will open. It looks and behaves just like a bin.

4. Drag-and-drop the clip(s) from the **Media** Tool into the bin discussed in step 1. There is no need to press any keys on the keyboard when you do this because Media Composer will automatically create a Clone of the Master Clip. Pretty cool, huh?

5. Close the **Media** Tool window.

How to do it...

1. Borrow a clip(s) by following either one of the methods found previously in the *Getting ready* section.

2. In the bin that you opened or created, and just Duplicated or Cloned a clip(s) into:

   ❑ Set the bin to **Text** display.

   ❑ Then, display the columns for Drive and Project. Do this by selecting the bin, then going to the **Bin** Menu and select **Choose Columns**, then in the **Column Selection** Dialog Window select Drive and Project, and then click **OK**.

   ❑ Rearrange the columns to make sure you can see the Drive and Project columns.

3. Notice that the **Project** column displays the name of the project from which you've borrowed the clip(s). This is telling you which project the media is associated with. In other words, which project the media belongs to.

4. Select the clip(s) you borrowed.

5. Go to **Clip** menu | **Consolidate/Transcode**.

6. In the **Consolidate/Transcode** dialog window, select the following:

   ❏ In the upper left corner, select **Consolidate**.

   ❏ Under the heading **Target Drives**, enable the checkbox for **Video, audio and data on same drive** (it will probably be enabled by default).

   ❏ In the **Video/Data** list box, select the destination drive/partition you want to place the new media file(s) onto.

   ❏ *Disable* (uncheck) the checkbox for **Delete original media files when done**. This is the key to *copying* the media files. For emphasis, *make sure to deselect* the checkbox for **Delete original media files when done**.

   ❏ **Skip media files already on the target drive** checkbox – if the original media you are copying resides on the same drive you want to place the copy, then you must deselect this checkbox in order for the copy to occur.

7. In the bottom right corner of the dialog window, click the **Consolidate** button to go to the next phase of the process.

8. The **Copying Media Files** dialog window will open.

9. Select the first option that reads, **Keep Master Clips linked to media on the original drive**. This makes sure that the original clip(s) stay linked to their original media and that you'll get a new **Master Clip** linked to its own, separate media.

10. Click the **OK** button.

11. Depending on the number of files, and the size of those files, this process may take some time.

12. If for any reason you need to stop the process (for example, it's taking a long time and you realize you better get back to editing and do the media copying later), you can do this at any time by pressing *cmd/Ctrl* + the period(.) key. This will stop the process for the media file currently being copied. Any previously copied media will remain intact on the target drive you selected. Note that if you are copying to a *different drive* than the original media resides, then when you return to this task later, follow the previous steps as well as enable one additional checkbox: **Skip media files already on target drive**. This will prevent copying files that are already copied and making the process take longer than necessary.

13. When the copy process is completed, every clip and the media that goes with it will have been duplicated. All the new clips will be at the *top* of the bin.

14. Take note of the clip name(s). You'll see that Media Composer has added **.new** to the end (so, they are frequently referred to as **Dot New Clips**).

15. Take note of the **Project** column. You'll see that the **.new** clip(s) are associated with *your* project.

16. Delete *the clips that you borrowed* so that you do not mistakenly edit with them. For emphasis, delete *only the clip(s)* but *not* the actual media files. To do this, continue with the following steps.

17. Select the original clips that you Duplicated or Cloned *from the other project* (these will *not* have the **.new** at the end of their names).

18. Press the *Delete* key.

19. The *Delete* dialog window will open.

20. Select *only* the checkbox that says **Delete Master Clips**. For emphasis, do *not* select any checkboxes that relate to media files.

21. Click the **OK** button.

22. Rest easy; all that is deleted in this instance is the **Master Clip** (the information that links/refers to the media). The media is untouched and nothing has been altered in the other project from which you originally borrowed the clip(s).

How it works...

For emphasis, this procedure works because you *disabled* the checkbox for **Delete original media files when done**. This is the key to *copying* the media files, rather than relocating them to another drive.

Sharing clips/backing-up clips

Please review items 1, 2, 3, 4, and 5 in the *Introduction* section of this chapter.

For this second recipe in this topic of actually copying media files (the previous one is the first recipe), the situation is as follows: you are *not* in a shared media situation (for example, Avid Unity, ISIS, or Interplay) and your workmate brings in a fixed hard drive and asks you to give them a copy of one or two *entire shots* (we'll cover making copies of/Consolidating Subclips later in this chapter). Or, similarly, you want to make a back-up copy of your media files onto another drive.

How to do it...

1. In a bin, select the clip(s) that you want to share or back up.

2. In the previous *Copying a borrowed clip's media* recipe, follow only steps 5 through 14.

3. If:

   ❑ If you are backing up the media files onto another drive, then you are done. The media files could be Relinked to in the future, and/or **Master Clips** could be created by using the second method (using the **Media Tool**) discussed in the previous *Copying a borrowed clip's media* recipe *Getting Ready* section. If you'd like to make a back-up bin as well, then follow steps 4 through 10.

   ❑ If you are giving copies to a workmate, follow the next additional steps, which will provide them with a bin. Sure, they could make Clones of the clips themselves using the **Media Tool** as discussed in the previous recipe's (*Copying a borrowed clip's media* recipe) *Getting Ready* section, but giving them a bin is a nice gesture.

4. Select the bin that contains the .new clips you created.

5. Go to the **File** menu | **Save Bin Copy As...**.

6. The **Save As** dialog window will open.

7. Name the bin.

8. Navigate to the drive you want to place the bin file copy (most likely the drive onto which you just placed the media).

9. Click the **Save** button.

10. On their drive they now have the media as well as a copy of the bin that they can then associate with their project.

How it works...

Let's follow one **Master Clip** (named **PATTY**) and its media files that are on drive **A** along their journey being copied onto drive **B**. The next picture is a simplified illustration of he following:

▸ The internal hard drive, which holds the Avid Projects folder (not pictured), which holds your Avid Project, which holds the bin file, which holds the **Master Clip** named **PATTY**

▸ The **Master Clip** named **PATTY** is linked to three media files on drive **A**

▸ Those three media files are inside a folder named `Avid MediaFiles`

▸ There are three media files, because one of them is the video, one of them is track 1 audio, and the other is track 2 audio

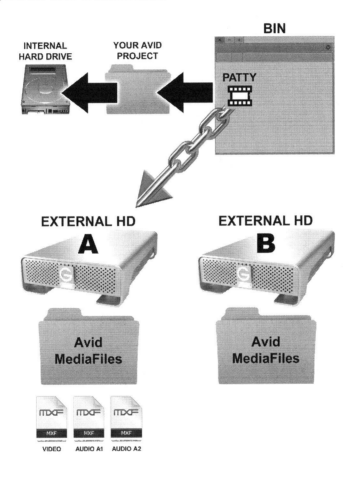

The image below shows the three media files being copied from drive **A** onto drive **B**:

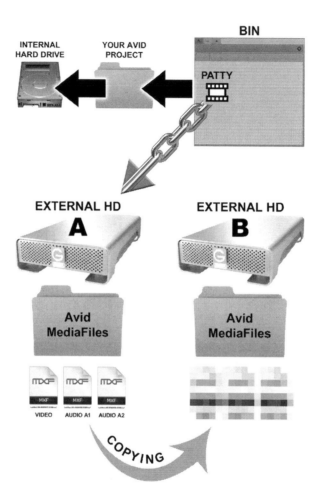

The final image (below) shows that once the media files are copied to drive **B**, that Media Composer creates a brand new **Master Clip** named PATTY.new. We can also see that the PATTY.new clip is linked to the media files on drive **B**.

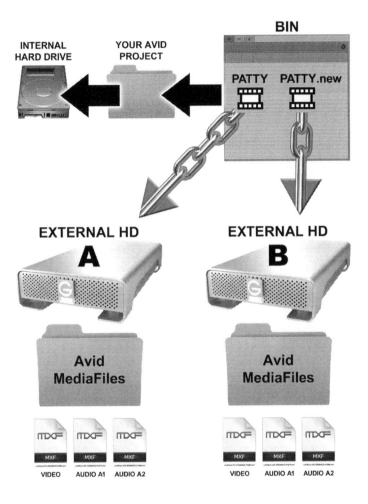

Consolidating Subclips

Please review items 1, 2, and 3 in the *Introduction* section of this chapter.

There are two common reasons why you may want to Consolidate Subclips:

▶ Situation 1: Reduce media (copying only portions you want and then deleting original media) – an example of this situation would be: you have ingested a very long duration of video and audio to create one **Master Clip** (for example, you captured a complete movie from a tape). Let's pretend that this single **Master Clip** is 90 minutes long. During the review process, you went through and created subclips of the portions you wanted to use. You've added up the duration of all the Subclips and they total just 30 minutes. This means that you have 60 minutes of media that you do not want to use and it is taking up valuable hard drive space. By Consolidating (copying) just the media that is being referenced by the Subclips (which makes brand new **Master Clips** for just those portions) and then *deleting the original* 90-minute long **Master Clip** *media*, you will be able to have the portions you want to use as well as free up the drive space.

▶ Situation 2: Share media (copying only portions you want and *not* deleting original media) – as an example, similar to the previous situation, you have a single 90-minute long **Master Clip** of a movie from which you are editing a trailer. Your workmate has been tasked with creating a short interview segment with the star of the film. He has come to you because he needs a bit of footage from the film to help make his project more interesting. He doesn't need or want the entire film, he only needs a few key shots (plus giving him a copy of the entire film would take a lot more time and drive space). He has brought his hard drive with him and connected it to your computer. In this situation you would make Subclips of the portions he wants, then you'd Consolidate (copy) them in order to make brand new **Master Clips** and media for him. Further, in this situation, you would *not* want to delete the original 90-minute long **Master Clip** media because you're using it.

Getting ready

▶ Make your Subclips

▶ Decide whether you want/need to delete the original media after the copies have been created

How to do it...

1. Select the Subclips.
2. Go to the **Clip** menu | **Consolidate/Transcode**.

3. The **Consolidate/Transcode** dialog window will open.

4. In the **Consolidate/Transcode** dialog window, select the following:

    i. In the upper left-hand side corner, select **Consolidate**.

    ii. Under the heading **Target Drives**, enable the checkbox for **Video, audio and data on same drive** (it will most likely be enabled by default).

    iii. In the **Video/Data** list box, select the destination drive/partition you want to place the new media file(s) onto.

    iv. In the **Handle length** entry box, enter a value. This will instruct Media Composer to make the new **Master Clips** longer than the original Subclips. For example, you have a Subclip that is 10 seconds long. You enter a duration of 60 frames for the handle. This will add 60 frames to the head (beginning) of the new **Master Clip** as well as 60 frames to the tail of the new **Master Clip**. So, in a 30-fps project, the total duration of the new **Master Clip** will be 14 seconds. Adding handle ensures that you have some additional material at the head and tail, just in case you made your Subclips slightly inaccurate.

    You may enter a value of zero if you want. However, be aware that Media Composer is programmed to always make both a new **Master Clip** and a new Subclip, even if no additional handle has been added. So, if you set the handle duration to **0**, this would produce a new **Master Clip** and a new Subclip that are the exact same duration. In this situation you may want to edit only with the new **Master Clips** because using the newly created Subclips may cause some confusion. The confusion would arise because a Subclip normally refers back to a longer **Master Clip**; and Match Framing from one of these Subclips back to the **Master Clip** could be confusing since they would be the exact same length. There is an exception to this, however. If, prior to Consolidating, you have renamed the Subclips, added comments, and descriptions to each, the **Consolidate** function will keep that information (metadata) on the .new Subclips but not on the .new **Master Clips**. Therefore, you may want to continue editing with the .new Subclips.

    v. Now comes the *all-important checkbox*, the one that says **Delete original media files when done**. *Stop*, and determine your needs.

    vi. If you are in situation 1 (reducing media) as described previously in the introduction to this section, then you will select this checkbox. For emphasis, this will delete the original media files once the copies (the new **Master Clips**) have been created. You will end up with media only for the portion that the Subclips referenced (plus any handle you added).

    vii. If you are in situation 2 (sharing media) as described previously, then you will not select this checkbox. For emphasis, this will not delete the original media files once the copies (the new **Master Clips**) have been created. You will end up with new **Master Clips** and media in addition to the originals.

    viii. **Skip media files already on the target drive** checkbox – if the *original* media you are copying resides on the *same drive* you want to place the copy, then you must *deselect* this checkbox in order for the copy to occur.

5. In the bottom right-hand corner of the dialog window, click the **Consolidate** button to begin the process.

6. Depending on the number of files, and the size of those files, this process may take some time.

7. When the process is completed:

    ❑ All the new clips will be at the top of the bin, and will have **.new** added to the end of their name.

    ❑ For each Subclip you selected, Media Composer is programmed to give you a new **Master Clip** and a new Subclip. The duration of each new **Master Clip** is the duration of the original Subclip, plus the duration of any handles you added. The new Subclip is the same duration as the original Subclip. Presumably, this would be of use if you set very long handles.

8. If you are giving copies to a workmate, who has brought you his/her hard drive, then you may want to follow the next additional steps that will provide them with a bin. Sure, they could make Clones of the clips themselves using the **Media Tool** as discussed earlier in this chapter (Copying a borrowed clip's media, in the Getting ready section), but giving them a bin is a nice gesture.

9. Select the bin that contains the `.new` clips you created.

10. Go to the **File** menu | **Save Bin Copy As…**.

11. The **Save As** dialog window will open.

12. Name the bin.

13. Navigate to the drive you want to place the bin file copy (most likely the drive you just placed the media).

14. Click the **Save** button.

15. On their drive they now have the media as well as a copy of the bin that they can then associate with their project.

How it works...

Let's follow two Subclips, named **Fire Ball** and **Big Punch**, and the media files that reside on drive **A** on their journey being copied onto drive **B** for our workmate, as in situation 2, described previously.

The next picture is a *simplified* illustration of the following:

▶ Inside the bin file are the two Subclips named **Fire Ball** and **Big Punch** that were created from a **Master Clip** named **Entire Movie**

▶ The **Fire Ball** Subclip is 20 seconds long

▶ The **Big Punch** Subclip is 10 seconds long

▶ The **Entire Movie Master Clip** is linked to three media files on drive **A**

▶ The media files are inside a folder named `Avid MediaFiles`

▶ There are three media files because one of them is the video, one of them is track 1 audio, and the other is track 2 audio

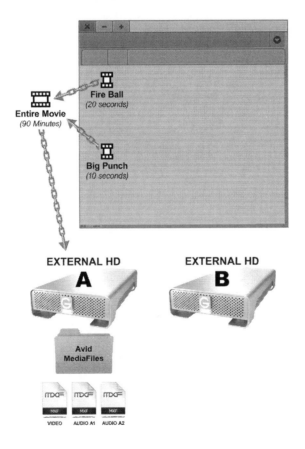

In this example, the Subclips are consolidated without deleting the original media, and the handle length is set to **60** frames. The final image (next) shows:

- ▶ Two sets of media files are copied onto drive **B**. One set is for the **Fire Ball** shot and the other is for the **Big Punch** shot.

- ▶ Media Composer creates *new* **Master Clips**, named after the *original* **Master Clip**, so they are named `Entire Movie.new.01` and `Entire Movie.new.02`.

- ▶ Media Composer creates new Subclips, named `Fire Ball.new` and `Big Punch.new`.

- ▶ The new **Master Clips** are the duration of the original Subclips, plus the 60 frames of handle at the head and tail. So, `Entire Movie.new.01` is 24 seconds long and `Entire Movie.new.02` is 14 seconds long.

- ▶ The new Subclips are the same duration as the originals. These new Subclips are linked to the new **Master Clips** and new media.

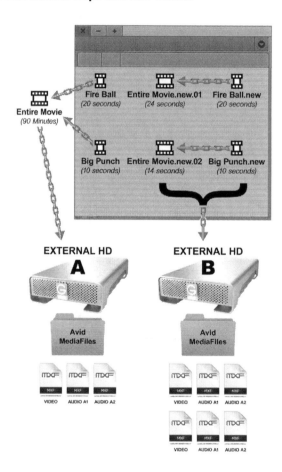

Consolidating Sequences

Please review items 1, 2, and 3 in the *Introduction* section to this chapter.

Two common reasons why you may want to Consolidate a sequence:

- ▸ Situation 1: Reduce media (copying and then deleting original media) – one example of this would be saving a copy of the low resolution version of a sequence and deleting the original media in order to clear space on the hard drives for the high resolution media you'll be creating during the finishing stages of the project (frequently referred to as the up-res). Doing this provides you with a sequence at the original, lower resolution that you can use to compare with the new, high resolution version to ensure that the correct material has been recaptured at high resolution. This is not a safeguard against anything regarding Avid Media Composer but rather against decks that don't cue up properly during the recapture/up-res (as I've had happen with DVCAM decks) or against human error (for example, a source has been incorrectly labeled). Performing the additional steps of a **Transcode** after Consolidating may free up additional hard drive space. So, you may also want to review the *Transcoding sequences for archiving or before up-res* recipe (immediately follows this topic in this chapter) to decide if also performing a **Transcode** is a useful addition/alternative to the Consolidate process.

- ▸ Situation 2: Share media – (copying and *not* deleting original media) – one example of this situation would be: you are *not* in a shared media situation (for example, using Avid Unity, ISIS or Interplay). You are editing a film and a workmate has been tasked with creating some titles and effects for one scene. She needs a copy of only that scene so she can use it as a reference while working in another edit bay. She has brought her hard drive with her and connected it to your computer. In this situation, you would make a Sub-Sequence of the scene she wants, then you'd Consolidate (copy) the Sub-Sequence's media in order to make brand new **Master Clips** of just the portions of media that are required to make her Sub-Sequence play. Further, in this situation, you would *not* want to delete the original media because you're using it. Lastly, you *must* also provide her with a bin containing the Consolidated Sub-Sequence.

What does consolidating a sequence do?

- ▸ Media Composer makes a brand new **Master Clip** for each and every segment (shot) that is in the sequence (additionally, if a shot was edited from a Subclip or a Group Clip, Media Composer will also create one of these). Each new **Master Clip** will have `.new` added to the end of the name (which is why they are frequently referred to as dot new clips).

▸ The new **Master Clips'** durations are *only* as long as what exists in the sequence, plus any handle you decide to add. Handle is additional material at the head (beginning) and tail of each **Master Clip** that doesn't appear in the Consolidated sequence. It is there only if you later need to Trim a Segment longer or need to add a transition effect, such as a dissolve. For emphasis, after Consolidating a sequence the Segments (shots) can only be trimmed as long as the handle duration.

▸ Once you make a Consolidated version of a sequence, it will link to the .new **Master Clips** that are created (which are *shorter* than the originals). This is one reason it is important to make a duplicate of your sequence before you Consolidate, Transcode, or Decompose it.

Getting ready

▸ Before you Consolidate (or Transcode, or Decompose) a sequence, it is *highly recommended* that you *make a duplicate of it* and place it in its own well-labeled bin (for example, **My Movie Before Consolidate**). This extra version will not only protect you in case you make an error, but also will help to keep your project organized for future reference.

▸ Before Consolidating, Transcoding, or Decomposing sequences: I highly encourage you to perform a small-scale test of the process with some clips that are for testing purposes only in order to familiarize yourself with the workflow, additional options, and final results.

▸ Decide whether you want/need to delete the original media after the Consolidated copies have been created.

How to do it...

1. Create a new bin by doing the following:

   ❑ If you are in a situation similar to situation 1 (discussed previously), this new bin will become the location of the duplicated sequence you create in step 2 (which will eventually be Consolidated). Duplicating the sequence and placing it in this bin protects the original and provides an extra back-up version that will not only help you in case you make an error but also will help to keep your project organized for future reference. You would label the bin along the lines of **My Movie Consolidated**.

   ❑ If you are in a situation similar to situation 2 (discussed previously), this new bin will be where you place the Sub-Sequence you create before Consolidating. When the **Consolidate** is completed, you must provide your workmate with a copy of this bin on their hard drive. You would label the bin along the lines of **Consolidated Sequence For My Workmate**.

2. Create the duplicate by doing the following:

    ❑   If you are in a situation similar to situation 1, then you will duplicate the entire sequence and place it into the bin you created in step 1. One method to duplicate a sequence is: select the sequence, then go to **Edit** menu | **Duplicate**.

    ❑   If you are in a situation similar to situation 2, then you will create a Sub-Sequence. One method to create a Sub-Sequence is:

        i.   Load the complete, original sequence into the **Timeline** Window.

        ii.   Enable the tracks you want/need to be included in the Sub-Sequence (for example, **V2**, **V1**, **A1**, and **A2**).

        iii.   Place a **Mark In** and a **Mark Out** around the portion of the original sequence that you want to isolate as a Sub-Sequence.

        iv.   Hold down the *option/Alt* key, then, click inside the **Record** Window and continue to hold down the mouse button. Then, as you continue to hold down the *option/Alt* key and the mouse button, drag-and-drop the Sub-Sequence you are creating into the bin that you made in step 1.

3. For an additional layer of protection, close all other bins except the bin you created in step 1. This will ensure you don't mistakenly Consolidate the wrong sequence when you're tired at 4 o'clock in the morning.

4. Select the sequence you placed into the new bin from step 1.

5. Go to the **Clip** menu | **Consolidate/Transcode**.

6. The **Consolidate/Transcode** dialog window will open.

7. In the **Consolidate/Transcode** dialog window, select the following:

    i.   In the upper left-hand corner, select **Consolidate**.

    ii.   Under the heading **Target Drives**, enable the checkbox for **Video, audio and data on same drive** (it will most likely be enabled by default).

    iii.   In the **Video/Data** list box, select the destination drive/partition you want to place the new media files onto.

    iv.   In the **Handle length** entry box, enter a value. This will instruct Media Composer to make the new **Master Clips** and media for each segment (shot) in the sequence longer than the current durations of the segments. For example, one of the segments (shots) is 10 seconds long. You enter a duration of 60 frames for the handle length. This will add 60 frames to the head (beginning) of the new **Master Clip** as well as 60 frames to the tail of the new **Master Clip**. So, in a 30-fps project, the total duration of the new **Master Clip** will be 14 seconds. Adding handle ensures that you have some additional material at the head and tail of each segment, just in case you need to trim a shot longer or add a transition effect (for example, a dissolve).

v.   Be *sure* to enable/check the box for **Create new Sequence** (note that some previous versions of Media Composer do not have this selection). Even though you manually created a duplicate earlier, this is yet one more layer of protection for you.

vi. The **Delete original media files when done** checkbox is very important. Stop, and determine your needs:

- If you are in a situation similar to situation 1 (reducing media, as described previoulsy), then you will select this checkbox. For emphasis, this *will delete* the original media files once the copies (the new **Master Clips** and media) have been created. You will end up with **Master Clips** and media *only* for the portion that each Segment (shot) referenced (plus any handle you added). The original media will be deleted and will be offline.

- If you are in a situation similar to situation 2 (sharing media, described previously), then you will *not* select this checkbox. For emphasis, this will not delete the original media files once the copies (the new **Master Clips** and media) have been created. You will end up with new **Master Clips** and media in addition to the originals.

vii. **Skip media files already on the target drive** checkbox – if the original media you are Consolidating (copying) resides on the same drive you want to place the copy, then you must de-select this checkbox in order for the copy to occur.

8. In the bottom right-hand corner of the dialog window, click the **Consolidate** button to begin the process.

9. Depending on the number of files, and the size of those files, this process may take some time. When the process is completed:

- All the new **Master Clips** will be at the top of the bin, and will have `.new` added to the end of their name. Because of this, these are frequently referred to as the dot new clips.

- You will have two sequences in the bin. One of them is the original that continues to link to the original **Master Clips** and media (of course if you deleted the media as in situation 1, then the media will be Offline). The new sequence was created by Media Composer because you enabled the **Create new Sequence** checkbox in step 7. The new sequence will have `.Consolidated` added to the end of the name. This sequence links to the `.new` **Master Clips** and media.

10. Follow one of these options:

- If you are clearing hard drive space of unneeded media (as in situation 1), you may want to review the later sections in this chapter on using the **Media** tool and methods of locking and deleting media.

❑ If you are in a situation similar to situation 2 (giving copy to a workmate who has brought you his/her hard drive), then you must follow the next additional steps in order to provide them with a bin containing the Consolidated sequence that links to the Consolidated .new **Master Clips** and media. To do this:

i. Select the bin that contains the .new clips and the .Consolidated sequence.

ii. Go to the **File** menu | **Save Bin Copy As...**.

iii. The **Save As** dialog window will open.

iv. Name the bin.

v. Navigate to the drive onto which you want to place the bin file copy (most likely the drive you just placed the media onto).

vi. Click the **Save** button.

vii. The final result is that on your workmate's drive is the media as well as a copy of the sequence bin that they will then need to associate with their project.

How it works...

Remember, as discussed at the beginning of this section, Media Composer makes a brand new **Master Clip** for each and every segment (shot) that is in the sequence, and that the new **Master Clips**' durations are only as long as what exists in the Sequence, plus any handle you decide to add. Further, making a backup of the original Sequence is important because once you make a Consolidated version of a Sequence, it will link to the ".new" **Master Clips** that are created (which are shorter than the originals).

Transcoding Sequences for archiving or before up-res

Please review items 1, 2, and 3 in the *Introduction* section of this chapter.

Before you Transcode (or Consolidate, or Decompose) a sequence, it is *highly recommended* that you first *duplicate it* and place the duplicate into its own well-labeled bin (for example, **My Movie Before Transcode**). This extra version is a protection in case you make an error, and it will help to keep your project organized.

Common reasons why you may want or need to Transcode a sequence:

▶ Situation 1 – archiving after finishing:

You have previously Decomposed the sequence (which made .new **Master Clips** for each segment in the sequence). You have already gone through the up-res process and recaptured the video at a high resolution (for example, 1:1). You have finished all of the final outputs. The project is officially completed, but you foresee a possible need in the future to have access to the project still in sequence form (for example, to make elements for the Internet, such as a teaser, a trailer, and so on). However, you feel that archiving the project at its present high resolution is not necessary, and you'd prefer to compress the video (to Transcode it) to a lower resolution. The resolution you select depends on your needs. It could be compressed a great deal in order to take up minimal hard drive space (for example, 15:1s or DNxHD36). While the image quality would be degraded because of the high compression, possibly you only need it in this form for reference purposes. On the other hand, you might compress it to a resolution that keeps the image quality acceptable for use as DVD extras or for the Internet while also reducing the hard drive storage required (for example, 3:1 or DNxHD145).

▶ Situation 2 – Consolidating and Transcoding to create a reference sequence:

❑ Note that Transcoding a Consolidated sequence is an additional step you may choose to perform in order to free up additional hard drive space, but it is not required.

❑ You are about to begin the finishing stage of the project where you'll be recapturing the video at a higher resolution (see situation 1 in the previous *Consolidating sequences* recipe).

❑ In addition to Consolidating the sequence, you want to further compress the video to free up additional hard drive space.

❑ Note that the **Transcoding** dialog window does not have any options to delete the original media after the Transcoded copies are created. If you want to free up drive space, then you will perform the media deletion manually.

▶ Situation 3: You have a sequence of mixed Standard Definition (SD) video and High Definition (HD) video. You need the sequence to be a consistent format throughout in order to output it. In other words, you need it to be entirely SD or entirely HD. This situation will be covered in the next *Transcoding sequences of mixed SD and HD video* recipe.

What does Transcoding a sequence do?

▸ When you Transcode a sequence, Media Composer makes a brand new **Master Clip** for each and every Segment (shot) that is in the sequence (also see important note that follows). The new **Master Clips'** durations are only as long as what exists in the sequence, plus any handle you decide to add. Handle is additional material at the head (beginning) and tail of each **Master Clip** that doesn't appear in the Transcoded sequence. It is there only if you later need to trim a segment longer or need to add a transition effect, such as a dissolve.

▸ Transcoding changes the compression scheme of the video – in other words, it changes the codec (method used to compress a video file for storage and to decompress it for playback). Transcoding can *not* increase the quality of the image. For example, if your footage came from a MiniDV tape (the resolution is DV25) and you Transcoded to a resolution of 1:1 (uncompressed), then the new file *will take up more space on your hard drive* but will *not* increase the quality to make it look any better. On the other hand, if you Transcoded to a resolution of 15:1s, then the file *will* be compressed further. So, along with a reduction in file size, *the image quality will be reduced as well*. Here's another example: transcoding SD video to HD does *not* increase the image quality. It is simply putting that image into the HD format. On the flip side, Transcoding HD video to SD will indeed reduce the quality of the image as it places it into that format.

▸ The **Transcoding** dialog window does not have any options to delete the original media after the Transcoded copies are created. If you want to free up drive space, then you will do that manually.

> Note a new behavior – Transcoding clips of a different frame rate will now take on all the attributes of the current project's frame rate, losing any history to what it was before the Transcode. This is something to consider if an EDL is needed for the original material or you ever wanted to link back to the original files. Don't worry, you will be presented with a dialog box alerting you that the Transcode will no longer allow the clip(s) to recapture, relink, and so on, to its original frame rate.
>
> Also, unlike **Consolidate**, **Transcode** will only make new **Master Clips** for the video by default. In other words, it does not make **Master Clips** that include audio by default. There is a workaround for this, described in step 13 of this recipe. However, this workaround will only apply to video and audio that originally came from the same clip and were cut into the sequence together (for example, an actor speaking dialog). For emphasis, the workaround will not affect audio-only clips (for example, music, sound effects, or dialog edited into the sequence without the video that was originally paired with it).

Getting ready

Please review items 1, 2, and 3 in the *Introduction* section of this chapter.

Make a duplicate of your sequence as discussed previously.

Note which situation you are in:

- ▶ Situation 1: Transcoding a Decomposed Sequence from high resolution to a lower resolution for archiving. This presumes the following:
    - ❏ You Decomposed your sequence (which created .new **Master Clips**).
    - ❏ You have already recaptured the video for the .new clips at high resolution for example, 1:1).
    - ❏ You have fully completed all the necessary outputs and masters and now want to archive the sequence at a lower resolution.

- ▶ Situation 2: Consolidating then Transcoding a sequence to create a reference sequence. Reminder: the goal of the process covered here is to further reduce the amount of media stored on the hard drive(s). Transcoding a Consolidated sequence is an additional step you may choose to perform in order to free up additional hard drive space, but it is not required.

- ▶ If you are in situation 1, then proceed to step 1 of this recipe.

- ▶ If you are in situation 2, then:
    - ❏ First, you will need to Consolidate your sequence. Follow all the steps for situation 1 in the earlier recipe of this chapter titled, *Consolidating sequences*.
    - ❏ Once completed, you will have a Consolidated sequence, but the video will be at the original resolution. If you want to further reduce the hard drive space required for the media, then you would follow the next Transcoding steps.

How to do it...

1. Create a new bin. This new bin will be the place where you put a duplicate of the sequence you will create in a moment (which will eventually be Transcoded). Duplicating the sequence and placing it in this bin protects the original and provides an extra back-up version that will not only help you in case you make an error but also will help to keep your project organized for future reference. Depending on your situation, you would label the bin along the lines of **My Final High Resolution Movie Transcoded**, or **My Consolidated Movie Transcoded**.

2. Create the duplicate of the high resolution or Consolidated sequence: select the sequence, then go to the **Edit** menu | **Duplicate**.

3. Place the duplicated sequence into the bin from step 1.

4. This is an optional step: For an additional layer of protection, close all other bins except the bin you created in step 1. This will ensure you don't mistakenly Transcode the wrong sequence when you're tired at the end of the day.

5. Go to the **Project** Window | **Format** tab.

6. In the **Format** tab, select the Project Type and Aspect Ratio. Avid states that, new clips created through the Transcode operation are in the project format. When you Transcode a clip across formats, for example, if you transcode a **16:9** clip in a **4:3** project, the **Reformat** bin setting determines how the clip is conformed to the new format. For details on the **Reformat** option, see the *Getting The AMA file's image to display as described* recipe in *Chapter 1, Getting Assets into your Media Composer Project* (this applies to non-AMA'd files as well).

7. Select the duplicated sequence you placed into the new bin from step 1.

8. Go to the **Clip** Menu | **Consolidate/Transcode**.

9. The **Consolidate/Transcode** dialog window will open.

10. In the **Consolidate/Transcode** dialog window, select the following:

    - In the upper left-hand corner, select **Transcode**.

    - Under the heading **Target Drives**, enable the checkbox for **Video, audio and data on same drive** (it will most likely be enabled by default).

    - In the **Video/Data** list box, select the destination drive/partition you want to place the new media files onto.

    - In the **Handle length** entry box, enter a value. If you enter a value that is equal to or longer than the handle length you set when you Decomposed or Consolidated the sequence, then the new, Transcoded **Master Clips** will be the same duration as those. Setting a shorter handle length here will create new, Transcoded **Master Clips** that are shorter than the Decomposed or Consolidated versions.

    - Be *sure* to enable/check the box for **Create new Sequence** (note that some previous versions of Media Composer do not have this selection). Even though you manually created a duplicate earlier, this is yet one more layer of protection for you.

    - Enable/check the box for **Convert Video**.

    - **Target Video Resolution** menu: select the resolution you want to Transcode the files to.

    - **Include reformatted clips already at target resolution** checkbox – Avid states, "*Select this option if you want to include reformatted clips in the sequence that are already at the target video resolution. Your Avid editing application does not normally Transcode clips in a sequence that are already at the target video resolution. However, you might want to include Reformatted clips at the target resolution to preserve the Reformatting.*"

11. **Convert Audio Sample Rate** checkbox and menu – selecting this is optional.

   ❏ *Not* selecting this checkbox – this produces new **Master Clips** and media for each segment (shot) in the sequence. *However,* they will be *video only* **Master Clips**. The audio will still play in the sequence because the audio is supplied by the *original* **Master Clips** and media. The possible problem with this is that if you ever needed to Match Frame back to one of the **Master Clips**, the clip loaded into your **Source** Window would be either **Video Only** or **Audio Only**.

   ❏ *Selecting* this checkbox – if you want/need to have the new **Master Clips** include *both* the video and audio that originally came from the *same* clip and which were *cut into the sequence together* (for example, an actor speaking dialog), then you *must* select this checkbox. Even if you select the existing sample rate of the audio, it will still work. *However,* this will *not* affect other audio in the sequence (for example, music, sound effects, or dialog edited into the sequence *without* the video that was originally paired with it). For emphasis, new **Master Clips** for these type of audio elements (music, sound effects, and so on). will not be created. The audio will still play in the sequence because the audio is supplied by the *original* **Master Clips** and media.

12. In the bottom right-hand corner of the dialog window, click the **Transcode** button to begin the process.

13. Depending on the number of files, and the size of those files, this process may take some time. When the process is completed:

   ❏ All the newly created `.new` **Master Clips** will be at the top of the bin.

   ❏ You will have two sequences in the bin. Depending on your situation, one of them is either the high resolution sequence or the Consolidated sequence, which continues to link to its original **Master Clips** and media. The new sequence was created by Media Composer because you enabled the **Create new Sequence** checkbox. The new sequence will have `.Transcoded` added to the end of the name.

14. You now have two sets of **Master Clips**: those at higher resolution and those at a lower resolution (the Transcoded clips). At this point, you will want to delete the higher resolution media. Before you do this, I highly suggest locking the Transcoded clips and media to make them difficult to delete by mistake. To do this, follow these steps:

15. Make a new bin. Name it something like `Lock All This Stuff`.

16. Duplicate the Transcoded sequence.

17. Place the duplicated sequence into the `Lock All This Stuff` bin.

18. Select the **Lock All This Stuff** bin to make it active.

19. Go to **Bin** menu | **Set Bin Display......**.

20. Enable these two checkboxes: **Rendered Effects** and **Show Reference Clips**.

21. Click **OK**. In the Lock All This Stuff bin, you will now see all the **Master Clips** and render files (also known as Precomputes) that are linked to the sequence. In other words, these are the elements that make that sequence play.

22. Select everything in the bin (*cmd/Ctrl + A*).

23. Go to **Clip** menu | **Lock Bin Selection**. This will lock the clips and media in order to make them difficult to delete.

24. You can choose to display the **Lock** column to see what elements are locked or unlocked. To do this, begin by setting the bin to Text View. Then, go to **Bin** menu | **Choose Columns**. The **Choose Columns** dialog window opens. Select **Lock** and then click **OK**.

25. Since you are clearing hard drive space of unneeded media (the higher resolution media), you would then delete it. You may want to review the later sections in this chapter on using the **Media Tool** and methods of deleting media.

Transcoding Sequences of mixed SD and HD video

Before Consolidating, Transcoding, or Decomposing sequences, I recommend that you perform a small test of the process, using unimportant clips to familiarize yourself with the workflow, additional options, and final results.

Before you Consolidate (or Transcode, or Decompose), a sequence I highly recommend that you make a duplicate of it and place it in its own well-labeled bin (for example, My Movie Before Transcode). This extra version is a protection in case you make an error, and will help to keep your project organized.

When you have a sequence of mixed Standard Definition (SD) video and High Definition (HD) video, you need the sequence to be a consistent format throughout in order to output it. In other words, it must be entirely SD or entirely HD.

What does Transcoding a sequence do? A discussion of this, along with some important notes, can be found in the introduction of the previous *Transcoding sequences for archiving or before up-res* recipe.

Getting ready...

Note that Transcoding only changes the video format and/or resolution of the media. It does not alter the aspect ratio.

▸ When you are in an SD project with an aspect ratio of **4 x 3** (also know as **1.33:1**), and outputting to SD at the same aspect ratio, then you'll most likely want to adjust any segments (shots) that are **16 x 9** (also known as **1.77:1**), so that they will display in the proper aspect ratio. One method to accomplish this is to use a **Reformat** effect: **Tools** menu | **Effect Palette** | **Reformat** category | **16:9 Letterbox**. Place this effect on each segment that should display as **16 x 9**.

▸ When you are in a HD project, or an SD project that has an aspect ratio of **16 x 9** (**1.77:1**), and outputting to the **16 x 9** aspect ratio, generally you want to adjust the segments that are **4 x 3** (**1.33:1**) in order to have them display in the correct aspect ratio. One way to do this is to apply a **Reformat** effect: **Tools** menu | **Effect Palette** | **Reformat** category | **4:3 Sidebar**.

How to do it...

1. Create a new bin. This new bin will be the place where you put a duplicate of the sequence you will create in step 2 (which will eventually be Transcoded). Duplicating the sequence and placing it in this bin protects the original and provides an extra back-up version that will not only help you in case you make an error but also will help to keep your project organized for future reference. Label the bin along the lines of **My Movie Transcoded for Output on [insert date]**.

2. Create the duplicate of the mixed SD/HD sequence. Select the sequence, then go to **Edit** menu | **Duplicate**.

3. Place the duplicated sequence into the bin from step 1.

4. This is an optional step: For an additional layer of protection, close all other bins except the bin you created in step 1. This will ensure you don't mistakenly Transcode the wrong sequence when you're tired or distracted.

5. First, determine the resolutions of the media in that sequence:

    i. Select the **My Movie Transcoded for Output** bin to make it active.

    ii. Go to **Bin** menu | **Set Bin Display...**.

iii. Enable these two checkboxes:

    ❑ **Rendered Effects**

    ❑ **Show Reference Clips**

iv. Click **OK**. In the **My Movie Transcoded for Output** bin, you will now see all the **Master Clips** and render files (also known as Precomputes) that are linked to the sequence. In other words, these are the elements that make that sequence play.

v. Now you'll determine the resolution of those clips. Go to **Bin** menu | **Choose Columns** | select **Video** | Click **OK**.

vi. Make note of the resolutions of the SD clips and the HD clips.

vii. Now that you've noted the resolutions, hide the Reference Clips by going to **Bin** menu | **Set Bin Display...**. Then, de-select the **Rendered Effects** and **Show Reference Clips** checkboxes and click **OK**.

6. Next you'll set the format (SD or HD) of the Transcoded clips that you will be creating. Go to **Project** Window | **Format** tab.

7. In the **Format** tab, select the Project Type and Aspect Ratio you are outputting to (SD or HD). Avid states, *"New clips created through the Transcode operation are in the project format. When you transcode a clip across formats, for example, if you transcode a 16:9 clip in a 4:3 project, the Reformat bin setting determines how the clip is conformed to the new format"*. For details on the **Reformat** option, see the *Getting the AMA file's image to display as desired* recipe in *Chapter 1, Getting Assets into Your Media Composer Project* (this applies to non-AMA linked files as well).

8. Next, you'll ensure that the highest quality Transcode process is used:

i. Go to **Project** Window | **Settings** tab | **Render Settings**.

ii. The **Render Settings** dialog window opens.

iii. You will see the heading labeled as **Image Interpolation**.

iv. From the **Image Interpolation** pull-down menu, select **Advanced (Polyphase)**.

v. Click **OK**.

9. Select the duplicated sequence you placed into the new bin from step 1.

10. Go to **Clip** menu | **Consolidate/Transcode**.

11. In the **Consolidate/Transcode** dialog window, select the following:

    i.   In the upper left-hand corner, select **Transcode**.

    ii. Under the heading **Target Drives**, enable the checkbox for **Video, audio and data on same drive** (it will most likely be enabled by default).

    iii. In the **Video/Data** list box, select the destination drive/partition you want to place the new media files onto.

    iv. In the **Handle length** entry box, enter a value. This will instruct Media Composer to make new Transcoded **Master Clips** that are longer than the original segments (shots) in the sequence. For example, you have a segment that is 10 seconds long. You enter a duration of 60 frames for the handle. This will add 60 frames to the head (beginning) of the new **Master Clip** as well as 60 frames to the tail of the new **Master Clip**. So, in a 30-fps project, the total duration of the new **Master Clip** will be 14 seconds. Adding handle ensures that you have some additional material at the head and tail, just in case you need to later trim a segment longer or add a transition effect (for example, a dissolve).

    v.   Be *sure* to enable/check the box for **Create new Sequence** (note that some previous versions of Media Composer do not have this selection). Even though you manually created a duplicate earlier, this is yet one more layer of protection for you.

    vi. Enable/check the box for **Convert Video**.

    vii. **Target Video Resolution** menu: Select the resolution you want to Transcode the mismatched files to. For example, in an example sequence, the SD clips are at **1:1** while my HD clips are at **DNxHD 220**:

         ❑ If I want to Transcode the SD to HD then, in this example, I would select **DNxHD 220**.

         ❑ If I want to Transcode the HD to SD then, in this example, I would verify that the project type (**Project** Window | **Format** tab) was set to SD and I would select **1:1**.

    viii. **Include reformatted clips already at target resolution** checkbox – Avid states, *"Select this option if you want to include Reformatted clips in the sequence that are already at the target video resolution. Your Avid editing application does not normally Transcode clips in a sequence that are already at the target video resolution. However, you might want to include Reformatted clips at the target resolution to preserve the Reformatting."*

12. Convert **Audio Sample Rate** checkbox and menu – this next step is optional, and I'll explain the results:

   ❑ *Not* selecting this checkbox – this produces new **Master Clips** and media for each segment (shot) in the sequence. *However*, they will be *video only* **Master Clips**. The audio will still play in the sequence because the audio is supplied by the *original* **Master Clips** and media. The possible problem with this is that if you ever needed to Match Frame back to one of the **Master Clips**, the clip loaded into your **Source** Window would be either **Video Only** or **Audio Only**.

   ❑ *Selecting* this checkbox – if you want/need to have the new **Master Clips** include *both* the video and audio that originally came from the *same clip* and which *were cut into the sequence together* (for example, an actor speaking dialog), then you *must* select this checkbox. Even if you select the existing Sample Rate of the audio, it will still work. *However*, this will *not* affect other audio in the sequence (for example, music, sound effects, or dialog edited into the sequence without the video that was originally paired with it). For emphasis, new **Master Clips** for these type of audio elements (music, sound effects, and so on.) will *not* be created. The audio will still play in the sequence because the audio is supplied by the *original* **Master Clips** and media.

13. In the bottom right-hand corner of the dialog window, click the **Transcode** button to begin the process.

14. Depending on the number of files, and the size of those files, this process may take some time. When the process is completed:

   ❑ All the newly created `.new` **Master Clips** will be at the top of the bin.

   ❑ You will have two sequences in the bin. One of them is the mixed format sequence that continues to link to the original SD and HD **Master Clips** and media. The new sequence was created by Media Composer because you enabled the **Create new Sequence** checkbox. The new Sequence will have `.Transcoded` added to the end of the name. This is the sequence that is now at one consistent format.

Changing the Sample Rate of clips in a bin before editing them into your Sequence

When you have audio with a Sample Rate that differs from what is set in the **Audio Project** settings (**Project** Window | **Settings** tab | **Audio Project**), Media Composer will actually allow it to be played. How great, you say. Well, it's great until you have to output your sequence to tape. When you output to a tape, the Sample Rate of all the audio elements must be the same (just in the same way that the video has to be all SD or all HD).

If you have imported audio at a Sample Rate that does not match the Sample Rate set for your project, this recipe will show you how to change the Sample Rate of clips in a bin *before* editing them into your sequence. It is advisable to correct the Sample Rate before editing clips into your sequence rather than after. If you have already edited mismatched audio into your sequence, then you will want to refer to the recipe that follows this one which is titled, *Changing the mismatched audio that has been edited into your sequence.*

Getting ready

It will be helpful to see the sample rate of a clip's audio in the bin:

1. Place the bin into **Text View**.

2. Go to **Bin** menu | **Choose Columns** | select **Audio SR** | Click **OK**.

Here are two things that may be helpful in the **Audio Project** settings located at: **Project Window** | **Settings** tab | **Audio Project**.

▶ If you are not already aware, check the Project Sample Rate. The Project Sample Rate will appear in the top right-hand side of the dialog window. The default setting is **48 kHz** (frequently abbreviated as 48K).

▶ Make sure that you can see which segments (shots) in your sequence are not at the sample rate of your project. There is a selection that reads **Show Mismatched Sample Rates as Different Color**. This should be set to **Yes**. More on this is next.

To see the segments in the sequence with mismatched sample rates, do one or both of the following:

▶ Display the Audio Waveform in the **Timeline** Window. One method to do this is: **Timeline Window Fast Menu** (hamburger) in the bottom left-hand corner of the **Timeline** Window | **Audio Data** | **Waveform** (note that previous releases referred to this as Sample Plot). Audio that is the same as the Project Sample Rate will display the waveforms as black. Audio that is not at the Project Sample Rate will display the waveforms as light gray.

▶ Display text that reveals the Sample Rate of the audio. To do this: **Timeline Window Fast Menu** (hamburger) in the bottom left-hand corner of **Timeline** Window | **Clip Text** | **Clip Resolutions**.

▶ You may need to make the audio tracks wider to better/easier see the waveforms and/or the Sample Rate text. One method to do this: enable the tracks, then use *cmd/Ctrl + L* to make the track(s) wider, and *cmd/Ctrl + K* to make them narrower.

How to do it...

1. Select the clip(s) in the bin.

2. Go to **Clip** menu | **Change Sample Rate**.

3. The **Change Sample Rate** dialog window opens.

4. From the **Sample Rate** pull-down menu, select the Sample Rate to convert the clip(s) into.

5. Set the **Quality** to **High**.

6. Delete **Original Media** checkbox:

▶ *If unselected (not checked):*

   ❑ This will create a new **Audio Only** Master Clip linked to its own media (at the new Sample Rate).

   ❑ If there is video with the **Master Clip**, then the video and new audio will be in separate **Master Clips**.

   ❑ The new clip will have .new added to the end of its name.

   ❑ If you have edited the original (incorrect Sample Rate) clip into the sequence, the instance(s) of it in the sequence will *not* be changed. You would need to manually re-edit the .new clip into the sequence where and as required.

▶ *If selected (checked):*

   ❑ New audio media will be created at the new Sample Rate and the old media (at the incorrect sample rate) will then be *deleted*. Media Composer will then link the **Master Clip** to the new audio media. If there is video with the **Master Clip**, then this will keep the video and audio together in one, single **Master Clip**. Further, if you have edited the clip into the sequence, the instance(s) in the sequence will also be changed because the sequence links to the **Master Clip**, which in turn links to the new media.

There's more...

In the **Audio Project** settings (**Project** Window | **Settings** tab | **Audio Project**) you will also see a menu for Audio File Format. The default setting is PCM, which will create a .mxf file, which will exist in the same folder as the video. On the other hand, the alternate selections of AIFF-C and WAVE create .omf files, which will reside in a separate folder (OMFI MediaFiles) from the .mxf media.

Changing the mismatched audio that has been edited into your Sequence

It is best if you can change the sample rate of mismatched clips before you edit them into your sequence, as covered in the previous recipe. However, if you weren't able to do that, the solution is given in the following sections.

Getting ready

Please refer to the *Getting ready* section of the previous *Changing the sample rate of clips in a bin before editing them into your sequence* recipe.

How to do it...

1. Create a new bin. This new bin will be the place where you put a duplicate of the sequence you will create in step 2 (which will eventually have the mismatched audio clips converted). Duplicating the sequence and placing it in this bin protects the original and provides an extra back-up version that will not only help you in case you make an error but also will help to keep your project organized for future reference. Label the bin along the lines of **My Movie With Sample Rate Converted for Output on [insert date]**.

2. Create the duplicate of the mixed sample rate sequence: Select the sequence, then go to **Edit** menu | **Duplicate**.

3. Place the duplicated sequence into the bin from step 1.

4. This step is optional. For an additional layer of protection, close all other bins except the bin you created in step 1. This will ensure you don't mistakenly convert the wrong sequence when you're tired or distracted.

5. Select the duplicated sequence.

6. Go to **Clip** menu | **Change Sample Rate...**.

7. The **Change Sample Rate** dialog window opens.

8. From the **Sample Rate** pull-down menu, select the sample rate you need to convert the mismatched clip(s) into.

9. Set the **Quality** to **High**.

10. Delete original media checkbox – in both cases detailed in steps 11 and 12, Media Composer creates new **Audio Only Master Clips** in their entirety. In other words, it does not create the **Master Clip**(s) only for the duration that is used in the sequence. For example, you have a song that is 3 minutes long. You edited only 20 seconds of that song into your sequence. Media Composer will create the new **Master Clip** for the full 3 minute duration of the song.

11. If the Delete original media checkbox is unselected:

  ❑ This will create new **Audio Only** Master Clips linked to their own media (at the new sample rate)

  ❑ If there is video with the original **Master Clip**, then the video and new audio will now be in separate **Master Clips**

  ❑ The new clips will have .new added to the end of their names

  ❑ The result – the original sequence remains linked to mismatched Sample Rate clips (which are still online and will play), while the new/converted sequence links to the new clips at the converted Sample Rate

12. If the Delete original media checkbox is selected:

  ❑ This is important: Choosing this with a sequence selected will delete the mismatched audio from the original **Master Clips**. This would make the video and audio (that previously were married together in one clip) into separate **Master Clips**. This is very likely undesirable, especially if you need to continue to edit. Instead, you would most likely want to select this only when changing the Sample Rate of the *clips in the bin*. See the previous *Changing the sample rate of clips in a bin before or after editing them into your sequence* recipe.

  ❑ This will create new **Audio Only** Master Clips linked to their own media (at the new sample rate).

  ❑ The old media (at the incorrect sample rate) will be deleted.

  ❑ The new clips will have .new added to the end of their names.

  ❑ The result – the original sequence remains linked to mismatched Sample Rate clips (which are now offline and will not play), while the new/converted sequence links to the new **Audio Only** clips at the converted Sample Rate.

How it works...

Remember that this creates new audio-only Master Clips that are at the converted Sample Rate. This affects what clips the sequence is linking to, and is why it is important to make a duplicate of the sequence as discussed in the previous step numbers 1 and 2.

Prevent editing with audio that does not match the Project's Sample Rate

While mixing clips with different audio Sample Rates is generally infrequent, it can occur (for example, when borrowing a clip from another project). This recipe will alert you to this issue before you've edited a mismatched clip into your sequence.

How to do it...

1. Go to **Project** Window | **Settings** tab | Double-click the **Audio Project** settings.
2. The **Audio Project** settings dialog window will open.
3. Set **Convert Sample Rates When Playing** to **Never**.
4. Close the **Audio Project** settings dialog window.

How it works...

By default, Media Composer is set to play audio that is *not* at the Project Sample Rate (**Project** Window | **Settings** tab | **Audio Project** | **Convert Sample Rates When Playing** | **Always**). By turning this feature *off*, if/when you load a clip into your **Source** Window with a mismatched sample rate, then you will *not* be able to hear the audio play. That's a pretty good sign that something is not as it should be. This will cause you to investigate to see if the audio is either Offline or at the incorrect Sample Rate. This way you can catch it and change the Sample Rate *before* editing it into your sequence (discussed earlier in this chapter in the recipe titled *Changing the sample rate of clips in a bin before editing them into your sequence*).

Setting the Media Tool display

In this recipe, we'll discuss opening the **Media Tool** and determining what gets displayed in the **Media Tool** window, and how it is displayed.

In the sections that *follow* this one, we'll discuss using the **Media Tool** for various tasks (for example, deleting unused media, deleting media for specific tracks of a clip, moving media from one drive to another, and so on.)

How to do it...

1. To open the **Media Tool** display dialog, go to **Tools** menu | **Media Tool**.

2. The **Media Tool** display dialog window opens. Let's discuss each section:

   ❑ **Media drive(s) display region**: This displays all the drives and/or partitions that Media Composer can see. You tell Media Composer to look at specific drives by using *Shift+Click* method, or you can quickly tell it to look at all the drives by clicking the **All Drives** button.

   ❑ **Project(s) display region**: Every time you create media files by capturing from tape, importing, rendering, Consolidating, or Transcoding, they become associated with the project that was open when they were created. In other words, they get a stamp on them that says **I belong to 'Project X**. In this way, you can have media from many different projects together in the same `Avid MediaFiles` (or `OMFI MediaFiles`) folder and still be able to deal with them individually when needed. You can tell Media Composer to look at specific projects' media by using *Shift+Click* method; or to tell it to look at only the media that is associated with the currently open project by clicking the **Current Project** button; or to tell it to look at all the different projects' media by clicking the **All Projects** button.

3. Now let's talk about the three checkboxes. However, let's talk about them in reverse order:

   ❑ **Media Files**: This will display all the types of media no matter how it was created (captured, imported, rendered, and so on), and it will display each individual media file just as it exists in your `Avid MediaFiles` (or `OMFI MediaFiles`) folder. This means that the names of the files are those created by Media Composer, and generally consist of numbers and letters that only make sense to a computer. So, this display may not be the most helpful or the one you'll use most often. To further illuminate how Media Composer works, it's helpful to know that one **Master Clip** can (and often does) link to (refer to) more than one media file. For example, in my bin, I have a **Master Clip** of an actor speaking with one video track and two audio tracks. That means that one **Master Clip** links to three separate media files: one video file, and two audio files. For emphasis, this selection will display each individual media file.

   ❑ **Precompute Clips**: This is Avid's term for what we've come to simply call `Render` files. In Media Composer, Precomputes are created whenever you render an effect, create a motion effect, or create a title.

   ❑ **Master Clips**: This places your media into a display that's easier for you to deal with. For emphasis, this is media displayed as **Master Clips**. This displays clips created by capturing, importing, consolidating, or transcoding.

4. Once you have configured the **Media Tool** display dialog window as you need, then click **OK**.

5. The **Media Tool** window will open. It looks and behaves just like a bin.

6. You can adjust what is displayed in the **Media Tool** window by first going to the **Media Tool Fast Menu** (hamburger-looking) in the bottom left side of the window. Then, from the menu, select **Set Media Display**, which will open the **Media Tool** display dialog window.

How it works...

The way Media Composer works with managed media files (meaning files not linked by AMA) is that it places them in a specific folder called `Avid MediaFiles` and/or `OMFI MediaFiles`. That means that media from multiple projects may be all mixed together. Along with the media files are two database files. The two files are labeled `msmFMID.pmr` and `msmMMOB.mdb`. The `msm` refers to a component of the Media Composer application called Media Stream Manager. These two files are a crucial component for Media Composer to keep track of media files and to keep media linked to clips and sequences.

Advantages of the **Media Tool**:

▶ Because the **Media Tool** works just like a bin, you can Sort and Sift media based on criteria, such as what drive it's located on, what resolution it is, its Sample Rate, its creation date, what Project it is associated with, and so on.

▶ You can move media from one drive to another, using the **Consolidate** function (see later in this chapter).

▶ You can delete specific file types. For example, if you wanted to delete only the **A3** and **A4** media files from a clip, you can do this when using the **Media Tool** (see later).

▶ You can locate all the media files associated with a particular project without having to go bin by bin in your project. This makes it easier to delete or move all the media at the conclusion of a project and avoid leaving extraneous, useless media files taking up space on your drives, as often happens with `Precompute` files (`Render` files).

▶ You can also use the **Media** tool to borrow a clip from another project (see later in this chapter).

Borrowing a clip from another Project

There will be times when you want to use clips that are already in use by another project (for example, music, graphics, and so on). This recipe will take you through that process.

How to do it...

Please review items 1, 2, and 3 in the *Introduction* section of this chapter.

1. Open the **Media Tool** and go to **Tools** menu | **Media Tool**.

2. Configure the **Media Tool** to display only **Master Clips** from the Project(s) you want to borrow from. This topic is discussed in more detail in the previous *Setting the Media tool display* recipe.

3. Simply drag a **Master Clip**(s) from the **Media Tool** window into any open bin. There is no need to hold down any keys on the keyboard. Media Composer will automatically create a Clone of the clip (the difference between a Duplicated clip and a Cloned clip is discussed in the *Mixing frame rates* in *Chapter 1, Getting Assets into Your Media Composer Project, in the There's more... section*).

4. *If* you need to make a copy of the *media* so that it will be permanently associated with *your* project, rather than the project from which it was borrowed, then see the *Copying a borrowed clip's media* recipe, earlier in this chapter.

How to determine where media files are stored and how to move them

Before you Consolidate or Transcode clips, I highly recommend that you perform a test of the process with some unimportant clips to familiarize yourself with the workflow, additional options, and final results.

Please note that the topics covered, and recipes of steps provided, are geared toward those using local media drives for storage, for example, the internal hard drive, fixed hard drive(s), and/or a relatively small, local RAID. Note that those working at a facility with Avid Unity, Avid ISIS, Avid Interplay, or another shared storage solution must consult with their facility's technical administrators or lead assistant editors before carrying out any media management functions in a shared storage environment. Failing to do so can cause inadvertent loss of media.

Getting ready

In this example situation, the **Media Tool** window is already open and you have configured it to display the following (details on this can be found earlier in the *Setting the Media tool display* recipe):

 ▸   *All* available media drives

 ▸   Media *only* from the *Current* Project

 ▸   **Master Clips** and **Precomputes**

The steps in the recipe will be using the Sort feature, and Sifting will be covered in the *There's more...* section. Before you can use the Sort and Sift features, you need to display the column(s) of information you need, for example, **Clip name**, **Tape name** (source), **Video** (video resolution), **Drive location**, **Sample Rate**, **Creation date**, and so on. To do this, follow these steps:

1. With the **Media Tool** window active, go to **Bin** menu | **Choose Columns**.

2. In the **Choose Columns** dialog window, select one or more columns of information that you need. In this example situation, your goal is to move media files from one drive onto another because you have mistakenly placed some clips onto a drive named `Cat` and they need to be moved off of that drive and onto a drive named `Dog`. So, displaying the Drive column will be helpful.

3. Click **OK**.

How to do it...

Now that you have prepared by following the *Getting ready* section, you can now Sort any column that is displayed (the *There's more...* section will cover Sifting). Sorting places data in a column in alpha-numeric order. In this example, we will display the Drive column.

1. In the Media Tool window, select the **Column Header** at very top of the column, so that the column becomes highlighted (for example, select where it says **Drive**, **Video**, **Creation Date**, and so on).

2. Right-click on the **Column Header**.

3. From the menu that appears, select either **Sort Ascending** or **Sort Descending**.

4. Once Sorted, it will be easier to select only the clips you want.

There's more...

Below are the steps to use the Sift feature as well as a discussion of another use of the Sort and Sift features.

Using the Sift feature

Sifting allows you to isolate the display to only what you need to see. This is accomplished by telling Media Composer to display only the clips that match a specific attribute (or criteria), such as **Clip name**, **Source name**, **Video resolution**, **Drive location**, **Sample Rate**, **Creation date**, and so on.

1. With the **Media Tool** window set as discussed in the *Getting ready* section, go to **Bin** menu | **Custom Sift...**.

2. The **Custom Sift** dialog window opens.

3. You will now tell Media Composer to restrict the display to only the clips that meet the attributes/criteria that you dictate:

   ❑ **Criterion** menu: Choose from **Contains**, **Begins With**, or **Matches exactly**.

   ❑ **Text to Find**: Type in the word or number to look for (for example, drive name, video resolution, and so on).

   ❑ **Column or Range to Search** menu: Only the columns that are currently displayed will appear in the list. Select a specific column in order to make Media Composer pay attention only to that column.

4. In this example, I have mistakenly placed some clips onto a drive called `Cat`, so in the **Custom Sift** dialog window, I do the following: I select **Contains**, I type in the word `cat`, and I select the **Drive** column.

5. Click the **Apply** button to see if the Sift criteria produces the results you expect/need. If not, then you can update the criteria and again press **Apply**.

6. If the display is as you need it to be, then click **OK**.

7. Note that the name of the **Media Tool** window has changed. It now includes the word **Sifted** in parentheses. This reminds you that you are not seeing all of the clips in the **Media Tool**. To return to seeing everything, go to **Bin** menu | **Show Unsifted**.

8. Scroll through the **Media Tool** window and verify that the display is indeed including only the clips you are concerned with.

9. Now that the display is restricted to only the media files (both **Master Clips** and **Precomputes**) that are on the incorrect drive (in this example, the `Cat` drive), you can select all of them (*cmd/Ctrl + A*) and Consolidate them. See the *Moving media files* recipe for the steps to use the **Consolidate** function to move the media file(s) from one drive to another.

Isolating video of a specific resolution

First, some background/context for you. It is common when working on large projects to bring the video into the system at a low resolution (to save drive space and/or to make it easier on the computer to play the media). Then, once the creative process is completed, the low resolution media is deleted and only the portions of media used by the sequence are recaptured at a higher resolution (for example, **1:1**) and all the effects are re-rendered at the higher resolution as well.

Just as common, is bringing in some video at low resolution and some video at the finishing resolution. For example, I might capture 100 hours of documentary footage at low resolution (**20:1**), but import all my graphic elements (stills and animations) at **1:1**. This way, when I reach the finishing stage of the project, all the graphic elements are already at high resolution and set to go. In this instance, I would only want to delete the video at the low resolution (**20:1**) to clear drive space to accommodate the high resolution media that I'll be capturing in the near future.

You can now see that using the Sort and/or Sift features would prove useful in the situation just described because you are able to utilize the **Video** column that displays the video resolution of the clips in your Project.

Deleting specific media files from clips (for example, just the A3 and A4 files)

Please review points 1, 2, and 3 in the *Introduction* section of this chapter.

Here's an example situation to put the steps in context:

▸ You have ingested several long clips that contain a video track and four audio tracks (**A1**, **A2**, **A3**, and **A4**)

▸ You realize that the audio on tracks **A3** and **A4** of each clip is unusable due to poor quality or is simply silent

Here is an overview of the goals in this example:

▸ First, delete the audio files only for tracks **A3** and **A4**.

▸ Second, modify the **Master Clips** so that they do not link to (refer to) media that is now Offline. Modifying the **Master Clips** after deleting the media is to avoid confusion. If you (or the editor you're working for) play a clip that has **A3** and **A4** tracks, but can't hear anything on those tracks, you would wonder if something is wrong (for example, media not captured, media corrupted, media mistakenly deleted, and so on), and possibly waste time dealing with a non-existent issue.

How to do it...

1. *Close all bins* except the bin containing the clips whose **A3** and **A4** media you want to delete.

2. Set the bin to **Text View**.

3. Go to **Bin** menu | **Choose Columns**.

4. The **Choose Columns** dialog window opens.

5. Select **Offline** and **Tracks**.

6. Click **OK**, then make sure you can see the **Offline** and **Tracks** columns in your bin.

7. Open the **Media Tool** display dialog window by going to **Tools** menu | **Media Tool**.

8. The **Media Tool** display dialog window opens.

9. Configure the **Media Tool** to display only **Master Clips** from the Current Project. This topic is discussed in the earlier *Setting the Media tool display* recipe, in this chapter.

10. The next steps assume that:

   ❑ The bin with the clips to be modified is open; and the **Offline** and **Tracks Columns** are displayed and easily visible

   ❑ The **Media Tool** window is open, displaying the media as **Master Clips**

11. In the next steps, you will locate the specific clips within the **Media Tool** window whose **A3** and **A4** media files will be deleted.

12. In the *bin*, select the clips to be modified.

13. Go to **Bin** menu | **Select Media Relatives**. This will locate and select the clips in the **Media Tool** display window.

14. Very carefully, click on the heading of the **Media Tool** window. You don't want to mistakenly click inside the **Media Tool** window and change the selections that have been made. Look in the **Media Tool** window. You'll see that the clips are selected (you may need to scroll up or down in the window to locate the highlighted clips).

15. With the **Media Tool** window active, and the clips selected, press *Delete*.

16. The **Delete Media** dialog window opens.

17. Here you can select which specific media files to *delete*. In this example, I want *only* the checkboxes for **A3** and **A4** to be selected. For emphasis, tracks **V1**, **A1**, and **A2** should *not* be selected.

18. *Stop and verify* that you have selected the correct tracks' media to *delete*. In this example, the only two checkboxes that should be selected are for **A3** and **A4**. Click **OK**.

19. A verification dialog window will open. If you are sure that you do indeed want to delete the media files you indicated, then click on the *Delete* button.

20. Close the **Media Tool** window.

21. Look at the clips in the bin. Look in the **Offline** column. Notice that the media is **Offline** for the **A3** and **A4** media you just deleted. Look in the **Tracks** column. Notice that the clips still refer to all the tracks, even though the media has been deleted. The next set of steps will take you through the clip modification process. Before we go through the steps, here's an overview of what you're going to do. First, you will Unlink the clips from the remaining media. Then you will use the **Modify** feature on the **Master Clips** to remove the unneeded tracks (in this example, tracks **A3** and **A4**). And the last thing you'll do is Relink the **Master Clips** back to the remaining media. Now let's do all of that step by step.

22. First, you will Unlink the clips. Start by selecting the clips you want to modify. Then, hold down the *Shift + cmd* keys (Mac) or the *Shift + Ctrl* keys (PC). While holding down the keys go to **Clip** menu | **Unlink** (if you don't hold down the correct keys, then the **Unlink** command will not appear and will instead read as **Relink**). Unlinking the clips from the media will cause them to become **Offline**. But because they are unlinked, they can now be modified.

23. The clips you're modifying should still be selected in the bin. If for any reason they are not, then re-select them.

24. Go to **Clip** menu | **Modify...**.

25. The **Modify** dialog window will open.

26. From the pull-down menu at the top of the **Modify** dialog window select **Set Tracks**.

27. Select the checkboxes *only for the tracks whose media still exists*. In this example, the selected checkboxes would be **V1**, **A1**, and **A2**. For emphasis, in this example, tracks **A3** through **A16** and **D** are *not* selected.

28. Click **OK**. The clips have now been modified. All that's left is to Relink the clips to the remaining media files. The next steps will take you through that process.

29. The clips you're modifying should still be selected in the bin. If for any reason they are not, then re-select them.

30. Go to **Clip** menu| **Relink**.

31. The **Relink** dialog window will open. Configure as necessary, though the default setting will generally be fine. Once configured, click **OK**. More information on Relinking is available in the **Media Composer Help**.

32. The clips relink and now link to (refer to) only the media that remains **Online**.

Deleting unused media files: Just Master Clips, just Precomputes, or both

Throughout the editing process, we create a good deal of media files by capturing off of tape, importing files, Consolidating, or Transcoding files linked by AMA, and of course by rendering effects. It is likely that you will want to determine what media is being used by your sequence(s) and what is not, so that you can delete it. This will not only free up drive space but also in some instances may even improve the performance of the system because the Media Composer software will have fewer media files to keep track of.

Deleting unused Precomputes is something you may want to do every few weeks. Deleting unused clips is generally something you'd do in the *very late stages* of a project in order to make room on the drives for some new footage that has arrived.

When deleting media, slow down, take your time, think things through, eliminate distractions, and don't do it when you're tired.

Getting ready

Before you dive into all the steps, I think it will be helpful to have a general overview of what is going to happen:

▸ Create duplicates: You'll place duplicates of all sequences and clips that link to (refer to) media that you do want to *keep* (in other words, the items that link to media you do *not* want to delete) into one common bin.

▸ Locking: As an additional layer of protection, before deleting unused media from a project, it is advisable to *lock* all critical and any as yet unused clips/media files that you feel you might want to use in the future. So, with all the sequences and clips that link to media that you want to keep all in one common bin, you will go through a locking process where you'll use the **Media Tool** and tell Media Composer to select this media and then lock it.

▸ Deleting: With all the sequences and clips that link to media that you want to keep all in one common bin, you will go through a multi-step deleting process where you'll use the **Media Tool** and tell Media Composer to select the media that is *not* being linked to by these sequences and clips (in other words, the media that is *not* being used by those specific sequences and clips), and then delete it.

How to do it...

Be very careful. The process detailed in the recipe will have you reference only specific sequences and clips in your project. This means that, in the end, *all* media files that are *not* referenced by (also known as linked to) these specific sequences and clips *will be deleted*.

1. Create a new bin. Name the bin along the lines of **Media Not To Delete**. This will be where you're going to place duplicates of:

   ❏ Any sequence that links to (refers to) media that you want to *keep*. This includes any other *versions* of a sequence that may link to different clips and/or Precomputes (renders).

   ❏ Clips you *haven't used in the sequence yet*, but want to protect from being deleted. Examples of these would be music, sound effects, voiceover, alternate performances, and any other clips you *haven't* edited into your sequence yet, but feel you might want to use in the future.

2. Go though each and *every* bin in your project and examine the **Master Clips**.

3. For each clip you haven't yet used in a sequence, but want to keep for future use, you will do the following: select the clip(s). Then go to **Edit** menu | **Duplicate**. Place the duplicate clips into the **Media Not To Delete** bin you created in step 1.

4. Go through *each* and *every* sequence bin in your project and examine the sequences. Determine if any of them are using media that should be saved (not deleted). These might be previous versions and/or alternate versions of your movie.

5. For *each* and *every* sequence whose media you want to save, you will do the following: select the sequence(s). Then go to **Edit** menu | **Duplicate**. Place the duplicate sequences into the **Media Not To Delete** bin you created in step 1.

6. Now you should have duplicates of all the clips and sequences that link to media that you want to *keep* in *one common bin* which you named along the lines of **Media Not To Delete**. The next thing you'll do is a few steps to lock the media that the *clips* link to, and then you'll go through some more steps to lock all the media that the *sequence(s)* link to (which will include Precomputes).

7. Now you will lock all the clips (you can display the **Lock** column to see what elements are locked or unlocked). Start by selecting all the clips and sequences in the **Media Not To Delete** bin (**Edit** menu | **Select All**). Next go to **Clip** menu | **Lock Bin Selection**. Note that for clips, this locks both the clips and the media files they link to. However, for sequences, it locks *only* the sequence, but *not* the media it links to. We'll do that in the next set of steps, using the **Media Tool**.

8. Keep the **Media Not To Delete** bin open, but close all other bins. This will help to avoid confusion.

9. Open the **Media Tool** dialog window by going to **Tools** Menu | **Media Tool**.

10. Set the **Media Tool** to display:

    ❑ Media from all drives

    ❑ Media *only* for your *Current Project*

    ❑ The goal here is to lock and protect *both* Precompute media files and **Master Clip** media files at the same time, so *select both of these checkboxes*

    ❑ See the *Setting the Media tool display* recipe for addition details, if you need them

    ❑ Click **OK** to open the **Media Tool** window

11. You may find it helpful to place the **Media Not To Delete** bin on one computer monitor and the **Media Tool** window on the other.

12. Now you'll *lock* just the media that *is* being referenced by the clips and sequences in your **Media Not To Delete** bin. To do this, follow the next steps.

13. In the **Media Not To Delete** bin, select everything. You can do this by going to **Edit** menu | **Select All**.

14. With everything selected, you'll now ask Media Composer to select all the media files in the **Media Tool** that link to (refer to) the selected clips and sequences in the **Media Not To Delete** bin.

15. With the clips and sequences in the **Media Not To Delete** bin still selected, and with the **Media Not To Delete** bin being the *active* bin, go to the **Media Not To Delete** bin's **Fast Menu** (hamburger) in the bottom left-hand corner. From the **Fast Menu**, choose the option that reads **Select Media Relatives**. The result is that all the media files that are linked to those sequences and clips will become selected in the **Media Tool** window.

16. The next goal is to lock all the selected media files in the **Media Tool** window. To do this, select the *very top* of the **Media Tool** window (where the name **Media Tool** appears), making sure you don't mistakenly click inside the **Media Tool** window and mistakenly deselect the highlighted media. **Next**; with the **Media Tool** window now active, and all the media files still selected, go to **Clip** menu | **Lock Bin Selection**. The result is that all of your selected media is now locked. If you try to delete it, Media Composer will tell you that it's locked with the message, **Locked selections can't be deleted**.

17. *Close* the **Media Tool** window so that we can reset the display in order to begin the deleting phase.

18. Open the **Media Tool** dialog window: **Tools** menu | **Media Tool**.

19. Set the **Media Tool** to display:

    ❑ Media from all drives or specific drives, depending on your situation and needs

    ❑ Media *only* for your *Current Project*

20. Now decide what you want to delete:

    ❑ If you want to delete only unused Precompute media files (renders), then select only the checkbox for **Precompute Files**

    ❑ If you want to delete only unused **Master Clip** media files (for example, captured clips, imported clips, Consolidated clips, Transcoded clips), then select only the checkbox for **Master Clips**

    ❑ If you want to delete both Precompute media files and **Master Clip** media files at the same time, in one step, then select both checkboxes

    ❑ See the *Setting the Media Tool display* recipe that is earlier in this chapter for addition details, if you need them

    ❑ Click **OK** to open the **Media Tool** window

21. You may find it helpful to place the **Media Not To Delete** bin on one computer monitor and the **Media Tool** window on the other.

22. Now you'll go through some steps (23 through 26) to select the media that's *not* being referenced by the clips and sequences in your **Media Not To Delete** bin.

23. In the **Media Not To Delete** bin, select everything. You can do this by going to **Edit** menu | **Select All**.

24. With everything selected, then in step 25 you will ask Media Composer to select all the media files in the **Media Tool** window that *do* link to (refer to), and *are* being used by, the selected clips and sequences in the **Media Not To Delete** bin.

25. With the clips and sequences in the **Media Not To Delete** bin still selected, and with the **Media Not To Delete** bin being the active bin. Go to the **Media Not To Delete** bin's **Fast Menu** (hamburger) in the bottom left-hand corner. Then, from the **Fast Menu**, choose the option that reads **Select Media Relatives**. The result is that all the media files that are linked to those sequences and clips will become selected in the **Media Tool** window. These are the files you do *not* want to delete. Therefore, now we'll tell Media Composer to select the opposite in the following steps.

26. Select the very top of the **Media Tool** window (where the name **Media** appears), making sure you don't mistakenly click inside the **Media Tool** window and deselect the highlighted media.

27. With the **Media Tool** window now active, and all the media files still selected, go to the **Media Tool** window's **Fast Menu** (hamburger) in the bottom left-hand corner. From the **Fast Menu**, choose the option that reads **Reverse Selection**. The result is that all the unused (not linked to) media is selected.

28. With the **Media Tool** window still active, press the *Delete* key on the keyboard.

29. The **Delete Media** dialog window will open.

30. Review the active checkboxes in the dialog window.

31. Click the **OK** button.

32. A verification dialog window will open.

33. If you do indeed want to delete the selected media files, then click the *Delete* button.

34. Depending on the number of files being deleted, this may take some time while the files are deleted and the Media Database files are updated.

Locking Clips and Sequences

Very often you will want to lock Clips and Sequences in order to make them more difficult to delete.

When you lock a clip in a bin, you are locking *both* the clip itself as well as the media it links to. Locking clips and media is not foolproof. Clips and media can be unlocked from within Media Composer as easily as they are locked. Additionally, someone who is determined can also very easily unlock media files at the Finder level without Media Composer even running.

When you lock a sequence in a bin, you are locking only the sequence itself. The *media* a sequence links to is *not* locked when the sequence is locked. See the *Deleting Unused Media Files: Just Master Clips, just Precomputes, or both* recipe that is earlier in this chapter for a discussion of how to lock the media files that a sequence is linked to.

It's also important to point out that locking a sequence in a bin does *not* prevent it from being edited. In other words, it will remain fully editable even though it's locked in a bin. How to make a sequence less easily editable is discussed in the recipe that follows this one.

How to do it...

1. Select the clips and/or sequences.

2. Go to **Clip** menu | **Lock Bin Selection**. Notice that in the **Clip** menu, right below the **Lock Bin Selection** choice, is the choice to *Unlock Bin Selection*.

3. You can display the **Lock** column to see what elements are locked or unlocked. To do this:

   i. Set the bin to **Text View**.

   ii. Go to **Bin** menu | **Choose Columns**.

   iii. The **Choose Columns** dialog window opens.

   iv. Select **Lock**.

   v. Click **OK**.

Locking sequences to make them less easily editable

It's important to make sure to communicate with others in your workgroup so they know a sequence has been locked and can't be edited, and ensure that they know how to unlock it if they need to. Not everyone knows about locking tracks in sequences and this may cause confusion in a workgroup.

There are two methods you can use to lock tracks in a sequence so that it is more difficult to perform an edit on those tracks. The first method will be presented in the *How to do it...* section, and the second will be in the *There's more...* section.

How to do it...

1. Load the sequence into the **Timeline** Window.

2. Using the Track Selectors, select the tracks you want to lock by enabling them. Only the enabled tracks will eventually become locked.

3. With the **Timeline** Window still active, go to **Clip** menu | **Lock Tracks**. Notice that in the **Clip** menu, right below the **Lock Tracks** choice, is *Unlock Tracks*.

4. Result – in the **Timeline** Window there is now a small lock icon where the Sync Lock icon normally resides. If you attempt to make an edit (for example, Spice, Lift, etc). on the locked tracks, then Media Composer will display a window telling you that it **Cannot edit a read-only track**. You will also find that you are unable to enter Trim or Segment Modes on locked tracks.

There's more...

Here's an alternate method for locking tracks.

1. Load the sequence into the **Timeline** Window.

2. Right-click on the Track Selector for the one track you want to lock.

3. Right-clicking will cause a **Contextual** menu to appear.

4. From the **Contextual** menu, select **Lock Track**. Notice that in the menu, right below the **Lock Track** choice, is **Unlock Track**.

5. You must perform this operation on *each* track you want to lock.

7

Mono and Stereo Audio Mixing

In this chapter, we'll cover:

- ▶ Understanding the Track Control Panel and Keyframe Selection Tool
- ▶ Understanding the Audio Mixer Tool – Clip Mode
- ▶ Understanding the Audio Mixer Tool – Auto Mode
- ▶ Understanding the Audio Tool (Audio Meters)
- ▶ Understanding Clip Gain and Pan versus Volume and Pan Automation
- ▶ Understanding Audio Project Settings
- ▶ Performing audio scrubbing: digital type scrubbing
- ▶ Performing audio scrubbing: analogue type scrubbing
- ▶ Displaying Audio Waveforms (also known as Sample Plot)
- ▶ Displaying Clip Gain, Volume Automation, and Pan Automation in the Timeline
- ▶ Clip Mode Level and Pan Adjustments
- ▶ Using Clip Mode with Dissolves to smooth Level and Pan adjustments
- ▶ Clip Mode: Setting a common Level or Pan to multiple segments
- ▶ Clip Mode: Adjusting multiple segments by a uniform amount
- ▶ Manually adding and adjusting Volume and Pan Automation keyframes
- ▶ Removing/Deleting Volume and Pan Automation Keyframes
- ▶ Adjusting multiple audio keyframes simultaneously
- ▶ Real Time Volume and Pan Adjustment
- ▶ Creating Stereo, 5.1 and 7.1 ("Multichannel") Tracks in a Sequence
- ▶ Converting a multichannel track into mono tracks in a Sequence
- ▶ Making Multichannel Clips (Stereo, 5.1 and 7.1)

- ▸ Using AudioSuite Plug-Ins
- ▸ Removing AudioSuite plug-ins
- ▸ Saving and Applying AudioSuite Templates
- ▸ Using Real Time Audio Suite (RTAS) Plug-Ins
- ▸ Removing RTAS plug-ins
- ▸ Saving and Applying RTAS Effect Templates
- ▸ Copying RTAS Effects between Tracks

Introduction

Avid Media Composer offers a great deal of audio manipulation capabilities, including volume adjustment, pan adjustment, equalization (EQ), both segment-based, and track-based effects (for example, reverb) and, now in Version 6, the capability to mix in 5.1 and 7.1 surround sound. This chapter will focus on many of the common audio mixing and effects tasks and challenges when working in a mono or stereo project.

- ▸ As Media Composer evolves, so does the terminology. At the time of writing, here are the audio related terminology changes to be aware of:
  - ❑ Sample Plot display has been renamed Waveform display
  - ❑ Energy Plot display has been removed
  - ❑ Auto Gain (short for Automation Gain) has been renamed Volume Automation

- ▸ At the time of writing, Media Composer provides 24 mono audio tracks, 24 stereo tracks, 24 Surround Sound Tracks, or any combination of them.

- ▸ At the time of writing, Media Composer provides the ability to hear any 16 of the displayed 24 tracks. In Avid ProTools lingo, they'd say that there are 24 tracks and 16 Voices. For most of us, 16 tracks are enough. For those that need to output more, they can perform an **Audio Mixdown** function (also known as Bouncing Tracks in the audio mixing world). **Audio Mixdown** is a selection from the **Special Menu**.

The smallest unit of time in Media Composer is essentially one frame (though in a 35-mm Film Project, it is possible to slip sync by 1/4 frame). Other applications created for the specific purpose of audio mixing (for example, Avid ProTools) can make adjustments at the Sample level (for example, 1/48,000th of a second).

The organization of your Sequence is important. It is advisable to keep specific audio elements on specific tracks. For example, track **A1** might be the designated track for the narrator of your film, and that is all that will ever be placed on that track. Separating audio elements onto specific tracks will make it easier to adjust levels, apply EQ, send the audio off to another mixer who is using ProTools, create Master Outputs with split tracks, generate EDLs, and so on.

Most productions will relate to you what elements should be placed on which track(s). If not, you should devise your own layout. Below is a written example of a track layout for a documentary, using only mono tracks (note that you can have both mono and stereo tracks in the same Sequence).

▸ **A1** is for Narrator Voice Over and whenever the Host appears on camera. It takes only one track because it is panned to the center (also known as mid or mono) so that the sound comes out of both the left and right speakers.

▸ **A2** and **A3** are for Interview Subjects. Again each track would be mono and panned to the center. There are two tracks in this example to allow for creating overlapping dialog of multiple Subjects, if required, or so that the Interviewer can be on **A2** and the Subject on **A3**.

▸ **A4**, **A5**, **A6**, **A7**, **A8** are for B-roll audio and sound effects. This provides room for multiple mono (one track) and stereo elements (two tracks).

▸ **A9** and **A10** are reserved for music. **A9** is the left channel and **A10** is the right channel of the stereo music.

Understanding the Track Control Panel and Keyframe Selection Tool

Becoming familiar with the locations of these tools and features will help with the discussions of using them, which are covered later in this chapter.

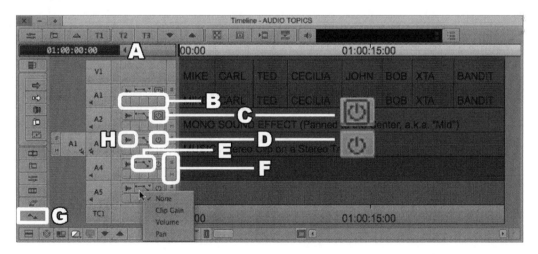

How to do it...

Open the **Track Control Panel** by either of these methods:

- ▶ **Timeline Window Fast Menu** (hamburger) in the bottom-left corner of the **Timeline Window** | **Track Control Panel**
- ▶ Click the **Track Control Panel** disclosure triangle found in the top-left of the **Timeline Window**, next to the **Timecode** display (see letter **A** in the previous screenshot)

How it works...

Now we'll take a look at the features in the previous screenshot:

- ▶ **B** – 5 **Real Time Audio Suite** (RTAS) buttons: The **RTAS Plug-Ins** are placed here. In addition, clicking on the buttons opens the **RTAS Tool**.
- ▶ **C** – **Active/Inactive Button** (with Outline): I think of these as the power button for each track, especially since that's the icon the designers chose.
  - ❏ Making a track Inactive is different than Muting it (see letter **F**). When you make a track Inactive, it means that there is less work for the computer to do because it will not have to process the **RTAS Plug-Ins**, **Volume Automation**, **Pan Automation**, or **Real Time** (unrendered) **EQ** effects on the track.
  - ❏ Making a track Inactive can be a convenient method of muting a track when the track is narrow and it is difficult to click on the actual **Mute Button** (see letter **F**).
  - ❏ The outline indicates that the track will be monitored during certain audio scrubbing processes. One example of this would be when you are playing in reverse at 60 fps, using the **J** key. The software allows only 2 of these types of tracks. So you can have either 2 Mono tracks or 1 Stereo track that has the **Active/Inactive Button** with the outline.
  - ❏ You can designate a track to be monitored (that is, to have the outline) by *option/Alt* + Clicking on the **Active/Inactive Button**. An example when this would be helpful is when you are using the **JKL** keys to shuttle around your Sequence. It may be that **A1** and **A2** (dialog) are the tracks with the outlined **Active/Inactive Button**, but you don't want to hear that as you shuttle quickly down the **Timeline**. Instead, it may be more helpful for you to hear tracks **A7** and **A8** (music) when you are shuttling forward at 90 fps or in reverse at 60 fps, and so on. So, in this example, you would *option/Alt* + Click on the **Active/Inactive Buttons** for tracks **A7** and **A8**.
  - ❏ Media Composer Version 6 provides 24 audio tracks. Please refer to the *Introduction* section of this chapter for additional details.
- ▶ **D** – **Active/Inactive Button** (Without Outline): See letter **C** for details.
- ▶ **E** – **Display Menu**: This allows you to display **Clip Gain**, **Volume Automation**, and/or **Pan Automation** on a track by track basis.

- ► **F** – **Solo and Mute** buttons: Multiple tracks can be set to **Solo** or to **Mute**. Soloing a track is essentially isolating it from the others. An example where using **Solo** would be helpful is if you had 12 audio tracks, but for a moment you wanted to hear only the dialog on **A1** along with the sound effect on **A5**. Muting is simply stopping the audio from being heard. Any **RTAS Plug-Ins**, **Volume Automation**, **Pan Automation**, or **Real Time EQ** effects are still being processed. To lighten the processing burden on the computer, you can make the track Inactive (see letter **C**).

- ► **G** – **Keyframe Selection Tool**: This is enabled by default, but it may be disabled to avoid accidentally adjusting a keyframe value when using the **Smart Tool**. For emphasis, it must be enabled in order to be able to manually adjust and/or remove keyframes using the cursor.

- ► **H** – **Waveform Display Button**: This allows you to display the **Waveforms** on a track by track basis.

Understanding the Audio Mixer Tool – Clip Mode

It's important to note that the **Audio Mixer Tool** has three different modes, each allowing different capabilities and functionality. The different modes are toggled using the **Audio Mixer Mode Button** (see letter **I** in the next screenshot). Two of the modes, **Clip** and **Volume Automation** (Auto), are discussed in this chapter.

Here's a screenshot of the **Audio Mixer Tool** – **Clip Mode**:

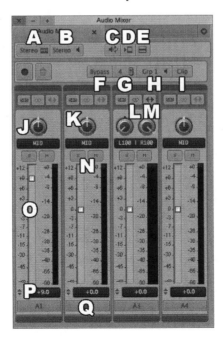

How to do it...

1. Open the **Audio Mixer** with any of these methods:

   i. **Tools Menu | Audio Mixer**.

   ii. **Windows | Workspaces | Audio Editing**.

   iii. Consider mapping the **Audio Mixer** menu selection to a convenient location on your keyboard. For example, I've placed this on *Shift + A*. More information on mapping buttons and menu selections can be found in the *Mapping buttons and menu selections* recipe in *Chapter 2, Customizing Your Work Environment*.

2. Click the **Audio Mixer Mode** button (letter **I** in the previous screenshot) so that it displays the text **Clip**.

How it works...

Later in this chapter we'll cover using the **Audio Mixer** when set to **Clip Mode**, but first let's examine the features in the previous screenshot:

▶ **A** (**Sequence Mix Format**): Informs Media Composer how the Sequence should be processed by the software. Selections are: Stereo, 5.1 and 7.1. Avid states, *"When you select a surround sound format, the Avid editing application displays the appropriate pan tools to use when you edit your sequence. Setting the surround sound format determines in which format you can mix your audio"*.

▶ **B** (**Monitor Mix**): Instructs Media Composer how the Sequence should be played back (monitored) in your edit suite. Selections include: Mono, Stereo, 5.1, and 7.1. See the **Avid Help** for additional details. The search term is Surround Monitoring. For example:

   ❑ If you are working on a Sequence that is in the 5.1 Surround Sound format and your edit suite is equipped to monitor all six channels, then you would set this to the appropriate 5.1 monitoring setting

   ❑ If you are working on a Sequence that is in the 5.1 Surround Sound format, but happen to be in an edit suite with only the ability to monitor 2 stereo channels, then in order to be able to hear all the channels you would need to monitor in Stereo

▶ **C** (**Audio Loop Play**): You can make adjustments while Media Composer loops. To do this, **Mark In/Out** for a portion of a Segment, one Segment, or multiple Segments. Then press the **Audio Loop Play** button. Make adjustments during the loop. Note that the changes will not be applied until the loop cycles back to the beginning. For this reason, you may find that selections of short durations work the best. Stop the looping playback by clicking the **Audio Loop Play** button. Any adjustments made during the audio looping will be applied.

▶ **D** (**Render Effect**): If you have applied an **AudioSuite Plug-In Effect** or an **EQ Effect** and rendered it, then adjusting the volume level or pan will require you to re-render the effect. You can use any method to perform the render; this button is provided as a convenience.

▶ **E** (**Audio Mixer Fast Menu**): Provides various functions, depending on the mode setting (**Clip**, **Auto**, or **Live**). Some of these selections are covered later in this chapter, in the sections that discuss using the **Audio Mixer** in **Clip Mode** and **Automation Mode** (Auto).

▶ **F** (**Bypass**): Avid states, *"Lets you temporarily turn off any Clip Volume or volume automation effects. This button functions the same as the Bypass panel in the Effects tab in the Audio Project Settings dialog box. (this control does not appear in Live Mix mode)".*

▶ **G** (**Mix Pane Size Toggle**): Allows you to toggle how many mixer channels are displayed. You can toggle between **4**, **8**, and **16**.

▶ **H** (**Mix Pane Display Toggle**): Toggles through the display of different mixer channels. For example, if you have chosen to display only 4 channels in the **Audio Mixer**, but your Sequence has 12 audio tracks. You can click this button to toggle between displaying channels **1** through **4**, then channels **5** through **8**, and then channels **9** through **12**.

▶ **I** (**Audio Mixer Mode Button**):

    ❑ **Clip**: Allows audio level and pan adjustment on a Segment basis. More information about using the **Audio Mixer** when in **Clip Mode** is included in this chapter.

    ❑ **Auto** (short for **Volume Automation**): Allows audio level and pan adjustment within a Segment by using keyframes. Further, keyframes can be added manually as well as recorded in Real Time. More information about using the **Audio Mixer** when in **Auto Mode** is included in this chapter.

    ❑ **Live:** Avid states, *"Lets you temporarily override any existing volume and pan automation settings. You can use the controls on the Audio Mixer tool or use an external controller to change volume and pan settings without modifying the existing volume and pan automation settings".* I'll add that these temporary adjustments can also be made permanent by using selections from the **Audio Mixer Fast Menu** when in **Live Mode**. I do not cover using this mode, but additional information is available in the **Avid Media Composer Help**. The search term is `Live Mix Mode`.

▶ **J** (**Pan Knob**): It may take a bit of getting used to using the knob. Your instinct may be to click on it and move your mouse up and down, but this will be frustrating. Instead, move your mouse left and right. Further, when a **Pan Knob** is selected, you can also type in a value to enter the pan value (be aware though, at the time of writing, the value does not appear as you type it). After typing in the value, *you must press the Return or Enter key*. Some helpful values are:

   ❑ **-100**: Panned 100 percent to the Left Channel

   ❑ **0**: Center Panned, which is indicated as **Mid**

   ❑ **100**: Panned 100 percent to the Right Channel

▶ **K** (**Group Button**): Note that in previous releases, this was referred to as the **Gang** button. Enable this for two or more channels. When channels are Grouped together, you will be able to adjust one slider and have the other Grouped slider(s) also be adjusted by the same amount.

▶ **L** (**Stereo Link**): Avid states, *"For stereo sequences, it links the two pan controls so that when you move one **Pan Location** cursor, the other moves in a parallel direction"*. Essentially, when you pan one channel more to the left or right, the other channel moves in the same direction, by the same amount.

▶ **M** (**Stereo Mirror**): This is only available by first enabling **Stereo Link**. Avid States, *"For stereo sequences, it links the two pan controls so that when you move one Pan Location cursor, the other moves in a mirrored direction—for example, if you drag the **Pan Location** cursor to the left, the corresponding cursor in the second X/Y grid moves to the right."* Essentially, when you pan one channel more to the left or right, the other channel moves in the opposite direction, by the same amount.

▶ **N** (**Solo and Mute** buttons): You can **Solo** or **Mute** multiple channels/tracks. Soloing a track is essentially for isolating it from the others. An example where using **Solo** would be helpful is if you had 12 audio tracks, but for a moment you wanted to hear only the dialog on **A1** along with the sound effect on **A5**. Muting is simply stopping the audio from being heard; any **RTAS Plug-Ins**, **Volume Automation**, **Pan Automation**, or **Real Time** (unrendered) **EQ** effects are still being processed. To lighten the processing burden on the computer, you can make the track Inactive (see the previous *Understanding the Track Control panel and Keyframe Selection tool* recipe).

▶ **O** (**Volume Level Adjustment Slider**): The value can be adjusted by:

   ❑ Use the cursor to grab and adjust the value up or down.

   ❑ Click on the dB numbers on the left-hand side of a channel to jump to one of the displayed values (for example, **+3**, **-7**, and so on).

   ❑ Select the **Slider** and type in a value (for example, **4.5**, **-12**, and so on). Note that you do not have to use the *Enter* or *Return* key after entering a value.

   ❑ *option/Alt* + Click anywhere within the **Slider Column** to set the level back to **0**.

▶ **P** (**Volume Level Display** and **Entry Box**): Displays the currently set value. You may also:

    ❑ Select the **Display/Entry Box** and type in a value (for example, **7.5**, **-17**, and so on.). Note that you do not have to use the *Enter* or *Return* key after entering a value.

    ❑ *option/Alt* + Click the **Display/Entry Box** to set the level back to **0**.

▶ **Q**: This is the **Channel/Track Enable** button.

Understanding the Audio Mixer Tool – Auto Mode

It's important to note that the **Audio Mixer Tool** has three different modes, each allowing different capabilities and functionality. The different modes are toggled using the **Audio Mixer Mode Button** (see letter **F** in the screenshot below).

Also see the previous *Understanding the Audio Mixer Tool: Clip Mode* recipe for additional information not presented here.

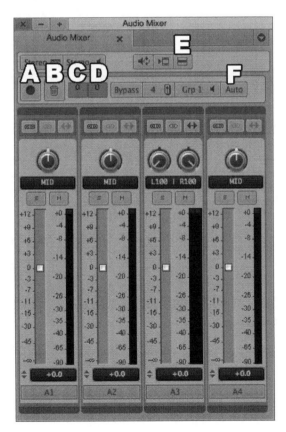

How to do it...

1. Open the **Audio Mixer** using either of the following methods:

    ❑ **Tools Menu | Audio Mixer.**

    ❑ **Windows | Workspaces | Audio Editing.**

    ❑ Consider mapping the **Audio Mixer** menu selection to a convenient location on your keyboard. For example, I've placed this on *Shift + A*. More information on mapping buttons and menu selections can be found in the *Mapping buttons and menu selections buttons* recipe in *Chapter 2, Customizing Your Work Environment.*

2. Click the **Audio Mixer Mode** button (letter **F** in the previous screenshot) so that it displays the text **Auto**.

How it works...

Later in this chapter we'll cover using the Audio Mixer when set to Auto Mode, but first let's get familiar with the tool itself:

▶ **A** (**Record Button**): Starts and stops the Real Time recording process. This process is discussed later in this chapter in the *Real Time Volume And Pan Adjustment Using Volume Automation And Pan Automation* recipe.

▶ **B** (**Cancel Button**): Stops the recording process and discards any keyframes that were recorded during that pass.

▶ **C** (**Preroll Entry Box**): Enter a value (for example, 5 = 5 seconds) for Media Composer to back up and play before the recording process begins. The Real Time recording process is discussed later in this chapter in the *Real Time Volume And Pan Adjustment Using Volume Automation And Pan Automation* recipe.

▶ **D** (**Postroll Entry Box**): Enter a value (for example, 2 = 2 seconds) for Media Composer to continue to play after the recording process has finished.

▶ **E** (**Audio Mixer Fast Menu**): Provides various functions, depending on the mode setting (**Clip**, **Auto**, or **Live**). Some of these selections are covered later in this chapter in the sections that discuss using the **Audio Mixer** in **Clip Mode** and **Automation Mode** (Auto).

▶ **F** (**Audio Mixer Mode Button**): Toggles between three settings: **Clip**, **Auto**, and **Live**. For additional details, please refer to letter **I** in the previous *Understanding the Audio Mixer Tool: Clip Mode* recipe.

Understanding the Audio Tool (Audio Meters)

In addition to evaluating a sound mix subjectively, we have to also evaluate it technically. The **Audio Tool** provides a variety of features to help us with the technical evaluation (and more).

How to do it...

▶   To open the **Audio Tool,** use either of the following methods:

    ❑   **Tools Menu | Audio Tool**

    ❑   *cmd/Ctrl + 1*

How it works...

Now lets take a closer look at the display and features of the **Audio Tool**.

- ▶ The measurement scale on the left-hand side is digital and uses the decibel scale, which is written as dB.

- ▶ The measurement scale on the right references the analog **Volume Units** scale, which is written as VU.

- ▶ On the digital scale, the highest value is zero. Audio above this level is clipped, and this is very *undesirable* as digital clipping causes distortion, making it sound terrible. On the VU scale, clipping occurs at *approximately* **20 VU**. After doing some mathematical calculations, it works out that **-20 dB** on the digital scale equates to **0 VU** on the analog scale. This is what Avid has set as the default, but it can be changed as needed (more on that in the next couple of bullet points).

- ▶ We mix so that generally the loudest average (also known as **Peak Average**) is around **-20 dB/0 VU**. However, it is generally allowed to have momentary peaks (called Transient Peaks) that can be louder. An example of a Transient Peak would be a single hand-clap, or a single drumbeat. It is generally allowed to have Transient Peaks extend as much as 6 dB higher. You'll see on the digital scale that the first value indicated above **-20 dB** is **-14 dB**, which is a difference of 6 dB. Also notice that the next level indicated above **-14 dB** is **-8 dB**, which again is a difference of 6 dB. As this information is only a general guide, it is a good idea to check with the broadcaster you are delivering to for the *exact* specifications that they require.

- ▶ The relationship of **-20 dB** to **0 VU** is not a hard and fast rule. On some productions, you may be asked to mix to a level of **-14 dB** (or some other level such as **-18 dB**). Generally, this is because you are outputting to an analog deck (for example, Beta-SP). When you are instructed to mix to a level such as **-14 dB**, you'll find it helpful to adjust the VU meter so that **0 VU** equates to **-14 dB** (or any other value dictated). How to adjust this (what is referred to as the Reference Level) will be covered just a bit later in this section (see the discussion of the Peak Hold Menu | "Set Reference Level").

- ▶ There is a grey button in the upper-left corner, labeled as **RP**. This is the Reset Peak button and its purpose is explained along with **Infinite Hold** just a few bullet points down.

There is what *appears* to be a grey button in the upper-right corner, labeled as **PH** (which stands for Peak Hold). When you click on it, you'll discover that it's not actually a button but a menu. Let's cover a few of the menu selections from the **Peak Hold Menu**:

- ▶ **Input Settings**: Opens the **Audio Project Settings** and reveals the **Input Tab**. **Audio Project Settings** can also be found here: **Project Window | Settings Tab | Audio Project**. The selections available here depend on what type of audio configuration you have with your system as well as what external hardware you are using.

▶ **Output Settings**: As with **Input Settings**, the selections available in **Output Settings** depend on what type of audio configuration you have with your system as well as what external hardware you are using. Take note of what Avid calls the **Mix Mode Selection Button**. When you click on it, you can toggle the output type. On software-only systems, it will toggle between **Stereo** and **Mono**. On systems with Avid hardware, there will be an additional option to send each track in your sequence out separately. This is called Direct Out. More information about Direct Out can be found in this chapter in the section that covers **Audio Project Settings**.

▶ **Peak Hold**: This is the default setting. This allows the peak loudness value to be displayed on the meter for an extra moment or two so that it is easier for us to see the peaks.

▶ **Infinite Hold**: This displays a horizontal line at the loudest/peak level. Because the line does not disappear automatically, they call it **Infinite Hold**. Since this holds a value on the meter, you will want to clear it when evaluating another portion of your film or capturing different footage. To do this, simply click the grey **RP** (**Reset Peaks**) button in the top-left corner. Infinite Hold can be useful in a variety of situations. Here are several:

   ❑ If you are having trouble noting the peak level value shown when the setting is **Peak Hold**, you can set it to **Infinite Hold**.

   ❑ If you'd like to watch a portion of your film and at the same time get information about audio peaks, this will allow you to concentrate on the film and then, after playback has ended, see the peak value.

   ❑ During capture, it's often common to leave that process unattended. If you use **Infinite Hold**, you can be aware of the peak audio value that occurred while capturing, and if it was too high.

▶ **Play Calibration Tone**: This plays out a reference tone, on all channels, at the value that is set in the **Set Reference Level** dialog (see next bullet point). This is a very useful feature for calibrating the devices, such as decks and mixers, that are connected to the editing system. It's also very useful for troubleshooting situations when you are unable to hear audio in your edit bay. This way you can send out a constant and uniform audio signal from your Avid system without having to loop a section of your Sequence. To stop the playback of the **Calibration Tone**, simply click anywhere on the **Audio Tool**.

▶ **Set Reference Level**: This allows you to enter an alternate value other than the default of **-20 dB**. This ensures that your digital value properly equates with **0 VU**.

▶ **Set Calibration Tone**: By default, Media Composer properly sets your **Reference Level** as the value for the **Calibration Tone**.

- **Create Tone Media**: Opens a dialog window allowing you to create a **Master Clip** of tone:

  - ❏ dB level defaults to the **Reference Level Setting**.
  - ❏ **Frequency of the tone**: The default is **1000 Hertz** (written as 1000 Hz). This is also referred to as a 1 kilohertz tone (1 kHz), and you'll hear people use a shorthand term as well and call it simply a 1 K tone. It can be adjusted if/when required.
  - ❏ **Tone Media Length**: This defaults to the commonly used 60 seconds (1 minute) that is used along with **Color Bars**, but you can set this to whatever length you need. Media Composer will not create media for the duration you set. It actually just creates one frame of media and tells the **Master Clip** to refer to that one frame over and over for the duration you specify. This is great because it is able to create the clip very quickly as well as take up a very small amount of space on the hard drive.
  - ❏ **Number of Tracks**: A nice convenience feature if you have to have tone on multiple tracks for a stereo output or a direct output (meaning each track in your Sequence goes out separately). This creates a **Master Clip** with the designated number of tracks so that when it comes time to edit it into the Sequence you can accomplish it with one edit rather than two or more.

Understanding Clip Gain and Pan versus Volume and Pan Automation

While the title of this section sounds complicated, this section is simply about understanding that the **Clip** setting of the **Audio Mixer** affects Segments *in their entirety*, while the **Auto** setting allows you to place keyframes *within* a Segment to affect *portions* of a segment differently.

You may find it helpful to first review the previous sections in this chapter that provide an overview of the **Audio Mixer**.

How to do it...

1. Open the **Audio Mixer** with any of the following methods:
   - ❏ **Tools Menu | Audio Mixer**.
   - ❏ **Windows | Workspaces | Audio Editing**.
   - ❏ Consider mapping the **Audio Mixer** menu selection to a convenient location on your keyboard. For example, I've placed this on *Shift + A*. For more information, go through *Mapping buttons and menu selections* recipe in *Chapter 2, Customizing Your Work Environment*.

2. Click the **Audio Mixer Mode** button so that it displays the text **Clip** or **Auto**.

3. Details on the **Audio Mixer** in these two modes can be found earlier in this chapter.

How it works...

Before covering these features in more depth, later in this chapter, I think it will be helpful to provide an overview of the differences between **Clip Gain** and **Clip Pan** versus **Volume Automation** and **Pan Automation** (referred to as **Automation Gain** and **Automation Pan** prior to Version 6).

▶ When the **Audio Mix Tool** is set to **Clip** (short for **Clip Gain**), the tool affects audio segments in their *entirety.* In other words it can only affect the level and pan for *whole* Segments; it can *not* affect only a *portion* of a Segment. Here, the software designers are using the term Clip and Segment interchangeably. This may help you remember what the **Clip** setting is programmed to do.

▶ You can divide a Segment into multiple, separate segments (that is, sections) using the **Add Edit** function. Then, each Segment's Level or Pan can be adjusted differently from the other(s). To smooth the transition of the Level or Pan from one Segment to another, you can add a dissolve. The longer the dissolve is, the longer (and more subtle) the level or pan change will be. This is discussed later in this chapter in the the *Using Clip Mode with Dissolves to smooth Level and Pan adjustments* recipe.

▶ **Volume Automation** and **Pan Automation** allow you to add keyframes and essentially graph changes of volume or pan *within* a single segment. In other words, with **Volume** and **Pan Automation** you do not have to cut a segment into separate segments (that is, sections) in order to affect different portions of it.

▶ New in Avid Media Composer Version 6, you do *not* have to display the **Volume** or **Pan Automation** in order to *add* keyframes *manually* to a segment *when using the level sliders or pan knobs.* In other words, moving a slider or pan knob when in **Auto** mode *will* add a keyframe. While convenient, it also means that you will need to be more aware of the **Clip/Auto** setting of your **Audio Mixer**. For emphasis, if you want to add a keyframe by pressing the **Add Keyframe** button, then you *must* have **Volume** or **Pan Automation** displayed in the **Timeline**. While this new programming is an interesting addition to the capabilities of the system, my instinct tells me that most will still want to display these the majority of the time, so that they can both see and adjust the keyframes.

▶ When you manually change the level or pan with the **Audio Mixer** set to **Clip**, it means that you will first make the adjustment and then, *in a second step,* play the adjusted region to evaluate it.

▶ When you *manually* add keyframes into the **Sequence**, and *manually* adjust them, it means that you will first make an adjustment and then, *in a second step,* play the adjusted region to evaluate it.

▶ When the **Audio Mix Tool** is set to **Auto**, it is possible to *record* your volume and pan adjustments *in Real Time.* In other words, you can make the changes while the Sequence plays in Real Time and *hear those changes occurring in Real Time.* This is discussed in the the *Real Time Volume and Pan adjustment* recipe.

▶ You can display any combination of **Waveforms**, **Clip Gain**, and **Volume Automation** in the **Timeline** at the same time. Or, you can display any combination of **Waveforms**, **Clip Gain**, and **Pan Automation** in the **Timeline** at the same time. In other words, you can not *display* **Volume** and **Pan Automation** at the same time. For emphasis, **Volume Automation** and **Pan Automation** changes (that is, using keyframes) *can be applied* to the same Segment, however, only one or the other can be *displayed* at a time.

▶ Adjustments made when the **Audio Mixer** is set to **Clip** are entirely separate from adjustments made with keyframes. Here are two examples where this is advantageous:

  ❑ Example 1 (**Low Audio**): In this example, I have a segment of audio that is very low, so I use **Clip Gain** to raise it up **+12dB** (the highest it will go). However, even after doing this, the audio is still too low. I can then use **Volume Automation** (keyrames) to raise that Segment (or a portion of that Segment) up as much as an additional **+12dB**. In other words, **Clip Gain** and **Volume Automation** are cumulative and I can raise a Segment's level up by as much as **+24dB** in total.

  ❑ Example 2 (**Quick Overall Change**): In my sequence, I have a long duration of music which I spent a good deal of time adjusting with many keyframes to make it louder in some portions and quieter in others. Then later, *without* my **Timeline** set to display the keyframes, I decide that I want to keep the volume keyframing as it is, but change the *overall* level of the music without having to switch the **Timeline View** and go through the other steps necessary to adjust the multiple keyframes. In this instance, I can use the **Audio Mixer** set to **Clip** to affect the overall level of the music without changing (or even having to display) the volume keyframes. Details on using the **Audio Mixer** set to **Clip Mode** begins with the *Clip Mode level and Pan Adjustments* recipe.

Understanding Audio Project Settings

Each time you create a new Project, Media Composer sets the **Audio Project Settings** to default values. However, you can adjust these settings if necessary.

How to do it...

Use either of these methods to access your **Audio Project Settings**:

▶ Go to **Project Window | Settings** tab and double-click the **Audio Project** settings to open them.

▶ Go to **Tools Menu | Audio Tool**. Click the **PH** button in the top-right corner to reveal the **Peak Hold Menu** and select **Input Settings**.

How it works...

Once you have opened the **Audio Project Settings**, you'll be presented with a window that has several sections (or tabs), that each offer various options.

In the tab labeled as **Main**, here are some options to be aware of:

▶ **The Sample Rate of your Project**: The default is **48 kHz**. This dictates the Sample Rate of audio when it is captured or imported as well as played during output.

▶ **Convert Sample Rates When Playing**: By default, Media Composer is set to play any audio that is not at the Project Sample Rate (the setting is **Always**). This is a handy feature until you have to output your Sequence to tape. When you output to a tape, the Sample Rate of all the audio elements must be the same (just in the same way that the video has to be all SD or all HD). This is discussed in Chapter 6 > "Changing Audio Sample Rate for Clips & Sequences."

▶ **Show Mismatched Sample Rates as Different Color**: The default setting is **Yes**. When you display the **Audio Waveforms** in the Sequence, audio that is at the same Sample Rate as the **Audio Project Sample Rate** setting will display as black. Audio that is not at the **Audio Project Sample Rate** will display as light grey.

In the tab labeled as **Input**, you can relate to the software where (what connection) the audio signal is coming from:

▶ The selections available here depend on what type of audio configuration you have with your system as well as what external hardware you are using. See the **Avid Media Composer Help** for additional information.

▶ **Input Source**: Allows you to select the available input sources, for example, **Host-1394** (also known as Firewire), **XLR**, **RCA**, **SDI**, **AES/EBU**, and so on.

In the tab labeled as **Output**, you can instruct how Media Composer will send the audio signal out of your system:

▶ The selections available here depend on what type of audio configuration you have with your system as well as what external hardware you are using. See the **Avid Media Composer Help** for additional information.

▶ **Output Gain**: Allows you to raise or lower the overall (also known as global) output of your system if required.

▶ **Mix Mode Selection Button**: When you click on it, you can toggle the output method, or as Avid puts it, *"How your system interprets audio values during playback."* On software-only systems, it will toggle between Stereo and Mono. On systems with hardware, there will be an additional option called **Direct Out**. This will send each track in your sequence out separately to the available output channels on the deck. By default it is set as a one-to-one relationship, but you can use the **Channel Assignment Menu** to set up whatever is required. The following is an example:

In my Sequence, I have eight tracks:

- ▶ **A1**: Narrator / Host on Camera
- ▶ **A2**: Interview Subjects
- ▶ **A3**: B-Roll audio (also known as Natural Sound or **Nats**)
- ▶ **A4**, **A5**, and **A6**: Sound effects
- ▶ **A7** and **A8**: Stereo Music

I am outputting to a tape format with only 4 available channels. If my goal is to create a Master Tape with the different audio elements split onto different channels, **Direct Out** allows me to assign specific tracks from my Sequence to specific channels on the deck. In this situation, I would assign (also known as **patch**) in the following way:

- ▶ **A1** and **A2** output to **Channel 1**
- ▶ **A3**, **A4**, **A5**, and **A6** output to **Channel 2**
- ▶ **A7** output to **Channel 3**
- ▶ **A8** output to **Channel 4**

The end result on the **Master Tape** is that I have the audio for the **Narrator, Host**, and **Interview Subjects** separate from the audio of the B-Roll and Sound Effects, and I keep the music in true stereo. This way if/when there is the need to repurpose the film, there will be greater flexibility. One example of this would be if I sold my English language documentary to a television station in Italy. Because all the dialog is separate from the other elements it will be easy to dub the film into Italian. Eccellente, eh?

Performing audio scrubbing: digital type scrubbing

Media Composer provides two types of audio scrubbing. One is a digital sounding scrub that might be described as staccato sounding (which is discussed in this recipe). The other is a more analogue sounding scrub that might be described as sounding like audio tape being rocked back and forth over the play-head on a tape machine (discussed in the recipe that follows this one).

How to do it...

1. Enable the **Digital Scrubbing** feature by either of these methods:

    i. Press and hold the *Shift* key.

    ii. Enable *Caps Lock*.

2. Scrub the audio by any of these methods:

    i. Moving the blue **Position Indicator**.

    ii. Use the **Step Forward** and **Step Backward** functions on the keyboard. By default, these are located on the *1, 2, 3,* and *4* keys. The *1* and *2* keys are **8** or **10** frames at a time (depending on Project Format), while the *3* and *4* keys are **1** frame at a time.

    iii. Use the **Step Forward** and **Step Backward** functions below the **Source** and **Record Windows**.

3. **Adjust the Digital Scrub Type**: By default, **Digital Audio Scrub** is set to **Fast Scrub** which smoothes out the playback of the scrubbing while also making it possible to scrub at nearly real time speed. If you'd like to have it slow down for a bit of additional precision then deselect the **Fast Scrub** feature which is found here: **Project Window | Settings Tab | Timeline Settings | Display Tab | Use Fast Scrub**.

Performing audio scrubbing: analogue type scrubbing

The more analogue sounding scrub (as opposed to digital scrub, discussed previoulsy) might be described as sounding like audio tape being rocked back and forth over the play-head on a tape machine.

How to do it...

1. Press and hold down the *Pause* Key. By default, this function is located on the *K* key.

2. While continuing to press the *K* key, do any of the following:

    i. Press and hold the *J* or the *L* key to scrub slowly either backward or forward.

    ii. Tap the *J* or *L* key quickly/momentarily to scrub one frame at a time either backward or forward.

How it works...

The multiple abilities of JKL are discussed in the *Moving around: Methods and tips* recipe in *Appendix A, Additional Tips, Tricks, and Explanations*.

Displaying Audio Waveforms (also known as Sample Plot)

Note that in earlier releases of Media Composer, **Audio Waveforms** were referred to as **Sample Plot** and that the display-type called **Energy Plot** has been removed.

It is also helpful to know that if you have audio with mismatched Sample Rates (meaning that a Clip's audio does not match the Project's Sample Rate as set in the **Audio Project Settings**), that those waveforms will be displayed as light grey, rather than black. There is more information about this in *Chapter 6, Changing Audio Sample Rate for Clips & Sequences*.

In this recipe, we'll cover the two methods available for displaying the **Audio Waveforms** in the **Timeline**, and in the *There's more...* section, we'll see how it's possible to display **Audio Waveforms** for **Source Material**.

How to do it...

This is the **first method** to **display waveforms in the timeline**. This method displays the audio waveform for *all* tracks, while the second method allows the waveforms to be displayed only on *selected* tracks.

1. Go to **Timeline Window Fast Menu** (hamburger-looking icon) in the bottom-left corner of the **Timeline Window**.

2. From the **Fast Menu**, select **Audio Data**.

3. From the **Sub-Menu**, select **Waveform**.

Alternatively, here's a second method to display waveforms in the timeline. This method allows the waveforms to be displayed only on selected tracks.

1. Open the **Track Control Panel** using one of these methods:

   i. **Timeline Window Fast Menu** (hamburger) in the bottom-left corner of the **Timeline Window | Track Control Panel**.

   ii. Click the **Track Control Panel** disclosure triangle found in the top-left of the **Timeline Window**, next to the **Timecode** display (see the next screenshot):

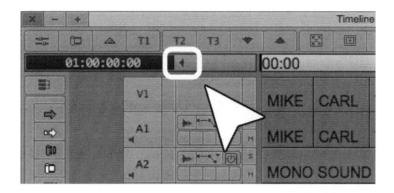

2. This reveals the **Audio Waveform Display** button for each individual track (see the next screenshot). Click this button to display or hide the waveform for a track.

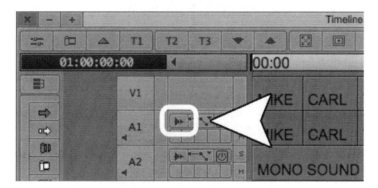

How it works...

Media Composer has to both calculate as well as draw the waveform display, so it may slow down the responsiveness of your system. This is why the per track display is a welcome addition. The more waveforms that must be drawn on screen, the more work for the computer, and the longer it will take. One method to reduce the redraw time is to zoom-in on the timeline, using the **More Detail** function or by using the **Focus** function (located, by default, on the letter *H* on the keyboard). See the *There's more...* section below for more related tips.

There's more...

There will be times when it is helpful to see the waveforms of material that is loaded into your **Source Window**, and there are a variety of helpful tips that relate to audio waveform display. We'll take a look at them below.

Displaying Waveforms for Source Material

Many users aren't aware that you can display the material that's loaded into your **Source Window** in the **Timeline Window**. Let's take a look at how easy it really is:

1. Load a Clip or Sequence containing audio into the **Source Window**.

2. Enable the **Audio Waveform Display**, using either method in the recipe of steps described earlier.

3. Step 4 will tell you how to switch the **Timeline** from displaying the Sequence that is loaded into the **Record Monitor** to instead displaying whatever (Clip or Sequence) has been loaded into the **Source Monitor**. To do this:

4. Click the **Toggle Source/Record In Timeline** button found in the bottom-left corner of the **Timeline** window, and next to the **Video Quality Menu** (see the next screenshot):

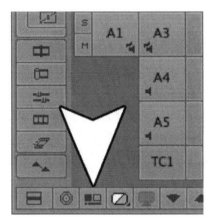

5. Notice that when you are viewing **Source Material** in the **Timeline Window**, Media Composer changes the color of the **Position Indicator** in the **Timeline** to green and that the icon for **Toggle Source/Record in Timeline** is also green. Additionally, the **Track Selectors** swap sides. In other words, while viewing **Source Material** in the **Timeline**, the **Source Track Selectors** will then be on the right and the **Sequence Track Selectors** will be on the left.

Tips When Displaying Waveforms

▶ The keyboard shortcut to make selected tracks wider or narrower is: *cmd/Ctrl + L*, and *cmd/Ctrl + K*, respectively (also located in the **Edit Menu**).

▶ Add one more key to the shortcut above and you will instead make the **Waveform Display** bigger or smaller on the selected tracks. The shortcut to make the waveform display larger or smaller is: *option/Alt + cmd/Ctrl + L*, and *option/Alt + cmd/Ctrl + K*, respectively.

▶ **Show Marked Waveforms:** By default, Media Composer will draw the waveforms for the entire duration of the Sequence, which can sometimes take a while. However, you can restrict it to drawing waveforms within a specific region by enabling this setting and then using a **Mark In** and **Mark Out** to define a shorter duration for the waveform display. For emphasis, no waveforms will be displayed unless you have placed both a **Mark In** and a **Mark Out** to define a region where the waveforms should be displayed. The setting to enable this feature is found here: **Project Window | Settings Tab | Timeline Settings | Display Tab | Show Marked Waveforms**.

▶ While the Waveforms are actually being drawn, if it is taking too long to draw them because you have a long Sequence and/or many audio tracks, you can stop the drawing process with the keyboard shortcut *cmd/Ctrl + the period key*.

▶ **Track Color**: You may find that when you are using the **Waveform** display, **Clip Gain** display and/or the **Volume/Pan Automation** display that you'd like to change the color of the track(s) to better see the display. You can do this by enabling the tracks you'd like to change, then going to: **Timeline Window Fast Menu** (hamburger) in the bottom-left corner of the **Timeline Window**, and then selecting **Track Color**. Here's an extra tip: if you hold down the *option/Alt* key while you select a color from the swatches, then you will open the color-picker window associated with your operating system (Mac or PC). This will give you a much wider selection of colors and brightness levels to choose from. For example, I sometimes like my tracks bright white.

▶ Make a **Timeline View** that includes the **Waveform Display**. This topic is covered in the *Creating Timeline views* recipe in *Chapter 2, Customizing Your Work Environment*.

▶ Map **Timeline Views** to the Keyboard. This topic is covered in the *Creating Timeline Views* recipe in *Chapter 2, Customizing Your Work Environment.*.

▶ Link a **Timeline View** to a Workspace. This topic is covered in *Linking Bin Layouts with Workspaces* in *Chapter 2, Customizing Your Work Environment*.

▶ Consider mapping the **Toggle Source/Record In Timeline** function (found in the **Command Palette | Other tab**) to a convenient location on your keyboard. Using the **Command Palette** to map button functions is covered in the *Mapping buttons and menu selections* recipe in *Chapter 2, Customizing Your Work Environment*.

▶ Consider mapping the menu selection that turns the waveform display on and off for all tracks to a convenient location on your keyboard. You can find it here: **Timeline Window Fast Menu** (hamburger) | **Audio Data** | **Waveform**. Using the **Command Palette** to map menu selections is covered in the *Mapping buttons and menu selections* recipe in *Chapter 2, Customizing Your Work Environment*.

Displaying Clip Gain, Volume Automation, and Pan Automation in the Timeline

In this recipe, we'll cover:

▶ Why you want/need to display **Volume/Pan Automation** and **Clip Gain**

▶ Two methods to display **Clip Gain** and **Volume Automation**

▶ The only method to display **Pan Automation** (due to the addition of 5.1 and 7.1 surround sound capabilities in Version 6)

Getting ready

First it is important to know *why* you would display **Volume/Pan Automation** and **Clip Gain**:

▶ Displaying **Volume Automation** and **Pan Automation** is required in order to be able to manually add keyframes, and manually adjust keyframes in Media Composer Version 5 and earlier. However:

  ❑ New in Avid Media Composer Version 6, you do *not* have to display the **Volume** or **Pan Automation** in order to *add* keyframes to a Segment *when using the* **Audio Mixer**'s *level sliders or pan knobs*. While this is convenient, it also means that you will need to be more aware of the **Clip/Auto** setting of your **Audio Mixer**. For emphasis, if you want to add a keyframe by *pressing the* **Add Keyframe** *button*, then you still *must* have **Volume** or **Pan Automation** displayed in the **Timeline**. While this new programming is an interesting addition to the capabilities of the system, my instinct tells me that most will still want to display these the majority of the time, so that they can both see and adjust the keyframes.

  ❑ If you are *recording* volume and/or pan changes in *Real Time,* then you do not have to have **Volume** or **Pan Automation** displayed (though you will most likely find it quite helpful). It's also helpful to know that **Volume Automation** and **Pan Automation** can *not* be *displayed* at the same time. For emphasis, you can certainly *apply* volume and pan changes to the same Segment using Automation keyframes, it's just that you can *not display* them at the same time.

▶ Displaying **Clip Gain** provides a helpful visual cue and/or reference so that you can see which segments, and how much those segments, have been adjusted using this method. Media Composer does this by displaying a black, horizontal line within segments that have been adjusted. For emphasis, the black, horizontal line will *not* appear within a segment unless it has been adjusted. This is a change from previous releases when the black line would appear immediately (at 0 VU), even if no adjustment had been made. It's also important to note that, even though there is a black line that you can see, you are *not* able to grab that line with your cursor and move it up or down in the Timeline; it is currently a display only.

How to do it...

There are two methods to display **Clip Gain** and **Volume Automation**, and one method to display **Pan Automation**.

This first method will allow you to display **Clip Gain** and/or **Volume Automation** for *all* tracks:

1. Go to **Timeline Window Fast Menu** (hamburger) in the bottom-left corner of the **Timeline Window**.

2. From the **Fast Menu**, select **Audio Data**.

3. From the **Sub-Menu**, select **Clip Gain**, **Volume Automation**, or **Pan Automation**.

4. Repeat this process to display additional audio data (for example, waveforms). Note that **Volume Automation** and **Pan Automation** can *not* be displayed at the same time.

This second method is the only way to display **Pan Automation**. It also allows **Clip Gain** and **Volume Automation**, or **Pan Automation**, to be displayed only on selected tracks.

1. Open the **Track Control Panel** using one of these methods:

   ❑ **Timeline Window Fast Menu** (hamburger) in the bottom-left corner of the **Timeline Window | Track Control Panel.**

   ❑ Click the **Track Control Panel** disclosure triangle found in the top-left of the **Timeline Window**, next to the **Timecode** display (see the next screenshot):

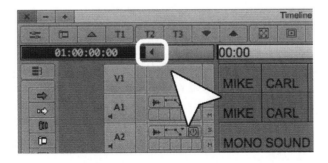

2. This reveals a menu for each individual track, allowing you to customize the display on a track by track basis (see the next screenshot):

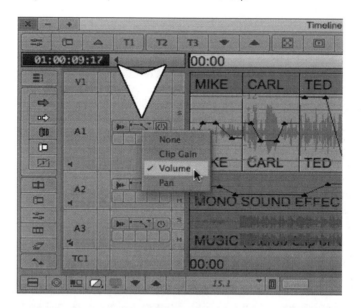

Clip Mode Level and Pan Adjustments

In the next several recipes, we'll be covering using **Clip Mode** with **Dissolves** to make Level and Pan adjustments, setting a common level to multiple segments simultaneously, and adjusting multiple segments simultaneously by a uniform amount. Once you understand these three things, then all the other available options from the **Audio Mixer Fast Menu** will make perfect sense.

First, let's open the **Audio Mixer** and get it set to **Clip Mode**:

How to do it...

1. Open the **Audio Mixer** with any of these methods:

   ❑ **Tools Menu | Audio Mixer**

   ❑ **Windows | Workspaces | Audio Editing**

   ❑ Consider mapping the **Audio Mixer** menu selection to a convenient location on your keyboard. For example, I've placed this on *Shift + A*. More information on mapping buttons and menu selections can be found in the *Mapping buttons and menu selections* recipe in *Chapter 2, Customizing Your Work Environment*.

2. Click the **Audio Mixer Mode** button so that it displays the text **Clip**.

How it works...

Following is some information that you will find helpful as you begin to use the **Audio Mixer**'s various functions as discussed in the several recipes later in this chapter.

▶ When the **Audio Mix Tool** is set to **Clip** (short for **Clip Gain**), the tool affects audio segments in their *entirety*. In other words, it can only affect the level and pan for *whole* segments; it can *not* affect only a *portion* of a Segment. Here, the software designers are using the term **Clip** and **Segment** interchangeably. This may help you remember what the **Clip** setting is programmed to do. We'll use a simple method, using dissolves, (detailed later in this chapter) to make it *seem* as if we have changed the level or pan within a segment and still used the **Audio Mixer** set to **Clip Mode**.

▶ For some operations (discussed below) found in the **Audio Mixer**'s **Fast Menu**, when there is no **Mark In** and/or **Mark Out**, then you will be affecting *all* the segments on the selected track(s). Avid refers to this as affecting the tracks Globally.

▶ For some operations provided in the **Audio Mixer Fast Menu** (discussed later), when you place a **Mark In** and/or a **Mark Out**, you are defining a *range of segments* to affect. Any segment that comes into contact with the **Mark In** and/or **Mark Out** (even if by only one frame), along with all the segments in between, will be affected. This leads some people to feel that they have to **Mark In** and **Mark Out** very precisely. Actually the opposite is true. This programming allows you to place your **Mark In** and **Mark Out** very *roughly*, only having to make sure that they are placed *somewhere* within the first segment you want to affect and somewhere within the last segment you want to affect. In the next screenshot, I would be affecting the **Reilly** Segment in its *entirety* through the **Kate** Segment in its *entirety*:

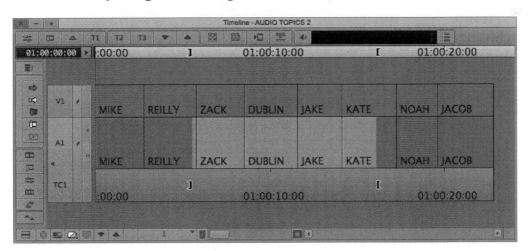

- ▸ For some operations provided in the **Audio Mixer Fast Menu** (discussed later), you can place only a **Mark In** and affect just the segments on the selected track(s) from the **Mark In** to the end of the Sequence.

- ▸ For some operations provided in the **Audio Mixer Fast Menu** (discussed later), you can place only a **Mark Out** and affect just the segments on the selected track(s) from the beginning of the Sequence to the **Mark Out**.

Using Clip Mode with Dissolves to smooth Level and Pan adjustments

While the **Audio Mixer** can only affect segments in their entirety, you can divide a Segment into multiple, separate segments (that is, sections) using the **Add Edit** function. Then, each Segment's Level or Pan can be adjusted differently from the other(s). To smooth the transition of the Level or Pan from one Segment to another, you can add a dissolve. The longer the dissolve is, the longer (and more subtle) the level or pan change will be.

How to do it...

1. Open the **Audio Mixer Tool**: **Tools Menu | Audio Mixer**.

2. Set the **Audio Mixer Mode** to **Clip**.

3. Enable the track(s) you want to affect.

4. Place the blue **Position Indicator** at the spot you want to divide a segment(s).

5. Press the **Add Edit** function. The **Add Edit** function's icon looks like the letter H turned on its side. By default, you'll find the **Add Edit** function in these locations:

    i. Under the **Record Monitor**, in the top row of buttons, on the right-hand side.

    ii. In the **Fast Menu Tool Palette** found between the yellow **Splice** arrow and the red **Overwrite** arrow.

    iii. In the **Command Palette**: **Tools Menu | Command Palette | Edit Tab**.

6. After dividing a segment of video or audio (but not **Filler**) you will of course see the cut, and you'll also notice a small, white equals symbol, which tells you two things:

    ❑ There is *no break in* **Timecode**. This is why Avid refers to this as a "Match Frame Edit."

    ❑ The white color tells you that there is no difference in level or pan between the segments. If/When there is a difference, the equals sign will be red. You can not remove a **Match Frame** edit if there is a difference between adjacent Segments. In other words, you can not remove a **Match Frame** edit when the equals symbol is red. See the *There's more...* section below for information on how to remove white **Match Frame** edits.

7. Place your blue **Position Indicator** onto the segment you want to adjust.

8. Use the **Audio Mixer Tool** in **Clip Mode** to adjust the level and/or pan.

9. Play the region you've adjusted to evaluate it.

10. Add a dissolve where you placed your **Add Edit**, using the **Quick Transition** function, to smooth the transition in level and/or pan. By default, you can find the **Quick Transition** function in these locations:

     i.   Back Slash Key, just above the *Return* key.

     ii. On the **Timeline Tool Bar** (by default it's the fifth button from the left).

     iii. In the **Fast Menu Tool Palette** found between the yellow **Splice** arrow and the red **Overwrite** arrow. It will be the first button on the top row.

     iv. **Command Palette**: **Tool Menu | Command Palette | FX Tab**.

How it works...

Remember that you are still affecting individual segments. The key is that there is no interruption or break in the flow of the actual content. Further, it's helpful to realize that you can trim a transition point early or later to adjust the position of the Pan and/or Volume change.

Added Trivia: The equals symbol comes from editing film when using a Workprint. It would be written at a cut-point on the Workprint very boldly, using a grease pencil. The equals symbol was used to communicate to the person conforming the film negative (known as the Conformer, or Negative Matcher) that a particular cut in the Workprint was an Unintended Splice and that they should not pay attention to it when cutting-up the negative.

There's more...

Removing **Match Frame Edits** – you can remove **Match Frame Edits** as long as the equals symbol at the cut point is white (not red). White indicates that there is no difference between the segments (for example, volume levels must be the same). Note that there will not be an equals symbol displayed when **Add Edits** (cuts) are placed in **Filler**. To remove **Match Frame Edits**, use either of the following methods:

Remove Match Frame Edits In Source/Record Mode

1. Enable the Track Selectors for the track(s) that contain **Match Frame Edits** you want to remove.

2. **Mark In/Out** to affect only a portion of **Match Frame** edits. Without Marks, you will be affecting all the white **Match Frame Edits** (and those in **Filler**) on the enabled track(s).

3. Do one of the following:

    i. **Clip Menu | Remove Match Frame Edits**.

    ii. Right-Click in the **Timeline** and select **Remove Match Frame Edits** from the contextual menu.

Remove Match Frame Edits In Trim Mode

Note that this method only works when the **Trim Rollers** are either Single (A-Side or B-Side), or **Double/Dual** (on both the A-Side and B-Side simultaneously). In other words, it does *not* work if you are in Slip or Slide.

1. Enter **Trim Mode** on a track(s) at a white **Match Frame Edit** or at a cut-point on a **Filler** track.

2. Press the *Delete* key.

3. Note that you will remain in **Trim Mode**. If there are no transitions with **Trim Rollers** on them, then the two monitors will display only black. Nothing is broken. Simply exit **Trim Mode** and notice that the **Match Frame Edits** have been removed.

Clip Mode: Setting a common Level or Pan to multiple segments

Overview example: imagine that you have many segments of narration (also known as Voice Over) on track **A1**. You edited them all in without making any changes to the original level they were recorded at. You recently added some music, ambience, and other sound effects and you have just adjusted one segment of Voice Over to mix better with the other audio elements. Now you want to make all the other Voice Over segments the same level as the one you just adjusted (rather than have to adjust them one by one).

How to do it...

This set of steps presumes that you have *already* adjusted one segment in your Sequence to a particular level and now want to make other segments on that same track to be the same level, as in the earlier Overview example.

1. Enable the Track Selectors for the track(s) you want to affect. In the situation described earlier, you would enable just track **A1**.

2. This step is optional: **Mark In** and **Mark Out** around a portion of the segments in order to define a region of segments to affect. If you do not have marks, then you will affect all the segments on the selected track(s) from beginning to end (that is, global). Details on using Marks to define a range/region of Segments to affect is above in *Clip Mode Level and Pan Adjustments*.

3. Place your blue **Position Indicator** on the segment that you have already adjusted. You can think of this segment as the guide segment, because you're going to tell other segments to be at the same level (or pan) setting as that one.

4. Go to the **Fast Menu** (hamburger-looking icon) located in the top row of buttons on the **Audio Mixer Tool**.

5. Select **Set Level On Track** (or **Set Pan On Track**) to set other segments to the same level (or pan value) as the guide segment you are parked on.

How it works...

Remember these things:

▶ For the active (enabled) track(s), the Segment that your blue **Position Indicator** is parked on is the guide Segment, and will tell the other Segments on that track(s) to be the same level (or pan) setting as that one.

▶ If you have no **Mark In** or **Mark Out**, then the command will affect all the Segments on the enabled track(s) Globally; and you can isolate portions of the track by using **Mark In**, **Mark Out**, or both.

Clip Mode: Adjusting multiple segments by a uniform amount

Overview example: imagine that you have many segments of dialog on tracks **A1** and **A2**. You edited them all in before adding other audio elements (for example, music). You have meticulously adjusted each segment of dialog to what you felt at the time was just the perfect level. Later, you added some music, ambience, and other sound effects and now realize the following:

▶ The various levels you set for the dialog segments are still perfect in relation to *each other* (meaning that all the actors are at an even level, one actor is not disproportionately louder or quieter than another)

▶ Now that you've added the other audio elements (music, and so on.), you need to adjust the dialog segments a bit louder without losing the relationship between them which you've already established

How to do it...

1. Enable the Track Selectors for the track(s) you want to affect. In the Overview example described earlier, you would enable just tracks **A1** and **A2**.

2. This step is optional: **Mark In** and **Mark Out** around a portion of the segments on the track(s) in order to define a region of segments to affect. If you do not have marks, then you will affect all the segments on the selected track(s) from beginning to end (that is, global). Details on using Marks to define a range/region of Segments to affect is earlier in *Clip Mode Level and Pan Adjustments*.

3. Go to the **Fast Menu** (hamburger-looking icon) located in the top row of buttons on the **Audio Mixer Tool**.

4. Select **Adjust Pan/Vols On Track**.

5. The **Adjust Pan/Volume** dialog window will open.

6. Enter a value for **Gain** (volume) or for pan.

    ❑   Positive values increase the level, or pan the audio to the right channel

    ❑   Negative values lower the level, or pan the audio to the left channel

7. Click **OK**.

How it works...

Remember these things:

▶   This process affects only Segments on tracks that are enabled

▶   If you have no **Mark In** or **Mark Out**, then the command will affect all the Segments on the enabled track(s) Globally; and you can isolate a range/region of Segments by using **Mark In**, **Mark Out**, or both

Manually adding and adjusting Volume and Pan Automation keyframes

Before reading this recipe, you may find it helpful to first read the previous sections in this chapter that discuss the topics of the Audio Mixer Tool, Clip Gain & Pan vs. Volume & Pan Automation, Displaying Clip Gain, Volume Automation and Pan Automation in the Timeline, and Clip Mode Level & Pan Adjustments.

In this recipe, we'll discuss how to manually add keyframes in order to adjust Volume levels and Pan values within a Segment.

Getting ready

The following points will be helpful when you want to make adjustments using keyframes:

- Displaying **Volume Automation** and **Pan Automation** is _required_ in order to be able to manually add keyframes (for example, clicking the **Add Keyframe** button), and manually adjust keyframes in Media Composer Version 5 and earlier.

- Now in Avid Media Composer Version 6, you do not have to display the **Volume** or **Pan Automation** in order to add keyframes to a Segment when using the **Audio Mixer**'s level sliders or pan knobs. This means that you will need to be more aware of the **Clip/Auto** setting of your **Audio Mixer**. For emphasis, if you want to add a keyframe by pressing the **Add Keyframe** button, then you still must have **Volume** or **Pan Automation** displayed in the **Timeline**.

- In order to manually adjust or remove/delete keyframes, the **Keyframe Selection Tool** must be enabled (it is enabled by default). This button is located on the left-hand side of the **Timeline Window**, at the bottom of what Avid calls the **Timeline Palette** (see the white arrow in the next screenshot). If this button is not enabled, then you will not be able to use the cursor as described later.

- You can not display **Volume** and **Pan Automation** at the same time. For emphasis, **Volume Automation** and **Pan Automation** changes (that is, using keyframes) can be _applied_ to the same Segment, however, only one or the other can be _displayed_ at a time.

- When you are manually adjusting volume level keyframes in the **Timeline**, using the cursor (the hand icon), the dB level will appear in the same location as the **Timeline View Menu** (see the next screenshot):

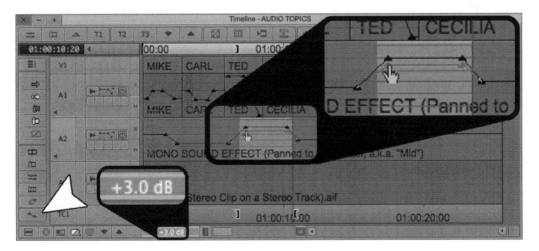

▶ Manually adding keyframes into the **Timeline**, and manually adjusting them, means that you will first make an adjustment and then, *in a second step*, play the adjusted region to evaluate it.

▶ When the **Audio Mix Tool** is set to **Auto**, it is possible to *record* your volume and pan adjustments *in real time*. In other words, you can make the changes in real time and *hear those changes occurring in real time*. This is discussed in this chapter, in the *Real Time Volume and Pan Adjustment* recipe.

How to do it...

Let's take a look at how to *manually* add keyframes for **Volume** and **Pan Automation**. Media Composer Version 6 provides two methods for adding keyframes manually.

1. Open the **Audio Mixer**: **Tools Menu | Audio Mixer**.

2. Set the **Audio Mixer** to the **Automation** (Auto) setting, rather than the **Clip** or **Live** setting.

3. Enable the Track Selector(s) for the tracks to which you want to add keyframes.

4. Add a keyframe with either one of these methods:

   ❑ Method 1 (without **Volume** or **Pan Automation** displayed): Make an adjustment using the Level Slider(s) and/or Pan Knobs. Even though **Volume** or **Pan Automation** is not displayed, in Version 6, you will still be adding a keyframe.

   ❑ Method 2 (with **Volume** or **Pan Automation** displayed): You can now:

   i. First, press the **Add Keyframe** button on the keyboard (by default on the Apostrophe key). Note that if your tracks are very narrow, this may not work. To make the tracks wider, use the keyboard shortcut *cmd/Ctrl + L*. To make them narrower the shortcut is *cmd/Ctrl + K*.

   ii. Next, make an adjustment using either the Level Slider(s) and/or Pan Knob(s) on the **Audio Mixer**, or by grabbing the keyframes with your cursor and moving them manually.

Removing/Deleting Volume and Pan Automation Keyframes

Media Composer provides two methods to remove/delete keyframes. The *How to do it...* section will present one method and the second method will be discussed in the *There's more...* section.

This first method will use the **Audio Mixer's Fast Menu**:

▶ Using this method does *not* require you to display **Volume** or **Pan Automation** (though you may), while the second method, in the *There's more...* section, *does* require it.

▶ This first method is used to remove *multiple* keyframes only. The second method, in the *There's more...* section, allows you to remove either a single keyframe or multiple keyframes.

How to do it...

1. Open the **Audio Mixer**: **Tools Menu | Audio Mixer**.

2. Set the **Audio Mixer** to the **Automation** (Auto) setting rather than the **Clip** or **Live** setting.

3. Enable the Track Selector(s) for the track(s) from which you want to remove/delete keyframes.

4. This step is optional: **Mark In** and **Mark Out** around a portion of one or more segments in order to define a range (or you could call it a region) of keyframes to remove. If you do not have marks, then you will affect *all* the keyframes within *all* the segments on the selected track(s) from beginning to end (that is, global). Details on using Marks to define a range/region of Segments to affect is earlier in the *Clip Mode Level and Pan Adjustments*.

5. Go to the **Fast Menu** (hamburger-looking icon) located in the top row of buttons on the **Audio Mixer Tool**.

6. Select any of the following, depending on your needs:

   ❑ Remove **Volume Automation On Track**

   ❑ Remove **Pan On Track**

   ❑ Remove **Pan/Volume On Track**

There's more...

This second method of removing keyframes uses the cursor. It's helpful to be aware of the following:

▶ Using this method does require you to display **Volume** or **Pan Automation**, while the method in the recipe does not.

▶ This method allows you to remove a single keyframe or multiple keyframes. The method in the recipe is used to remove multiple keyframes only.

Follow these steps:

1. Make sure that the **Keyframe Selection Tool** *is enabled* (it is enabled by default). This button is located on the left-hand side of the **Timeline Window**, at the bottom of what Avid calls the **Timeline Palette** (see the white arrow in the next screenshot). If this button is not enabled, then you will not be able to use the cursor as described later.

2. Enable the Track Selector(s) for the track(s) from which you want to remove a single keyframe or multiple keyframes.

3. This is an an optional step: **Mark In** and **Mark Out** around a portion of one or more segments in order to define a range (or you could call it a region) of keyframes to remove. If you do not have **In/Out Marks**, then you will only be affecting *one keyframe at a time on any enabled track.*

4. Park your cursor arrow over a single keyframe so that the Hand Icon appears (see the next screenshot). You do not have to click on the keyframe, only to park your cursor over it to make the Hand Icon appear. This is important because if you do not see the hand icon, then Media Composer will think you want to delete the entire track itself, rather than just a keyframe(s) on that track(s).

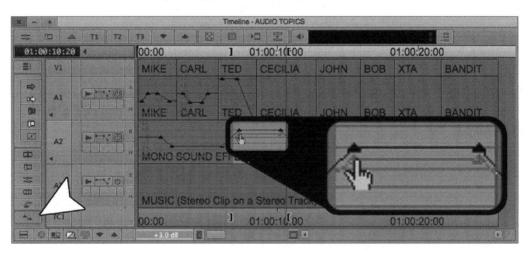

5. Press the *Delete* key.

6. These are the two possible results:

   ❑ If you do *not* have **In/Out Marks** defining a range of keyframes, *and* if you have *multiple tracks enabled, and* if there is a keyframe on the *same frame* on multiple tracks, then a single keyframe will be removed from *each* of the *enabled* tracks

   ❑ If you have **In/Out Marks** defining a range of keyframes, then *all* the keyframes within that range will be deleted from *all* the *enabled* tracks

How it works...

The key factors for adjusting and deleting keframes in the **Timeline Window** are:

▸ Make sure that the **Keyframe Selection Tool** is enabled.

▸ Make sure that the **Hand Icon** is visible before grabbing/adjusting, or deleting, a keyframe

Adjusting multiple audio keyframes simultaneously

Media Composer provides two methods to adjust multiple keyframes at the same time. The *How to do it...* section will cover one method, while the *There's more...* section will present the second.

This first method uses the **Audio Mixer**'s **Fast Menu**. Here are some differences between the two methods before we start the recipe:

▸ Using this method does *not* require you to display **Volume** or **Pan Automation** (though you may), while the second method, in the *There's more...* section, does require it.

▸ This method is used to adjust *multiple keyframes only*. The second method allows you to adjust either a single keyframe or multiple keyframes.

How to do it...

1. Open the **Audio Mixer**: **Tools Menu | Audio Mixer**.

2. Set the **Audio Mixer** to the **Automation** (Auto) setting, rather than the **Clip** or **Live setting**.

3. Enable the Track Selector(s) for the track(s) on which you want to adjust keyframes.

4. This is an optional step: **Mark In** and **Mark Out** around a portion of one or more segments in order to define a range (or you could call it a region) of keyframes to adjust. If you do not have marks, then you will affect *all* the keyframes within *all* the segments on the selected track(s) from beginning to end (that is, global). Details on using Marks to define a range/region of Segments to affect is earlier in the *Clip Mode Level and Pan Adjustments* recipe.

5. Go to the **Fast Menu** (hamburger-looking icon) located in the top row of buttons on the **Audio Mixer Tool**.

6. Select **Adjust Pan/Volume On Track**.

7. The **Adjust Pan/Volume** dialog window will open.

8. Enter a value for **Gain** (volume) or for Pan.

   ❑ Positive values increase the level, or pan the audio to the right channel

   ❑ Negative values lower the level, or pan the audio to the left channel

9. Click **OK**.

There's more

In this section, we'll take a look at a second method of adjusting multiple keyframes at the same time, and following that you'll find some additional tips for when you're using keyframes.

This second method uses the cursor directly in the **Timeline**. Before we go through the steps, it's helpful to be aware of the following:

▸ Using this method *does* require you to display **Volume** or **Pan Automation**, while the method in the recipe above does not

▸ This method allows you to adjust either a single keyframe or multiple keyframes, while the first method is used to adjust *multiple keyframes only*

Now let's go through the steps for the second method:

1. Make sure that the **Keyframe Selection Tool** *is enabled* (it is enabled by default). This button is located on the left-hand side of the **Timeline Window**, at the bottom of what Avid calls the **Timeline Palette** (see the white arrow in the next screenshot). If this button is not enabled, then you will not be able to use the cursor as described later.

2. Enable the Track Selector(s) for the track(s) on which you want to adjust a single keyframe or multiple keyframes.

3. This step is optional: **Mark In** and **Mark Out** around a portion of one Segment, an entire Segment or multiple Segments in order to define a range/region) of keyframes to adjust. If you do not have **In/Out Marks**, then you will only be affecting *one keyframe at a time on any enabled track*. Details on using Marks to define a range/region of Segments to affect is earlier in the *Clip Mode Level and Pan Adjustments* recipe.

4. Park your cursor arrow over a single keyframe so that the Hand Icon appears (see the next screenshot):

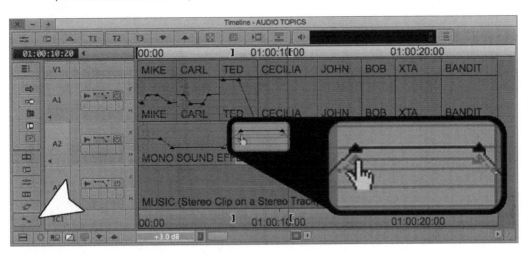

5. Press the mouse button to grab the keyframe and adjust it.

6. These are the two possible results:

- ❑ If you do *not* have **In/Out Marks** defining a range of keyframes, *and* if you have *multiple tracks enabled*, *and* if there is a keyframe on the *same frame* on multiple tracks, then a single keyframe will be adjusted on *each* of the *enabled* tracks.

- ❑ If you have **In/Out Marks** defining a range of keyframes, then *all* the keyframes within that range will be adjusted on *all* the *enabled* tracks. For emphasis, when you **Mark In** and **Mark Out** you're defining a range of keyframes that you want Media Composer to pay attention to on the tracks that you've enabled.

The following are some helpful tips when using keyframes:

▶ When manually adjusting volume level keyframes in the **Timeline**, the dB level will appear in the same location as the **Timeline View Menu** (see the next screenshot):

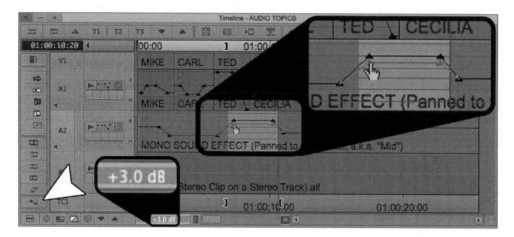

▶ Make the keyframe(s) snap to the decibel lines of the **Volume Automation Display** by pressing the *cmd/Ctrl* key as you adjust them. You may find that for this to be useful that you'll need to adjust the track height much wider. One way to do this is to use the keyboard shortcut *cmd/Ctrl + L* (*cmd/Ctrl + K* will make selected tracks narrower).

▶ To move a *single* keyframe horizontally, in order to lengthen or shorten the duration of the change between keyframes (that is, the "ramp"), then follow these steps:

    i.   Make sure that the **Keyframe Selection Tool** is enabled (it is enabled by default). This button is located on the left-hand side of the **Timeline Window**, at the bottom of what Avid calls the **Timeline Palette** (see the white arrow in the previous screenshot). If this button is not enabled, then you will not be able to use the cursor as described later.

    ii.   Enable the Track Selector(s) for the track(s) on which you want to adjust a single keyframe.

    iii. First, park your cursor arrow over a single keyframe so that the Hand Icon appears.

    iv. Then, press and hold the *option/Alt* key.

    v.   Then click on that keyframe and adjust the keyframe's position horizontally. Note that when you are adjusting horizontally, you can not adjust vertically (so that you don't accidentally change the value).

Real Time Volume and Pan Adjustment

When you make adjustments to pan or volume level using the **Audio Mixer** set to **Clip Mode**, or by manually adding and adjusting keyframes, you do not get instant feedback about how well that adjustment sounds. In other words, you first make an adjustment and then, in a second step, you go back and play the section you just adjusted in order to listen to it and evaluate it.

However, using the method discussed in this recipe, you'll be able to make level and pan adjustments while Avid Media Composer is actually playing, and you'll also be able to hear the result of those adjustments immediately in Real Time. Additionally, while you're making those adjustments, Media Composer is recording them as keyframes and you can adjust them after the recording is completed if you need to.

This recipe will be covering how to use the Media Composer software to accomplish **Real Time Volume** and **Pan Adjustment**. However, it's also good to know that it's possible to attach certain hardware mixers (for example, Avid's **Command 8** mixer) that allow you to make adjustments, by physically moving faders on the attached mixer, and have those adjustments translated into keyframes and applied to your Sequence in Real Time.

How to do it...

1. Open the **Audio Mixer**: **Tools Menu | Audio Mixer**.

2. Set the **Audio Mixer** to **Automation Mode** (Auto), rather than **Clip Mode** or **Live Mode**. An overview of the Audio Mixer can be found in the previous *Understanding the Audio Mixer Tool – Auto Mode recipe*.

3. Display **Volume** or **Pan Automation**. While this is not required to record volume level and pan adjustments in Real Time, I think you'll find it helpful.

4. Enter a value in the **Preroll** entry box (for example, 5 = 5 seconds). This tells Media Composer an amount of time to back up and play before actually beginning the recording process. This will give you some time to move your cursor from the **Record Button** to a level slider or pan knob, and to get your bearings before needing to make adjustments.

5. This step is optional: Enter a value in the **Postroll** entry box. This tells Media Composer an amount of time to continue to play after the recording process has actually stopped. This only applies if there is a **Mark Out** in the Sequence (Marks are discussed in more detail in the *How it works... section*).

6. Determine the area you want to perform **Volume** or **Pan Automation** recording. To do this, you can do any of the following:

   ❏ Have *no* **Mark In** or **Mark Out** placed in your Sequence: If there are no marks, then Media Composer will consider wherever your blue **Position Indicator** is placed to be the spot where you want to begin recording. In this situation, you will have to *manually* stop the recording process (discussed later in this recipe).

   ❏ Place only a **Mark In**: Just as with placing no marks, you will have to *manually* stop the recording process. Placing a **Mark In** tells Media Composer *exactly* where you want to begin recording, as well as protects any keyframes that already exist before the **Mark In** from being accidentally recorded over and also, marks that spot to make it easy to repeat the recording process, if the first attempt didn't produce a good result.

   ❏ Place only a **Mark Out**: This tells Media Composer *exactly* where to stop the recording process, as well as protects any keyframes that already exist after the **Mark Out** from being accidentally recorded over.

   ❏ Mark a **Region**: Place both a **Mark In** and a **Mark Out** to define a specific region for recording.

7. Click the **Record** button to begin the recording process. The **Record** button (with a red dot in the center) is in the top, left corner of the **Audio Mixer**.

8. The **Record** button will blink red to tell you when the recording process is in progress.

9. You can manually stop the recording process at any time by:

   ❏ Clicking the **Record** button – This stops the recording process and *keeps* any keyframes you recorded during that pass.

   ❏ Clicking the **Trash Can Icon** (Avid calls it the **Cancel** button) – If during the recording process you want to stop and also have Media Composer *throw away* the keyframes that were recorded during that pass, you can click the **Trash Can Icon**.

How it works...

During the recording process, Media Composer creates many keyframes as you adjust the pan knobs and/or the volume sliders. You may need to zoom in on the **Timeline** (for example, using **More Detail**) to actually see all the keyframes.

You can use the following tips in order to make adjustments to the keyframes that were recorded:

▶ Use the methods discussed earlier in this chapter in the section titled "Adjusting Multiple Keyframes Simultaneously."

▶ If you would like to reduce the number of keyframes that were recorded, you can follow the steps below:

  ❑ First, enable the Track Selector(s) for the track(s) you want to affect.

  ❑ Second, **Mark In/Out** around a region of keyframes you would like to reduce.

  ❑ Third, go to the **Fast Menu** (hamburger) at the top of the **Audio Mixer**.

  ❑ Lastly, select **Filter Volume Automation** or **Filter Pan Automation**, depending on your situation. Each time you select either of these from the **Fast Menu**, approximately 10 percent of the keyframes are removed and the graphing is simplified. Repeat this as many times as desired. Once the graph reaches its most simple form, then no more keyframes will be removed.

Creating Stereo, 5.1 and 7.1 ("Multichannel") Tracks in a Sequence

Before we dive into the recipes, let's go over some information about the differences between **Mono** tracks and **Stereo** tracks in a Sequence:

▶ At the time of writing, Media Composer provides up to 24 audio tracks in a Sequence and provides the ability to hear any 16 of the displayed 24 tracks. In Avid ProTools lingo, they'd say that there are 24 tracks and 16 Voices. For most of us, 16 tracks are enough. For those that need to output more, they can perform an **Audio Mixdown** (also known as Bouncing Tracks in the audio mixing world). **Audio Mixdown** is a selection from the **Special Menu**.

▶ Avid refers to **Clips** and **Tracks** that are Stereo, 5.1 and 7.1 as being Multichannel.

▶ **Clips** and their **Audio Tracks** can be Mono, Stereo, 5.1 Surround Sound, or 7.1 Surround Sound. A recipe a bit later in this chapter discusses how to create **Multichannel Clips**.

▶ You can have any combination of track-types in a Sequence.

▶ Only Mono elements can be edited onto Mono tracks, Stereo elements onto Stereo tracks, and so on.

- In a Sequence, you can convert Stereo, 5.1, and 7.1 tracks into separate Mono tracks. However, you can *not* do the reverse.

- In Version 6, Media Composer relates the track type with an icon or text placed on the **Audio Track Selector** (see the next screenshot):

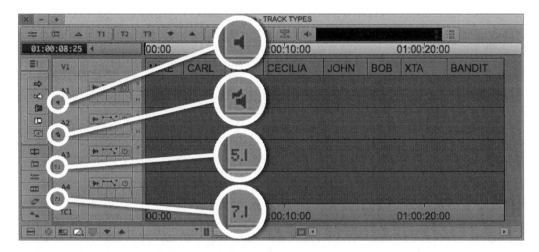

Now that you have an overview of Multichannel tracks, let's look at the two methods to create Multichannel tracks in a Sequence.

How to do it...

This is the first method you can add a Multichannel track to a Sequence:

1. Create a new Sequence, or load an existing Sequence into the **Timeline Window**.
2. Go to **Clip Menu**.
3. Select **New Audio Track**.
4. From the **Submenu**, select **Mono**, **Stereo**, **5.1 Surround**, or **7.1 Surround**.

You can also add a Multichannel track to a Sequence this way:

1. Create a new Sequence, or load an existing Sequence into the **Timeline Window**.
2. Right-click in the **Timeline Window**.
3. Select **New Audio Track**.
4. From the **Submenu**, select **Mono**, **Stereo**, **5.1 Surround**, or **7.1 Surround**.

Converting a multichannel track into mono tracks in a Sequence

First, it's important to note that you can convert a Multichannel track into separate mono tracks, but you can *not* do the reverse.

You can convert a Multichannel track(s) into separate mono tracks in two ways. The first method allows you to convert specific tracks, individually, while the second method will convert *all* the tracks in the Sequence.

How to do it...

This first method will let you convert individual Multichannel tracks into separate Mono tracks.

1. Duplicate the Sequence(s) before converting tracks. To do this, first select the Sequence(s) in the bin. Then go to **Edit Menu | Duplicate**. Lastly, amend the Sequence name(s) to indicate which is Multichannnel and which is Mono.

2. Make sure the correct Sequence is loaded in the **Record Monitor/Timeline** (that is, the one that is to have a Multichannel track converted to mono tracks).

3. In the **Timeline**, right-click on the **Track Selector** of the Multichannel track you want to convert.

4. From the **Contextual Menu** that appears, select **Split Track To Mono**.

This second method is a fast way to convert *all* of the Multichannel tracks in a Sequence(s) into separate Mono tracks:

1. In a bin, select the Sequence(s) for which you want to have *all* the Multichannel tracks converted into individual Mono tracks.

2. Go to: **Clip Menu | Split All Tracks To Mono**.

3. Media Composer will automatically create a duplicate Sequence and convert all Multichannel tracks to individual Mono tracks.

4. Amend the Sequence name(s) to indicate which are Multichannnel and which are Mono.

See also

▶ The *Making Multichannel Clips (Stereo, 5.1 and 7.1)* recipe

Making Multichannel Clips (Stereo, 5.1 and 7.1)

A Clip can have all its audio tracks as separate Mono tracks, or you can have a clip with two or more audio tracks *interpreted* by Media Composer as Stereo, 5.1 Surround Sound, or 7.1 Surround Sound. With regard to **Stereo Clips**, the benefit is rather than have two mono channels (Left and Right) take up two tracks in the Sequence, you can have the Stereo pair take up just one track. In Sequences with many Stereo elements (for example, music, ambiance, layers of sound effects, and so on) this means that if you treat them as one Stereo track, rather than two mono tracks, you'll have more space available. Further, you may find that adjusting volume level is faster and easier as well.

As I mentioned, at the beginning of this chapter, my discussions in this book will be focusing on **Mono** and **Stereo Clips** and **Tracks**, though in this instance the same methods used to make **Stereo Clips** can also be used to make 5.1 and 7.1 Surround Sound clips.

The recipe itself will present how to convert **Mono Clips** into **Multichannel Clips** *after* they have been Captured or Imported. In the *There's more...* section we'll take look at how to instruct Media Composer to make Clips Multichannel during the Capture and/or Import.

Getting ready

If you haven't already read the previous *Creating Stereo, 5.1 and 7.1 ("Multichannel") Tracks In A Sequence* recipe, you may find it helpful either before or after reading this section.

How to do it...

Here we'll focus on making **Mono Clips** into **Multichannel Clips** *after* they have been Captured or Imported. Note that Clips can be modified at *any time* to be either mono or multichannel:

1. Import or Capture your file(s) into a bin.
2. Select the clip(s) you want to affect.
3. Go to: **Clip Menu | Modify** (you may also right-click on the selected clips and choose **Modify**).
4. The **Modify** dialog window opens.
5. From the pull-down menu, select **Set Multichannel Audio**.
6. From the menu below the tracks, configure how you want the audio tracks to be interpreted by Media Composer.
7. Click **OK**.
8. This step is optional: Display the **Track Formats** column in the bin to indicate which clips are Stereo, 5.1 Surround, or 7.1 Surround.

There's more

The recipe focused on how to convert Clips *after* they have been Captured or Imported. Now we'll take a look at how to have Clips automatically configured to the Mutlichannel setting that you prefer *during* the Import or Capture process.

Making Multichannel Clips During Import

1. Open the **Import Settings**: **Project Window | Settings** tab and double-click **Import** settings.

2. Select the **Audio** tab.

3. In the section labeled **Multichannel Audio**, click the button labeled **Edit**.

4. The **Set Multichannel Audio** dialog window opens.

5. From the menu below the tracks, select how you want the audio tracks to be interpreted by Media Composer during import.

6. Click **OK**. Now when you import clips containing audio, they will automatically be configured as you've just set.

7. This step is optional: Display the **Track Formats** column in the bin to indicate which clips are Stereo, 5.1 Surround, or 7.1 Surround.

Making Multichannel Clips During Capture

1. Open the **Capture Tool**.

2. From the **Audio Channel Grouping** menu below the audio track selectors, select how you want the audio tracks to be interpreted by Media Composer. Now when you capture clips containing audio they will automatically be configured as you've just set.

3. This step is optional: Display the **Track Formats** column in the bin to indicate which clips are Stereo, 5.1 Surround, or 7.1 Surround.

Using AudioSuite Plug-ins

The AudioSuite provides plug-in effects that are applied to *individual Segments*, and they must be rendered in order to play. On the other hand, **RTAS Plug-In** effects (discussed later in this chapter) are applied to audio *tracks* and they affect *every* Segment on that track. Additionally, they do *not* require rendering.

While the **AudioSuite Plug-Ins** are definitely useful, they have one potential drawback in that they are not easily combined (you must perform an **Audio Mixdown** found in the **Special Menu** and apply the second effect to the newly created **Master Clip**), whereas you can place as many as five **RTAS plug-ins** on a track.

The **AudioSuite** plug-ins are located at: **Tools Menu | AudioSuite**. Before we get into the specifics, let's get familiar with the **AudioSuite Window** (see the next screenshot):

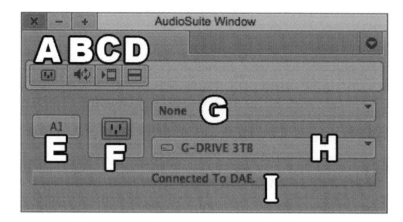

- ▶ **A** (**AudioSuite Effect Icon**): Drag this to any open bin to create an Effect Template that can be applied to Segments in the future.

- ▶ **B** (**Audio Loop Play Button**): Useful for quickly playing a Segment after you have applied *and rendered* an **AudioSuite Plug-In Effect**.

- ▶ **C** (**Render Effect Button**): If you make adjustments to an effect that you previously rendered then it will need to be re-rendered. You can use any render method; this button is provided as a convenience.

- ▶ **D** (**Fast Menu**):

  - ❑ Provides various functions to more efficiently add, remove and render multiple **AudioSuite Plug-In Effects**. For additional details about **Global** functions and/or using **Mark In/Out**, see the *Clip Mode Level and Pan Adjustments* recipe earlier in this chapter.

  - ❑ Provides quick access to two preset effects: Compressor and Normalizer. These presets *can* be adjusted after applying them.

- ▶ **E** (**Track Selector Menu**): You can select multiple tracks in the **Timeline**, or you can use this menu along with the *Shift* key.

- ▶ **F**: Avid calls this the **Activate Current Plug-In Button**. Click on it to reveal the parameter controls for a **Plug-In** effect after it has been applied (see letter **G**). Each **Plug-In** will have a different interface and varying controls.

- ▶ **G** (**Plug-In Selection Menu**): When a plug-in is selected it is applied to the Segment(s) on the enabled track(s).

▶ **H (Target Drive Menu)**: Dictates where the media file(s) will be placed when the effect is rendered.

▶ **I (Status Display)**: You'll see the progress of the **DigiDesign Audio Engine (DAE)** starting-up the first time the **AudioSuite** is opened during an editing session. If there is a problem opening the **AudioSuite**, then a message will appear here.

How to do it...

Now that you have an overview of the AudioSuite Window, let's take a look at how to apply, adjust, and modify the AudioSuite plug-in effects.

1. Enable the Track Selector(s) in the **Timeline** for the track(s) you want to place an **AudioSuite Plug-In** onto.
2. Place your blue **Position Indicator** over the Segment(s) you want to affect.
3. Open the **AudioSuite: Tools Menu | AudioSuite**.
4. Select a **Plug-In** from the **Plug-In Selection Menu**. By default this pull-down menu will say **None**.
5. After selecting a plug-in from the list, it will be applied to the Segment on each enabled track.
6. Access the **Plug-In**'s controls. Click the large, purplish icon that resembles a three-pronged electrical socket. This will open the parameters window. Note that each plug-in will have its own unique interface and parameters.
7. Click the **Preview Button** to test the effect before rendering. Note that some plug-ins are too complex to fully preview their effects, so you will need to render to test the complete effect.
8. This step is optional: While the Preview is *in progress* you can use the **Bypass** button to hear the Segment with or without the effect applied.
9. Click the **Render** button to create the media with the effect baked in to allow it to playback in real time.
10. To later modify an **AudioSuite** effect that has already been applied to a Segment you will take the following steps:

    i. First, enable the Track Selector(s) in the **Timeline** for the track(s) that contain an **AudioSuite Plug-In** you want to modify.

    ii. Second, place your blue **Position Indicator** over the Segment(s) you want to affect. Next, open the **AudioSuite Window: Tools Menu | AudioSuite**.

    iii. Now you can access the **Plug-In**'s controls by clicking the large, purplish icon that resembles a three-pronged electrical socket, which will open the parameters window.

Removing AudioSuite plug-ins

There are three methods available to remove **AudioSuite** plug-ins. The recipe will focus on one method, while the *There's more...* section will provide two additional methods.

How to do it...

This first method will remove *one* **AudioSuite Effect** at a time (per enabled track):

1. Enable the Track Selector(s) for the track(s) that contain a Segment(s) with an **AudioSuite Plug-In** that you want to remove.

2. Park the blue **Position Indicator** on the Segment(s) with **AudioSuite Plug-in** to be removed.

3. Click the **Remove Effect** button (which resembles the octagonal Stop sign in the U.S with a Slash through it). By default, the **Remove Effect** button can be found in these locations:

   ❑ In the **Fast Menu Tool Palette**, located between the yellow **Splice** arrow and the red **Overwrite** arrow

   ❑ Below the **Record Monitor**, in the second row of buttons

   ❑ On the **Timeline Tool Bar**

   ❑ In the **Command Palette**: Tools Menu | Command Palette | FX Tab

There's more

Now, let's discuss two additional methods to remove **AudioSuite plug-ins**. The first uses the **AudioSuite** window, while the second uses **Segment Mode**.

Using The AudioSuite Window to remove effects

This method is best used to remove multiple effects.

1. Open the **AudioSuite**: Tools Menu | AudioSuite.

2. Enable a Track Selector(s) in the **Timeline** or select a track from the **AudioSuite Window**'s **Track Selection Menu**.

3. Go to: **Fast Menu** (hamburger) at the top of the **AudioSuite Window**.

4. Select **Remove AudioSuite Plug-Ins On Enabled Tracks**. Note that without placing a **Mark In** and **Mark Out**, you will be removing all the plug-ins on the track from beginning to end (that is, Global).

Using Segment Mode to remove effects

This method is good for removing either single effects or multiple effects:

1. Enable either the **Lift/Overwrite** (red) or the **Extract/Splice-In** (yellow) **Segment Mode Arrow**. It doesn't matter which you enable; it's just being used as a way to make a selection.

2. Select one or more Segments containing **AudioSuite Plug-Ins**. Multiple Segments can be selected by using the *Shift* key.

3. Once the Segment(s) are selected, press the *Delete* key.

Saving and Applying AudioSuite Templates

If you're going to be using a particular effect frequently, or if you want to save a particular combination of settings before experimenting with alternate adjustments, you can save a template of the effect in a bin for use at any time in the future.

How to do it...

1. Click and hold on the **Effect Icon** located in the top-left corner of the **AudioSuite** window. The icon is a smaller version of the purplish icon that resembles a three-pronged electrical socket.

2. Drag that icon to any open bin and release the mouse button.

3. To later apply the effect, simply drag-and-drop it from the bin onto a Segment(s).

4. Render the effect. Note that you may have to first open the **AudioSuite** in order to launch the software components that process the **AudioSuite** effects. The components are part of what is called the **Digidesign Audio Engine** (**DAE**). You can render the effect using any method you like, including:

    ❑ Clicking the **Render Effect Button** (located, by default on the **Timeline Tool Bar**)

    ❑ Right-clicking in the Timeline and selecting either **Render at Position** or **Render In/Out**

    ❑ If the **AudioSuite** is open, you may use the **Render** button there

Using Real Time Audio Suite (RTAS) Plug-Ins

The **RTAS plug-in** effects are different from the **AudioSuite plug-ins** in three ways. First, as their name implies, they do not require rendering. Secondly, the **RTAS plug-ins** affect entire tracks, rather than individual Segments. And lastly, you can apply up to five **RTAS effects** to a track at one time.

It's important to note the following about **RTAS plug-in** effects:

- ► They are processed in order from left to right, in other words from **Insert a** to **Insert e**
- ► You may get different results depending on the order of the effects

RTAS Plug-Ins are accessible from the following places:

- ► **Tools Menu | Effect Palette | RTAS** category. Also note that there are sets of **RTAS Plug-Ins** that apply specifically to Mono, Stereo, 5.1, and 7.1 tracks
- ► From within the **RTAS Tool: Tools Menu | RTAS**
- ► Right-click on an **Audio Track Selector | RTAS Tool**
- ► Right-click on an **Audio Track Selector | RTAS Effects**, choose one of the five inserts (**a** through **e**), and select a preset from the submenu(s)

Before getting into applying and adjusting the **RTAS Plug-ins**, let's take a look at the **RTAS Tool** itself (see the next screenshot):

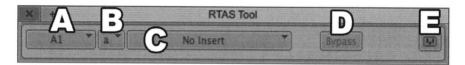

- ► **A** (**Track Selector Menu**): Only one track can be selected at a time.
- ► **B** (**Insert Selector Menu, a** through **e**): An Insert is essentially what holds each effect.
- ► **C** (**RTAS Effect Selector Menu**): If there is not a plug-in effect assigned to the selected Insert, then the menu will read as **No Insert**.
- ► **D** (**Bypass Button**): Instructs Media Composer to ignore the **RTAS** effect on the selected track and Insert. Both the **Bypass Button** and the **Insert Button** in the **Track Control Panel** will turn blue when an effect is being bypassed.
- ► **E** (**Save Effect**, also known as the **Effect Icon**): Click on, and then drag this to any open bin to save a template for future use.

How to do it...

Now that we've gotten an overview of the **RTAS Window**, let's turn our attention to how to apply, adjust, and modify the **RTAS plug-in** effects.

There are three methods available to apply, adjust, and modify **RTAS Plug-ins**. This section will present one method, and there will be two additional methods presented in the *There's more...* section.

The first method that we'll go through will be using the **RTAS Tool**.

1. Open the **Track Control Panel** to reveal the five RTAS plug-in inserts that are named **a** to **e**. These are the five small squares (these are actually buttons) in the second row of controls. Open the **Track Control Panel** by either of these methods:

   ❑ Go to **Timeline Window Fast Menu** (hamburger) in the bottom-left corner of the **Timeline Window | Track Control Panel**

   ❑ Click the small, black disclosure triangle found in the top-left of the **Timeline Window**, next to the **Timecode** display

2. Open the **RTAS Tool** using any of these methods:

   ❑ **Tools Menu | RTAS**

   ❑ Right-click on an **Audio Track Selector | RTAS Tool**

   ❑ Click on any of the five **RTAS Buttons** in the **Track Control Panel**

3. In the **RTAS Tool**, select a Track from the pull-down menu. Note that **RTAS** are applied just one track at a time.

4. Select an **Insert** to place the Plug-In (that is, **a** though **e**). As a reminder, the **RTAS plug-in** effects are processed in order from **a** to **e** and you may get different results depending on the order of effects.

5. From the **Select Plug-In** pull-down menu, choose an effect category, and then a specific effect from that category's submenu.

6. Once the plug-in is applied, the parameter controls window for that effect will open and you may make adjustments. The adjustments are immediately applied, and you can play the Sequence with or without the **RTAS Tool** open.

7. To later modify a **RTAS plug-in**, you can follow either of these methods:

   ❑ Method 1: First, open the **RTAS Tool**. Second, select a Track from the Pull-down menu. Third, select the insert containing the effect you want to modify. Lastly, once the insert is selected, the parameter controls window for that effect will open and you will be able to make modifications.

   ❑ Method 2: First, open the **Track Control Panel** to reveal the five **RTAS plug-in Insert** buttons. Second, click on the Insert button containing the plug-in you want to modify. After clicking on the Insert button, the **RTAS Tool** will open and the controls for that plug-in will be displayed.

There's more...

Media Composer's flexibility provides two additional ways to apply **RTAS Plug-Ins**. The first method focuses on working in the **Timeline**, while the second method uses the **Effect Palette**.

Applying RTAS Plug-ins in the Timeline

1. This step is optional. Open the **Track Control Panel** to reveal the five **RTAS plug-in Inserts** as discussed in the recipe earlier.

2. Right-click on an **Audio Track Selector** for the track to which you want to apply an **RTAS** effect.

3. From the contextual menu that appears, select **RTAS Effects**, choose one of the five inserts (**a** through **e**), and select a preset from one of the submenu(s).

4. To later modify the preset you can use either of methods discussed in the previous recipe.

Applying RTAS Plug-ins from the Effect Palette

1. This step is optional. Open the **Track Control Panel** to reveal the five **RTAS plug-in Inserts** as discussed in the recipe earlier.

2. Open the **Effect Palette**: **Tools Menu | Effect Palette**.

3. In the **Effect Palette**, select a **RTAS category** from the left column.

4. From the right column, drag-and-drop a specific **RTAS** effect in either of the following ways:

   ❏ If the **Track Control Panel** is open, then you can drag the effect to any one of the 5 insert buttons.

   ❏ You may also drag the effect onto a track (whether the **Track Control Panel** is open or closed). This will open a dialog window that will allow you to select an insert to place the effect onto.

5. To later modify the preset you can use either of methods discussed in the recipe.

Removing RTAS plug-ins

There are two methods available to remove **RTAS Plug-ins**.

How to do it...

This first method allows you to remove a single **RTAS** effect at a time:

1. Open the **RTAS Tool** by using any of these methods:

   ❏ **Tools Menu | RTAS**

   ❏ Right-click on an audio **Track Selector** and choose **RTAS Tool**

   ❏ Click on one of the five **RTAS Insert Buttons** found in the **Track Control Panel**

2. In the **RTAS Tool**, Select a Track from the pull-down menu.

3. Select an insert (that is, **a** though **e**).

4. From the **Select Plug-In** pull-down menu, choose **No Insert**.

This second method will let you remove *all* of the **RTAS** effects from a track in one step:

5. Right-click on an **Audio Track Selector** and choose **RTAS Effects**.

6. From the **Submenu**, select **Remove All**.

Saving and Applying RTAS Effect Templates

If you'd like to save a particular **RTAS** effect for later use, or if you want to save a particular combination of settings before experimenting with alternate adjustments, you can save a template of the effect.

How to do it...

There are two methods available to save an **RTAS Effect Template**. The first method utilizes the **RTAS Tool**.

1. In the **RTAS Tool**, on the top-right side, you will see a small, purplish icon that resembles a three-pronged electrical socket. This is the **Save Effect** icon. Click-and-hold onto that icon.

2. As you hold down the mouse button, move your cursor over to any open bin.

3. Once you're over a bin, you'll see that your arrow cursor icon has changed to a hand icon. You can now release the mouse button to drop the **Effect Template** into the bin.

4. The Template can be applied directly from the bin using the same methods discussed above in the *There's more...* section of the *Applying RTAS Plug-ins from the Effect Palette* recipe.

The second method available to save a **RTAS Effect Template** is directly from a **RTAS Insert** button in the **Track Control Panel**.

1. Open the **Track Control Panel** to reveal the five **RTAS Insert** buttons using either of these methods:

   ❑ Go to **Timeline Window Fast Menu** (hamburger) in the bottom-left corner of the **Timeline Window | Track Control Panel**

   ❑ Click the small, black disclosure triangle found in the top-left of the **Timeline Window,** next to the **Timecode** display

2. Click-and-hold on any of the five **RTAS Insert** buttons that contains an effect.

3. As you hold the mouse button down, move your cursor over to any open bin.

4. Once you're over a bin, you'll see that your arrow cursor icon has changed to a hand icon. You can now release the mouse button to drop the **Effect Template** into the bin.

Copying RTAS Effects between Tracks

Rather than first having to make an **RTAS Effect Template** (as discussed earlier), and then apply that template to another track, it is possible to copy a RTAS effect and place it onto another track directly.

How to do it...

1. You must open the **Track Control Panel** to reveal the five **RTAS Insert** buttons. You can do this using either of these methods:

   - Go to **Timeline Window Fast Menu** (hamburger) in the bottom-left corner of the **Timeline Window | Track Control Panel**

   - Click the small, black disclosure triangle found in the top-left of the **Timeline Window**, next to the **Timecode** display

2. Press and hold down the *option/Alt* key.

3. Click and hold on any of the five **RTAS Insert** buttons that contains a **Plug-In**.

4. As you continue to hold down the mouse button, move your cursor over to any **Insert Button** on another track. The selected **Insert Button** will become highlighted.

5. Release the mouse button to apply the **RTAS** to the highlighted **Insert Button**.

8

Editing with Group Clips and MultiCamera Mode

In this chapter, we'll cover:

- ▶ Syncing and Grouping clips with common timecode
- ▶ Syncing and Grouping Clips with common reference points
- ▶ Creating a syncing Sequence for syncing and grouping clips
- ▶ Using the Group Clip Menu
- ▶ Using The MultiCamera display and methods of switching camera angles
- ▶ Swap Cam Bank: Toggling the MultiCamera Display
- ▶ Editing with a Group Clip – not using MultiCamera Mode
- ▶ MultiCamera Mode Editing
- ▶ MultiCamera Mode Settings

Introduction

In the past, the most common use of shooting with multiple cameras was during the taping of television shows (for example, sitcoms and variety shows), sporting events, and concerts in order to capture different angles and shots of the same event at the same time. Now that cameras have become less expensive and smaller, more and more productions are shot using multiple cameras. Just a few examples include documentaries, music videos, and reality television shows.

For an editor, having more creative choices is always welcomed. However, the issues that come up are how do we sync up all the different cameras, and how do we edit with footage from multiple cameras in an efficient way? That's what we'll cover within this chapter. Also, be aware that there is additional information about Multicamera editing available in *Appendix C, Helpful Details about MultiCamera Editing*.

Media Composer helps us to edit with footage from multiple cameras by allowing us to create a single clip that refers to many **Master Clips**. This single clip is referred to as a **Group Clip**, and the process of making a **Group Clip** is referred to as Grouping.

Before you create the **Group Clips**, you have to have a way to sync the different cameras' footage together. In the beginning of this chapter, we'll look at three ways in which you can sync source clips (**Master Clips** and/or **Subclips**) in order to create **Group Clips** (and/or **MultiGroup Clips** if all your clips share common **Timecode**, and that timecode is sequential). The three methods presented are some of the more common methods, but not the only methods. We'll start with the easiest and fastest method and progress to the one which is a bit more challenging and definitely more time consuming.

Syncing and Grouping clips with common timecode

This is syncing and Grouping method number one of three presented in this chapter. It refers to syncing and creating **Group Clips** (also known as Grouping) when all the footage shares the exact same timecode. This is frequently referred to as Common or Jam-Synced timecode.

This is the fastest and easiest method as long as the production prepared properly before shooting. See *Appendix C, Helpful Details about MultiCamera Editing* and the *There's more* section for additional details.

Getting ready

For this recipe, we'll use the example of a narrative television show (commonly a situation comedy) that was shot with four cameras: A, B, C, and D. In actuality, in television, the fourth camera is generally labeled as X, which I presume is to avoid confusion between cameras B and D during a live production when the Director tells the Technical Director (in the UK referred to as the Vision Switcher) which camera to switch to.

This recipe presumes that:

- All the cameras shared common timecode.

- All the footage is of the same frame rate.

- Each camera's **Master Clips** have been placed into their own separate bins during the capture process. In other words, you have four bins for your footage, one for camera A, one for camera B, and so on. While this is not required, it is good for organization.

- Each Clip has been named in some *consistent fashion* to reference which camera recorded it. Examples of labeling might be:

  - **18A/1** (meaning: Scene 18, Camera A/Take 1)

  - **18/1_A** (meaning: Scene 18/Take 1 – Camera A)

  - **18/A** (meaning: for an interview, Question 18/Camera A)

How to do it...

This recipe refers to the situation presented in the *Getting ready* section:

1. Create a new bin for each scene. This bin will be where you'll place copies of your **Master Clips** of all the footage for that scene, and also create the **Group Clips**. Name the bin along the lines of **Scene 18 Group Clips**.

2. Open the individual bins of footage for each camera.

3. Copy the clips (using your preferred method) into the bin you made in step 1. I choose to use the **Clone** method, since I find it to be a faster process, and I don't like having `.copy` added to the end of a Duplicated clip. To Clone a clip, you will *option/Alt +* Drag it into the **Scene 18 Groups** bin. More information on the differences between Duplicating and Cloning clips can be found in the *Mixing frame rates* recipe in *Chapter 1, Getting Assets into Your Media Composer Project*.

4. Repeat the copying process for all the different cameras' clips from Scene 18, placing them all into the **Scene 18 Groups** bin.

5. A suggested option is to perform a sort of the **Name** column to quickly place the clips into sets of clips that will be grouped together (see the next screenshot), and also to place them in alphabetical order. To sort a column, one method is to right-click on the column header (in this case the word **Name**). A contextual menu will be displayed, and you can select **Sort Ascending** (**A** to **Z**) or **Sort Descending** (**Z** to **A**). The result of my ascending-sort of the clips is seen in the next screenshot:

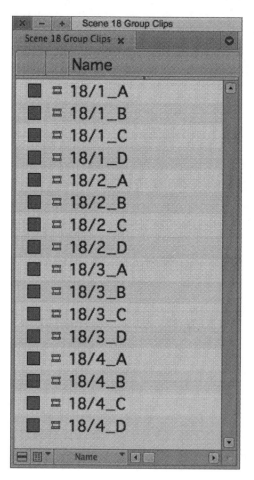

Having the clips in take order and alphabetical order will make it easier to figure out which clips need to be grouped together, since all the clips from Take 1 will be together, Take 2 will be together, and so on. Further, it can be helpful when you get to the editing stage and are viewing multiple angles simultaneously in either the **Quad Split** or **9 Split** display because the clips are initially displayed in the same order in which they were grouped (for example, Camera A, then Camera B, and so on).

6. There are two choices listed in this step:

   ❑ If you are creating **Group Clips** individually (one at a time), then move on to step 7.

   ❑ If you are working on a situation comedy television program, or a similar type of production, where multiple takes of each scene were recorded *sequentially*, then follow the next steps to create a **MultiGroup Clip** *as well as* individual **Group Clips** all in one step:

   i. Select all the clips in the bin that are to be *MultiGrouped*.

   ii. Go to **Bin menu | MultiGroup**.

   iii. A dialog window will open.

   iv. In the top section titled **Sync Clips Using**, select **Source Timecode** and click **OK**.

   v. Media Composer will then create one **MultiGroup Clip**, as well as the individual **Group Clips** that are contained within the **MultiGroup Clip**. For example, if you had four takes for Scene 18, then Media Composer would create one **MultiGroup Clip** that contains takes 1 through 4, as well as an individual **Group Clip** for Take 1, an individual Group Clip for Take 2, and so on. This gives you the flexibility to edit with either the **MultiGroup Clip**, or the individual **Group Clips**. The benefits of the **MultiGroup Clip** are that all the footage for that scene is available in one clip, and that you can jump from take to take in the **Source Window** using the **Fast Forward** and **Rewind** buttons.

   vi. Rename the **MultiGroup Clip** to reflect its contents. In this example, I'd rename it `18/1,2,3,4`. This completes the Grouping process.

7. Select the clips to be grouped together (for example, in this example, we would first select only clips **18/1_A**, **18/1_B**, **18/1_C**, and **18/1_D**).

8. Go to **Bin Menu | Group Clips** (or use the keyboard shortcut *Shift + cmd/Ctrl + G*). A dialog window will open.

9. In the top section titled **Sync Clips Using**, select **Source Timecode** and click **OK**.

10. Media Composer creates a **Group Clip** and places it at the top of the bin.

11. Repeat steps 7 through 10 for any and all additional takes.

12. Rename the **Group Clips**. By default, the **Group Clip** gets its name from the first clip in the Group, and it gets appended with `.Grp.01`. I prefer to have the name of the **Group Clip** be simplified to **18/1**, **18/2**, and so on.

There's more...

You should explain to the producers that a small bit of preparation can (and will) save a lot of time in the editing process; and as we all know, time is equal to money. During production, if the camera team can do the following, it will save a good deal of time for the editorial team:

▸ The cameras should be set to generate **Timecode** based on the time of day (rather than the setting which is called **Record Run**). This is often referred to as **TOD** or **Free Run Timecode**.

▸ Make sure that all the cameras or decks are forced to record using the *exact same* timecode. This is often referred to as Jam-Syncing. This can be done by either feeding (supplying) the same timecode from a single timecode generator to all the cameras or decks (as is often the case in studio productions), or cameras can be Jam-Synced with one camera acting as the main camera which tells the others what their timecode should be (this is sometimes referred to as the cameras being *master* and *slaves*). With regard to cameras in the field, this timecode syncing process can usually be done without having to keep all the cameras connected together with cables. Instead, they can be synced at the beginning of the shooting day. As there is the possibility that the timecode will drift from camera-to-camera throughout the day, it is advisable to re-sync the cameras several times each shoot day.

▸ *If at all possible*, make sure the camera operators start and stop recording at approximately the same time. In the scheme of things, Tape and/or SSD card space is cheap. Assure the camera team that it's okay that they continue recording while they are repositioning, recomposing, and focusing. It will save a good deal of time and frustration in post production if they do not frequently stop and start recording during an event. For emphasis, in a perfect situation, all the camera operators will stop and start at about the same time for each take. If there will be very long takes, then it may be necessary to stagger the starting and stopping of each camera (or deck), so that none of the event goes unrecorded. But again, the operators should record continuously until directed to stop.

See also

▸ The *Syncing and Grouping Clips with common reference points* recipe
▸ The *Creating syncing Sequence for syncing and grouping clips* recipe

Syncing and Grouping Clips with common reference points

This is syncing and Grouping method number two of three that are presented in this chapter.

If it is not possible to have all the cameras record the exact same timecode (as discussed in the previous recipe), then the next best thing is to make sure that all the cameras share a common sync reference point (for example, a Clapper Slate), and making sure that the camera operators recorded each take continuously (meaning that all the camera operators started and stopped recording at approximately the same time for each take).

The best case in this situation would be that the production team used a Clapper Slate (or a utility on an iPad or similar device) to provide a common sync reference point. This recipe will use the example of four cameras where:

▸ All the cameras began recording at approximately the same time.

▸ Once recording, all the camera operators pointed their cameras to a Camera Assistant holding a Clapper Slate.

▸ Once the camera operators had framed up a good, clear image of the slate, the Camera Assistant clapped the slate (banged the top portion down onto the bottom portion), providing both a visual and an audible sync reference point for use in post production.

▸ All the cameras *recorded continuously* for each take until instructed to stop.

▸ Each Camera's **Master Clips** have been placed into their own separate bins during the capture process. In other words, you have four bins for your footage, one for Camera A, one for Camera B, and so on.

▸ Each Clip has been named in some *consistent fashion* to reference which camera recorded it. Examples of labeling might be:

    ❑ **18A/1** (meaning: Scene 18, Camera A/Take 1)

    ❑ **18/1_A** (meaning: Scene 18/Take 1 - Camera A)

    ❑ **18/A** (meaning: for an interview, Question 18/Camera A)

Getting ready

Perform steps 1 through 5 from the *Syncing and Grouping Clips with common timecode* recipe.

How to do it...

Now that you have performed steps as directed in the previous *Getting ready* section, we can now begin the syncing and Grouping process. The following steps presume that you have placed Duplicates or Clones of all the clips you want to Sync and Group into a common bin.

1. An optional step is to enable **Waveform Display: Timeline Window Fast Menu** (bottom-left corner of the **Timeline Window**) | **Audio Data** | **Waveforms**.

2. Another optional step is to display Source material in the **Timeline Window** by enabling the **Toggle Source/Record In Timeline** function. This is located, by default, in the bottom-left corner of the **Timeline** window and next to the **Video Quality Menu**. When you are viewing **Source Material** in the **Timeline Window**, Media Composer changes the color of the **Position Indicator** in the Timeline to green and the icon for **Toggle Source/Record In Timeline** will also be green.

3. A third optional step is to enable **Digital Scrubbing** by pressing the *Caps Lock* key, and make sure that it is active. Now when you move your **Position Indictor**, you will hear audio as well. This will allow you to hear the Clapper Slate being clapped.

4. Load the first **Master Clip** or **Subclip** into the **Source Window** (for example, in this example, we would load shot **18/1_A**).

5. Locate the general area where the slate is clapped together.

6. Move one frame at a time by using the **Step Forward** and **Step Backward** functions (by default located on the *3* and *4* keys), to find the exact point when the slate is clapped. In other words, the exact point when the top portion of the slate first makes contact with the bottom portion.

7. Place a **Mark In** on the clip at the point described in step 6.

8. You have now created a sync reference for Media Composer. Repeat steps 4, 5, 6, and 7 for the remaining clips to be grouped together. In this example, we'd repeat the process on shots **18/1_B**, **18/1_C**, and **18/1_D**.

9. Now that all the clips to be Grouped have a **Mark In** at the exact same point when the slate was clapped together: Select all the clips to be Grouped. In this example, we select four clips: **18/1_A**, **18/1_B**, **18/1_C**, and **18/1_D**.

10. Go to **Bin Menu** | **Group Clips** (or use the keyboard shortcut *Shift + cmd/Ctrl + G*). A dialog window will open.

11. In the top section titled **Sync Clips Using**, select **Inpoints**. Click on **OK**.

12. Media Composer creates a **Group Clip** and places it at the top of the bin.

13. Repeat the previous steps for any and all additional takes.

14. The last optional step is to rename the **Group Clips**. By default, the **Group Clip** gets its name from the first clip in the Group, and it gets appended with `.Grp.01`. I prefer to have the name of the **Group Clip** be simplified to **18/1**, **18/2**, and so on.

See also

▶ The *Creating a syncing Sequence for syncing and grouping clips* recipe

Creating a syncing Sequence for syncing and grouping clips

This is syncing and Grouping method number three of three that are presented in this chapter.

This manual syncing method may be the solution for you if:

▶ The footage does *not* share common timecode

▶ There is no visible sync reference (for example, a Clapper Slate, someone setting down a glass, and so on) within the video for one or more of the multiple camera angles

▶ All the cameras recorded the *same audio* (this *is the crucial, key requirement* to use this method)

▶ Possibly (because this is *not* a requirement to use this method), you had a camera operator(s) that started and stopped recording multiple times within a take

Getting ready

First, you will want to map the **Match Frame** function to at least one of these locations:

▶ Below the **Record Monitor**

▶ On the **Timeline Toolbar**

▶ On the keyboard

Details on mapping buttons can be found in the *Mapping buttons and menu selections* recipe in *Chapter 2, Customizing Your Work Environment*.

Let's start by taking a look at the key concepts of this method, which relies on using the **Match Frame** function. When you use the **Match Frame** function from the Sequence, then Media Composer will do the following:

▶ Load the **Source Clip** into the **Source Window.**

▶ Whatever frame you are positioned upon in the Sequence will be the same frame that you will be positioned upon in the **Source Window** (that's why it's called the **Match Frame** function).

▶ Media Composer will automatically place a **Mark In** on the matched-frame in the **Source Window.**

▶ Any location/common sync point within synced clips in the Sequence can be used when using this method. It does not have to be the beginning or end.

▶ The **Grouping** function can (and will) be instructed to pay attention to the **Mark In** points on the clips as sync reference points.

▶ If a camera operator(s) started and stopped multiple times (each at different times) within a take, you will have to create multiple **Group Clips** for each common section of the take.

Next, it will be helpful to look at an *overview* of the workflow:

1. Create a sequence with the clips you want to sync.

2. Stack the clips to be synced onto different tracks and visually align the waveforms of the clips in the Sequence.

3. Use the **Match Frame** function on all the clips to establish a common sync point on each source clip (**Master Clip** or **Subclip**).

4. Group the Clips.

5. An optional step is to use the Syncing Sequence as a guide and add in the **Group Clips**.

6. Note that once you get familiar with the essential aspects of this recipe/process, you will undoubtedly make adjustments that better suit your specific needs.

Lastly, before we get to the recipe of steps, I want to point out that to help illustrate the process, I will reference a fictitious sit-down interview where:

▶ There were four cameras during production:

  ❑ Camera A: Interviewer

  ❑ Camera B: Interview Subject 1 (President Barack Obama)

  ❑ Camera C: Interview Subject 2 (First Lady Michelle Obama)

  ❑ Camera D: Roams between a two-Shot of the Interview Subjects and a Wide-Shot that includes both the Interviewer and the Subjects

▶ All the cameras recorded the same audio on at least one channel.

▶ There is no common timecode or a Clapper Slate to help with the syncing/Grouping.

▶ The camera operators were conscientious, and made sure to stop and start their cameras at approximately the same times for each interview question. Note that in a real situation, the camera operators would more likely let their cameras record for multiple questions and for many minutes at a time. I'm just using this scenario to help illustrate the process.

▶ Each Camera's **Master Clips** have been placed into their own separate bins during the capture process. In other words: You have four bins for your footage, one for Camera A, one for Camera B, and so on.

▶ You have labeled the **Master Clips** for each question and answer in the following fashion: **Q1A** (meaning: Question 1, Camera A), **Q1B**, **Q1C**, and **Q1D**. Of course then, the second question and answer **Master Clips** would be labeled as **Q2A**, **Q2B**, **Q2C**, and **Q2D**.

How to do it...

Now we'll go through the process of syncing and then Grouping the footage:

1. Please take a moment to:
   - Review the information in the *Getting ready* section
   - Then, begin by following steps 1 through 5 in the earlier recipe titled *Syncing and Grouping clips with common timecode*

2. At this point you will have Duplicates or Clones of your clips all together in a common bin. With the bin active, create a new Sequence: **Clip Menu | New Sequence**. Name it something along the lines of **Scene 18 Syncing**, or **Obamas Interview Syncing**.

3. Enable **Waveform Display**: **Timeline Window Fast Menu** (bottom-left corner of the **Timeline Window**) | **Audio Data** | **Waveforms**.

4. An optional step is to enable **Digital Scrubbing**. Press the *Caps Lock* key, and make sure that it is active. Now when you move your **Position Indictor** in either the **Source Window** or within the Sequence, you will hear audio as well.

5. Load the first clip into the **Source Window**. In this example, I'd load clip **Q1A**.

6. Locate the beginning of a word that you know has been recorded by all the cameras. In this example, let's pretend that our Interviewer begins by saying, "Welcome viewers. I'm fortunate today to be speaking with President Barack Obama and the First Lady, Michelle Obama." The letter "P" in President is a good clear sound that you can use as a reference (see the tip box at the end of this recipe for additional details). So, place a **Mark In** just a tiny bit *before* the interviewer says the "P" in President. Don't worry about being overly precise.

7. Edit this clip into the Syncing Sequence, making sure that you include the audio that is common to *all* of the clips. In this example, we would edit clip **Q1A** onto tracks **V1** and **A1**.

8. An optional step is to trim the Head (the beginning) of the segment longer, so that the entire clip is represented in the Sequence (this depends on your preferred method for aligning the segments, which is covered in step 16).

9. Load the next clip into the **Source Window**. In this example, we would load clip **Q1B**. Just as we did before, with clip **Q1A**, we'll place a **Mark In** just a tiny bit *before* the Interviewer says the P in President.

10. In the *Sequence*, place a **Mark In** just a bit *before* the Interviewer says the "P" in President.

11. Edit the Source clip into the Syncing Sequence, making sure that you include the audio that is common to *all* of the clips. In this example, I would edit clip **Q1B** onto tracks **V2** and **A2**.

12. An optional step is to trim the Head (the beginning) of the segment longer, so that the entire clip is represented in the Sequence (this depends on your preferred method for aligning the segments, which is covered in step 16).

13. Repeat steps 9 through 12 for all of the remaining clips that you want to sync. In this example, we would repeat this process on clips **Q1C** and **Q1D**. We would edit clip **Q1C** onto tracks **V3** and **A3**, and clip **Q1D** onto **V4** and **A4**. Note that once you are familiar with this method/recipe, you may very well find that you really only need to edit the audio tracks into the Sequence, depending on your needs.

14. At this point, you should have the following:

    ❑ All the clips to be synced have been edited into the Sequence, and very roughly aligned. In this example, we used the letter "P" in "President" as the guide for roughly syncing the clips.

    ❑ The **Waveforms** displayed on all tracks.

15. Suggested options:

    ❑ Make the audio tracks wider. One method to do this is to enable just the Track Selectors for the audio tracks. In this example, we'd enable just **A1**, **A2**, **A3**, and **A4**. Then, use the keyboard shortcut *cmd/Ctrl + L* as many times as you like to increase their width. Note that this command is located within the **Edit Menu**, and that you can reduce the width of the track(s) with *cmd/Ctrl + K*.

    ❑ Make the **Waveform Display** larger or smaller as needed to make it easier to see them and to eventually align them visually. Enable the Track Selector(s) for whichever track's waveform you want to adjust. Then add one more key to the shortcut mentioned earlier. The key you'll add is *option/Alt*. So, for example, the final keyboard shortcut to adjust the **Waveform Display** *larger* would be *option/Alt + cmd/Ctrl + L*.

16. Now it's just a matter of adjusting the segments so that all of the waveforms align as best as possible. You may need to zoom in (Avid calls this More Detail) to get a more precise look at the Waveform). To accomplish the alignment you could use any of the following methods:

    ❑ Method 1: Enable the **Link Selection Toggle** function (located above the **Smart Tool** on the left-hand side of the **Timeline Window**). Next, use the *red* **Lift/Overwrite Segment Mode** to select one set of segments (for example, **Q1B** that is on tracks **V2** and **A2**). Then use the Trim keys on the keyboard (by default located on the keys *M*, comma, period, and forward slash) to *nudge* that set of segments left or right to place them into alignment with the **Q1A** segments, by using the **Waveform Display** as your visual guide. You would then repeat this process for all the other segments in the Sequence.

❑ Method 2: Note that this method uses Slipping, so you *would* need to have some handle at the Head and Tail of the segments in the Sequence, otherwise you will not be able to Slip with this method and Media Composer will give you some sort of alert sound (for example, Beep, or Bonk). Place your blue **Position Indicator** at a point in one of the segments that you want to use as the syncing guide. For example, you would first place the position indicator on track **A1**, *exactly* where the Interviewer first says the letter "P" in the word President, or the "B" in Barack. Next, enable *only* the track selectors for the segments you want to Slip. In this example, it would be segment **Q1B** (so we would enable *only* tracks **V2** and **A2**). Lastly, use the *Trim Keys on the keyboard* to Slip the segments into alignment with the **Q1A** segments by using the **Waveform Display** as your visual guide. You would then repeat this process for all the other segments in the Sequence. More information about this method of Slipping can be found in *Appendix B, Details on Trimming, Slipping, Sliding, and Segment Mode.*

❑ Method 3: Use Slipping or Sliding in **Trim Mode** to adjust the segments into alignment. More information about Slipping and Sliding in **Trim Mode** can be found in *Appendix B, Details on Trimming, Slipping, Sliding, and Segment Mode*. Note that, just as with Method 2, to use *Slipping,* you *would* need to have some handle at the Head and Tail of the segments in the Sequence, otherwise you will not be able to Slip and Media Composer may give you some sort of alert sound (for example, Beep, or Bonk).

17. Now that all the segments are in alignment, the next phase will be to use the **Match Frame** function to set a sync reference (a **Mark In**) in all the source clips, using the steps that follow. Make sure that in the following steps you use the **Match Frame** function that you previously mapped below your **Record Monitor**, onto the **Timeline Toolbar**, or onto the keyboard.

18. Park the blue **Position Indicator** at any location in the Sequence where it comes into contact with *all* the clips you want to Group together. Once you have selected this location in the Sequence, *do not move* the **Position Indicator**. For emphasis, *do not move* the blue **Position Indicator** until *all* the clips have gone through the **Match Frame** process detailed in the next steps.

19. Enable all the Audio tracks, as well as *Disable* all the video tracks. In this example the only tracks enabled would be **A1**, **A2**, **A3**, and **A4**.

20. It's helpful to know that the **Match Frame** function only pays attention to the uppermost track that is enabled. So in this example, even though multiple tracks are enabled, it will initially pay attention only to Track **A1**.

21. Click the **Match Frame** button that you previously mapped below the **Record Monitor**, onto the **Timeline Toolbar**, or onto the keyboard. Details on mapping buttons can be found in *Chapter 2, Customizing Your Work Environment.*

22. Now that you have clicked the **Match Frame** function, the source clip (in this example, clip **Q1A**) is loaded into the **Source Window** and Media Composer has placed a **Mark In** on that frame. You have accomplished what is necessary for that clip. Now return to your Sequence in the **Timeline Window**.

23. Deselect the Track Selector for Track **A1**. This will make Track **A2** the upper-most track that is enabled.

24. Click the **Match Frame** button.

25. Now that you have clicked the **Match Frame** function, the source clip (in this example, clip **Q1B**) is loaded into the **Source Window** and Media Composer has placed a **Mark In** on that frame. You have accomplished what is necessary for clip **Q1B**. Now return to the **Timeline Window**.

26. Repeat steps 23, 24, and 25 for the remaining clips that need to be Grouped. In this example, I would deselect Track **A2**, and then **Match Frame**. Then I would deselect Track **A3**, and then **Match Frame**.

27. Now all the source clips (in this example, **Q1A**, **Q1B**, **Q1C**, and **Q1D**) have a **Mark In** at a common location. The next phase is to use them to create a new **Group Clip**.

28. In the bin, select all the clips to be Grouped.

29. Go to **Bin Menu | Group Clips** (or use the keyboard shortcut *Shift + cmd/Ctrl + G*).

30. A dialog window will open. In the top section titled **Sync Clips Using**, select **Inpoints**, then click **OK**. Media Composer then creates a **Group Clip** and places it at the top of the bin.

31. An optional step is to rename the **Group Clips**. By default, the **Group Clip** gets its name from the first clip in the Group, and it gets appended with `.Grp.01`. I prefer to have the name of the **Group Clip** be simplified to **18/1** or **Q1**, and so on.

There's more...

Here we'll discuss syncing footage with starts and stops, as well as creating a Sequence that will help you be aware of where the cameras stopped and started.

Syncing Staggered Start and Stop Footage

The steps in the previous recipe presume that *all* the camera operators started and stopped recording at roughly the *same time*. However, many times you will have a camera operator(s) that stops and starts recording while the others are continuously recording. In that case, it will be helpful to use the Syncing Sequence as a map where you can place all the clips in sync and see the portions/sections of time when all the cameras were recording at the same time, and where an operator stopped and started.

Once all the Segments are in sync within the Sequence, you would create a **Group Clip** for each portion/section of time where all the cameras were recording at the same time, using the **Match Frame** method detailed earlier.

Once you have a **Group Clip** for each section, follow these steps to create a Sequence that contains the **Group Clips**, which I refer to as a **Group Clip Map**.

1. Duplicate the Syncing Sequence (select it, then go to: **Edit Menu | Duplicate**).

2. Rename the Sequence along the lines of **Scene 18 Group Clip Map**.

3. Use the **Replace Edit** function along with **Source Timecode** (displayed above the **Source Window** as well as the **Record Window**) to replace the Segments in the Sequence with the **Group Clips**. Details on using the Replace Edit function can be found in the *Replace edit: How and why* recipe in *Chapter 3, Polishing Gems*.

4. Duplicate the **Group Clip Map** Sequence you just created. That will be the one that you will use to actually edit with. Duplicating it makes sure you have an unedited back-up copy if you ever needed to refer to the unedited original in the future.

Software Help

If you're in this type of situation frequently, then you may want to investigate an application called PluralEyes, or any other similar syncing application(s).

Plosives as sync references

Words that you'll find easier to use as sync references will contain the hard sounds of consonants such as B, D, G (as in the word Game), K, P, and T. In phonetics, the sounds these letters produce are called plosives.

Using the Group Clip Menu

Whenever you load a **Group Clip** into the **Source Window**, an additional menu will appear above it. Its icon is very similar to that of a **Group Clip** (see the next screenshot).

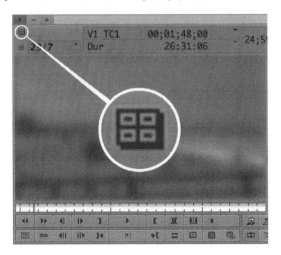

From the menu, you can select what elements from the contents of the **Group Clip** (the **Master Clips** and/or **Subclips**) are being referenced (that is, played and/or edited into the Sequence). For example, let's say I have a **Group Clip** from Scene 23, take number 7, which is made up of four Master Clips named **23/7_A**, **23/7_B**, **23/7_C**, and **23/7_D**; and that each of these **Master Clips** has two audio tracks (that is, **A1** and **A2**). In this instance, the **Group Clip Menu** would display as in the next screenshot (note that the check Marks tell you what source is active):

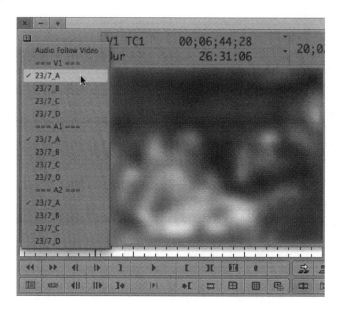

What this allows you to do is choose which clip's video you want to see or edit into the Sequence as well as which clip's audio you want to hear or edit into the Sequence. In this way, you can mix things if you need to. In other words, it's possible to play or edit with video from Camera B, but play or edit with the **A1** audio from Camera C, and the **A2** audio from Camera D.

How to do it...

While you can mix and match the video and audio from different source clips when editing with a **Group Clip**, what if instead you want to make sure that when you select (also known as Switch to) a different camera that the audio that belongs with that video is also selected? That's easy:

1. Go to **Group Clip Menu**.

2. Select **Audio Follow Video** (it's at the very top of the drop-down menu).

3. Note that the **Group Clip Menu** icon will turn bright green to indicate that **Audio Follow Video** is enabled.

4. From the **Group Clip Menu**, select a different video source. Note that the audio tracks from that source will automatically be selected for you.

5. See the next *There's more...* section for more information on changing camera angles (that is, Switching to different clips).

How it works...

The **Audio Follow Video** feature is particularly helpful when the clips that are grouped together contain very different audio and you want to keep the video and audio paired together. For example, let's say that you're editing with a **Group Clip** from an American Football game where Camera A is one of the coaches shouting, Camera B is the Quarterback yelling the count, Camera C is a close-up of a fan cheering, and Camera D is a close-up of another fan jeering.

There's more...

Another method to Switch from one clip's video to another within a **Group Clip** is to use the functions called **Previous in Group**, and **Next in Group**. By default, these functions are already mapped to the Up Arrow and Down Arrow on your keyboard. You can also map them to any location you like, using the **Command Palette: Tools menu | Command Palette | MCam Tab**. Details on mapping buttons and menu items can be found in the *Mapping buttons and menu selections* recipe in *Chapter 2, Customizing Your Work Environment*.

Using the Multicamera display and methods of switching camera angles

In the previous section, we discussed Switching camera angles (that is, changing to different clips within the **Group Clip**) by using the **Group Clip Menu**. While the **Group Clip Menu** is certainly useful, there are faster methods to switch to the different video angles which we'll cover in this section. Further, we'll also discuss the **MultiCamera Display**, which is referred to as the **Quad Split** when four clips are shown at the same time, or **9 Split** when nine clips are shown at the same time.

How to do it...

This recipe will first take you through mapping the necessary functions and then will present the various methods to Switch camera angles.

1. First, you'll map the necessary functions to a convenient location(s). Go to **Tools menu | Command Palette | MCam tab**.

2. In the bottom-left corner of the **Command Palette**, enable **Button to Button Reassignment**.

3. Drag-and-drop the **Quad Split** display function to a convenient button location below your **Source Monitor**.

4. Drag-and-drop the **Nine Split** display function to a button below your **Source Monitor**.

5. Close the **Command Palette**. Details on mapping buttons and menu items can be found in the *Mapping buttons and menu selections* in *Chapter 2, Customizing Your Work Environment*.

6. Now that you've mapped the **Quad Split** and **Nine Split** display functions to buttons below your **Source Window**, let's look at several methods to Switch the active camera:

   i.   Method 1: Using the Cursor, first, enable either **Quad Split** or **Nine Split** display by clicking on the button you mapped in the previous steps. You can then select which camera angle is active by simply clicking your cursor directly on the image you want to be active. When you make a camera's video active, you'll see a green line appear under that camera's display.

   ii. Method 2: **Previous in Group** and **Next in Group** – by default, these functions are already mapped to the up arrow and down arrow on your keyboard. This method can be used in the following cases:

        ❑ If you're still only displaying one clip at a time in the **Source Window** (Avid calls this as Full Monitor Display).

        ❑ If you've enabled either **Quad Split** or **Nine Split** display – when a camera's video is active, you'll see a green line appear under that camera's display.

   iii. Method 3 – Numeric Keypad. This feature *only works when*:

        ❑ You are in **MultiCamera Mode** (**Special Menu | MultiCamera Mode**). **MultiCamera Mode** is covered later in this chapter

        ❑ You are using the numeric keypad

        ❑ You are *playing* in Real Time

7. If you are using Method 3, then the numeric keypad will activate the camera angles as follows:

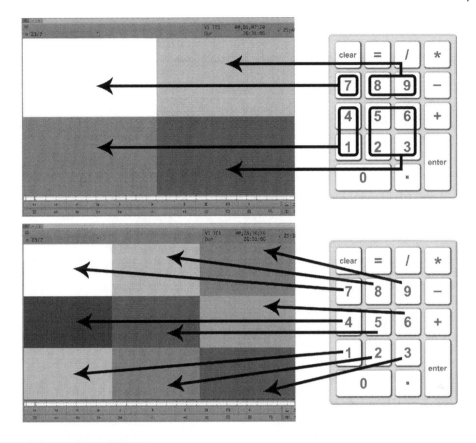

There's more...

First, it's important to remember that all we've done in the previous steps is to display and/or edit with a **Group Clip**. We were *not* in **MultiCamera Mode**. **MultiCamera Mode** will provide you with additional editing capabilities, but is not required in order to edit with a **Group Clip**. **MultiCamera Mode** editing is covered a bit later in this chapter.

Now let's take a closer look at the behaviors of the **Quad Split** and **Nine Split Display** function.

How Split display affects Multicamera Mode

Later you may want to use **MultiCamera Mode** for editing. It's helpful to know that, by default, whichever **Split** display you used last tells Media Composer how you'd like your display to be when you use **MultiCamera Mode**. For example, let's say I'm *not* in **MultiCamera Mode** and then I enable the **Nine Split** display for a minute, and then I turn it off, so that I'm back to viewing only one camera angle at a time (Avid calls this Full Monitor Display). Well, Media Composer remembers that, and later in the day when I do enable **MultiCamera Mode** editing, the display will be **Nine Split**. If you haven't set a preference, then it will default to the **Quad Split** display.

If you map **Quad Split** and **Nine Split** below the **Record Monitor**, onto the **Timeline Toolbar**, and/or onto the keyboard, then you will get three behaviors with one button-push:

- ▸ Enables **MultiCamera Mode**
- ▸ Enables the selected **Split Display** type that you clicked/pressed
- ▸ *While you are using* **MultiCamera Mode**, you can press the **Split Display** buttons to toggle between the display types

Also see the the *MultiCamera Mode Settings* recipe for more information on settings which control the **Split Display** in the **Source Window** as well as on your **Client Monitor** (if you have one connected to your system).

Setting-Up The MultiCamera (Quad Split and Nine Split) Displays

We have discussed using the **Quad Split**, and **Nine Split** displays. But how do you know what camera angle (clip) is shown in each of the 4 or 9 camera angle display regions?

Situation 1 – Sorting before Grouping

The clips are placed into the different **MultiCamera** display regions based on their order in the bin. So, rather than letting the order be random, *if prior to Grouping the Master* **Clips** *and/ or* **Subclips** together into a **Group Clip**, you *first* performed a Sort on the **Name Column** in the bin, so that all the clips were in alpha-numeric order before you Grouped them, then the clips will already be in a logical order for you in the **MultiCamera** display regions. Specifically, when a **Group Clip** is shown in the **Quad Split** display or **Nine Split** display, the clips are placed in order from left to right, and from top to bottom, essentially in the same order that those in the West read a book.

For example, let's say that *before you grouped* four **Master Clips** together, you *first perform a Sort on the* **Name Column** in the bin (for Scene 23, Take 7, cameras A, B, C, and D). The result of the Sort would be that the **Master Clips** in your bin are then in the following order:

- ▸ **23/7_A**
- ▸ **23/7_B**
- ▸ **23/7_C**
- ▸ **23/7_D**

Now, after the four clips are made into a **Group Clip**, and then shown in the **Quad Split** display: the first clip in the Group (**23/7_A**) is placed in the top-left display region, the second clip is in the top-right display region, the third in the lower-left, and the fourth (**23/7_D**) in the lower-right. The result would look like this:

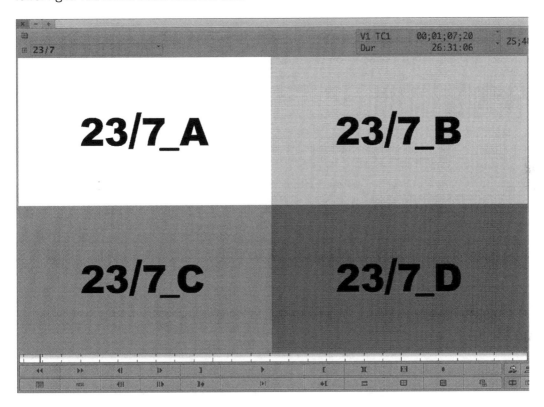

Situation 2 – Customizing the Order

The different clips' (camera angles') positions can be customized by pressing the *cmd/Ctrl* key. When you press the *cmd/Ctrl* key, you'll see that below each of the **MultiCamera** display regions, a label will appear, telling you the name of the clip that is being displayed in that region. That display is also a menu (Avid calls this the **Multi-Angle View Menu**). So, while holding down *cmd/Ctrl*, just click your cursor on the menu-display (actually, you can click anywhere in the display region) and select a different clip/angle from the drop-down menu that appears.

It's important to remember that even though we just discussed **Quad Split** and **Nine Split** displays, all we've done in the previous steps is to display and/or edit with a **Group Clip**. We were *not* in **MultiCamera Mode**. **MultiCamera Mode** will provide you with additional editing capabilities, but is not required in order to edit with a **Group Clip**. **MultiCamera Mode** editing is covered a bit later in this chapter.

Swap Cam Bank: Toggling the MultiCamera Display

In the previous *There's more...* section, we discussed how to display **Group Clips** in the **Source Monitor** using the **Quad Split** and **Nine Split** displays. However, what if you have more than four or nine camera angles (clips within a **Group Clip**)? For this situation, Avid provides a feature called **Swap Cam Bank**.

How to do it...

First, you'll map the **Swap Cam Bank** function to a convenient location(s).

1. Go to **Tools menu | Command Palette | MCam tab**.

2. In the bottom-left corner of the **Command Palette**, enable **Button to Button Reassignment**.

3. Drag-and-drop the **Swap Cam Bank** function to a convenient button location below your **Source Monitor**. Note that you could also map this onto your keyboard. A discussion of keyboard mapping is in *Chapter 2, Customizing Your Work Environment*.

4. Close the **Command Palette**.

5. Load a **Group Clip** with more than four or nine angles/clips within it into the **Source Window**.

6. Enable either the **Quad Split** or **9 Split Display**.

7. Do one of the following methods to use the **Swap Cam Bank** feature:

    ❏   Click on the **Swap Cam Bank** button. This will work whether you are using **MultiCamera Mode** or not. However, if you are in **MultiCamera Mode**, this function will have to be mapped to your keyboard, under the **Record Monitor**, or in the **Timeline Toolbar**.

    ❏   Right-click with the mouse *while in* **MultiCamera Mode**. For emphasis, you *must* be using **MultiCamera Mode** in order to **Swap Cam Banks** with the mouse.

How it works...

No matter how many clips you may have Grouped together, the **Swap Cam Bank** function *only toggles back and forth*. Here are some examples:

▸ Example 1: You have eight clips in one **Group Clip** (for ease of discussion, let's call the clips 1, 2, 3, 4, 5, 6, 7, and 8). You load that **Group Clip** into the **Source Window** and you set the display to **Quad Split** (showing just four of the clips at the same time). Initially, you would be viewing clips 1, 2, 3, and 4. Then when you clicked the **Swap Cam Bank** button, you would see clips 5, 6, 7, and 8. When you press the **Swap Cam Bank** button a second time, the display will toggle back to displaying the first four (1, 2, 3, and 4).

▸ Example 2: You have 10 clips in one **Group Clip**, (for ease of discussion, they're named 1 through 10). You load the **Group Clip** into the **Source Window** and you set the display to **Quad Split** (showing just four of the clips at the same time). Initially, you would be viewing clips 1, 2, 3, and 4. Then when you clicked the **Swap Cam Bank** button, you would see clips 5, 6, 7, and 8. When you press the **Swap Cam Bank** button a second time, the display will toggle back to displaying the first four (1, 2, 3, and 4). To see camera angles 9 and 10, you could do any of the following:

   ❑ Use **9 Split Display**.

   ❑ Make a selection from the **Group Clip Menu**.

   ❑ Use the **Previous in Group/Next in Group** functions (mapped to the up and down arrow keys by default).

   ❑ Press and hold the *cmd/Ctrl* key to reveal the **Display Region Labels** (Avid calls this the **Multi-Angle View Menu**). Click in a display to show the **Selection Menu**, and then select a clip to be displayed.

Editing with a Group Clip – not using MultiCamera Mode

When a **Group Clip** has been edited into your Sequence, Media Composer helps you differentiate a **Group Clip** from other types of source clips in your Sequence by placing **(G)** after the clip's name.

It is possible to edit with a **Group Clip** without using **MultiCamera Mode**. We'll discuss that in this recipe and later in this chapter, we'll examine editing with **MultiCamera Mode**.

How to do it...

First, select what you'd like to edit into the Sequence (Steps 1 through 4).

1. Load a **Group Clip** into the **Source Window**.

2. Select the video angle you'd like to edit into the Sequence to start out with. For example, possibly you'd prefer to start with the **Wide Shot/Master Shot**. Honestly, this is an option and is not required because you can quickly and easily change angles/shots at any time after it has been edited into the Sequence (covered in the steps later). To select the video, you could:

    ❑ Make a selection from the **Group Clip Menu** that's above the **Source Window**.

    ❑ Use the **Previous in Group/Next in Group** functions (mapped by default on the up and down arrow keys).

    ❑ If you are in **Quad Split** or **9 Split Display**, click on one of the camera angle's display regions to activate it. A green line appears below the active camera angle.

    ❑ Press one of the **MultiCamera Angle Buttons** (also known as the M keys) on the keyboard (see the *There's more...* section later for details).

3. From the **Group Clip Menu**, select which audio sources you want to edit into the Sequence. An option is to enable the **Audio Follow Video** feature (discussed earlier in this chapter in the *Using the Group Clip menu* recipe).

4. Edit all of, or a portion of, the **Group Clip** into your Sequence.

5. Now that you've edited a **Group Clip** into the Sequence, the following steps will take you through the basic editing process. See the *There's more...* section later for additional techniques.

6. In your *Sequence*, place the blue **Position Indicator** where you'd like to change to (Switch to) another camera angle.

7. Enable the tracks you'd like to affect. For example, if you want to Switch only the video, then enable only the **Video Track Selector**. If you want to affect both audio and video tracks, then enable the appropriate Track Selectors (for example, **V1** and **A1**).

8. Click the **Add Edit** function, as shown in the following screenshot:

9. The **Add Edit** function icon looks like the letter H on its side, as seen in the previous screenshot. It is located by default:

   ❑ In **Tools Menu | Command Palette | Edit tab** (consider mapping this to a convenient location on your keyboard since you'll be using it a lot with **Group Clips/MultiCamera Mode**)

   ❑ In the **Fast Menu Tool Palette**

   ❑ Below the **Record Monitor**, first row of buttons, on the right side

   ❑ On the **Timeline Toolbar**, towards the center of the row

10. Now that you've created a cut using the **Add Edit** function, and your blue **Position Indicator** is placed over the shot you want to change, then you can switch the *video* by one of the following methods:

    ❑ Make a selection from the **Group Clip Menu** that appears above the **Record Monitor**. For emphasis, when your blue **Position Indicator** is placed on a **Group Clip** *in the Sequence*, a **Group Clip Menu** will become available above the **Record Monitor**.

    ❑ Use the **Previous in Group/Next in Group** functions which are mapped to the arrow keys on the keyboard by default.

    ❑ Right-click on the **Video Segment** in the Sequence and make a selection from the menu that appears.

    ❑ Press one of the **MultiCamera Angle Buttons** on the keyboard (also known as the M keys). You do *not* have to be in **MultiCamera Mode,** or even in **Quad Split** or **Nine Split Display** in order to use these buttons. See the *There's more...* section later for additional details about the M keys.

11. If you want to Switch the *audio*, you can do any of the following:

    ❑ Make a selection from the **Group Clip Menu** that appears above the **Record Monitor**.

    ❑ Right-click on an **Audio Segment** in the Sequence and make a selection from the menu that appears.

    ❑ Option: is to enable the **Audio Follow Video** feature from the **Group Clip Menu** above the **Record Monitor**. The **Group Clip Menu** will turn green to indicate that this feature is enabled. If enabled, when you switch *video* angles (using any method *except* the right-click menu), then the audio that comes from that video's source clip will also be switched automatically.

How it works...

While not as fast as editing in Real Time with **MultiCamera Mode**, the methods described earlier are still wonderfully fast. It's also helpful to keep in mind that:

▸ You can combine portions of different **Group Clips** to form a complete scene.

▸ All standard editing methods and techniques are still available when you're editing with a **Group Clip**. However, you get the added advantage of having multiple camera angles (clips) available to switch to whenever you like.

▸ You can use audio from one angle/clip with video from another.

▸ You can adjust when the camera angles switch by trimming the cut-point (using **Double-Roller Trim**).

▸ See the *There's more...* section for additional information.

There's more...

The following is another method of editing with **Group Clips**, how to remove unwanted edit points in a **Group Clip**, methods to remove **Match Frame Edits**, some valuable information about the **MultiCamera Angle** keys (also known as the M Keys), and a tip about color coding your clips.

Premapping Edit Points (also known as Transitions)

Rather than placing cut-points one at a time, you can place a series of cut points in Real Time and then go back in a second pass to switch the camera angles and/or to adjust the cut-points. Here are the steps:

1. In order to use this technique, the **Add Edit** function must be mapped to your keyboard. The **Add Edit** function can be found at: **Tools Menu | Command Palette | Edit tab**. Details on mapping buttons can be found in the *Mapping buttons and menu selections* recipe in *Chapter 2, Customizing Your Work Environment*.

2. Edit a **Group Clip** into your Sequence.

3. Enable the Video and/or Audio Track Selectors for the tracks you want to edit in the Sequence. For example, you might have four camera angles of a person giving a speech that are within a **Group Clip**, but are using just one audio track because it was a direct feed from the sound system. Therefore, in that instance, you would enable only the Video Track Selector.

4. Since you will already have a general idea of the different camera angles within the **Group Clip** (for example, Wide Shot, Close-up, Profile, Audience Reaction, and so on), you can make the decisions about where you think you'd like to switch angles (premapping), using the next steps.

5. Play the Sequence.

6. As the Sequence plays, any time you feel is a good point to switch camera angles, simply press the **Add Edit** function that you mapped to your keyboard. Note that you will *not* see the cuts you made until *after you've stopped the playback*. Don't worry that you may have made a cut in the wrong place. You can adjust that position later, using **Double-Roller Trim**. Also, see the next section for information on removing unwanted cuts.

7. Stop the playback. All the cuts (**Add Edits**) will now appear.

8. Use whatever technique (detailed earlier in the recipe steps) that you like to change the video angle and/or audio source.

Removing unwanted edit points

Here are two methods for removing transitions/edit points:

▶ Method 1: Enter **Trim Mode** at the cut-point (transition) that you want to remove. By default, you will be placed into the **Double-Roller Trim** configuration. This is exactly what you want. Use your mouse/cursor to drag the **Double-Roller Trim Rollers** until they come into contact with another transition. Avid Media Composer's programming will automatically stop the trim from progressing beyond that point. So, you could do this with your eyes closed! After you release the mouse button and then grab the **Trim Rollers** a second time, then you could continue to trim further if you like. You can also use the **Play Reverse**, **Pause**, and **Play Forward** functions (by default on the *J*, *K*, and *L* keys) while in **Trim Mode**. Note that the programming in earlier releases *may* be different with regard to JKL Trimming and transitions. In earlier releases, you *might* find that the programming tells Media Composer to stop a **Double-Roller Trim 1** frame before contacting a transition.

▶ Method 2: If the transition is what Avid calls a **Match Frame Edit** (with a white equals symbol appearing on it), then you will find a discussion about removing these in the *Using Clip Mode with dissolves to make level And pan adjustments* recipe in *Chapter 7, Mono and Stero Audio Mixing* (specifically, see step 6, as well as the *There's more* section).

Details about the MultiCamera Angle Keys (The M Keys)

Following is some useful information about using the **MultiCamera Angle** keys.

▶ By default, they are mapped on the following keys:

- ❑ *F9*: **MultiCamera Angle 1 (M1)**
- ❑ *F10*: **M2**
- ❑ *F11*: **M3**
- ❑ *F12*: **M4**
- ❑ *Shift* key + *F9*: **M5**
- ❑ *Shift* key + *F10*: **M6**

           ❑   *Shift* key + *F11*: **M7**

           ❑   *Shift* key + *F12*: **M8**

▸   You can map the M keys anywhere you like. The M keys can be found at **Tools Menu | Command Palette | MCam tab**. For example, I have a separate keyboard mapping for when I'm editing with **Group Clips/MultiCamera Mode** (see *Chapter 2, Customizing Your Work Environment* for more information on alternate settings and keyboard mapping). I've chosen to place the **MultiCamera Angle** functions onto the F keys; and because I'm on a Mac I can also use the *F1* key (on a PC the *F1* key cannot be customized because it's reserved by the operating system for Help). I make it easy for myself to remember what M function is mapped where by placing **M1** onto the *F1* key, **M2** onto the *F2* key, and so on.

▸   The **MultiCamera Angle** function does *not* switch the audio. The exception to this would be if you have the **Audio Follow Video** feature enabled.

▸   You *can* use the M keys when you're *not* in **MultiCamera Mode**. Further, you do not even have to be using the **Quad Split** or **9 Split Displays**. **M1** will be the first clip/angle within the **Group Clip**, **M2** would be the second clip, and so on. This is one reason performing a **Sort** on the **Name Column** before Grouping the Clips is helpful. More details on this topic are earlier in this chapter within the *Syncing and grouping clips with common reference points* recipe.

▸   You do *not* have to use the **Add Edit** function before using any of the M keys. When you press an M key, it makes a cut as well as switches the camera angle.

▸   The M keys correspond to activating the **Quad Split** and **9 Split Displays** as follows:

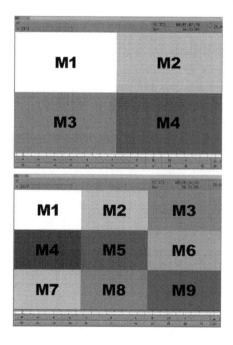

Color Coding Clips/Camera Angles

If you'd like to be able to have a very quick visual reference of what camera angles you're using in your Sequence, you can color code the clips. For example, let's say we are editing a scene with three characters. The camera angles are:

▸ **Master Shot** of all three characters

▸ **Close-Up** of **KATIE**

▸ **Close-Up** of **LEAH**

▸ **Close-Up** of **SAMANTHA**

We can choose to color code the **Master Shot** as green, **KATIE** as purple, **LEAH** as pink, and **SAMANTHA** as yellow. Here's how to make it all work:

1. In Media Composer Version 6, the programmers have displayed the **Color Column** in the bin by default and placed it to the left of the **Name Column**. In earlier releases, you can choose to display the **Color Column** from **Bin Menu | Choose Columns**.

2. Right-click on the small color swatch next to a clip's name and select a color from the palette that appears. In earlier releases, you will left-click within the **Color Column**.

3. In all releases of Media Composer, you may also color code a clip by select it/them and then going to **Edit Menu | Set Clip Color**.

4. Repeat steps 2 or 3 for additional clips if needed.

5. Though you have color coded the clips in the bin, these colors will not be visible in the **Timeline** unless you choose to have them displayed, using the next steps.

6. Go to **Timeline Window Fast Menu** (the hamburger-looking icon in the bottom-left of the **Timeline Window**) | **Clip Color** and then enable the option **Source Color**.

7. An optional step is to save a **Timeline View** with **Clip Color** enabled. More information about **Timeline Views** is in *Chapter 2, Customizing Your Work Environment*.

MultiCamera Mode Editing

MultiCamera Mode editing (MultiCam for short) provides additional editing features that are not available when simply editing with a **Group Clip**. To be clear, *you can still use all the features and editing techniques discussed previously in this chapter* while in **MultiCamera Mode**, however you get more. Specifically, you get the ability to switch camera angles in real time! This is accomplished by using the **MultiCamera Angle Keys** (also known as the M Keys) on the keyboard. See the previous *There's more...* section for the *Details about the MultiCamera Angle keys*.

Getting ready We'll get ready by first setting up the **Split Display**. See the previous *Using The MultiCamera display and methods of switching camera angles* and *Swap Cam Bank: Toggling the MultiCamera display* recipes for more information on this topic.

Also see the next *MultiCamera mode settings* recipe for more information on settings which control the **Split Display** in the **Source Window** as well as on your **Client Monitor** (if you have one connected to your system).

- ▸ Method 1: By default, *before you enter* **MultiCamera Mode**, whichever Split display you used last tells Media Composer how you'd like your display to be when you use **MultiCamera Mode**. For example, let's say I'm *not* in **MultiCamera Mode** and then I enable the **Nine Split** display for a minute, and then I turn it off, so that I'm back to viewing only one camera angle at a time (Avid calls this Full Monitor Display). Well, Media Composer remembers that, and later in the day when I do enable **MultiCamera Mode** editing the display will be **Nine Split**. If you haven't set a preference, then it will default to the **Quad Split** display.

- ▸ Method 2: If you map **Quad Split** and **9 Split** below the **Record Monitor**, onto the **Timeline Toolbar**, or onto the keyboard, then you will get these three behaviors:

  - ❑ Enables **MultiCamera Mode**
  - ❑ Enables the selected **Split Display** type you clicked/pressed
  - ❑ *While you are using* **MultiCamera Mode**, you can press the **Split Display** buttons to change the display type

How to do it...

Here we'll go through the process of editing **Group Clips** in real time, using **MultiCamera Mode**:

1. First, select what you'd like to edit into the Sequence; so start by loading a **Group Clip** into the **Source Window**.

2. Select the video angle you'd like to edit into the Sequence to start out with. For example, possibly you'd prefer to start with the Wide Shot/Master Shot. Honestly, this is an option and is not required because you can quickly and easily change angles/shots at any time after it has been edited into the Sequence. To select the video, you could use one of the following options:

   - ❑ Make a selection from the **Group Clip Menu** that's above the **Source Window**.
   - ❑ Use the **Previous in Group/Next in Group** functions (mapped by default on the up and down arrow keys).
   - ❑ If you are in **Quad Split** or **9 Split Display**, click on one of the camera angle's display regions to activate it. A green line appears below the active camera angle.

❑ Press one of the **MultiCamera Angle Buttons** (also known as the M keys) on the keyboard.

3. From the **Group Clip Menu**, select which audio sources you want to edit into the Sequence. Optionally, you can enable the **Audio Follow Video** feature (discussed earlier in this chapter in the *Using the Group Clip menu* recipe).

4. Edit all of, or a portion of, the **Group Clip** into your Sequence.

5. Place your blue **Position Indicator** *over the* **Group Clip** in your Sequence wherever you'd like to begin editing it.

6. Make sure that the Video Track Selector is enabled. The Audio Track Selector(s) can also be enabled if you want to simultaneously affect the audio as well. An example for doing this would be when the audio from each camera angle is different and you're using the **Audio Follow Video** feature. See the earlier *Using the Group Clip menu* recipe for details.

7. Enter **MultiCamera Mode** using any of these methods:

❑ Go to **Special Menu | MultiCamera Mode**.

❑ Use the keyboard shortcut *Shift + cmd/Ctrl + M.*

❑ If you have mapped the **Quad Split** and/or **9 Split Display** function(s) below the **Record Monitor**, on the **Timeline Toolbar**, or on the keyboard, then when you click/press one of these buttons, then two things will happen: You will enable **MultiCamera Mode**, and the display type you selected will be activated.

8. After entering **MultiCamera Mode**, the following will have occurred:

❑ Media Composer instantly and automatically gangs (locks) the Sequence and the **Multiple Camera Angle Window** (also known as the **Source Window**) into sync with one another. You'll see that when you move the blue **Position Indicator** that all the displays are in sync and move together.

❑ No buttons will appear under the **Multiple Camera Angle Window** (also known as the **Source Window**). This is a useful visual reminder what editing mode you're in. This is especially helpful if, when you're not in **MultiCamera Mode**, you also have the **Source Window** set to one of the Split displays as well. It's also helpful to know that in releases of Media Composer before Version 6 if you click in the non-button, gray area below the **Multiple Camera Angle Window**, then *you will be taken out* of **MultiCamera Mode**. In Version 6, this is not available. So, in order to exit **Multicamera Mode**, you can either go to the **Special Menu | MultiCamera Mode**, or use the shortcut *Shift + cmd/Ctrl + M.*

9. To edit in **MultiCamera Mode**, you can use any of the four methods:

    ❑   Method 1 (Non-Real Time): First, move the blue **Position Indicator** to a point in the Sequence where you'd like to switch camera angles. Then click your cursor in the **Multiple Camera Angle Window** onto one of the different camera angles. A green line will appear below the active camera and you'll see that Media Composer placed a cut in the Sequence as well as switched the camera angle for you.

    ❑   Method 2 (Real Time): First, place your blue **Position Indicator** over the **Group Clip** in your Sequence wherever you'd like to begin editing it. Second, play the Sequence. Then, while the Sequence is playing, press any of the M keys mapped to your keyboard. See the previous *There's more...* section for the recipe titled *Details about the MultiCamera Angle keys (the M keys)* for more information. You will see the image change in your **Record Monitor** and you'll see the green line update in the **Multiple Camera Angle Window**. However, you will not see the actual cut-points appear in the Sequence until after the playback has stopped.

    ❑   Method 3 (Real Time – Numeric Keypad): This feature only works when you are in **MultiCamera Mode**, and you are *playing* in Real Time. The numeric keypad will activate the camera angles as seen in the following screenshot:

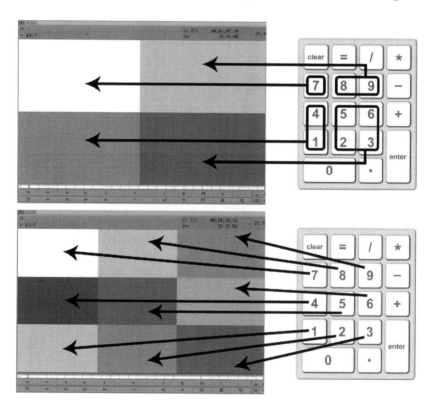

❑ Method 4 (Non-Real Time): While in **MultiCamera Mode**, you can still use all the methods discussed earlier in this chapter in the *Editing with a Group Clip: Not using MultiCamera mode* recipe. Note that this includes using the M Keys that you mapped to the keyboard. For emphasis, you do *not* have to be playing in Real Time in order to use the M Keys.

How it works...

When you are in **MultiCamera Mode**, Media Composer will automatically display the source **Group Clip** in the **Multiple Camera Angle Window** (also known as the **Source Window**), as well as sync (also known as gang) them all together if:

▸ You are positioned over a **Group Clip**

▸ The appropriate Video Track Selector is enabled

There's more...

Here are two methods of Swapping the **Cam Bank** when in **MultiCamera Mode**.

Swap Cam Bank In MultiCamera Mode

Map the **Swap Cam Bank** function (**Tools Menu | Command Palette | MCam tab**) to any of these locations:

▸ Below the **Record Window**

▸ Within the **Timeline Toolbar**

▸ On your keyboard

The second method is to right-click with the mouse while in **MultiCamera Mode**. For emphasis, you *must* be using **MultiCamera Mode** in order to use this feature with the mouse.

See also

▸ The *Editing with a Group Clip – not using MultiCamera mode* recipe

▸ The *MultiCamera Mode Settings* recipe

MultiCamera Mode Settings

There are some settings that control a couple different aspects of **MultiCamera Mode**:

▶ The display type in the **Source Window** when you are in **MultiCamera Mode**.

▶ The display type on your Client Monitor when you are in **MultiCamera Mode**. To be clear, this refers to the display on a PAL, NTSC, or SECAM monitor connected to your editing system.

How to do it...

Here's how to access and customize the **MultiCam** settings:

1. Go to **Project Window | Settings tab | Composer Settings | MultiCam tab**.

2. From the **Split Mode Play** menu, you can:

   ❑ Leave it set to the default setting of **Quad** or **Nine Split**. More information about **Quad** or **Nine Split** display is earlier in this chapter in the the *Using the MultiCamera display and methods of switching camera angles* recipe.

   ❑ Select **Fullscreen**. Fullscreen will display only for the active camera.

3. From the **MultiCam Mode Client Monitor** menu, you can:

   ❑ Leave it set to the default setting of **Quad** or **Nine Split**. An example of when this is useful would be when you're working with the director and he/she wants to tell you which camera angles to switch to. You will still be able to see the Sequence as normal in the **Record Monitor**.

   ❑ Select **Linecut**. Selecting this will display the Sequence.

   ❑ Select **Off** if you don't want any video displayed on the **Client Monitor** while in **MultiCamera Mode**.

9

Output Tips and Tricks

In this chapter, we will cover:

- ▸ Creating accurate Color Bars and Tone
- ▸ Methods for setting Sequence Timecode
- ▸ Adding Filler for Color Bars, Tone, and Slate
- ▸ Exporting a still image
- ▸ Exporting multiple still images using Markers
- ▸ Exporting a QuickTime Reference Movie
- ▸ Exporting a QuickTime Movie (Self Contained)
- ▸ Using the Timecode Burn-In effect

Introduction

This chapter will focus on topics that sometimes cause some frustration for users when they're *outputting*. First, we'll look at creating bars and tone, along with how to adjust your Sequence to accommodate them. Then we look at methods to export still images and QuickTime movies. Lastly, we'll examine the **Timecode Burn-In** effect.

Creating accurate Color Bars and Tone

First, it's helpful to understand what **Color Bars** and **Tone** are for. The goal when mastering is to make sure that the image and sound meet broadcast standards, and that you do as much as possible so that your program is viewed and heard outside of your facility just as you created it. In order to do this, we all agree to use a common reference for picture and a common reference for audio. This way, when your film or program is broadcast or duplicated, if there are any deviations from these agreed upon reference values on the **Master Tape** or **Master Digital File**, then adjustments can be made, so that the image and audio remain within broadcast specifications as well as are consistent to the levels they were when mastered at your facility.

Before mastering, we start by using **Color Bars** and **Tone** to calibrate the equipment in our edit bay/facility. We'd use **Color Bars** to properly calibrate the external NTSC, PAL, and/or HD monitor that is connected to the editing system; and we'd use **Tone** to calibrate the audio signal as it leaves the editing system and makes its way through all the different devices in our editing bay. For example, you'd play a 0VU (zero Volume Units) tone out of your Media Composer (see the *Understanding the Audio Tool* recipe in *Chapter 7, Mono and Stereo A udio Mixing*) in order to adjust the mixing board's input and output to 0VU, and then from the mixing board the signal would flow to a deck, which would also be adjusted to receive the signal at 0VU.

There are different types of **Color Bars** for both PAL and NTSC. We'll focus on the commonly used **Society of Motion Picture and Television Engineers** (**SMPTE**) Color Bars which are used in North America, though the concepts will be the same even if you're using PAL.

Keeping things simple, Color Bars obviously contain different colors in them, but they also contain varying levels of brightness. In professional lingo, we refer to color as Chrominance (Chroma, for short) and brightness as Luminance (Luma, for short). We analyze the Chroma and Luma values using devices called Oscilloscopes (Scopes, for short). A **Waveform Monitor** oscilloscope is used to analyze the Luminance values of the video signal and a **Vectorscope** is used to analyze the Chrominance.

With regard to tone, we set it so that its analogue value is **0VU**. On the digital side of things, **0VU** can be set to equate to any digital value. However, a very common digital setting is **-20dB**. There is some additional discussion about this in the *Understanding the Audio Tool* recipe in *Chapter 7, Mono and Stereo Audio Mixing*.

Now that you've gotten a brief introduction to Bars and Tone, let's get to making them (and making them properly).

Getting ready

Before we get to the actual recipe, it is important to do the following:

- Set the proper format for your **Color Bars**. Go to: **Project Window | Format** tab.
- Set the desired resolution for your **Color Bars** (for example, 1:1). Go to: **Tools Menu |Media Creation | Import Tab**.
- This step is optional. Make a new bin. Name it `Bars` and `Tone`.

How to do it...

You can certainly create bars and tone in whichever order you like, but let's start with the less complicated procedure first. So, let's begin by creating tone.

1. Click on the menu button next to the **Audio Meters** in the **Timeline Toolbar**. Note that there is an alternate method to open the **Create Tone Media** dialog window in the *There's more...* section.

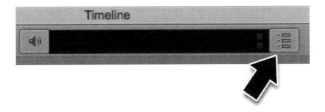

2. From the menu, select **Create Tone Media**. A dialog window will open:

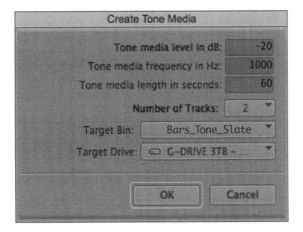

3. In the **Create Tone Media** dialog window, customize the following based on your needs (frequently, the default values will be appropriate):

    ❑ **Tone media level in dB**: The default is **-20** dB. If you've mixed to a different level (for example, -14 dB) then you would enter the appropriate value here.

    ❑ **Tone media frequency in Hz**: The default is **1000** Hz (also known as 1 Kilohertz, or commonly referred to as 1K). This is the standard reference tone. However, you may be asked to include tone at a different frequency. If so, you can enter the required value here.

    ❑ **Tone media length in seconds**: The default is **60** seconds. Note that Media Composer doesn't actually create media for the duration you specify. It actually just creates one frame of it and then refers to that one frame over and over for the duration you set for the **Master Clip**. This allows the creation to go very quickly, and for the media file to take up a very small amount of space on your hard drive.

4. Set the **Number of Tracks** you'd like from the pull-down menu. The default is **1**, though you may need more. A common example would be if you were outputting in stereo, then you'd want two tracks of tone. This will save you time when editing it into your sequence since it will be one edit rather than two.

5. **Target Bin**: Select the bin you'd like place the **Master Clip** for the tone.

6. **Target Drive**: Select the drive where you'd like to place the media that will be created.

7. Click **OK**. Very quickly the tone media and **Master clip** will be created.

8. Next will be the process to import **Color Bars** properly. The next steps apply to using NTSC, SMPTE Color Bars.

9. Select the open bin into which you'd like to import the **Color Bars** in order to make it active.

10. Go to **File Menu | Import** (or right-click inside the bin and select **Import** from the menu that appears).

11. Navigate into the folder that contains the Media Composer application.

12. Inside the folder that contains the Media Composer application, you will see several folders. The one you want to navigate to next is the **Supporting Files** folder.

13. Inside the `Supporting Files` folder, navigate inside the **Test_Patterns** folder.

14. Inside the `Test Patterns` folder, you will see the following four folders:

    ❑ **HD_720** (for 1280 x 720 raster)

    ❑ **HD_1080** (for 1920 x 1080 raster)

    ❑ **SD_NTSC** (for Standard Definition in the NTSC Standard)

    ❑ **SD_PAL** (for Standard Definition in the PAL Standard)

15. Navigate inside of the appropriate folder (listed in step 14) for your situation/needs. For the remainder of this recipe's steps, I'll navigate inside the HD_1080 folder *as an example.*

16. *After navigating into the appropriate folder, and before you select a file*, perform the next steps.

17. In the dialog window, use the pull-down menu to select the hard drive you want the media you'll be creating to be placed when the file is imported.

18. In the dialog window, select the resolution for the media you'll be creating. It should already be set, if you followed the steps in the *Getting ready* section. However, you can double-check it here, or select a different resolution.

19. The next step is *crucial to correctly importing the file.*

20. Click on the **Options** button. This will open the **Import Settings** dialog window.

21. Click on the **Image** tab, if it is not already displayed.

22. Set the following:

    ❑ **Image Size Adjustment**: In the *Getting ready* section, I had you make sure to set the correct format for your project. Since the file you will import should be the same dimensions as the format you've set, then enable the choice labeled as **Image sized for current format**.

    ❑ **Field Ordering In File**: Since the file is a graphic file, with no separate fields, then enable the choice labeled as **Ordered for current format**.

    ❑ **File Pixel to Video Mapping**: The file you're going to import is already at broadcast levels (as opposed to RGB levels which are used in graphics), so you'll enable the choice labeled as **601 SD or 709 HD (16 - 235)**. For emphasis, this is a very important part of the recipe that ensures that the Chroma and Luma levels are correct when the file is imported. For details, see the *How it works...* section after this recipe.

    ❑ **Alpha Channel**: This relates to any transparency information that may be in a file. The Color Bars file you'll be importing does not have an Alpha Channel, so it honestly doesn't matter which selection you make here. However, if it makes you feel more comfortable, feel free to select **Ignore**.

    ❑ **Frame Import Duration**: The default is **60** seconds, but you can enter any value you like. Just as when creating tone, Media Composer doesn't actually create media for the duration you specify. It actually just creates one frame of it and then refers to that one frame over and over for the duration you set for the **Master Clip**. This allows the creation to go very quickly, and for the media file to take up a very small amount of space on your hard drive.

23. Click the **OK** button to close the **Import Settings** dialog window.

24. Now you're ready to select the file you'd like to import. In my example, we would select SMPTE_Bars.tif.

25. To start the import, you can do one of the following:

    ❏ Double-click on the file you want to import

    ❏ Select the file, then click the "**Open**" button in the bottom-right of the dialog window

26. The **Color Bars** will then quickly be imported into your selected bin.

How it works...

While the audio tone is generated by Media Composer, the **Color Bars** are created by importing a special file which Avid provides for us. The file is special because it is not at the Chroma and Luma levels used in the graphics field (referred to as RGB). Instead, this file's Chroma and Luma values are at television broadcast standards. Technically, these standards are referred to as ITU-R BT.601 for SD video and ITU-R BT.709 for HD video. I mention these two standards because you see the numbers **601** and **709** in the **Import Settings** dialog window, and it explains where those numbers come from.

There's more...

The following is an additional method to create tone, along with some helpful supporting information.

Accessing the Create Tone Media Dialog Window

There is an alternate method for opening the **Create Tone Media** dialog window from the one presented in the recipe of steps:

1. Open the **Audio Tool: Tools Menu | Audio Tool**.

2. Click on the button labeled as **PH**. Avid calls this the **Peak Hold Menu**.

3. From the menu, select **Create Tone Media**.

The Test Pattern Files

Inside the `Test_Patterns` folder there are some test patterns in the `.pct` file format. These files are 8 bit. The files inside the folders are in the `.tif` file format (`.tif`) and are 16 bit.

Color Bars I and Q Blocks

Avid states that, if you must have **I** and **Q** blocks correct in a sequence, do one of the following:

- ▶ Record **SMPTE** bars from a signal generator.

- ▶ Use the **Video Output** tool to generate **SMPTE** bars, and record them to tape using the controls on the deck. Then, capture them back into the system from the tape.

Methods for setting Sequence Timecode

These topics are presented within the context of adding **Color Bars** and **Tone** at the beginning of your Sequence prior to output. However:

- ▶ You can change **Timecode** values and/or types (that is, **Drop Frame** or **Non-Drop Frame**) whenever you need.

- ▶ Note that it is okay to first add the **Filler** to accommodate the **Color Bars**, **Tone**, and **Slate**, and then to change the **Timecode**. I'm simply showing you to change the **Timecode** first because this is my personal preference.

- ▶ See the *There's more...* section after the recipe of steps for discussion of other methods and situations for setting Sequence Timecode.

Before we get into the recipe of steps, let's start with some helpful background information. When mastering in a professional situation, we must:

- ▶ Make sure that the very first frame of the content (for example, film, TV show, commercial, and so on) is placed *precisely* in the Sequence, so that its **Timecode** value is on the hour frame *exactly*. For example, in the U.S., we would typically make sure that the very first frame of the content in our Sequence is at 01;00;00;00 (or any other hour value as is required). Other countries may use different values (for example, content typically begins at 10:00:00:00 in the UK).

- ▶ **Add Filler** at the beginning of the Sequence to accommodate the **Color Bars** and **Tone**, **Slate**, and any other elements required (for example, a countdown clock) before the content begins. Adding **Filler** is discussed in the following the *Adding Filler for Color Bars, Tone, and Slate* recipe.

▶ For television broadcast in the U.S. (and other countries that use the NTSC standard), we use a type of Timecode that is referred to as **Drop Frame Timecode** (as opposed to **Non-Drop Frame Timecode**). For anyone unfamiliar with these two types of Timecode, I'll avoid the technical reason for the two types and simply relate that **Drop Frame Timecode** *is* temporally accurate. In other words, it *does correspond* to clock time: 1 hour of **Drop-Frame Timecode** equals 1 hour of time on a clock. On the other hand, **Non-Drop Frame Timecode** is *not* temporally accurate. In other words, it does *not* sync with regular clock time. Here's an example:

   ❑ Start playing a Sequence (or tape) beginning at 01:00:00:00 in **Non-Drop Frame Timecode** at the exact same time as you start a stop-watch.

   ❑ When the Sequence (or tape) shows that it has played for 1 hour (reaching the Timecode value of 02:00:00:00) stop both the Sequence and the stop watch at the same time.

   ❑ What you'll find is that while the Sequence time indicates that 1 hour has passed, that the stop watch indicates, correctly, that 01:00:03:18 (1 hour, 0 minutes, 3 seconds, and 18 frames) of time has gone by. So you see **Non-Drop Frame Timecode** is not clock accurate, which is why those countries that use the NTSC standard use **Drop Frame Timecode**, which is clock accurate for television broadcast purposes. Note that for a great explanation of the technical reason why **Drop Frame Timecode** was implemented, and what the math involved is, I recommend the book *Nonlinear, 4th edition, Michael Rubin, Paperback.*

Now that you have a bit of background on **Drop Frame** versus **Non-Drop Frame Timecode**, a logical question that needs to be answered is how do I know which type of Timecode is on a tape or that my Sequence is using? The answer is simple: Look at the symbol (referred to as the **separator**) that appears between the numbers. When looking at the Timecode of a tape while it's in a tape deck, if all of the separator symbols between the numbers are colons (:), then the **Timecode** type is **Non-Drop Frame**. If you see that any separator deviates from this in any way, then the **Timecode** type is **Drop Frame**. Here's just one example of various deviations you might encounter: If you paused a tape in a deck and saw that the Timecode was **06:11:18.04**, then you'd know that the **Timecode** type was **Drop Frame**. Did you notice that between the numbers **18** and **04** there wasn't a colon, but instead it was only a period? That is the deviation that indicates **Drop Frame Timecode**. However, Media Composer makes it much easier to tell which type of **Timecode** your Sequence is using:

▶ **Non-Drop Frame Timecode** will have colons (**:**) as separators between *all* the numbers

▶ **Drop Frame Timecode** will have semi-colons (**;**) as separators between *all* the numbers

Getting ready

The context of this recipe of steps is that you are changing the starting **Timecode** value to make room for the **Bars**, **Tone**, and **Slate**; and that your content needs to begin at the even hour position, as is required in professional situations. See the discussion earlier for details on **Timecode**.

Note that this recipe of steps applies to Media Composer Version 5.x and later. Prior to Version 5.x, you would use one of the following methods:

▶ Click on the **Record Monitor** to make it active, then go to the **File Menu** and select **Get Clip Info**

▶ Click on the **Record Monitor** to make it active, then use the shortcut *cmd/Ctrl + I*

How to do it...

There are two methods available for changing the starting **Timecode** value and/or the **Timecode** type. The following is one method and later, in the *There's more...* section, you will find the other.

1. Load the Sequence into the **Timeline**.

2. Right-click on the **Record Monitor**.

3. From the menu that appears, select **Sequence Report**.

4. The **Sequence Report** dialog window will open. In the **Starting TC** entry box, you can do the following:

   ❏ If the **Timecode** *type* (**Drop Frame** or **Non-Drop Frame**) is already set to the type you need, then to change the **Timecode** *value*, all you have to do is highlight the current entry value and type the new numbers. Media Composer will take care of adding the separator symbols for you.

   ❏ If all you need to do is to change the **Timecode** type (but not the value), you do not need to change every separator symbol. All you have to do is place your cursor anywhere in the **Starting TC** entry box and then type either a colon or a semi-colon. Media Composer will change all the separators for you.

5. Note that this example is based on a Sequence that was already set to use **Drop Frame Timecode**. Additionally, after setting the new starting **Timecode** value, you would add 1 minute and 30 seconds of **Filler** at the beginning of the Sequence, into which you would later place the **Color Bars**, **Tone**, and **Slate** (adding FIller for bars, tone and slate is covered in the recipe that follows this one).

6. In the **Starting TC** entry box, I enter `00583000`. Media Composer automatically adds the separator symbols for me and the result is **00;58;30;00**.

7. Click the **Apply Changes** button.

8. This next step will seem strange and counter-intuitive. However, to complete the process, you will then click on the **Cancel** button.

9. You have now successfully changed the starting **Timecode** value and/or the **Timecode** type.

There's more...

Following are some additional tips regarding Sequence timecode.

Changing Timecode in the Bin

Rather than have to load a Sequence into the **Timeline Window** in order to modify the starting **Timecode** value, you can do it directly in a Bin.

1. Make sure that the **Start** column is displayed.

2. To change the starting **Timecode** value, highlight the existing numbers and then simply type in the new numbers. Media Composer will add the separator symbols for you.

3. To change the **Timecode** type (**Drop Frame** or **Non-Drop Frame**), *highlight* any one of the separators and enter the separator type that you need. Media Composer will change all the other separator symbols for you.

Setting a default starting Timecode value and type

Since I'm in the U.S. and work primarily in television (which uses **Drop Frame Timecode** at all times), I set my default starting **Timecode** for all new Sequences to **01;00;00;00** (one hour straight up); and I set the **Timecode** type to **Drop Frame** (semi-colon as the separators). To set the default Starting timecode for each new Sequence you make:

1. Go to **Project Window | Settings** tab | **General**.

2. Double-click the **General** settings to open the dialog window.

3. Enter the default starting **Timecode** value and/or type that you require.

4. Click the **OK** button.

5. Now each time you create a new Sequence, it will begin with the value and **Timecode** type you have set. For emphasis, this only affects new Sequences; it does not affect existing sequences.

See also

▶ The *Adding Filler for Color Bars, Tone, and Slate* recipe

Adding Filler for Color Bars, Tone, and Slate

While editing we generally do not have any additional material at the beginning of the Sequence, and we have the **Timecode** value of the first frame set to **01;00;00;00** (in the U.S.) or **10:00:00:00** (in the UK). It is very common to first add **Filler** to the beginning of the Sequence and then to add the **Color Bars**, **Tone**, and **Slate** into that region.

Getting ready

If you have not already read the previous *Methods For Setting Sequence Timecode* recipe, then you may find it helpful prior to reading this section if you are unfamiliar with that process.

This discussion presumes these two things:

▶ You are using the NTSC broadcast standard (which uses **Drop Frame Timecode**), as discussed in the previous section. If you are not, then make adjustments to the recipe of steps as required.

▶ You have *already changed* the starting **Timecode** value of your Sequence to **00;58;30;00** as discussed in the previous *Methods For Setting Sequence Timecode* recipe.

How to do it...

There are several methods you could use to add **Filler** at the beginning of your Sequence. However, I will present two of the more straightforward methods. The recipe of steps will present one method and we will see the other in the *There's more...* section.

1. Load your Sequence into the **Timeline Window**.

2. Do one of the following:

    ❑ Enable *all* video and audio tracks

    ❑ Enable the **Sync Locks** for *all* tracks

3. Go to the **Clip Name Menu** above your **Source Monitor** (see the next screenshot):

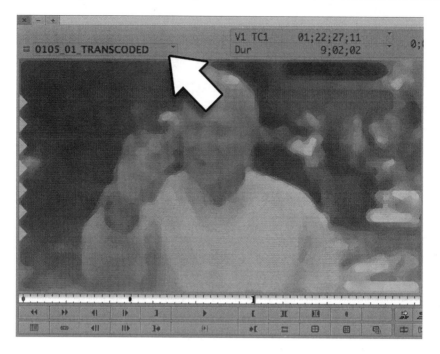

4. From the **Clip Name Menu**, select **Load Filler**. Media Composer will then load 2 minutes of **Filler**.

5. Place a **Mark In** at the beginning.

6. Using the Numeric Keypad, type in a + (plus symbol), and you'll see an entry box appear. *Note that* for those on a laptop, without an extended keyboard, press the *Ctrl* key twice in quick succession and the entry box will appear.

7. Now type in the amount of **Filler** you want to add. In this example, I'm going to type in a very specific value that compensates for **Drop Frame Timecode**, which will save me some work later (though I'll touch on that too in step 12, in case you choose not use this specific value). I will now type in the numbers 12927. Media Composer automatically adds the separators for me and the result is **+1:29:27** (1 minute, 29 seconds, and 27 frames).

8. Press the *Enter* key. The blue **Position Indicator** moves forward.

9. Place a **Mark Out**. You will have marked a duration of **1:29:28** (1 minute, 29 seconds, and 28 frames).

10. Go to the *very beginning* of your Sequence.

11. **Splice** the **Filler** into the Sequence.

12. In this example, we're using **Drop Frame Timecode** and the Sequence was previously set to begin at **00;58;30;00**. Therefore, after Splicing in the **Filler**, the result will be the following:

   ❑ You now have **Filler** at the beginning, ready for you to add **Bars**, **Tone**, and **Slate**.

   ❑ The Content in your Sequence has been pushed down and now begins at precisely **01;00;00;00,** as it should (see the *Methods For Setting Sequence Timecode* recipe for more information).

   ❑ Note that if, after adding the **Filler**, for any reason your content does not begin precisely at **01;00;00;00**, then you can use **Trim Mode** (specifically, yellow **Ripple Trim**) to add or remove **Filler** until the first frame of your content does properly start at **01;00;00;00**. When you trim, make sure that you are either trimming *all* the tracks, or that you have enabled **Sync Locks** for *all* tracks.

There's more...

You can instruct Media Composer to add **Filler** at the beginning of the Sequence by either:

▸ **Clip Menu | Add Filler at Start**

▸ Right-click in the **Timeline Window | Add Filler at Start**

A nice benefit of using this method is that it will maintain the starting **Timecode** value for the first frame of the Sequence. For example, when I'm editing, I will have no Filler at the beginning of my Sequence and the starting Timecode will be set to **01;00;00;00**. When I add **Filler** at the beginning, using the **Add Filler at Start** method, the content is pushed down by the **Filler** and Media Composer automatically compensates and keeps my content beginning at **01;00;00;00**. Nice, huh? Further, I instruct Media Composer to add exactly the amount of **Filler** I need for my **Bars**, **Tone**, and **Slate**. I do this by adjusting the default amount of **Filler** that Media Composer adds. By default, the **Add Filler at Start** feature adds 30 seconds of **Filler**. However, you can set whatever amount you'd like it to add by following these steps:

1. Go to **Project Window | Settings** tab | **Timeline** settings | **Edit** tab.

2. In the **Start Filler Duration** entry box, you can enter whatever value you want. For example, if you're using **Drop Frame Timecode**, then you might set the value to **00:01:29:28** to get the results I described in the previous recipe.

See also

▸ The *Methods For Setting Sequence Timecode* recipe

Exporting a still image

It's pretty common to have to export still images for use on the web, use in print materials, or to manipulate in another application (for example, Photoshop) and then to import the altered frame back into your project and edit it into your Sequence.

How to do it...

Here is how to export a still image:

1. In either the **Source Window** or **Record Window**, pause on the frame you want to export.

2. Enable the video track for the source clip or Sequence where the image resides (for example, **V2**).

3. To begin the Export process, you can use any of the following methods:

   - Right-click on **Source Monitor** and select **Export**

   - Right-click on the **Record Monitor** and select **Export**

   - Go to **File Menu | Export**

4. The **Export As...** dialog window will open. Enter a name for the file you will be exporting.

5. From the pull-down menu, select where you'd like the file to be placed when it's created (for example, Desktop).

6. Click on the **Options** button. The **Export Settings** dialog window will open.

7. From the **Export As** pull-down menu, select **Graphic**.

8. From the **Graphic Format** pull-down menu, Select your preference from the list of available formats. I particularly like that one of the choices is Photoshop.

9. Click the **Format Options** button to customize the quality of the exported file (this is available only for some formats, for example, JPEG).

10. From the **Width x Height** menu, select the setting that correctly reflects your format.

11. In the **Color Levels** section:

    - If you are exporting the file for use in print or on the web, then select **RGB**

    - If you are exporting the file to be manipulated in another application and later re-imported into your project, then select **609/701**

12. In the File Field Order section, Avid states:

   ❑ This defines which field is the upper field during export. For 23.976p, 29.97p, 24p, 25p, 50p, and 59.94p projects, these options do not appear, and all fields are automatically exported as progressive (still) frames.

   ❑ Use **Odd (Upper Field First)** if you are in a PAL project. Field 1 becomes the upper field (its lines become the odd-numbered lines) in the frame. Field 2's lines become the even-numbered lines. There is an exception to this. If your footage is PAL DV, then you will select **Even** (lower field first).

   ❑ Use **Even (Lower Field First)** if you are in an NTSC project. Field 1 becomes the lower field (its lines become the even-numbered lines) in the frame. Field 2's lines become the odd-numbered lines.

   ❑ Use **Single Field** if you want the output file to consist of only Field 1. For example, with SD video, your Avid editing application resizes the single field of 243 lines for NTSC (288 lines for PAL) to fit the frame as specified in the width and height selection.

13. Once you have set all the necessary options, click the **Save** button. This will close the **Export Settings** dialog window and take you back to the **Export As...** dialog window.

14. In the bottom-right of the **Export As...** dialog window, click the **Save** button.

15. Your single image will be exported.

Exporting multiple still images using Markers

It is possible to place Markers (previously called **Locators** in earlier releases) into your Source clip and/or your Sequence and then instruct Media Composer to export the images where the Markers have been placed. One example where this might be useful is if you've gone through your movie with the Producer or Director and used Markers to select many frames which they would like to give to the website designer to use. Rather than have to export all of the images one at a time, you can do them all at the same time.

How to do it...

Here we'll export multiple still images using Markers.

1. In either the **Source Window** or **Record Window**/Sequence, place Markers on the images you want to export.

2. Follow steps 2 through 12 in the previous *Exporting A Still Image* recipe.

3. While still displaying the **Export Settings** dialog window, enable the choices for *both*:

   ❏ **Sequential Files**

   ❏ **Markers Only**

4. Once you have set all the necessary options discussed in the *Exporting A Still Image recipe*, click the **Save** button. This will close the **Export Settings** dialog window and take you back to the **Export As...** dialog window.

5. In the bottom-right of the **Export As...** dialog window, click the **Save** button.

6. All images with a Marker will be exported.

How it works...

If you do *not* select the **Markers Only** option, then all frames that exist (or just those between a **Mark In** and a **Mark Out**, depending on your situation and **Export Settings**) will be exported. This creates what is often referred to as an **Image Sequence**. An **Image Sequence** is another method that you can use to provide images for use/manipulation in another application.

Exporting a QuickTime Reference Movie

Exporting to the `QuickTime` file format has become a very common way to get your content out of Media Composer and into another application (for example, for DVD encoding, for use as a reference with **ProTools**, to upload to the web, and so on).

There are a few things to be aware of when exporting a QuickTime Reference Movie out of Media Composer:

▸ **QuickTime Reference** is not the same as a **QuickTime Movie**. A QuickTime reference is a very small file that simply points (refers) to the Avid Media Composer media files from your project. It allows you to fool another application (for example, a compression application like QuickTime Pro, Sorenson Squeeze, or Adobe Media Encoder) into thinking that it's looking at a `QuickTime` file, so that you can then resize it and/or encode/compress it as you need. QuickTime Reference is convenient because they are created very quickly. However, they can *not* be shared with someone whose computer is not able to also reference your Avid Media Composer media files. For emphasis, if you have to send a `QuickTime` file to someone, then it needs to be what is referred to as Self Contained, meaning that the `QuickTime` file is a standalone file whose media is totally separate and independent from the Avid media files. To make a Self-Contained QuickTime file, you will select QuickTime Movie. This is discussed in the recipe that follows this one.

▸ Many Avid Media Composer editors report having better success in exporting QuickTime movies by first creating a **Video Mixdown** within Media Composer (found in the **Special Menu**), editing the file that is created into the Sequence, and then exporting only the mixdown track (and audio if desired) by using either of the methods listed (depending on your needs and preferences):

❑ Video resolution set to **Same As Source**, which creates a Self Contained QuickTime movie

❑ QuickTime Reference

▸ Be aware of the following:

❑ You can not create a QuickTime Reference if any of the media in the Sequence is linked through **AMA** (**Avid Media Access**). An export set to **Same As Source** or a Video Mixdown will be required.

❑ You can not perform a **Same As Source** export with Long-GOP video formats (for example, HDV, AVCHD, XDCAM-HD). You will need to first perform a Video Mixdown.

Suggestion: Before exporting a long Sequence, or a long selection from a **Master Clip**, perform what I refer to as a Small Scale Test. For example, rather than exporting your entire 25 minute short film as a Self Contained QuickTime file (which will take quite a long time), and then discover that the aspect ratio is not displaying correctly, or that the color levels are incorrect (or some other negative issue), I suggest you export a 5 to 10 second portion. This will export much faster and allow you to review it and make sure that all the settings are producing the results you want. Once you have the settings as they need to be, then you can export your content in its entirety.

How to do it...

Now we'll export a QuickTime Reference movie.

1. This is a recommended step, but it is not mandatory. If you have decided not to first perform a **Video Mixdown** (from the **Special Menu**) and then edit the resulting file into the Sequence before exporting (as mentioned earlier), then follow these additional steps.

   i. First, enable all the tracks (*cmd/Ctrl + A*).

   ii. Second, place a **Mark In** at the very beginning of the Sequence and a **Mark Out** at the very end.

   iii. Third, go to **Clip Menu | Expert Render In/Out** (you can also right-click in the **Timeline Window** to access **Expert Render In/Out**). This rendering step will help the export process to go faster.

2. Follow one of these options:

   ❑ If you want to export only a portion of your content (for example, movie, TV show, and so on), then place a **Mark In** and a **Mark Out** around the portion you want (discussed in step 9 will be how you tell Media Composer to pay attention, or not, to those Marks).

   ❑ If you want to export only certain tracks of your content (for example, video but not audio, or video along with specific audio tracks, and so on), then enable only the tracks you want to export. (discussed in step 9 is how you tell Media Composer to pay attention, or not, to only the enabled tracks).

3. To begin the **Export** process, you can use any of these methods:

   i. Right-click on the **Source Monitor** and select **Export**.

   ii. Right-click on the **Record Monitor** and select **Export**.

   iii. With the **Source** or **Record Monitor** active, go to **File Menu | Export**.

   iv. In a Bin, select one or more Clips and/or Sequences that you want to export. Then go to **File Menu | Export**. Note that you can also right-click and select **Export** from the menu. Just be sure that when you right-click that you do so on one of the selected items.

4. The **Export As...** dialog window will open.

5. Enter a name for the file you will be exporting.

6. From the pull-down menu, select where you'd like the file to be placed when it's created (for example, Desktop).

7. Click on the **Options** button. The **Export Settings** dialog window will open.

8. From the **Export As:** pull-down menu, select **QuickTime Reference**.

9. Some of the following settings are suggested only (you may need to make modifications, depending on your specific situation and requirements). You can consult **Avid Media Composer Help** for additional details:

   ▶ **Use Marks**: Select this if you want Media Composer to export only the material that is between the **In** and **Out Marks** in your Clip or Sequence. If you do not enable this selection, then the entire Clip or Sequence will be exported.

   ▶ **Use Enabled Tracks**: Select this if you want Media Composer to export only the material from specific tracks in a Clip or Sequence. If you do not enable this selection, then all the tracks in the Clip or Sequence will be exported. If you have performed a **Video Mixdown**, and edited the mixdown into your Sequence, then you will want to select this option, as well as to enable only the Track Selector for the track on which the **Video Mixdown** exists (along with any audio tracks you require).

   ▶ **Defaults** pull-down menu: Set this to **Digital Mastering**. See the *How it works...* section for more information.

10. The following selections *should be enabled*; in other words, they *should* have a check mark next to them (see the *How it works...* section for more information about these):

▸ **Flatten Video Tracks**

▸ **Fill Spaces with Black**

▸ **Render All Video Effects**

11. Additional settings are as follows:

▸ From the **Display Aspect Ratio** pull-down menu, select what you need. Generally the **Native dimensions** setting will produce the result you want. If you are exporting NTSC or PAL anamorphic material that needs to seen as 16:9, then you will want to select the **16:9** option.

▸ **Mixdown Audio Tracks**: This selection should be enabled. This will mix all the audio into a separate, standalone file. Even for a long program, this does not add much time to the process.

▸ **Audio Format**: Avid states, "Select the format that is supported by the application into which you will be importing the QuickTime reference movie".

   ❏ **WAVE**: Definitely compatible with Windows applications (and is a common standard used across other platforms as well).

   ❏ **AIFF-C**: Compatible with many third-party applications.

   ❏ Select **AIFF-C** for all audio media files you plan to transfer directly to a **ProTools** system for sweetening.

▸ **Sample Rate**: Set this to **Project** (meaning that it will mirror the audio sample rate as set in your **Audio Project Settings**) or choose a specific setting from the pull-down menu, depending on your situation and needs.

▸ **Sample Bit Depth**: Set this to **Project**, or choose a setting from the pull-down menu, depending on your situation and needs.

▸ **Use Network Media References**: If you're not accessing Avid media over a network, then you can ignore this, and leave it deselected. Avid states: "When this option is selected, the exported movie uses the machine and drive share name of the media drive in the QuickTime reference movie instead of a drive letter. Select this option when the media files referenced by the movie are accessed remotely over the network. If the media files are stored on the same drive as the QuickTime reference movie, you do not need to select this option. When this option is deselected, you cannot select Add Shares for Media Drives".

▸ **Add Shares for Media Drives**: If you're not accessing Avid media over a network, then you can ignore this, and leave it deselected. Avid states, "When this option is selected, your Avid editing application creates a new drive share for referenced media files stored on unshared network drives. The drive share is hidden, so other users do not see the shared drive when browsing your computer. You do not need to select this option when media is stored on the same drive as the QuickTime reference movie."

▸ **Use Avid Codecs**: Avid states, "Deselect this option when you are working in a cooperative environment where one or more non-Avid systems also have access to the media. Select this option if the non-Avid systems have the Avid DV Codec installed".

▸ **Color Levels**: This is a very important setting.

  ❑ If you are exporting the file for use only on a computer (for example, the web, or a PowerPoint presentation), then you would select **RGB**.

  ❑ If you are exporting in order to use the QuickTime file in another application (for example, After Effects), with the final goal being to create a new file that will be imported back into your project, or as a broadcast master, then select **601/709**. Further, if you are exporting in order to use the file for DVD encoding (for example, using Adobe Media Encoder), in order to you will want to use the **601/709** setting.

  ❑ These are exceptions to the previous point: If you are using Apple's application called Compressor, then you will export as **RGB** since that is the setting Compressor is programmed to expect. Also note that the application Sorenson Squeeze defaults to expecting the file you give to it to be **RGB**. However, you can adjust this in the encoding parameters to tell it that the file is at broadcast levels (**16-235**).

  ❑ Performing a small scale test, as discussed in the earlier information box, is advisable to ensure proper levels before exporting the entire Sequence.

▸ **Save As...** button: Clicking this does not begin the export. Its purpose is to allow you to save your own customized **Export Settings**.

▸ **Save** button: Clicking this will make Media Composer remember the settings you've just made and then take you back to the **Export As...** dialog window.

12. Click the **Save** button. Once you are back in the **Export As...** dialog window, then you will click its **Save** button in order to begin exporting the files. Using the settings above will produce two exported files:

  ❑ An audio file of your mixed down audio tracks.

  ❑ QuickTime Reference file. This file refers (points) to the mixed down audio file and the Avid Media Composer video media files.

How it works...

The following are details about some selections which are available when creating a QuickTime Reference Movie:

▸ **Defaults Menu**: You have two choices. Avid states the following:

- ❑ **Fast Draft** – When this option is selected, export is faster. This option automatically selects Flatten Video Tracks and Fill Spaces with Black, and automatically deselects Render All Video Effects and Premix Audio Tracks.

- ❑ **Digital Mastering** – When this option is selected, your Avid editing application renders all video effects and premixes audio tracks before exporting the file. This option automatically selects **Flatten Video Tracks**, **Fill Spaces with Black**, **Render All Video Effects**, and **Premix Audio Tracks**.

▸ **Flatten Video Tracks**: Avid states the following: "When this option is selected, your Avid editing application exports the composition as one video track. When this option is deselected, your Avid editing application generates one QuickTime video track for each video track in the composition, and you cannot select Fill Spaces with Black. Because most third-party applications do not understand multiple QuickTime video tracks, it is a good idea to select this option. This option is automatically selected if you select Fast Draft Defaults and Digital Mastering Defaults".

▸ **Fill Spaces with Black**: Avid states the following: "When this option is selected, your Avid editing application fills blank spaces in video tracks [Filler] with black in the QuickTime reference movie. Because QuickTime reference movies do not recognize blank spaces, it is a good idea to select this option. When this option is deselected, a QuickTime reference movie might interpret spaces in the video track as gray or as the background of the player. This option is automatically selected if you select Fast Draft Defaults and Digital Mastering Defaults".

▸ **Render All Video Effects**:" When this option is selected, Media Composer renders all unrendered video effects, including matte keys and titles, before the export begins. When this option is deselected, your Avid editing application ignores any unrendered effects. This option is automatically selected if you select Digital Mastering Defaults".

Exporting a QuickTime Movie (Self Contained)

Exporting to the QuickTime file format has become a very common way to get your content out of Media Composer and into another application (for example, for DVD encoding, for use as a reference with **ProTools**, to upload to the web, and so on).

Getting ready

Please review the following:

- ▶ The introduction to the previous *Exporting a QuickTime Reference Movie* recipe as it contains helpful information

- ▶ The previous information box that discusses performing a small scale test before exporting an entire sequence

How to do it...

Now that you have reviewed the information mentioned in the *Getting ready* section, let's export a Self Contained QuickTime movie.

1. Follow steps 1 through 7 in the previous *Exporting a QuickTime Reference Movie* recipe.

2. From the **Export As:** pull-down menu, select **QuickTime Movie** (not Quick Time Reference).

3. Some of the following settings are *suggestions only*, based on selecting the **Same as Source** option. You can consult **Avid Media Composer Help** for additional details.

- ▶ **Same as Source**: This is the fastest and easiest selection to make, and it maintains the same video quality you have in your Sequence. Avid states: *"When you select this option, your Avid editing application copies the media files directly with no resolution change. This method is fast and creates output that uses the same quality as your source files. This is the best method to use if you plan to process the video with another application,"* such as Adobe Media Encoder, After Effects, and so on. Be aware that you can not perform a Same As Source export with Long-GOP video formats (for example, HDV, AVCHD, XDCAM-HD). You will need to first perform a **Video Mixdown**. This is discussed in the *Exporting a QuickTime reference movie* recipe.

- ▶ **Use Marks**: Select this if you want Media Composer to export only the material between the **In** and **Out Marks** in your Clip or Sequence. If you do not enable this selection, then the entire Clip or Sequence will be exported.

- ▶ **Use Enabled Tracks**: Select this if you want Media Composer to export only the material from specific tracks in a Clip or Sequence. If you do not enable this selection, then all the tracks in the Clip or Sequence will be exported.

- ▶ **Video and Audio/Video Only/Audio Only**: This allows you to select what elements to export.

▸ **Use Avid Codecs**: Avid states, "Deselect the Use Avid Codec sub-option when you are working in a cooperative environment where one or more non-Avid systems also have access to the media. [I add: Only select this if the other non-Avid systems have the Avid codecs installed] – if you export DV media from a 24p or 23.976 project using Same as Source, you must use the Avid DV Codec to ensure the QuickTime movies retain all of the progressive information. If you do not use the Avid DV Codec, your Avid editing application treats movies as interlaced sources when you re-import them".

▸ **Custom**: Selecting this will reveal more options. A large **Format Options** button will appear. When you click on the **Format Options** button, then QuickTime's **Movie Settings** dialog window will open. Avid states, "When you select this option, your Avid editing application decompresses the files, processes them, and compresses the files at the requested resolution and audio format. This method is slower and often loses quality. Use this option only if you have to directly export a clip or sequence in a particular file format." For more information about these settings, see **Avid Media Composer Help**. The search string is QuickTime Movie Settings.

▸ **Video Format**: This will only be displayed if you have selected **Custom**. Avid states, "Width x Height: Defines the size of the clip. You can type in values or select from the predefined values in the Fast Menu. The values in the Fast menu suggest a typical use for each size, for example, 320 x 240 (Internet video, large). The Size to Fit sub-option sizes to fit the specified width and height. The Crop/Pad sub-option instructs your Avid editing application not to scale or resize the frames. If necessary, it adds black lines to the top and bottom of the frame to achieve the correct size".

▸ **File Field Order**: This will only be displayed if you have selected **Custom**. Avid states, "File Field Order: Defines which field is the upper field during export. For 23.976p, 29.97p, 24p, 25p, 50p, and 59.94p projects, these options do not appear, and all fields are automatically exported as progressive (still) frames". Refer to the following:.

   ❑ Use the **Odd (Upper Field First)** sub-option if you are in a PAL project. Field 1 becomes the upper field (its lines become the odd-numbered lines) in the frame. Field 2's lines become the even-numbered lines. There is an exception to this. If your footage is PAL DV, then you will select **Even** (Lower Field First).

   ❑ Use the **Even (Lower Field First)** sub-option if you are in an NTSC project. Field 1 becomes the lower field (its lines become the even-numbered lines) in the frame. Field 2's lines become the odd-numbered lines.

   ❑ Use the **Single Field** sub-option if you want the output file to consist of only Field 1. In this case, your Avid editing application resizes the single field of 243 lines for NTSC (288 lines for PAL) to fit the frame as specified in the width and height selection."

▶ **Audio Format**: Avid states, "If you select Direct Out as your audio format, you should select Same as Source for your export option for media that includes surround sound audio. This allows you to export the track assignments in your source sequence accurately".

▶ **Color Levels**: This is a very important setting. If you are exporting for use only on a computer (for example, the web, or a PowerPoint presentation) then you would select **RGB**. If you are exporting in order to use the `QuickTime` file in another application (for example, After Effects), with the final goal being to create a new file that will be imported back into your project, or as a broadcast master, then select **601/709**. Further, if you are exporting to then use the file for DVD encoding (for example, using Adobe Media Encoder), then you will want to use the **601/709** setting.

  ❑ Exceptions to the above: If you are using Apple's application called Compressor, then you will export as **RGB** since that is the setting Compressor is programmed to expect. Also note that the application Sorenson Squeeze defaults to expecting the file you give to it to be **RGB**. However, you can adjust this in the encoding parameters to tell it that the file is at broadcast levels (16 - 235).

  ❑ Performing a small test on 5 to 10 seconds of your Sequence, as discussed in the earlier information box, is advisable to ensure proper levels before exporting the entire Sequence.

▶ **Display Aspect Ratio**: Generally **Native dimensions** will produce the results you want. Avid states, "Defines an image size for the video you want to export: Native, 4:3, or 16:9. This lets you control the display format without modifying the source file". Also refer to the following:.

  ❑ If you are exporting NTSC or PAL **anamorphic** material that needs to be seen as **16:9**, then you will want to select the **16:9** option. Note that if you have any problems obtaining the proper display, you may also have to specify the **Size** settings within the **QuickTime** dialog window to a **16:9** frame size (see **Custom** settings earlier for more information).

  ❑ This option creates metadata (information that is stored with the QuickTime movie). Some applications, such as the QuickTime Player, can interpret this metadata and scale the image at display time.

  ❑ This option is useful for the **Same as Source** option because that option also preserves the original format. When you select **Same as Source**, the selections in the **Display Aspect Ratio** area are based on the resolution of the media you are exporting and the project type (NTSC or PAL).

  ❑ When you select **Custom**, your Avid editing application calculates the **Display Aspect Ratio** selections from the values you enter for Width x Height in the **Video Format** tab.

❑ Performing a test on a short portion of your Sequence is highly advisable to ensure proper aspect ratio before exporting the entire Sequence.

▶ **Save As...** button: Clicking this does not begin the export. Its purpose is to allow you to save your own customized **Export Settings**.

▶ **Save** button: Clicking this will make Media Composer remember the settings you've just made and then take you back to the **Export As...** dialog window.

4. Click the **Save** button. Once you are back in the **Export As...** dialog window, then you will click its **Save** button in order to begin exporting the file.

Using the Timecode Burn-In effect

It is very common to have to supply an output of your content with a Timecode overlay (commonly referred to as a **Timecode Burn-In**) for reasons such as:

▶ Provide a visual Timecode reference (or other data, for example, film edgecode) for a visual effects artist, music composer, sound designer, sound mixer, or film negative conformer

▶ To indicate the version and/or date of the output, who is receiving the output, and/or to place a copyright notice

For this recipe, we'll be using the relatively new **Timecode Burn-In** effect found in the **Generator** category of the **Effects Palette**. Not only does it play in Real Time (and if rendering is required, it will render much faster than a Non-Real Time effect), but it has multiple displays and a great deal of customizability.

How to do it...

This simple recipe of steps will tell you how to create what Avid calls an **Effect Template**. Once customized and saved, you can then re-apply it at any time in the future and have all your customizations already configured, which saves you time and trouble.

Additional details about the **Timecode Burn-In** effect can be found in the *There's more...* section as well as in the **Avid Media Composer Help** by using the search string `timecode burn-in`.

1. This step is optional. Create a new bin specifically for holding **Effect Templates**.

2. In your Sequence, create a new, empty video track: **Clip Menu | New Video Track** (or use the shortcut *cmd/Ctrl + Y*).

3. Make sure that the **Video Monitor** is moved up to the empty track that you created (see the next screenshot).

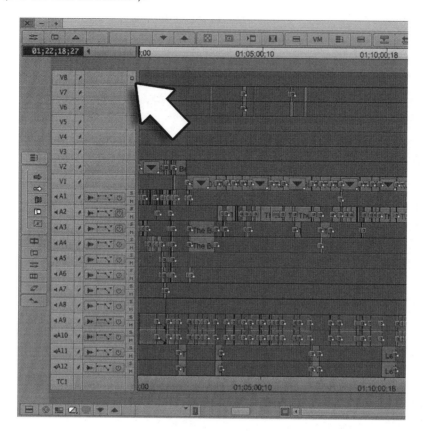

4. Open the **Effect Palette**: **Tools Menu | Effect Palette** (or use the shortcut *Cmd/Ctrl + 8*).

5. Select the category in the left column called **Generator**. All the effects in the **Generator** category will then be displayed in the right-hand column.

6. In the right-hand column, select the **Timecode Burn-In** effect.

7. Apply the **Timecode Burn-In** effect to the empty track you just created. One method to apply the effect is to drag-and-drop it.

8. Customize the effect as required. See the *There's more...* section for an overview of some of the features available.

9. To save this effect (or any effect) as an **Effect Template**, follow the next steps.

10. In the **Effect Editor**, next to the name of an effect, you will see an icon (see the next screenshot). For obvious reasons, Avid refers to this as the **Effect Icon**. Drag-and-drop the **Effect Icon** into any open bin. This creates the **Effect Template**.

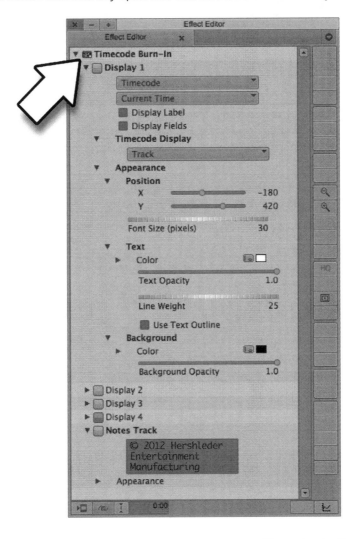

11. Label the **Effect Template** to reflect its purpose or specific customizations.

12. Use an **Effect Template** from a bin just as you would from the **Effect Palette**.

13. There's more...

Following is some additional information about the **Timecode Burn-in** effect.

Overview of Features

Here are some of the **Timecode Burn-in** effect features:

- When you place it/apply it into your Sequence, it automatically (instantly) accesses all the information (that is, metadata) about it such as **Sequence Timecode**, **Source Timecodes**, **KeyKode**, **clip names**, and so on

- Four information displays; this is very helpful. Here's just one example: When making a film, it is often necessary to simultaneously display **Sequence Timecode**, **Film KeyKode**, **Video Source Timecode**, and **Audio Source Timecode**.

- A **Notes Track** where you can enter whatever information is required, such as output date, version number, copyright notice, name of individual receiving the output, and so on

- All of the displays can be customized. Each **Display**, as well as the **Notes Track**, has a section labeled **Appearance** (a screenshot of the **Effect Editor** appears at the end of the recipe of steps earlier). Parameters include:

  - **Position on the screen**
  - **Font Size**
  - **Text Color**
  - **Text Opacity**
  - **Background Color**
  - **Background Opacity**

The other Timecode Burn-In effect

Depending on what version of Media Composer you are using, you *may* have two different **Timecode Burn-In** effects available in the **Effects Palette**. The one discussed in the recipe earlier is far superior to the other.

The other timecode effect can be found in the **Illusion FX** category. This is an older effect which does not play in Real Time. In other words, it has to be rendered. That is not its only negative trait; it also has only one display, and very few parameters available.

Additional Tips, Tricks, and Explanations

While writing, there were instances when there was some additional helpful information that did not fit the format of a cookbook. Therefore, I've placed a good deal of useful information into the several appendices. This appendix covers the following topics:

- ▶ Find Bin function tips
- ▶ Moving around: Methods and tips
- ▶ Getting more use from the Grid
- ▶ cmd/Ctrl + L and K: Several uses
- ▶ Locking and unlocking

Find Bin Function Tips

The **Find Bin** function is found by default below the **Source** and **Record Windows** in the far left of their button bars (below the **Rewind** button on both **Source** and **Record Windows**).

The **Find Bin** function has two default abilities:

- ▶ **Record Window/Timeline**: When you click the **Find Bin** function below the **Record Window** (or from the keyboard when either the **Record Window** or **Timeline Window** is active), then Media Composer will display the bin in which the currently loaded *Sequence* is stored. This is helpful when the Sequence Bin might be hidden under other windows, or when you might be working on several Sequences at the same time, which reside in different Bins.

> ▶ On the **Source Window**: When you click the **Find Bin** function below the **Source Window** (or from the keyboard when then **Source Window** is active), then Media Composer will display the bin in which the loaded source *Clip* is stored. This is quite a valuable feature, and the information later will explain two methods of using it.

The context

First, an explanation of the situation and the goal:

In your Sequence, you have a shot of a white cat that you liked last week, but now you'd like to change it to a shot of an orange cat. Your documentary project is large and has 150 bins in it. You have one bin that's filled with many shots of cats, including the white one that's currently in the Sequence as well as the orange one that you have in mind. The goal is to be able to locate and open the bin of all the cats as quickly and easily as possible.

Method 1: Using the Source Window

This is a multi-step process that uses two functions.

1. From the **Record Window/Timeline**, use the **Match Frame** function to load the clip of the white cat into the **Source Window** (see the *Using the Match Frame function* recipe in *Chapter 3, Polishing Gems*).

2. Now that the clip (white cat) is loaded in the **Source Window**, press the **Find Bin** function on the **Source Window** button bar.

3. The Bin that holds the Clip of the white cat will be displayed (even if it's closed, Media Composer will open it) and the clip of the white cat will be highlighted. Now you know which Clip you've already used, and you can now locate the new footage you want to use (orange cat).

Method 2: Directly from the Timeline

This is a process that only uses the **Find Bin** function:

1. Enable the track that contains the clip you want to use **Find Bin** with (I'll call that the Target Track). In this example, it would be the track that contains the white cat. Also, make sure that no other video track selector that's above your Target Track is enabled. In other words, your Target Track must be the top-most enabled track.

2. On the **Record Window/Timeline**, use *option/Alt* + **Find Bin**.

3. The bin that holds the clip of the white cat will open and the clip of the white cat will be highlighted.

There's more...

If you want to make Method 2, described earlier, to work by pressing/clicking just one button, you can do this by adding the *option/Alt* modifier directly to the **Find Bin** button:

1. Open the **Command Palette**: **Tools | Command Palette**.

2. Enable the **Button to Button Reassignment** selection in the lower-left of the **Command Palette**.

3. On the **Command Palette**, select the tab labeled as **Other**.

4. In the first column of buttons on the **Command Palette**, you'll see a button labeled **Add Option Key** (Mac) or **Add Alt Key** (PC).

5. Drag-and-drop the **Add Option/Alt Key** function right onto the **Find Bin** button under the **Record Monitor**.

6. If you look very closely, you'll see a small black dot has appeared on the button to indicate that the *option/Alt* modifier has been added.

7. This is an optional step. First, map the **Find Bin** function to your keyboard. Then include the **Add Option/Alt Key** function with it.

Moving around: Methods and tips

Media Composer provides a variety of methods to help you move around Clips and Sequences, as well as to locate specific **Timecode** points. Reading the *Understanding Track Sensitivity* and *Snapping actions for the Position Indicator line and in Segment Mode* recipes in *Chapter 3, Polishing Gems* will also be helpful along with this information.

Play Reverse, Pause, and Play Forward (also known as JKL or Three-Button Play)

By default these functions are placed on the *J*, *K*, and *L* keys. The **Play Reverse**, **Pause**, and **Play Forward** functions can be used not only while editing, but when trimming too. When you become accustomed to using them while trimming, you'll find yourself working even faster and more intuitively. So, I highly encourage you to give them a try when trimming and to also check out the section titled *Keyboard mapping ideas* in the *Mapping buttons and menu selections* recipe in *Chapter 2, Customizing Your Work Environment* for a discussion on a particularly popular remapping choice for these.

It's also helpful to be aware that when you're capturing from tape, and the **Capture Tool** is active, you can use these functions to control the tape deck. This not only makes the process easier but, since you're not using the **Capture Tool**'s deck shuttle control, it's healthier for your wrist too.

Here are all the things you can do when editing or trimming with **Play Reverse**, **Pause**, and **Play Forward**. Note that **Capture Tool** will not go one frame at a time as described later. Instead you could use the **Step Forward One Frame** button.

▸ Press **Play Forward** or **Play Reverse**:

    ❑ One time – plays/trims at the frame rate of your project (for example, 25 fps or 30 fps).

    ❑ Two times in quick succession (for example, tap, tap) – plays/trims at two times (2x) the frame rate of your project (for example, 50 fps or 60 fps).

    ❑ Three times in quick succession – plays/trims at three times (3x) the frame rate of your project.

    ❑ Four times in quick succession – audio is intentionally muted. It plays/trims at five times (5x) the frame rate of your project.

    ❑ Five times in quick succession – audio is intentionally muted. It plays/trims at eight times (8x) the frame rate of your project.

▸ Press **Pause** *at the same time as pressing* either **Play Forward** or **Play Reverse**. If you're using these functions in their default positions, then you would be holding down both the *K* and *J* keys or both the *K* and *L* keys. This will play back or trim at 8 fps in NTSC projects, 6 fps in PAL projects, and 6 fps in 24-p projects. The sound will have a quality similar to when analogue audio tape is scrubbed across a play head.

▸ One Frame at a time – first, press and hold down the **Pause** button. Then quickly tap either the **Play Reverse** key or the **Play Forward** key. If you're using these functions in their default positions, then you would be holding down the *K* key and quickly tapping either the *J* key or the *L* key.

Fast Forward and Rewind

When you're editing, these functions are programmed to take you from one edit point (transition) to another. See the *Understanding Track Sensitivity* recipe in *Chapter 3, Polishing Gems* for important information about how this function is programmed and how to control its behavior.

▸ **Fast Forward** and **Rewind** will jump you from one key frame to the next when you're in **Effect Mode**, and either the **Effect Editor** window or the **Key Frame Position Bar** below the **Effect Monitor** (also known as the **Record Monitor**) is active.

▸ Stops at the **Head Frame** (first frame) of a clip by default. You can adjust this behavior by going to: **Project Window | Settings tab | Composer | FF/REW**.

▸ Will stop at Markers if this behavior is enabled. Enable this by going to: **Project Window | Settings tab | Composer | FF/REW**.

Go to Previous/Next Edit

These functions are placed on the *A* and *S* keys by default. They are designed to take you from one edit point (transition) to the next and to also place you into **Trim Mode**. See the *Understanding Track Sensitivity* recipe in *Chapter 3, Polishing Gems* for important information on how this function is programmed and how to control its behavior.

Home and End (also known as Go To Start and Go To End)

You'll find these functions on your extended keyboard above the arrow keys. Further, if you're on a Mac, then they're just to the right of the *Delete* key, and if you're on a PC then they're just to the right of the *Backspace* key.

These functions are mentioned not so much because they will quickly take you to the beginning or end of whatever is loaded in your **Source Window** or **Timeline**, but because they can be mapped wherever you want. Being able to map them is especially helpful for anyone without an extended keyboard, like those editing on a laptop in the field. You can find these functions here: **Tools menu | Command Palette | Move tab**. More information about mapping can be found in the *Mapping buttons and menu selections* recipe in *Chapter 2, Customizing Your Work Environment*.

Frame Offset – Jumping Forward or Backward by Typing

A **Frame Offset** is simply a way to tell Media Composer to move the **Position Indicator** (the blue line) a specific number of minutes, seconds, and/or frames forward (later in time) or backward (earlier in time).

First, let's get familiar with entering numeric values:

- ▶ In order for this feature to work properly, it is important to make sure that timecode is displayed in the **Tracking Information Menu** above the **Source** and **Record Monitors**. Further, if you have both **Tracking Information Menus** displayed above each monitor (enabled in **Project Window | Settings tab | Composer Settings | Window Tab | Always Display Two Rows of Data**), make sure that the menu on *top* is displaying timecode.

- ▶ When using the numeric keypad on an extended keyboard, the moment you begin typing a white entry box will appear in whichever window is active (**Source** or **Record**). For emphasis, you don't have to do anything other than begin entering numbers on the numeric keypad. When you're finished typing, press the *Enter* key on the numeric keypad.

- ▶ When using a laptop (which doesn't have a numeric keypad) you first tap the *Ctrl* key two times in quick succession (tap, tap) in order to make the white entry box appear. When you're finished typing, press the *Return* key (Mac)/*Enter* key (PC).

- ▶ You must type either a minus or a plus symbol before any numbers, otherwise Media Composer thinks you are entering a **Timecode** value (entering a timecode number is discussed in the section immediately following this one).

- ▸ Type a minus symbol before any numbers to move the Blue Line to the left of its current position (moving it to an earlier point in time).

- ▸ Type a plus symbol before any numbers to move the Blue Line to the right of its current position (moving it to a later point in time).

- ▸ You do not have to type a colon between the numbers. Media Composer will add them for you automatically as you type.

Now, let's focus on performing the **Frame Offset**:

- ▸ The way you type is identical to the format for timecode. In other words, Hours:Minutes:Seconds:Frames. For example, to move the **Position Indicator** forward by 2 seconds and 15 frames in a NTSC 30-fps project, you would type +215. Then you'd press the *Enter* key. Another example is to move the **Position Indicator** backward by 20 frames, you would type -20, and then press the *Enter* key.

- ▸ To make Media Composer always calculate in terms of frames (for values over 99 frames), rather than seconds and frames, type a *lower case* letter f. For emphasis, do not type a capital letter F or it won't work. For example, if you were in a NTSC 30-fps project and wanted to move forward 200 frames, you would type in +200f. If you didn't type the lower case letter f, then you would only go forward by 2 seconds (only 60 frames).

- ▸ When **Marking In** and **Out** – when you use this feature along with marking in and out, be aware that the first frame you are parked on is included in your selection. For example, when you place your **Mark In**, this tells Media Composer that you want that frame as part of your selection. Then you type +20, enter (moving forward 20 frames), and then you place the **Mark Out**. The result is that you have told Media Composer you wanted the first frame and then to add 20 more. If you look at your **Center Duration** display, you'll see that the total selection you've made is 21 frames. If, in the previous example, you wanted to select exactly 20 frames, you could have either made the adjustment when typing by entering +19, or before placing your **Mark Out** you could have used the **Step Backward 1 Frame** function to move back one frame.

- ▸ **Numeric Keypad Memory** – a nice feature is that the numeric keypad remembers whatever value you've typed in until a new value is entered. For example, let's say you wanted to place shots exactly 2 seconds apart. First, type in +200 and hit the *Enter* key. When you want to move forward again by 2 seconds, simply hit the *Enter* key.

Timecode

You can make the **Position Indicator** jump to a specific timecode point in either the **Source Window** or **Record Window/Timeline**. If the timecode number exists, the **Position Indicator** will jump to it. If it does not exist, then the **Position Indicator** will not move and you may hear an alert sound from your computer (for example, bonk).

If you're not familiar with entering numeric values, please see the section above titled *Frame Offset – Jumping Forward or Backward by Typing* which includes a helpful overview of how to enter numeric values.

Type fewer numbers tips – for this example, let's say you have loaded a very long **Master Clip** into the **Source Window**. First, you glance at the **Tracking Information Menu** above the **Source Window** and you see that you are currently parked in the **Master Clip** at **02:01:11:18**. Then, you look at your script notes and see that the producer has indicated that the shot she wants is at **02:09:00:00**. Rather than having to type all those numbers, you could reduce it to pressing just three keys:

▶ You do not need to type the 02 value for the hours since you're already parked in that timecode region.

▶ Since the minutes value begins with a zero, you can ignore it and type just a 9 value.

▶ You do not need to type two zeroes for the seconds value. Instead, you can press once on the decimal key on the numeric keypad or the period key on the main keyboard. When you do this, you will be given two zeroes with just the one-button push.

▶ Press the decimal key or the period key a second time to type two more zeroes for the frames value.

▶ Pressing *Enter* would be button press number 4.

Step Forward and Step Backward by Frames

These functions will move you forward or backward by a set number of frames. By default, these functions are found in these locations and work as follows:

▶ *1* key and *2* key in the top-left of the main keyboard – moves 1/3rd the number of frames of the frame rate of your project. Specifically, in a 24-fps project, you'll move eight frames, while in a 30-fps project, you'll move 10 frames.

▶ *3* key and *4* key – moves one frame at a time.

▶ Left Arrow key and Right Arrow key – Moves one frame at a time.

Step Forward and Step Backward by Fields

When you are stepping through interlaced video, Media Composer only shows you **Field 1**. However, when you play the video and watch it on your NTSC or PAL broadcast monitor (which displays both fields), you may see a dropout (a flaw) in the image every now and then. So, how do you verify there is a dropout on **Field 2** if you can only see **Field 1** when using the **Step Forward/Backward by Frames** function? Well, Media Composer does allow you to step through the video one field at a time.

You can find these functions here: **Tools menu | Command Palette | Move tab**.

▸ Since the function pertains to fields in interlaced video, this feature is not available if your video format is progressive.

▸ It is very helpful to make sure that timecode is displayed in the **Tracking Information Menu** above the **Source** or **Record Monitors**. As you step forward or backward by one field, watch the **Frames** region of the timecode. You'll notice that the value changes every two clicks of the **Step Forward/Backward by Fields** function. When you see the number change, you are on **Field #1** and when the number does not change, you are on **Field #2**.

▸ You *should* see a small, white number **2** in the top-right corner of the image area in the **Source** or **Record** window when you are on **Field 2**. My current experience is that this number only appears intermittently, which is most likely a small bug (error) in the programming that will be fixed in later releases.

▸ Make sure that you have returned to viewing **Field 1** before going back to editing, otherwise as you navigate, you will be viewing **Field 2** when you move the **Position Indicator** (blue line) forward or backward.

▸ When you are in **Effect Mode** and are using interlaced video the **Step Forward/ Backward by Frames** function will actually move you by **Fields**.

Getting more use from the Grid

This useful feature is often overlooked, so I wanted to make sure you know that it exists, and mention a few of its useful features.

The **Grid** is displayed in either the **Source Window** or **Record Window** by using the **Grid** button found in the **Fast Menu Tool Palette** or on the **Effect Editor Window**. To map the **Grid** button to a custom location, it can be found in the **Tools menu | Command Palette | FX tab**. See the *Mapping buttons and menu selections* recipe in *Chapter 2, Customizing Your Work Environment* for more information if you are unfamiliar with mapping.

The **Grid Setting** is found in the **Project Window | Settings Tab | Grid**:

▸ **Coordinates | Scale Mode** – allows you to display a grid that reflects a different aspect ratio than the one you are currently viewing. For example, let's say you're working with a **Project Aspect Ratio** of **16:9** but have to make sure to place titles and graphics, so that they will also be seen properly when the film or TV program is reformatted to show only the center **4:3** area of the image (also known as Center Cut or Center Extraction). In this example, you would select **4:3 Inside 16:9 Monitor**. When you don't need this, be sure to set it back to **Normal**.

▸ **Coordinates | Fields Increments Entry Box** – changing the value in the **Fields** box will increase or decrease the number of Tick Marks and the number of Points (a grid of dots). Tick Marks and Points are enabled in the grid's **Display** tab.

- ► **Display tab | Safe Title** – the innermost of the two rectangles represents 80 percent of the image. For broadcast delivery, titles must not sit outside this area. They may be right on it, as is often the case when you place a speaker's name on screen (also known as Lower Thirds or Chyrons).

- ► **Display tab | Safe Action** – this area is also called the Broadcast Safe Area. It's the outermost of the two rectangles and represents 90 percent of the image. While we can see the entire image, viewers at home are guaranteed to see only the image that's inside the **Safe Action** area. As an aside, when you're outputting for the Internet (a QuickTime movie, for example), the entire image (not just the **Safe Action** area) is output.

- ► **Display tab | Color** – you can change the color of the **Grid** from the default setting of white to one of several other choices. I've settled on green as I find that it shows up well on both light and dark backgrounds.

- ► **Display tab | Axes** – will display the **X** and **Y** axes. This is helpful for positioning video elements when creating effects.

- ► **Display tab | Tick Marks** and **Points** (a grid of dots) – helpful for positioning video elements when creating effects. You can increase or decrease the number of **Tick Marks** and the number of **Points** by using the **Coordinates | Fields Increments** entry box. In addition, Roger Shufflebottom (one of the technical reviewers of this book) relates that when **Points**, **Tick Marks**, and **Axes** are displayed, then when you are in **Effect Mode** some effects (for example, **Picture In Picture**) will snap to them.

- ► **Duplicate Grid** settings – you can have multiple **Grid** settings. See the the *Settings overview* recipe in *Chapter 2, Customizing Your Work Environment* for more information on duplicating, naming, restoring and activating settings.

cmd/Ctrl + L and K: Several uses

These keyboard shortcuts relate to selections found in the **Edit Menu** and are for enlarging and reducing several displays. *cmd/Ctrl + L* makes sense and is easy to remember because it makes things Larger. *cmd/Ctrl + K* well, if you speak German, then *Cmd/Ctrl + K* makes sense as well, because in German the word for smaller is Kleinere. For those of us that don't speak German, you'll notice that the letter K is to the left of the letter L on the QWERTY keyboard.

These keyboard shortcuts will do different things, depending on which window is active when you use them:

- ► **Bin Window** – when a bin is in either **Frame View** or **Script View**, using these shortcuts will enlarge/reduce the size of the thumbnail image for the clip.

- ► **Timeline** – will enlarge or reduce the height of tracks that have their Track Selectors enabled (on either the **Source** side or the **Record/Timeline** side). More information on **Track Height** is given later.

▶ **Record Window** or **Source Window** – the purpose for the shortcuts here are to **Enlarge/Reduce** (zoom in/out) the display image. This is useful in the **Effect Monitor** (also known as the **Record Monitor**) when creating various video effects (for example, enlarging is helpful when Corner Pinning). Sometimes users find themselves enlarging or reducing the display image by mistake when they mean to use these keyboard shortcuts to enlarge/reduce the width of their timeline tracks and don't realize that the **Record** or **Source** window is selected instead. More information on this is given next.

Enlarge/reduce display image tips:

Following are a few tips that will come in handy while enlarging or reducing the display image:

▶ When enlarged or reduced, a small white number will appear in the upper-right corner to indicate the zoom level (for example, 2x, or 50 percent).The normal display will not have any number appearing. So, do not be confused when you see **1x**. This is relating that there is a 1:1 (one- to-one) relationship between the pixels in the video and the pixels on the computer monitor. This actually makes the image larger, and the entire image is not seen.

▶ When the image is enlarged, you can reposition it by first pressing, and holding, *option + cmd* (Mac) or *Alt + Ctrl* (PC). This will change your arrow cursor into a hand cursor. Then, at the same time you press the keys, hold down the left mouse button and you can then drag the image around to reposition it.

▶ You can quickly return to a normal display size with the shortcut *option + cmd + L* (Mac) or *Alt + Ctrl + L* (PC).

More on track height:

Let's take a look at couple of options to adjust the track height:

▶ You can also adjust the track height dynamically using the *option/Alt* key. Press and hold *option/Alt* (if *Alt* does not work, try the *Ctrl* key), then place your cursor between two Track Selectors. The resize icon will appear (a black line with arrows pointing up and down). You will be adjusting the height for the track which is *above* the resize icon. Hold down the mouse button and drag up or down to resize the track.

▶ *cmd/Ctrl + K* and *L* adjusts track height, but of you add *option/Alt*: *option/Alt + cmd/Ctrl + K* or *option/Alt + cmd/Ctrl +L*, then you will be adjusting the height of the Waveform, if it is displayed.

Locking and unlocking

You can lock Clips, Sequences, and Timeline Tracks.

- ▶ Ways to lock clips:
  - ❑ Select the clip(s) and go to **Clip menu | Lock** or **Unlock**; or select the clip(s) and right-click on the selected clip(s), and select **Lock** or **Unlock**.
  - ❑ When a clip is locked, you can not easily delete the clip or the media files that it links to. Notice that I didn't say that it's impossible to delete the clip or the linked media files. First, it's obvious from the **Unlock** selection that clips and media can be unlocked from inside of Media Composer. But what's not obvious is that media files can be unlocked at the Operating System Level even when Media Composer isn't running.
  - ❑ You can determine which clips are locked by displaying the Lock column when the bin is in **Text View**. Details on displaying columns of data and creating **Bin Views** are in the *Creating Bin views* recipe in *Chapter 2, Customizing Your Work Environment*.

- ▶ Ways to lock Sequences:
  - ❑ Select the Sequence(s) and go to **Clip menu | Lock** or **Unlock**; or select the Sequence(s) and right-click on the selected Sequence(s), and select **Lock** or **Unlock**.
  - ❑ When a Sequence is locked, it only locks it from being deleted.
  - ❑ When a Sequence is locked, it does not lock the media it refers to.
  - ❑ When a Sequence is locked, it can still be edited just as if it weren't locked.
  - ❑ You can determine which Sequences are locked by displaying the **Lock** column when the bin is in **Text View**. Details on displaying columns of data and creating **Bin Views** are in the *Creating Bin views* recipe in *Chapter 2, Customizing Your Work Environment*.

- ▶ Ways to lock **Timeline Tracks**:
  - ❑ Enable the track(s) you want to lock and select **Clip menu | Lock** or **Unlock**; or lock/unlock tracks one at a time by right-clicking on a **Track Selector | Lock** or **Unlock**.
  - ❑ When a track is locked, you can not perform any editing functions on it. If you attempt to **Spice**, **Overwrite**, **Lift**, or **Extract**, you will be alerted that you **Cannot edit a read-only track**.
  - ❑ When a track is locked, a small lock symbol will appear in the **Sync Locks** column.

Details on Trimming, Slipping, Sliding, and Segment Mode

This appendix includes the following topics:

- ▶ Trimming terminology
- ▶ Trimming icons and colors
- ▶ How Trimming works
- ▶ Enabling and congiguring the Trimming Tools
- ▶ Trimming methods
- ▶ Monitoring during Trimming
- ▶ Slipping with Trim Mode
- ▶ Slipping outside of Trim Mode
- ▶ Sliding in Trim Mode
- ▶ Trimming and effects
- ▶ Smart Tool overview
- ▶ Using the Trim functions in the Smart Tool
- ▶ Using Segment Mode with the Smart Tool
- ▶ Nine Segment Mode Tips

Trimming terminology

Before we get into Trimming, it will be helpful to be familiar with a couple of terms. So, in this section, we'll discuss A-Side and B-Side as well as the concept of **HANDLE**.

A-Side/B-Side

When you are editing (for example, using **Splice** and **Lift**, and so on), the **Composer Window** displays two monitors. The **Source Monitor** is on the left-hand side and the **Record Monitor** is on the right-hand side.

However, when you are Trimming shots longer or shorter (we'll talk about Slipping and Sliding later), monitors of the **Composer Window** change their display. The left monitor is displaying the tail frame (the last frame) of the shot on the left-hand side of the transition (the cut), while the right monitor is displaying the head frame (the first frame) of the shot on the right-hand side of the cut. However, we need a more generic and succinct way to describe them. So, we refer to the shot on the left-hand side of the transition as the **A-side** shot and the shot on the right-hand side, as you guessed it, the **B-side** shot. You may also hear people refer to the A-side shot as the outgoing shot and the B-side as the incoming shot. I'll be sticking with the terms A-side and B-side.

Handle

Handle is the material that was *not* edited into the Sequence, but is *still available* in the clip.

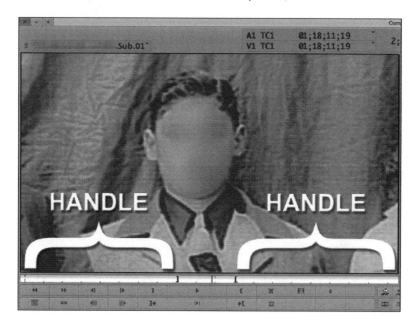

Handle gets revealed when you trim a Segment longer (of course, once it's revealed it's no longer **Handle**). On the other hand, when you trim a Segment shorter you are creating **Handle**. Further, **Handle** also comes into play whenever you apply a transition effect (for example, a dissolve). The transition effect uses the material in the **Handle** to do its job creating the effect.

Trimming icons and colors

With the introduction of the **Smart Tool** in Media Composer 5, there are more things to be aware of. Here's an overview of what the **Trim Rollers** and the colors indicate.

- **Single Roller**: When you have just one roller, at a transition on a track, it means that you are trimming just one side of the transition on that track. In other words, you are only trimming just the A-side or just the B-side shot at the transition on that track (see the previous *Trimming terminology* section).

- **Double Rollers**: When there are two rollers side by side at a transition it means that you are affecting both shots on either side of the transition at the same time. In other words, you are trimming both the A-side and the B-side, adding material to one shot (extending it) while simultaneously removing the exact same amount of material from the other (shortening it).

- **Yellow**: Yellow tools indicate that they have the power to change duration of tracks. For example, **Splice** adds material to the track, which lengthens it, and pushes other segments down the **Timeline** to the right. Extract removes material from the track, which shortens it, and the remaining material on the track then moves to the left. When trimming with a single roller which is yellow, Avid refers to this as a **Ripple Trim**. For those that have used the software prior to the **Smart Tool**, the behavior of yellow, single roller trimming is identical to single roller trimming in the past. When you're adding material to a segment (a shot) with the yellow **Ripple Trim**, shots to the right-hand side of it are pushed down the timeline to the right. When you're removing material from a segment, shots to the right of it are pulled up the **Timeline** to the left.

- **Red**: Red tools indicate that they do not change the duration of tracks. For example, **Overwrite** places new material into the **Timeline** on top of whatever was there. It's not adding additional material, it's simply replacing it. So, the duration of the track remains the same. **Lift** removes material from the **Timeline**, and it maintains the duration of that track by leaving behind an equal amount of **Filler**. When trimming with a single roller which is red, Avid refers to this as an **Overwrite Trim**. I quibble with this name a bit as I think it should be called Overwrite-Lift Trim. When you're *adding* material to a segment (a shot) with the red **Overwrite Trim**, the adjacent segment that's in the path of the trim is actually overwritten. In other words, material from the segment you're extending (adding to) is replacing the adjacent shot's material. Note that when you're *extending* a segment with the red **Trim Roller**, the result is identical to using **Double Roller Trim**. On the other hand, when you're *removing* material from a segment (shortening it), the red **Trim Roller** leaves **Filler** behind in order to maintain the duration of that track (just like when you perform a **Lift**).

- **Purple**: Whenever you have two **Trim Rollers** on a track, they will be purple. Purple rollers will appear when you are in **Double Roller Trim**, **Slipping**, and **Sliding**.

How Trimming works

To be concise, the way that editing works with Media Composer (and other nonlinear editing applications) is that rather than make permanently destructive changes to the actual picture and audio files (the media), it instead makes changes to the *references* to the media. However, let me give you some detail.

Let's start at the beginning. A clip (for example, **Master Clip**) in your bin is not actually the picture and/or audio file. It's just a reference to it. The classic analogy (most likely given to me by Greg Staten many years ago) is this:

In a time before computers, libraries used a card catalog to help you locate books. These were filing cabinets which held small, paper index cards.

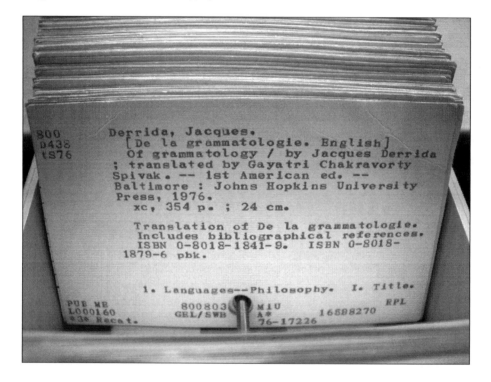

Photo Credit: David Fulmer

The cards contained helpful information about a book such as the author, publication date, number of pages, a short synopsis, and so on. It also contained the all-important Dewey Decimal System number that was assigned to that book, so you could locate it in the expansive library. Obviously, that small card was not the book. Its purpose was to point you to the book. Well, that's similar to how clips and media work together too. A clip is a small collection of information that points to (in Avid terminology, **links** to) the media:

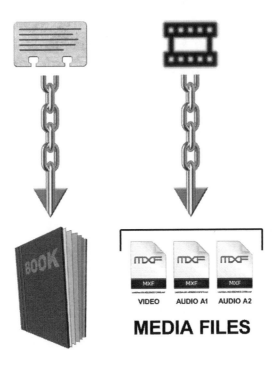

MEDIA FILES

Now let's turn to Sequences. A sequence is really just a collection of references. Each shot (known in Avid terminology as a Segment) is a reference that tells Media Composer what image to show and/or what audio to play from a media file when you press play.

My analogy is this: the media are like books and the Segments in the Sequence are like reading assignments for Media Composer. The reading assignment of each Segment can be lengthened or shortened (trimmed) with no affect on the actual book (the media).

Enabling and configuring the Trimming Tools

Media Composer provides editors with multiple ways to do things so you can have flexibility, depending on your personal preference or on what will work best at a particular moment. In this section we'll cover the different ways to enable the Trim tools (also known as **Trim Mode**) as well as the different methods for selecting (configuring) what to trim.

Methods for entering Trim Mode

There are four methods to enter **Trim Mode**:

▸ Method 1 is to park the **Position Indictor** (the blue line) near the transition of the shot(s) you want to trim, enable the Track Selector(s) for the track(s) you want to trim, then click/press the **Trim Mode** button. By default, the **Trim Mode** button can be found in the following locations:

   ▫ On the **Composer Window** (also known as the **Source/Record Window**), underneath the **Splice** and **Overwrite** buttons

   ▫ On the far left-hand side of the **Timeline Toolbar**

   ▫ Mapped to the keyboard on the letter *U*

   ▫ Some of the trim tools can be found on the **Smart Tool**. More information about Trimming and the using the **Smart Tool** is later in this appendix

▸ Method 2 is to use the **Go To Previous** and **Go To Next Edit** functions. By default, these are mapped to the *A* and *S* keys on the keyboard. See the the *Understanding Track Sensitivity* recipe in *Chapter 3, Polishing Gems* for more information on using them.

▸ Method 3 is to Lasso. Lassoing to select segments and lassoing to enter **Slip** or **Slide** mode are discussed in sections later in this appendix. Right now we're focusing on lassoing single transitions on one or more tracks. This is done by clicking and holding the mouse button in the **Timeline Window** (the area outside the actual tracks) and then drawing a selection box (the lasso) around the transition(s) you want to trim. If you're not already in **Trim Mode** when you lasso, then it will be activated, which makes it a really great, fast way to get into **Trim Mode**. Following are some examples of lassoing to get into **Trim Mode**. The last example (lassoing inside the **Timeline**) is particularly helpful.

❑ **Single transition**: The next image attempts to illustrate clicking in the **Timeline Window**, holding down the mouse button, and drawing the selection box (the lasso) around just one transition. It's important to note that the lasso must totally surround the transition in order to select it and enter into **Trim Mode**.

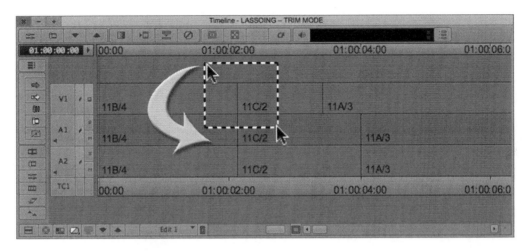

❑ **Multiple transitions**: The next image attempts to illustrate clicking in the **Timeline Window**, holding down the mouse button, and drawing the lasso box around multiple transitions. Note that even **Split Edits** can be lassoed and trimmed.

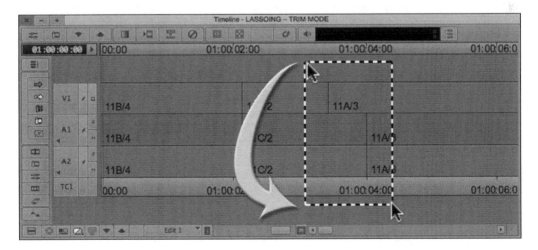

❑ Lasso inside the **Timeline**. When you have many tracks in your Sequence, there's a pretty good chance that you won't have easy access to the **Timeline Window** background area in order to click and make a lasso. Even so, it's still possible to lasso. All you have to do is press and hold the *option/Alt* key as you click inside the **Timeline** tracks and lasso the transition(s) you want.

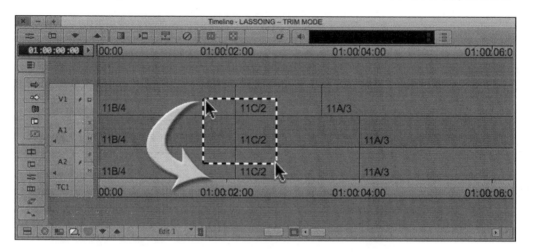

▶ Method 4 is to return to the last used **Trim roller** configuration. This is a very useful feature, especially when you've just performed a multi-track **Asymmetric** trim (discussed in *Chapter 4, Creating Split Edits* which covers making **Split Edits** as well as in *Chapter 5, Maintaining and Regaining Sync*. After exiting **Trim Mode,** you can re-enter **Trim Mode** and have the **Trim Rollers** placed into the very last configuration you used. To do this:

i. Press and hold *option/Alt.*

ii. Do one of the following:

❑ Press the **Trim Mode** button on the keyboard (by default on the letter *U*)

❑ Click on the **Trim Mode** button in the interface (for example, on the **Composer Window**, below the **Splice** and **Overwrite** buttons)

Configuring the Trim Rollers

Once you're in **Trim Mode**, the next thing you have to do is tell Media Composer exactly what you want to trim on each track by configuring the **Trim Rollers**. Here's how:

▶ Clicking on the **Composer Window**:

❑ **A-Side Monitor** (left window): When you're in **Trim Mode** and hover your cursor over the A-Side monitor, you'll see that the cursor icon has changed from an arrow to what looks a bit like a film canister (it's actually the **Trim Roller** icon) with a piece of film extending out from it. Since the cursor is hovering over the A-Side monitor (the left of the two monitors) the piece of film extends out to the left-hand side. If you click at this time, then you'll see that the **Trim Roller**(s) in the **Timeline** have been placed onto the A-Side (left-hand side) shot at the transition. This is known as a **Ripple Trim**.

❑ **B-Side Monitor** (right window): Just like A-Side earlier, except that you'll be hovering over the B-Side monitor and the piece of film in the icon extends out to the right. Clicking the mouse at this time will configure the **Trim Rollers** onto the B-Side (right-hand side) shot at the transition. Again, this is known as a **Ripple Trim** and you'll see that the **Trim Rollers** are yellow.

❑ **Between the A-Side and B-Side Monitors:** Rather than hovering your cursor over the A or B-Side Monitor, you'll place it in a region between the two. When the cursor is in this region, it will display two pieces of film, each extending out in both directions. Clicking the mouse at this time will configure the **Trim Rollers** in the **Timeline** onto *both* the A-Side and the B-Side shots at the transition. This is called **Double Roller Trim** or **Dual Roller Trim**.

▶ Clicking on the **Trim Counters**: When you're in **Trim Mode**, you'll see two purple boxes right below the monitor screens. These will display how much you have trimmed for the A-Side and/or the B-Side shot at the transition. You can also click on these displays as a way to configure the **Trim Rollers** in the **Timeline**.

▶ *P*, *[*, and *]* keys: – By default, Avid has mapped the **Trim Roller** configuration buttons to the following three keys: *P*, *[*, and *]*. Pressing the *P* key will configure the **Trim Rollers** onto the A-Side. The *[* key will place them on both the A-Side and B-Side (**Double Rollers**). The *]* key will configure the **Trim Rollers** onto the B-Side.

▶ **Cycle Trim** – in the **Command Palette** (**Tools** menu | **Command Palette** | **Trim** tab), you'll find the **Cycle Trim** function that lets you press this one button to shuffle through the different configurations. When you're in **Trim Mode**, each time you press it, it switches to the next configuration, cycling through them. Information on mapping this to the keyboard can be found in the *Mapping buttons and menu selections* recipe in *Chapter 2, Customizing Your Work Environment*.

▶ *Shift* + click to add or remove **Trim Rollers**: – This technique allows you to manually configure any trimming setup you want, and is *essential* to be able to perform the highly useful **Asymmetric Trim** (discussed in *Chapters 4, Creating Split Edits* and *Chapter 5, Maintaining and Regaining Sync*). It's very important to pay attention to the cursor icon in the **Timeline** when Shift-Clicking. The direction the piece of film extends indicates which side of the transition you are over. The following are two images to help describe the *Shift* + click feature:

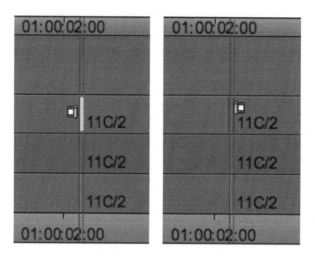

In the image on the left, *Shift* + click at this moment would *add* a **Trim Roller** on the A-Side (left-hand side) of the transition. In the image on the right, *Shift* + click at this moment would *remove* the Trim Roller on the B-Side.

Trimming methods

Media Composer provides you with multiple methods to perform a trim to give you flexibility, depending on your personal preference, or for what will work best at a particular moment.

▶ **Trim Keys** (Interface) – the **Trim Keys** can be accessed on the interface when in **Trim Mode** (see the next screenshot). The only caution here is not to click on the **Step Forward/Reverse** keys by mistake, since they do not trim and will exit you from **Trim Mode**. You can, however, use **Fast Forward** and **Rewind** to jump from transition to transition and remain in **Trim Mode**.

▶ **Trim Keys** (Keyboard) – found on the keyboard in the bottom-right corner. By default, they are on the keys *M*, comma, period, and forward slash. It's important to note that the **Trim Keys** on the keyboard also have a function even when you're not in **Trim Mode**. Specifically, they Slip segments (discussed in this appendix in the section titled *Slipping Outside of Trim Mode*).

▶ Numeric Keypad – you can type in a specific number of seconds and frames (or feet and frames if you're in a film project) that you'd like to trim. When you do this, the two purple trim counter displays will be replaced by a value entry box. The important thing to know here is that Media Composer needs to know which direction you want the **Trim Roller**(s) to trim. To instruct it to trim to the left, you type a minus sign before entering a numeric value and pressing the *Enter* key. To trim to the right, type a plus sign before entering a numeric value and pressing the *Enter* key. Here are two examples:

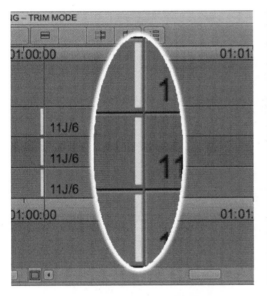 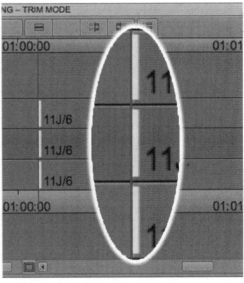

In the image on the left, the **Trim Rollers** are on the A-Side (left-hand side) shot of the transition. To make this shot *longer* by 48 frames, using the numeric keypad, you'd type in +48, then press the *Enter* key. The + tells Media Composer to trim to the *right* (in a *positive* direction). In the image on the right, the **Trim Rollers** are on the B-Side shot of the transition. To make this shot *longer by* 60 frames, using the numeric keypad, you'd type in −60, then press the *Enter* key. The − tells Media Composer to trim to the *left* (in a *negative* direction). What can be confusing is that the plus and minus signs are not telling Media Composer to add or subtract. They are instead telling it which *direction* to perform the trim.

A bonus feature of using the Numeric Key Pad is that after you have used it to make a trim, the value you entered remains in its memory. So, if you want to trim by that same amount in the future, just press the *Enter* key. The value remains in the memory until you type in a new value.

▸ **JKL** Trimming – also referred to as Three Button Trimming or Dynamic Trimming. This is one of the most (if not the most) useful editing features. If you haven't used it before, give it a try. The more you use it, the more comfortable with it you'll become. And once you're comfortable with it, you'll find yourself trimming faster and more intuitively than ever. For more information on all that JKL can do, see the *Moving Around: Methods and tips* section in *Appendix A, Additional Tips, Tricks, and Explanations*. For a discussion on remapping the JKL functions, see the *Mapping buttons and menu selections* recipe in *Chapter 2, Customizing Your Work Environment*.

▸ Dragging in the **Timeline** – you can click to grab the **Trim Rollers** directly in the **Timeline** and drag left or right in order to perform a trim. The addition of the **Smart Tool** increased these abilities (more information about the **Smart Tool** is later in this appendix). The one issue to be aware of when grabbing **Trim Rollers** is making sure that you are indeed grabbing the roller and not mistakenly instructing Media Composer to change the **Trim Roller** configuration to the opposite side. The key to this is to pay attention and make sure that the **Trim Roller** in the **Timeline** and your cursor's trim icon indicate the *same* side of the transition. Following are two examples:

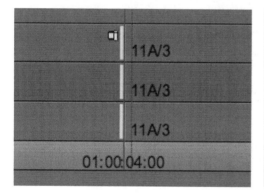 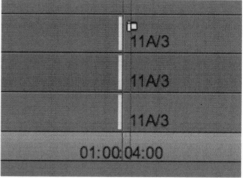

Screenshot on the left: If the goal is to trim the A-Side (left-hand side) shot at the transition, then the picture on the left is correct. It's correct because the cursor icon has its little piece of film extending out of it pointing to the left (facing to the A-Side) while it's hovering over a **Trim Roller** in the **Timeline** which is also on the A-Side. In this situation, clicking and holding the mouse button and then dragging will indeed trim the A-Side shot.

Screenshot on the left: If the goal is to trim the A-Side shot at the transition, then the picture on the right is *not* correct. It's incorrect because the **Trim Rollers** in the **Timeline** are on *the A-Side,* but the cursor icon has its little piece of film extending out of it pointing to *the B-Side.* Clicking the mouse button in this situation would tell Media Composer to move the **Trim Rollers** to the B-Side.

The exception to the previous rule is **Double Roller Trim**. In this case, it doesn't matter which direction your cursor's piece of film extends when you grab. In other words, when you're in **Double Roller Trim**, you can grab the rollers when the cursor icon faces *either* direction. Why? The reason it doesn't display a **Double Roller** icon is that when you're using the *Shift* + click method to configure the **Trim Rollers**, you need the cursor icon to display as either A-Side or B-Side (the *Shift* + click method is discussed earlier in this appendix in the the *Enabling and configuring the Trim tools* recipe).

► Trim while Looping – when you enter **Trim Mode**, the **Play** button automatically transforms into the **Play Loop** function wherever it's located (for example, on the Space bar). What's sometimes useful is that when you are looping the transition you can also trim. To be clear, you must have pressed the **Play Loop** button and the loop must be in progress for the following abilities to work:

  ❑ Use the **Trim Keys** on the keyboard (by default on the *M*, comma, period, and forward slash keys) – while the loop is in progress, tap any of the **Trim Keys** on the keyboard as many times as you like. For example, to trim three frames to the right while the looping is in progress, you'd tap the period key three times in quick succession (tap, tap, tap). It may take a moment for the trim to actually take effect, so you may need to let the loop complete its cycle to see the result. This is a particularly useful ability when you need to trim just one or two frames at a time.

  ❑ **Mark In** or **Mark Out** – while the loop is in progress, press either the **Mark In** or **Mark Out** button on the keyboard (it doesn't matter which) and the segment will be trimmed to the point at which you pressed the **In** or **Out Mark**.

► Isolate the Loop – when using the **Play Loop** trimming tricks previously, you may find it helpful to change the loop from playing both the A-Side and the B-Side to only playing one or the other side. While the loop is in progress, press the **Go To Mark In** button on the keyboard (by default on the letter *Q* key). The loop will then occur only on the A-Side. While it's looping just the A-Side, if you press the **Go To Mark In** button (*Q* key) a second time, the loop will return to looping both sides. The same behavior is true for the **Go To Mark Out** button (by default on the letter *W* key), except that it loops only the B-Side of the transition.

Monitoring during Trimming

When you're **Double Roller** trimming, **Slipping**, or **Sliding**, there is a simple method to tell Media Composer what you want to hear, or to focus on visually, as you're trimming. This is done with what Avid calls the **Trim Monitors**. These are the green lights below the purple trim counters. The arrow in the next screenshot points to the green monitor light for the A-Side, while the light on the B-Side is off and is colored gray.

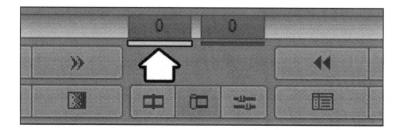

When you're in **Double Roller Trim Mode**, all you have to do is momentarily hover (don't click) your cursor over either the **A-Side Trim Monitor** (the left monitor displaying the image) or over the **B-Side Trim Monitor**. Notice that if you move your cursor back and forth across the two that the green monitor light will change as well.

- ▸ Example 1: You're in **Double Roller Trim Mode** on track **A2**. On the A-Side (left-hand side) of the transition is audio and on the B-Side is **Filler**, which of course is silent. In this case I'd want to have the green monitor light on the A-Side, so that as I trimmed in real time, using **JKL**, I could hear the audio at the same time.

- ▸ Example 2: When Slipping a shot, you can choose to monitor either the **Head Frame** (the first frame) of the shot or the **Tail Frame** by momentarily hovering your cursor over one or the other to set the green monitor light. Then, as you trim in real time using **JKL**, you'll also see the selected image update in real time. Also note that if you have a third **Client Monitor** (a PAL or NTSC monitor) attached to your editing system, then the image you have selected for monitoring is also displayed there.

Slipping with Trim Mode

Slipping is part of the trimming set of features. It is used for shifting a shot's contents to reveal earlier or later material. It has a brother, called Sliding and it has a cousin that can also Slip a shot, except it does it without being in **Trim Mode**. All of this is covered in this appendix, but let's begin with Slipping.

Slipping allows you to adjust a shot in your Sequence to reveal earlier or later material from its source clip without changing the shot's duration. First, here's what Slipping a video segment (the **FRANKY** segment), along with the audio that belongs with it, looks like in the following screenshot:

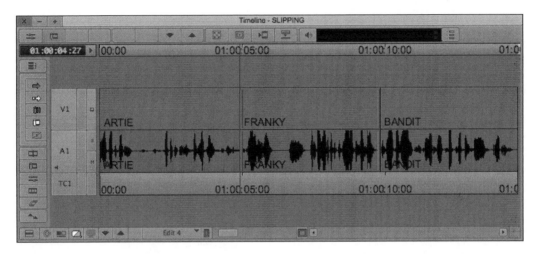

After the list of steps to perform a Slip, below, you will find an example that illustrates what Slipping is doing.

Method 1 is a very fast way to enter **Slip Mode** (also known as Slipping) and methods 2, 3, 4, and 5 are important to know in case you need to Slip the first or last Segment (shot) in a Sequence where lassoing may not work.

▸ Method 1: Lasso while in **Trim Mode** or **Source/Record Mode**:

◻ In this instance, you'll be lassoing a very specific direction (see earlier in the *Enabling and configuring the Trimming Tools* recipe for details on lassoing). You'll *lasso from right to left* entirely around a *Segment* in order to tell Media Composer that you want to Slip it. You can lasso around just a video Segment, or just the audio segment(s), or you can lasso both the video and the audio that goes with it if the two need to stay in sync. It's important to note that while Media Composer will allow you to lasso from right to left around multiple Segments that are next to each other, here I am talking about lassoing only one segment and any others that belong with it (for example, a video segment and the audio that belongs with it, as with the **FRANKY** shot in the next screenshot):

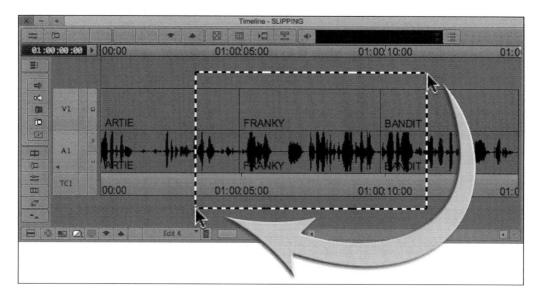

▸ Method 2: Double-click while already in **Trim Mode**:

i. Enter **Trim Mode** at any transition.

ii. For the Segment (shot) you want to Slip, place the cursor at one of its transitions, either the head or the tail. For emphasis, you will be placing your cursor either on an existing **Trim Roller** or in the location where a **Trim Roller** would appear if it were there (see the next screenshot).

iii. Pay close attention to the cursor icon. Make sure that the little piece of film that extends from the roller is facing the *Segment you want to Slip*. In the next screenshot, I want to Slip the shot of **FRANKY**. So, before I double-click, I've made sure that the cursor icon's piece of film extends towards the shot of **FRANKY**:

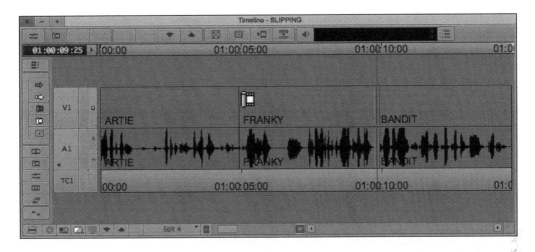

iv. When the cursor's icon is facing the Segment that you want to Slip, then double-click, in order to enter **Slip Mode**.

v. If you need to select an additional segment(s) in order to stay in sync (for example, you've initially entered **Slip Mode** on the video segment, but now want to include the audio segment that belongs with it), you can either **Shift** + double-click on the audio segment(s) as you did with the video segment or you can enable the required Track Selector(s).

▸ Method 3: *Shift* + click to configure the **Trim Rollers** while already in **Trim Mode**. The *Shift* + click method to configure the **Trim Rollers** is explained earlier in this appendix in the *Enabling and configuring the trimming tools* recipe.

▸ Method 4: Using **Segment Mode**:

i. Enable either **Overwrite/Lift Segment Mode** (red arrow) or **Extract/ Splice-In Segment Mode** (yellow arrow). It doesn't matter which one as this is just being used to make a selection.

ii. Select the video Segment you want to Slip. If there is audio that belongs with that video, then *Shift* + select that Segment(s) as well. Note that you can slip audio and video separately if/when needed.

iii. With the Segment(s) selected, press/click the **Trim Mode** button on the keyboard or on the interface and you will be placed into the **Slip** configuration of trimming.

▸ Method 5: While you are in **Trim Mode**, right-click on a Segment and, from the menu that appears, choose **Select Slip Trim**.

Now let's take a closer look at the configuration of the **Trim Rollers** as well as the display that is presented to us when we're Slipping in **Trim Mode**.

The Rollers – frequently, people will describe Slipping as when the **Trim Rollers** are on the inside of the segment. Rather than saying that the rollers are on the inside, I prefer to point out that the rollers are touching only that segment. The idea here is that whatever shot the Trim Rollers are touching is the shot that is being affected. This will become even more apparent when I talk about Sliding just a bit later.

The Four Image Display – when you're Slipping a video segment Media Composer will display four images.

In the screenshot below, we are Slipping the **FRANKY** Segment, and the the images in the display are the following:

- ▸ **A** is the last frame in the **ARTIE** segment
- ▸ **B** is the first frame in the segment you're Slipping (the **FRANKY** segment)
- ▸ **C** is the last frame in the segment you're Slipping
- ▸ **D** is the first frame in the **BANDIT** segment

What's happening – first, when you slip, you are not changing the duration of the shot that is in your Sequence. What you are doing, however, is shifting (Slipping) what images and/or audio is referenced (played) from the original **Master Clip** during that same amount of time. The following screenshots will take you through an example.

The following screenshot illustrates all the frames that are within a **Master Clip** of a ball rolling across the floor.

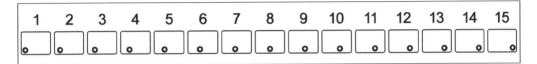

The screenshot below shows the shot of the ball as it was originally edited into the Sequence.

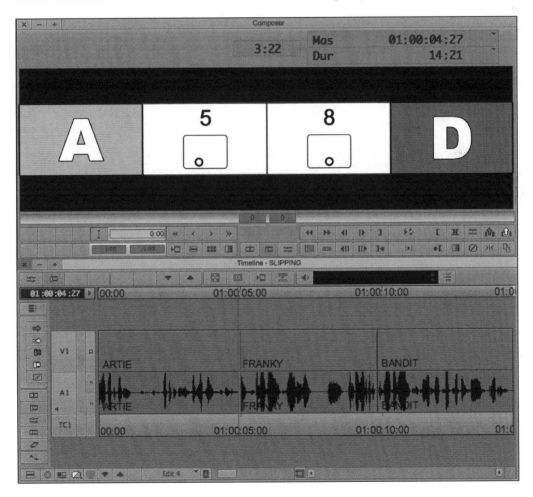

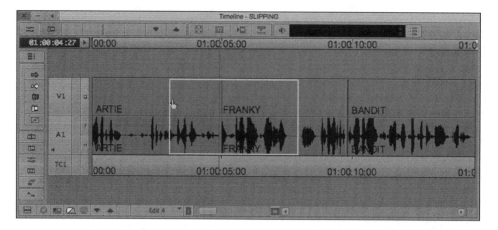

In the screenshot above, I've grabbed the **Trim Roller** and dragged a bit to the left. During the Slipping process, Media Composer displays a ghosted outline of the segment. Often this is confusing. What that ghosted outline is telling you is that it is looking (referring) to earlier or later material within its original **Master Clip**. In this instance, as I Slip to the left, the ghosted outline is telling me that it is looking at *earlier* material from its Master Clip.

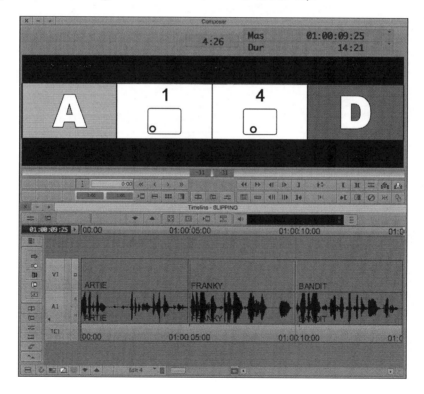

The previous screenshot shows the result of Slipping the shot to the *left*, revealing earlier frames from the **Master Clip**. For emphasis, the duration of the **FRANKY** shot has not changed, but now we see *earlier* frames from the **Master Clip**.

Slipping outside of Trim Mode

Slipping allows you to adjust a shot in your Sequence to reveal earlier or later material from its source clip without changing the shot's duration.

The previous section discussed Slipping a shot in **Trim Mode** and, as usual, the helpful engineers at Avid have programmed Media Composer to be able to Slip a shot in more than one way. This second method also provides you with a syncing ability that's not inherently available with Slipping in **Trim Mode**.

While you will *not* be in **Trim Mode**, you *will* be using the **Trim Keys** on the keyboard. For emphasis, *this feature only works when using the **Trim Keys** on the keyboard when not in **Trim Mode***.

The "how" part is very easy, and the steps are below. After the steps, are an explanation, and an example that will provide some context for you:

1. Park the **Position Indicator** (the blue line) on a Segment.

2. Enable only the track(s) you want to Slip.

3. Press any of the **Trim Keys** on the keyboard to Slip the segment(s). By default, you'll find the **Trim Keys** on the *M*, comma, period, and forward slash keys.

Remember that Slipping allows you to adjust a shot in your Sequence to reveal earlier or later material from its source clip without changing the shot's duration.

Imagine that the Segment you're Slipping is a window that reveals the selected frames from the **Master Clip** behind it (see the following screenshot). When you Slip a segment using the **Trim Keys**, it's as if the window is locked in place and you're shifting the **Master Clip** left or right behind it.

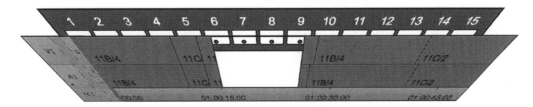

When you shift (Slip) the shot to the *right, all the frames within it are shifted to the right, and the result is that the* frame at the Head (beginning) of the shot will come from an *earlier* part of the **Source Clip**. In the previous screenshot, we can see frames **6**, **7**, **8**, and **9** through the window. If we shifted the numbered frames to the *right*, then it would reveal frames **2**, **3**, **4**, and **5**.

When you shift (Slip) the Segment to the *left*, the result is that the frame at the Tail (end) of the Segment will come from a *later* part of the **Source Clip**. In the previous screenshot, we can see frames **6**, **7**, **8**, and **9** through the window. If we shifted the numbered frames to the *left*, then it could reveal frames **11**, **12**, **13**, and **14**.

This is often confusing since this behavior is the opposite of when you're Slipping a shot using **Trim Mode**.

How to do it...

Let's take a look at a specific example where Slipping outside of **Trim Mode** is very helpful. In the example provided in a moment, you could achieve the same result by Slipping with **Trim Mode**. However, it would involve a bit more work on your part using at least one Marker, and who wants extra work, right? In the particular situation that I'll be describing, the Slipping outside of **Trim Mode** method would be the most direct path to the objective and also showcases the syncing ability that's not inherently available when Slipping in **Trim Mode**.

Here is the situation: You are editing a commercial for a company that makes tools. The ad features close-up shots of various tools (a drill, a saw, a hammer, and so on) that are being used in a workshop. Along with the images, you've edited in some upbeat music.

At one spot in the commercial, you notice that there is a loud drum beat (arrow **A** in the next screenshot), and about half a second later in the video the hammer strikes a nail (arrow **"B"** in the next screenshot). You think that it would work well if the hammer struck the nail at the same time as the drum beat. You decide to Slip the video segment of the hammer (without using **Trim Mode**) to sync with the drum beat.

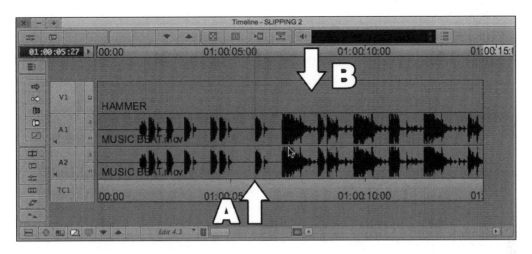

1. Park the **Position Indicator** at the point where the drum beat occurs (arrow **A** in the screenshot above).

2. Enable *only* the **V1** Track Selector (since you only want to slip the video).

3. Watch the image in the **Record Monitor**. You are seeing whatever frame is occurring where the **Position Indicator** (blue line) is placed.

4. Press the **Trim One Frame Left** key (by default on the comma key) several times. Keep tapping it until the image of the hammer hitting the nail appears in the **Record Monitor** and syncs with the drum beat.

5. You have now shifted (Slipped) the video segment to the left. In the Sequence, the shot of the hammer hitting the nail remains the same duration, but it now starts and ends on later frames from the **Master Clip** than it did before the Slip.

Sliding in Trim Mode

Like Slipping, Sliding is part of the trimming set of features. Sliding allows you to move one or more segments (shots) earlier or later in the Sequence. In other words, Sliding let's you move one or more shots to the left or to the right in the Sequence.

After the list of steps, there is an example to illustrate what Sliding is doing and how it might be used.

There are four methods available to enable Sliding (also known as **Slide Mode**). Let's take a look at each:

> ▸ Method 1 is to Lasso while in **Trim Mode** or **Source/Record Mode**:
>
> > ❑ First, if you're unfamiliar Lassoing, it is discussed in more detail in this appendix in the *Enabling and configuring the trimming tools* recipe.
> >
> > ❑ In this instance, you'll be pressing both the *Shift* key + *option/Alt* key at the same time as lassoing a very specific direction: from right to left around a Segments(s). You can lasso around just a video segment, or just the audio segment(s), or you can lasso both the video and the audio that goes with it/ them if they need to stay in sync. The next screenshots show *Shift + option/ Alt* + lassoing the **SAMMY** video segment and then the resulting Slide configuration of the **Trim Rollers** after lassoing.

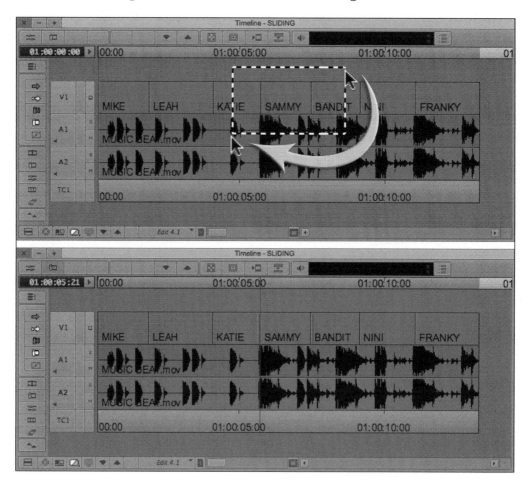

- Method 2: While already in **Trim Mode**, here are the steps:

    i. Enter **Trim Mode** at any transition.

    ii. For the Segment (shot) you want to Slide, place the cursor at one of its transitions, either the head or the tail (see the next screenshot). For emphasis, place the cursor either where a **Trim Roller** already exists, or where it would appear if one was there.

    iii. *Pay close attention to the cursor icon.* Make sure that the little piece of film that extends from the roller is *facing the Segment you want to Slide.* In the next screenshot, the **Trim Roller** icon is set up for the **KATIE** shot.

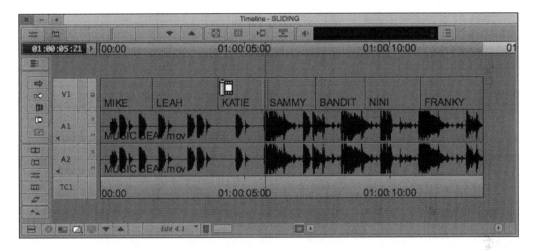

    iv. When the cursor's icon is facing the Segment you want to Slide, then double-click. This will initially place you into Slip Mode (also known as Slipping).

    v. Without changing the position of your cursor, *double-click again.* This will place you into **Slide Mode** (also known as Sliding).

    vi. If you need to select an additional segment(s) in order to stay in sync, for example, you've initially entered **Slide Mode** on the video segment but now want to include the audio segment(s) that belongs with it, you can either *Shift* + double-click as you did with the first Segment, or you can enable the required Track Selectors.

- Method 3 is to perform *Shift* + click method to configure the **Trim Rollers** while already in **Trim Mode**:

    - The *Shift* + click method to configure the **Trim Rollers** is explained earlier in this appendix in the *Enabling and configuring the trimming tools* recipe

- Method 4: While you are in **Trim Mode**, right-click on a Segment and, from the menu that appears, choose **Select Slide Trim**.

Now that you know how to enable Sliding, let's take a closer look at the **Trim Rollers** and the **Four Image Display** when Sliding.

The Rollers – frequently, people will describe Sliding as when the **Trim Rollers** are on the outside of the segment (see the next screenshot). Rather than saying that the rollers are on the outside, I prefer to point out that *the rollers are touching the adjacent segments.* The idea here is that whatever shots the **Trim Rollers** are *touching* are the shots that are being made longer or shorter while the shot(s) between the rollers get shifted (Slid) either to the left or to the right. When you Slide, it's as if the shot(s) between the rollers are on a moving conveyor belt. For emphasis, in the next screenshot, we can see that the **Trim Rollers** are touching the Segments (shots) labeled as **MIKE** and **SAMMY**. Therefore, the Segments that we will be Sliding are labeled as **LEAH** and **KATIE**.

The Four Image Display (see the next screenshot) – when you're Sliding a video segment(s), Media Composer will display four images. In the next screenshot, I've set up to Slide two shots, the **LEAH** and **KATIE** shots. The four images in the display are the following:

- ▸ **A** is the last frame of the **Mike** shot
- ▸ **B** is the first frame of the **Leah** shot
- ▸ **C** is the last frame of the **Katie** shot
- ▸ **D** is the first frame of the **Sammy** shot

As you're Sliding, it will be images **A** and **D** that will change, since those are the shots that are being trimmed.

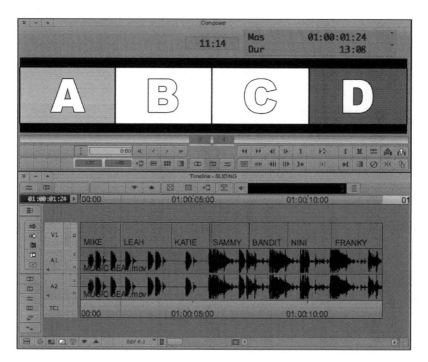

What's happening – First, when you Slide, you are *not* changing the duration of the shot(s) that you are *moving* in your Sequence (in this example, **LEAH** and **KATIE**). What you are doing, however, is lengthening and shortening the *adjacent* shots (**MIKE** and **SAMMY**). The next screenshot will take you through an example:

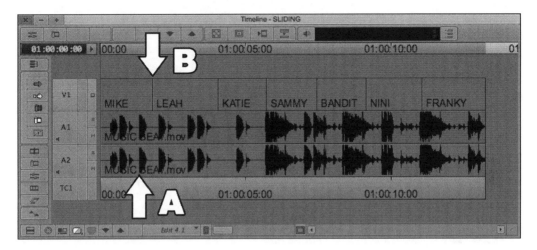

The previous screenshot illustrates a situation where there is a distinct drum beat in the music (arrow **A**). Arrow **B** points to the transition between shots that we'd like to have occur at the same time as the drum beat. After more closely examining the Sequence, we decide that we want to slide not just the **LEAH** shot, but also the **KATIE** shot that comes right after it.

Here are the steps:

1. Press *Shift + option/Alt and lasso from right to left* around *both* the **LEAH** and **KATIE** video segments.

2. Use the **Trim Keys** (or any trimming method you prefer) to shift (Slide) the **LEAH** and **KATIE** segments to the left until the transition syncs with the drum beat.

3. The next screenshot shows the **LEAH** and **KATIE** shots after they have been shifted (Slid) to the left (earlier in the Sequence). The arrows show that the transition and the drum beat now occur at the same time. The results to the shots are as follows:

    ❑ Shot **A** (**MIKE**) is now shorter

    ❑ Shots **B** and **C** (**LEAH** and **KATIE**) are the same duration, but now occur earlier in the Sequence

❑   Shot **D** (**SAMMY**) is now longer

Trimming and effects

There is a feature that tells Media Composer to compute and display an effect (for example, a dissolve or a Picture-in-Picture) whenever the **Position Indicator** is placed on it. This feature is called **Render On-The-Fly**, and is found in two locations.

The first location it can be found is: **Special** menu | **Render On-The-Fly**. When you're in **Source/Record Mode**, this feature is enabled by default. This is why when you place the **Position Indicator** on a dissolve (or another effect) that you can see it.

The second location you'll find **Render On-The-Fly** is in your **Trim Settings**: **Project Window** | **Settings** tab | **Trim** settings | **Features** tab. Here you'll notice that this feature is *disabled* by default. This is because it can often be frustrating to have to deal with seeing an effect (for example, a dissolve) when you're attempting to trim a shot. However, what if you're trimming a layered video effect you've constructed that includes multiple video tracks? In that case, there's a good likelihood that being able to see what is happening in the video layers as you trim would be helpful. So, now you know where to enable that feature when you need it.

Smart Tool overview

At its most basic, the **Smart Tool** is a palette of tools that can be enabled/disabled individually, just like you're used to doing with the Red and Yellow **Segment Mode** Arrows. However, its real power is providing the ability to enable two or more individual tools simultaneously, which provides access to them in the **Timeline** simultaneously. What's nice is that with the addition of the **Smart Tool**, the engineers didn't remove the original methods from the software and simply gave us more options.

Following is a screenshot of the **Smart Tool**:

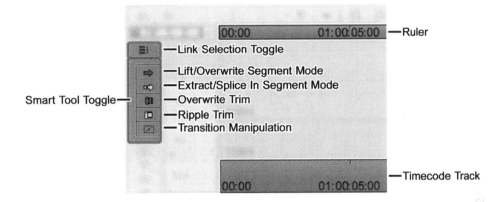

Enabling/disabling the Smart Tool

Individual Tools – each of the five tools can be enabled/disabled individually by:

▸ Clicking on them in the **Smart Tool**

▸ From their default locations on the keyboard:

  ❑ *Shift + A* = **Lift/Overwrite Segment Arrow** (Red)

  ❑ *Shift + S* = **Extract/Splice In Segment Arrow** (Yellow)

  ❑ *Shift + D* = **Overwrite Trim** (Red)

  ❑ *Shift + F* = **Ripple Trim** (Yellow)

▸ Mapped to locations of your choice using the **Command Palette**. The **Smart Tools** have their own tab on the **Command Palette**.

Smart Tool – enabling one or more functions on the **Smart Tool** essentially tells Media Composer that those are the functions you like to use. Then you can enable/disable them all simultaneously by:

▸ Clicking on the Left Edge of the **Smart Tool** (labeled above as **Smart Tool Toggle**).

▸ *Shift + Tab* key

▸ Mapping the **Smart Tool Toggle** button to a location(s) of your choice using the **Command Palette**.

▸ After enabling the **Smart Tool**, you are provided access to multiple tools (of your choosing) based on where you place your cursor in the **Timeline**, allowing you to potentially work faster. The next sections discuss using both the **Trim** functions and the **Segment Mode** functions with the **Smart Tool**.

Link Selection and Smart Tool functions

Link Selection allows you to select one segment or transition and have those that are related become selected at the same time. By default, you can enable/disable **Link Selection** from the keyboard with *Shift + L*. **Link Selection** allows you to select multiple transitions and segments when:

▸ The segments come from the same clip.

▸ The related segments overlap by at least one frame.

▸ The **Link Selection Toggle** is enabled.

▸ Press the *option*/Alt key – if you'd prefer to work with **Link Selection** disabled, you may still get the Linking behavior whenever you want by using *option/Alt* + Clicking. The opposite is also true: if you've enabled **Link Selection**, and you want to select a segment or transition without also selecting all that are associated with it, then you can use *option/Alt* + Clicking.

Navigating the Timeline when using Smart Tool

When any of the functions within the *Smart Tool* are active, you can no longer click inside the **Timeline** in order to move the **Position Indicator** (the blue line) since the cursor is transformed into an active tool. Instead, Media Composer provides you with several places that you can click and/or drag to update your location:

▸ **Timecode track** at the bottom of the **Timeline** (see the screenshot at the beginning of this section)

▸ The **Ruler** (which also displays **Timecode**) that runs along the top of the **Timeline Window**, directly below all the buttons on the **Timeline Toolbar** (see the screenshot at the beginning of this section)

▸ The position bar that is directly below the **Record Monitor**

Disabling the Smart Tool

There are several ways that you can disable (exit) the **Smart Tool**, which will then disable all the functions within it.

▸ Clicking the left edge of the **Smart Tool** palette (labeled in the previous screenshot as **Smart Tool Toggle**).

▸ By default you can enable/disable the **Smart Tool** by using *Shift + Tab*.

▸ You can map the **Smart Tool Toggle** button from the **Command Palette**: **Tools** menu | **Command Palette** | **Smart Tools** tab.

▸ You can instruct Media Composer to disable the **Smart Tool** whenever you click onto either the **Timecode Track** at the bottom of the **Timeline** or on the **Ruler** at the top of the **Timeline Window** (see the screenshot at the beginning of this section), which is a behavior that many long-time Media Composer editors have become accustomed to. To do this: **Project Window** | **Settings** tab | **Timeline Settings** | **Edit** tab, and select the option that states **Clicking the TC Track or Ruler Disables Smart Tools**.

Using the Trim functions in the Smart Tool

You can enable as many of the functions in the **Smart Tool** that you like. When you enable multiple functions, then you can then access them directly in the **Timeline**, simply based on where you place your cursor. This saves you time from having to turn functions on or off. Let's start by focusing on using just the trimming functions.

1. Within the **Smart Tool**, enable *both* the red **Overwrite Trim** function as well as the yellow **Ripple Trim** function. Note that enabling a function(s) within the **Smart Tool** also enables the **Smart Tool** itself. Use any of the methods described in the *Smart tool overview* recipe to disable and/or re-enable the **Smart Tool** as a whole at any time.

2. When multiple **Smart Tool** functions are enabled, you access them right in the **Timeline** based on where you place your cursor. Remember, in this example, we're discussing only the red **Overwrite Trim** function and the yellow **Ripple Trim** function, though you can have any combination of functions enabled that you like.

   ▫ Placing the cursor near a transition, on either the A-Side or B-Side, *towards the top half of the segment* indicates red **Overwrite Trim** (discussed earlier in this appendix in the *Trimming icons and colors* section).

   ▫ Placing the cursor near a transition, on either the A-Side or B-Side, *towards the bottom-half of the segment* indicates yellow **Ripple Trim**.

   ▫ Placing the cursor exactly over the transition will display a white icon of one **Trim Roller** with the film extending out from it in both directions. This icon indicates **Double-Roller Trim**.

   ▫ Once you have displayed the tool you want (**Overwrite Trim**, **Ripple Trim**, or **Double-Roller Trim**), then click the mouse to engage it.

Notice that the **Smart Tool** palette reminds you where to position your cursor in the **Timeline** by placing the red tools above the yellow tools.

Using Segment Mode with the Smart Tool

While it is possible to have as many of the **Smart Tool** functions enabled as you like at any time, here we'll focus on just enabling the **Segment Mode** functions. And, just as with the **Smart Tool** trimming functions (discussed earlier), once the **Segment Mode** functions are enabled, they can be accessed in the **Timeline**, based on where you place your cursor. Let's take a closer look:

- ▸ Within the **Smart Tool**, enable *both* the red **Lift/Overwrite Segment Mode** as well as the yellow **Extract/Splice In Segment Mode**. Note that enabling a function(s) within the **Smart Tool** also enables the **Smart Tool** itself. Use any of the methods described in the the *Smart tool overview* section to disable and/or re-enable the **Smart Tool** as a whole at any time.

- ▸ When multiple **Smart Tool** functions are enabled, you access them directly in the **Timeline** based on where you place your cursor. Remember, in this example, we're discussing only the red **Lift/Overwrite Segment Mode** and the yellow **Extract/Splice** - In **Segment Mode**, though you can have any combination of functions enabled that you like.

  - ❑ Placing your cursor in the upper portion of a segment displays the Red Arrow, while placing it in the lower portion displays the Yellow Arrow (notice that the **Smart Tool** palette reminds you where to position your cursor in the **Timeline** by placing the red tools above the yellow tools)

  - ❑ Once you have displayed the tool you want (red arrow or yellow arrow), then click the mouse to engage it

  - ❑ There are additional **Segment Mode** tips next.

Nine Segment Mode Tips

The following are a variety of tips that will help you get more out of using **Segment Mode**.

Sync Locks

By default, **Extract/Splice In Segment Mode** does not pay attention to the **Sync Locks**. However, you can force it to. Go to **Project Window | Settings Tab | Timeline Settings | Edit Tab | Segment Drag Sync Locks**. There is a discussion of this in the *Segment Mode: Methods for staying in sync* recipe in *Chapter 5, Maintaining and Regaining Sync*.

Snapping

There are two methods available to make segments snap in a specific manner. The default method uses keyboard shortcuts which are discussed in the *Snapping Actions for the Position Indicator and in Segment Mode* recipe in *Chapter 3, Polishing Gems*. The second method involves this setting: **Project Window | Settings Tab | Timeline Settings | Edit Tab | Default Snap-To Edit**.

When the **Default Snap-To Edit** setting is enabled:

▶ The Head (left side) of the segment(s) you're moving will automatically snap to transitions, **Mark In** or **Mark Out**, and the **Position Indicator** (blue line)

▶ Press the *option/Alt* key to make the Tail (right side) of the segment(s) you're moving snap

▶ Note that the **Position Indicator** will also snap, so you'll need to navigate using **JKL**, the **Step Forward/Backward** keys, or within the position bar below the **Record Monitor**

Selecting Methods

Media Composer provides several ways for you to select Segments:

▶ *Shift* + Click – if you're already in **Segment Mode**, you can add (or remove) segments from your selection by pressing and holding the *Shift* key and then clicking on a segment.

▶ **Select Left**, **Select Right**, **Select Between In/Out Marks** – by default, you'll find these functions on your **Timeline Toolbar**. They can also be mapped anywhere you'd like. They can be found in the **Tools menu | Command Palette | Edit** tab, and you'll find them in the fourth column. To use one of these three functions, you must do the following:

    ❑ Step 1: Enable the track(s) on which you want to select segments.

    ❑ Step 2: You will use one of these, depending on your situation. To use **Select Left** or **Select Right**, for this step you will park your **Position Indicator** on the first segment you want to select. To use **Select In/Out**, then you'll place Marks that include the segments you want to select. The marks do not have to totally surround the segments you want to select. In other words, the marks only need to be partially within the segments you want to select.

    ❑ Step 3: Once you have prepared as discussed in step 2, then press the required function (**Select Left**, **Select Right**, or **Select In/Out**).

▶ Lassoing – you can select segments and place them into **Segment Mode** by Lassoing around them in a very specific way. Lasso *entirely* around them, moving your cursor from *left to right*. Lassoing is discussed and pictured in more detail as it relates to Trimming earlier in this chapter. See the *Enabling and configuring the trimming tools* recipe (and don't miss the portion that discusses lassoing inside the **Timeline** with the *option/Alt* key).

Moving Segments

It is important to note that in versions of Media Composer, up to and including version 6.0, if you are trying to move multiple segments, then all the segments have to be touching each other; and this includes any **Filler** that may be between two Segments. In other words, all the Segments must be adjacent to one another. If you attempt to move multiple Segments that do not all touch each other, then they will not move, and you may get a system alert sound (for example, Beep). Note, however, that for those using Version 6.5 or later, you *can* move Segments that are not touching each other when you use the red **Lift/Overwrite Segment Mode** arrow. For emphasis, this is new programming that only applies to Version 6.5 and later.

Exiting Segment Mode

Just as there are multiple ways to enable **Segment Mode**, there are several ways to disable it. You'll find that you'll use some methods more than others, but it's helpful to be familiar with all of them:

▶ Click on either the red and/or yellow segment arrow to toggle it off.

▶ You can map the **Segment Mode Arrows** from the **Command Palette** to any location on the keyboard or interface that you like.

▶ Click the left edge of the **Smart Tool** palette.

▶ By default, you can enable/disable the **Smart Tool** by using *Shift + Tab*.

▶ You can map the **Smart Tool Toggle** button from the **Command Palette**: **Tools** menu | **Command Palette** | **Smart Tools** tab.

▶ You can instruct Media Composer to disable the **Smart Tool** whenever you click onto either the **Timecode Track** at the bottom of the **Timeline** or on the **Ruler** at the top of the **Timeline Window**. To do this, **Project Window** | **Settings** tab | **Timeline Settings** | **Edit** tab and select the option that reads: **Clicking the TC Track or Ruler Disables Smart Tools**.

Segment Mode Track Placement

If you have selected both video and audio segments, and if you have multiple tracks in your timeline, it is possible to move segments not only horizontally but vertically as well. Whichever element, video or audio, that you want to move vertically should be the last thing selected before moving them. The entire selection will move horizontally and the last element selected will also move vertically.

For example, you have three video tracks and six audio tracks in your Sequence. You'd like to move a shot that has video and two tracks of audio to a later position in the Sequence, and at the same time move the shot's audio from tracks **A1** and **A2** to tracks **A3** and **A4**. Here are the steps:

1. Select the video segment and its related audio segments in order to place them into **Segment Mode** using any method described earlier in the *Selecting Methods* recipe.
2. Select and hold down the mouse button on either of the audio segments (the video segment also remains selected).
3. As you move the segments horizontally, simultaneously move the audio segments vertically to tracks **A3** and **A4**.

Link Selection

Link Selection allows you to select one segment or transition and have other segments that are related become selected simultaneously. By default, you can enable/disable **Link Selection** from the keyboard with *Shift + L*.

Link Selection allows you to select multiple segments (and transitions) when:

▶   The segments come from the same clip.

▶   The related segments overlap by at least one frame.

▶   The **Link Selection Toggle** is enabled.

▶   You press the *option/Alt* key – if you'd prefer to work with **Link Selection** disabled, you may still get that behavior whenever you want by using *option*/Alt + Clicking. The opposite is also true: if you've enabled **Link Selection**, and you want to select a segment without selecting the others that are associated with it, then you can use *option/Alt* + Clicking.

Setting a Preference

When you lasso to select segments, or when you use the **Select Left/Right/Between Marks** buttons, by default you will be placed into the **Extract/Splice In Segment Mode** (yellow arrow). However, you can change that, if you prefer, by going to **Project Window | Settings** tab | **Timeline Settings | Edit** tab | **Default Segment Tool | Segment Overwrite**.

One at A Time

Prior to the introduction of the **Smart Tool**, it was only possible to have one **Segment Mode** arrow enabled at a time. If you prefer this behavior, you can tell Media Composer to do this by going to **Project Window | Settings** tab | **Timeline Settings | Edit** tab | **Only One Segment Tool Can Be Enabled At A Time**.

Helpful Details about MultiCamera Editing

Editing with **Group Clips** and **MultiCamera Mode** can be a bit confusing. So, the first goal with this appendix is to provide some additional background information to help reduce confusion. Additionally, for those already familiar with **Group Clips/MultiCamera Mode**, at the very least, you may find the last *Understanding System Performance with Group Clips and MultiCamera Mode* recipe to be helpful.

This appendix will cover the following topics:

- ▶ Uses for Group Clips and MultiCamera Mode
- ▶ Definition of a Group Clip
- ▶ Definition of a MultiGroupClip
- ▶ Definition of MultiCamera Mode
- ▶ Overview: Syncing Methods
- ▶ Editing multiple camera angles without Group Clips
- ▶ MultipleCamera Editing Resolutions
- ▶ Understanding System Performance with Group Clips and MultiCamera Mode

Uses for Group Clips and MultiCamera Mode

Group Clips and **MultiCamera Mode** editing are especially useful in any situation where footage from multiple cameras is recorded at the same time and/or shares a common sync reference. For example:

▸ **Music Videos**: Even though you may have shot your music video with just one camera, all the different angles and locations in the footage still have at least one common sync reference: the song. Professional music video shoots will also use a timecode reference tied along with the music track to aid with syncing footage.

▸ **Small Shoots**: This relates to shoots with two or three cameras, such as an interview, a lecture, or a presentation. It's always preferred to have all the cameras share the exact same timecode (referred to as Common Timecode) and that the cameras be exactly synced together (frequently referred to as Jam Synced). Unfortunately, this may not always be possible (due to the capability, or in this case the incapability, of the cameras being used). However, you can still provide a common sync reference point for all the cameras by using a **Clapper Slate** (see screenshot and discussion later in the *Overview: Syncing Methods* recipe).

▸ **Large Shoots**: This relates to shoots of various kinds with multiple cameras, covering a large expanse, and/or not necessarily recording the same image and audio at the same time, yet all the footage needs to be synced (Grouped) together. In these instances, using a **Clapper Slate** is most likely not practical and you would want to make sure that all the cameras (or decks, if you're feeding the signal to a control truck or control room) are jam-synced together so that they share identical timecode. Some examples would be:

  ❑ A music concert where one camera records the singer, another camera the drummer, another camera the entire band, another camera the audience, and so on

  ❑ An American Football game where one camera records the Quarterback, another camera a coach, another camera the fans in the stadium, and so on

  ❑ A studio production like a situation comedy (for example, The Big Bang Theory), a talk show (for example, The Ellen DeGeneres Show or The Graham Norton Show), or a court show (for example, Judge Judy)

Definition of a Group Clip

First, I think it's good to know that you can edit with a **Group Clip** *without* using **MultiCamera Mode**. **MultiCamera Mode** editing gives you some additional editing abilities, but is *not required* to edit a **Group Clip**.

A **Group·Clip** is a single clip that *you create* from multiple **Master Clips** and/or **Subclips**. During the process of creating **Group Clips** (referred to as Grouping), you instruct Avid Media Composer how to sync the clips. Examples of syncing methods include a common **Mark In** point on all the clips, or matching timecode on all the clips.

A **Group Clip** is able to **Link** to (you could also say point to, or refer to) up to 99 **Master Clips** and/or **Subclips** at one time. For example, let's say you're editing a sit-down interview with one Interviewer and two people being interviewed (the Subjects) which was shot with four cameras, and the recording was *continuous* on *all* the cameras for the *entire duration* of a 45-minute interview. Each of the four cameras would produce one **Master Clip** (each about 45-minutes long) which you would then combine into a single **Group Clip**. In the end, that one single **Group Clip** would link to/refer to all four **Master Clips** (camera angles) at the same time:

- ▸ Camera A: Interviewer
- ▸ Camera B: Interview Subject 1
- ▸ Camera C: Interview Subject 2
- ▸ Camera D: Roams between a Two-Shot of the Interview Subjects and a Wide-Shot that includes both the Interviewer and the Subjects

The benefits of editing with Group Clips include:

- ▸ Having all the different camera angles contained in one clip means that it will only have to occupy one video track in your **Timeline** (the alternative is discussed later in the *Editing multiple camera angles without Group Clips* recipe)
- ▸ You can quickly and easily change video angles from one to another, and/or from one audio source to another (the various methods are discussed in the chapter about **Group Clips** and **MultiCamera Mode**)

The duration of the **Group Clip** is dictated by the longest clip in the Group. That means that while editing, if you change to (also known as Switch to) one of the camera angles (that is, **Master Clips**) at a point in time when that clip does not have any video (for example, at the beginning or end of a **Group Clip**), Media Composer will display black.

The icon for a **Group Clip** is a square that is divided into four parts. This symbol is inspired by the four-image display, known as the **Quad Display** which is frequently used when editing with **Group Clips**. This icon is pictured in the next screenshot:

Definition of a MultiGroupClip

A **MultiGroup Clip** is one clip that contains two or more **Group Clips**. You could say it's a *Group of* **Group Clips**. *As a matter of fact, if you look at a* **MultiGroup Clip** *while it's loaded in the* **Source Monitor** *(using the* **Toggle Source/Record In Timeline** *function), then you'll actually be able to see the individual* **Group Clips** *that are within it.*

While you might think that you would first create the separate **Group Clips** and then, in a second operation, instruct them to be MultiGrouped together, that is actually not the case. Instead, like **Group Clips**, **MultiGroup Clips** are created from **Master Clips** and/or **Subclips**. Further, they can only be correctly created from **Master Clips** and/or **Subclips** that have sequential timecode. Avid states, "The MultiGroup function is designed primarily for situation comedies and similar productions that record multiple takes sequentially on the same source tapes. MultiGrouping does not provide any benefit when you edit with clips that do not share common timecode or were not recorded sequentially, and might even cause the wrong clips to be grouped together."

The icon for a **MultiGroup Clip** looks like the icon for a regular **Group Clip**, however, you will also see a small Plus Symbol on the left of it. Honestly, the plus symbol is so small that it looks like a dot when it's viewed at normal size. See the next screenshot:

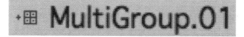

Definition of MultiCamera Mode

As mentioned earlier, it's good to know that you can edit with a **Group Clip** *without* using **MultiCamera Mode**. In other words, it is *not required* to use **MultiCamera Mode** to edit a **Group Clip**. However, **MultiCamera Mode** editing gives you some additional abilities which include:

- ▸ Two methods that allow you to switch to (cut to) a specific camera angle by using the keyboard.

- ▸ Being able to Switch camera angles *while you are playing* your Sequence. In other words, you are able to switch from one camera angle to another in *Real Time*, in a way that is very similar to switching cameras during a live production.

Overview: Syncing Methods

When you create **Group Clips**, you have to tell Media Composer how the multiple clips should be synced together. The chapter on editing with **Group Clips** and **MultiCamera Mode** will discuss the specifics of syncing and Grouping clips that all share the same timecode (frequently referred to as **Common** or **Jam-Synced** timecode), as well as syncing and Grouping clips that may not share the same timecode, but do have a common reference point (for example, a Clapper Slate or the same audio).

Since syncing multiple clips that all share the exact same timecode is relatively easy, I thought an overview of two other methods of syncing clips so that they can then be used to create **Group Clips** would be helpful.

Clapper Slate

Screenshot of **Clapper Slate**:

Using a **Clapper Slate** during production works like this. You would begin recording with all the cameras, making sure that they can all see the **Clapper Slate**. You would then **Clap** (also known as, Mark) with the **Slate**. The slate being clapped (that is, the two parts of the slate being banged together) provides both a visual and an audible common sync reference point when recorded by all the cameras at the same time. This is then used during editing to sync up the footage from the various cameras. If you're really in a bind, and don't have a **Clapper Slate**, you could position your hands parallel to the ground, one above the other, and clap your hands to provide a common sync reference point.

Once the cameras are recording, *if at all possible, it is advisable not to stop them independently of each other.* In other words, the most desirable thing is to have the cameras start and stop recording at roughly the same time. This will make the syncing process a great deal easier and faster. If this is not possible, it's not the end of the world. It just means that there will be some additional work required. This additional work is introduced later in the *Audio Waveform Display* recipe.

Audio Waveform Display

Multiple cameras can also be synced by aligning their audio waveforms (presuming they all recorded the same audio, of course). The chapter on editing with **Group Clips** discusses how to do this manually by *visually* aligning the waveform displays. If you do a lot of **MultiCamera** editing with footage that does not have common (jam-synced) timecode, or even a common sync reference point (for example, a **Clapper Slate**), then you may want to investigate a Third-Party application called PluralEyes. It also syncs multiple cameras by analyzing the waveforms, but it potentially does it much faster than the manual method covered in the chapter. While I have not personally used this software, I have heard positive things about it, and it could be a big time-saver if you're in this situation frequently.

Editing multiple camera angles without Group Clips

Just for purposes of comparison, let's examine how we would have to edit without the benefit of **Group Clips**. Let's use our previous example of a sit-down interview with one Interviewer and two people being interviewed:

- ▶ Camera A: Interviewer
- ▶ Camera B: Interview Subject 1
- ▶ Camera C: Interview Subject 2
- ▶ Camera D: Roams between a two-Shot of the Interview Subjects and a Wide-Shot that includes both the Interviewer and the Subjects

Without the ability to create **Group Clips**, you would have at least four video tracks; and you'd have at least two audio tracks (presuming the interviewer was recorded on one audio channel, while both subjects were recorded together on a different channel). Likely you'd have at least three audio tracks in this situation (each person recorded on a different audio channel), and possibly a fourth that was recorded with all the cameras' audio channels mixed into one (as a safety/reference). In the Sequence, the video would be stacked onto different tracks and placed in sync with each other. You might configure the stacked clips like this (depending on your own preferences):

- ▶ **V1**: Camera A
- ▶ **V2**: Camera B

- ► **V3**: Camera C
- ► **V4**: Camera D

While editing like this is not impossible (there are a couple of different methods you might use, though I won't bother you with detailing them), it is a great deal slower and more cumbersome than using **Group Clips**, whether you're using **MultiCamera Mode** or not.

MultipleCamera Editing Resolutions

In the past (in the days before High Definition video) it was necessary to use specific, optimized video compressions (resolutions) in order to be able to play multiple Standard Definition (SD) video clips at the same time in the **Quad Split** and **Nine Split** displays (which are frequently used when editing **Group Clips** and when using **MultiCamera Mode**). These SD resolutions were denoted with the letter **m** following them, for example, **4:1m**. Today, with the improvements in both hardware and software, using the **m** resolution is not mandatory with **Group Clips/MultiCamera Mode**. However, using it will provide increased performance. Avid states that you will see *the best real-time playback performance when you play [SD] material that was recorded at* **10:1 m**, **4:1 m**, *or* **1:1** *resolutions*. Further, you can certainly edit **Group Clips** comprised of HD video. However, since the amount of data for each frame of HD is so much more than SD, there are some issues and features to be aware of, which are discussed in the next section.

Understanding System Performance with Group Clips and MultiCamera Mode

Playing multiple video clips at the same time requires a lot of processing work from the computer. So, when editing with higher resolution video (for example, HD), you may see that the system drops frames (stutters) during playback. In addition to using a lower resolution of video to improve playback performance, you can also temporarily decrease the quality of the video playback by using the **Video Quality Menu** (located in the bottom left of the **Timeline Window**).

When you're using **MultiCamera Mode** and you change the **Video Quality Menu** to a different setting, Media Composer will remember that setting each time you enable **MultiCamera Mode** during your current editing session. For example, let's say you're editing your Sequence not using **MultiCamera Mode** and the **Video Quality Menu** is set to **Full Quality** (green). Then you come to a portion of your Sequence that has some **Group Clips**, so you enter **MultiCamera Mode** while you edit that section. At this point, the **Video Quality Menu** is still set to **Full Quality** and you experience some dropped frames (stuttering) during playback. So, while still in **MultiCamera Mode**, you set the video **Quality Menu** to **Draft Quality** (yellow/green) to get smooth playback. Later, when you leave **MultiCamera Mode**, the **Video Quality** will automatically shift to **Full Quality** again; and then later, when you re-enter MultiCamera Mode it will automatically shift to **Draft Quality** for you.

Lastly, when you have finished editing a **MultiCamera** Sequence and you are happy with all the edits you made, meaning that you are at the point in your project that you feel 100 % comfortable locking-in (in other words, committing to) the camera-angle-choices you've made, then you can use a feature called **Commit MultiCam Edits**. This changes all the **Group Clips** in your Sequence into regular clips. Doing this accomplishes the following:

- ▸ Lessens the processing burden on the computer. Avid states,"You can remove the grouped clips in a sequence and replace each of them with its selected clip. This might be useful if you experience poor performance with a very complex MultiCamera sequence on a slower system, for example, a sequence that uses many MultiCamera clips and many effects or color corrections." The result is that each Segment will reference only the original **Master Clip**, rather than the **Group Clip**. While you will no longer be able to switch to the other angles/cameras, you will be able to continue to edit with these clips (for example, Trim them longer or shorter).

- ▸ Ensures that only the video and/or audio media that is actually used in the Sequence is placed into an AAF file export that also includes embedded media. If you do not **Commit MultiCam Edits**, then all of the media from every clip in the **Group Clips** is included in the AAF file, and the file becomes needlessly very large. If you're unfamiliar with exporting AAF files, they are frequently used as a way to transfer audio files and Sequence data over to the audio mixing application called ProTools.

How to do it...

This recipe of steps will take you through the process of using the **Commit MultiCam Edits** command.

1. In the bin, right-click on the Sequence.

2. A menu will appear. Select **Commit MultiCam Edits** (it's in the middle of the menu list).

3. Media Composer will then display a dialog window telling you that you will lose all the references to the alternate angles, and that it will also create a duplicate of the Sequence, so that you'll have the original as a backup. Click the **OK** button.

4. The new Sequence, with the **Group Clips** removed, is created and appears at the top of the bin. Media Composer adds .NoGroups to the end of its name.

5. If all went well, then Media Composer will display a dialog window informing you that **All MultiCam Groups were modified in the selected Sequence**.

6. Click the **OK** button to close the dialog window.

Index

Thank you for buying
Avid Media Composer 6.x Cookbook

About Packt Publishing

Packt, pronounced 'packed', published its first book "*Mastering phpMyAdmin for Effective MySQL Management*" in April 2004 and subsequently continued to specialize in publishing highly focused books on specific technologies and solutions.

Our books and publications share the experiences of your fellow IT professionals in adapting and customizing today's systems, applications, and frameworks. Our solution based books give you the knowledge and power to customize the software and technologies you're using to get the job done. Packt books are more specific and less general than the IT books you have seen in the past. Our unique business model allows us to bring you more focused information, giving you more of what you need to know, and less of what you don't.

Packt is a modern, yet unique publishing company, which focuses on producing quality, cutting-edge books for communities of developers, administrators, and newbies alike. For more information, please visit our website: www.packtpub.com.

Writing for Packt

We welcome all inquiries from people who are interested in authoring. Book proposals should be sent to author@packtpub.com. If your book idea is still at an early stage and you would like to discuss it first before writing a formal book proposal, contact us; one of our commissioning editors will get in touch with you.

We're not just looking for published authors; if you have strong technical skills but no writing experience, our experienced editors can help you develop a writing career, or simply get some additional reward for your expertise.

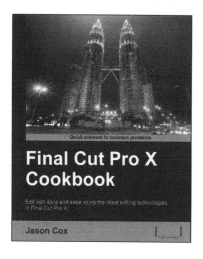

Final Cut Pro X Cookbook

ISBN: 978-1-84969-296-0   Paperback: 452 pages

Edit with style and ease using the latest editing technologies in Final Cut Pro X!

1. Edit slick, professional videos of all kinds – music videos, promos, documentaries, even feature films

2. Add hundreds of built-in animated titles, transitions, and effects without complicated keyframing

3. Learn tons of time-saving workflows to tricky, yet common editing scenarios

4. Fix common (and uncommon) sound and image issues with a click or two of the mouse

Learning VirtualDub: The Complete Guide to Capturing, Processing and Encoding Digital Video

ISBN: 978-1-90481-135-0   Paperback: 212 pages

The complete guide to capturing, processing, and encoding digital video

1. This book is available as a free download, scroll down for more information

2. Capture and process broadcast, digital, home, streaming video

3. Cut, paste and edit ads, trailers, clips

Please check **www.PacktPub.com** for information on our titles

Sony Vegas Pro 11
Beginner's Guide

ISBN: 978-1-84969-170-3   Paperback: 264 pages

Edit videos with style and ease using Vegas Pro

1. Edit slick, professional videos of all kinds with Sony Vegas Pro

2. Learn audio and video editing from scratch

3. Speed up your editing workflow

4. A practical beginner's guide with a fast-paced but friendly and engaging approach towards video editing

Cinema 4D R13 Cookbook

ISBN: 978-1-84969-186-4   Paperback: 292 pages

Elevate your art to the fourth dimension with Cinema 4D

1. Master all the important aspects of Cinema 4D

2. Learn how real-world knowledge of cameras and lighting translates onto a 3D canvas

3. Learn Advanced features like Mograph, Xpresso, and Dynamics.

4. Become an advanced Cinema 4D user with concise and effective recipes

Please check **www.PacktPub.com** for information on our titles

Made in the USA
San Bernardino, CA
13 September 2016